GREECE, MACEDON AND PERSIA

GREECE, MACEDON AND PERSIA

*Studies in Social, Political and Military History
in Honour of Waldemar Heckel*

edited by

Timothy Howe, E. Edward Garvin
and Graham Wrightson

Oxbow Books
Oxford & Philadelphia

Published in the United Kingdom in 2015 by
OXBOW BOOKS
10 Hythe Bridge Street, Oxford OX1 2EW

and in the United States by
OXBOW BOOKS
908 Darby Road, Havertown, PA 19083

Hardcover Edition: ISBN 978-1-78297-923-4
Digital Edition: ISBN 978-178297-924-1

A CIP record for this book is available from the British Library

Printed in the United Kingdom by Short Run Press, Exeter

For a complete list of Oxbow titles, please contact:

UNITED KINGDOM
Oxbow Books
Telephone (01865) 241249
Fax (01865) 794449
Email: oxbow@oxbowbooks.com
www.oxbowbooks.com

UNITED STATES OF AMERICA
Oxbow Books
Telephone (800) 791-9354
Fax (610) 853-9146
Email: queries@casemateacademic.com
www.casemateacademic.com/oxbow

Oxbow Books is part of the Casemate group

Cover illustration: (top) Hellenistic victory monument, Dion, Greece; (bottom) detail of Attic Black Figure, 6th century (object: Yale University Art Gallery; photo: Hood Museum of Art)

CONTENTS

WALDEMAR HECKEL, BIBLIOGRAPHY

Books

Quintus Curtius Rufus: The History of Alexander, tr. by J. C. Yardley, with introduction, notes and appendices by W. Heckel. (Penguin Classics: Harmondsworth, 1984) pp. 337. ISBN 0140444122. Reprinted with corrections 2001; repr. with updated bibliography 2004; republished by BCA 2004.

Ancient Coins of the Graeco-Roman World: The Nickle Numismatic Papers, edited by W. Heckel and R. D. Sullivan (WLU Press: Waterloo, 1984) pp. xvi, 307. ISBN 0889201307. Papers of the Nickle Numismatics Conference, Calgary, October 19–23, 1981.

The Last Days and Testament of Alexander the Great: A Prosopographic Study. Historia Einzelschriften, Heft 56 (Stuttgart, 1988) xiv, 114.

The Marshals of Alexander's Empire (Routledge: London and New York, 1992), xxvi, 416. ISBN 0415050537. Out of print, but available in Kindle electronic version.

Justin: Epitome of the Philippic History of Pompeius Trogus, Volume I. Books 11–12: Alexander the Great, trans. by J. C. Yardley, commentary by W. Heckel, Clarendon Ancient History Series (Oxford, 1997) xxiv, 360. ISBN 0198149077 (hbk); 0198149085 (pbk).

Livy. The Dawn of the Roman Empire, Oxford World's Classics, translation of Books 31–40 by J. C. Yardley, introduction, notes and indices by Waldemar Heckel (Oxford, 2000). ISBN 019283293X.

The Wars of Alexander the Great: 336–323 BC, Osprey Essential Histories series, no. 26 (Oxford: Osprey, 2002) 95 pages. ISBN 18417604736 (pbk). Republished by Routledge 2003 (hbk).

Alexander the Great: Historical Sources in Translation, J. C. Yardley and Waldemar Heckel, (Oxford: Blackwell Publishers, 2003). ISBN: 0631228217.

Crossroads of History. The Age of Alexander, Waldemar Heckel and Lawrence A. Tritle (eds). Regina Books: Claremont, CA, 2003. 276 pp. ISBN 1930053282 (hbk) 1930053290 (pbk).

The Greeks at War. From Athens to Alexander, Philip de Souza, Waldemar Heckel and Lloyd Llewellyn-Jones. Forward by Victor Davis Hanson (Osprey, 2004).

Who's Who in the Age of Alexander the Great. Prosopography of Alexander's Empire (Oxford: Blackwell Publishers, 2006). ISBN 1405112107.

The Macedonian Warrior: Alexander's Elite Infantryman, Waldemar Heckel and Ryan Jones; Christa Hook (Illustrator). Warrior series. (Osprey, 2006) ISBN 1841769509.

Alexander's Empire. Formulation to Decay, edited by Waldemar Heckel, L. A. Tritle and P. V. Wheatley (Claremont, CA: Regina Books, 2007). ISBN 1930053452.

The Conquests of Alexander the Great. Key Conflicts of the Ancient World. (Cambridge: Cambridge University Press, 2007). ISBN 9780521842471.

Alexander the Great: A New History. Edited by Waldemar Heckel and L. A. Tritle. (Wiley-Blackwell, 2009). ISBN 97811405130813 (cloth); ISBN 97811405130820 (pbk).

Justin: Epitome of the Philippic History of Pompeius Trogus, Volume 2. Books 13–15: The Successors of Alexander the Great, trans. by J. C. Yardley, commentary by P. V. Wheatley and W. Heckel, Clarendon Ancient History Series (Oxford, 2011). ISBN 9780199277599.

Chapters in Books

'Philip II and Olympias (337/6 BC)', *Classical Contributions. Studies in Honour of Malcolm Francis McGregor*, edited by G. S. Shrimpton and David Macargar (Locust Valley, N.Y., 1981) 51–7.

'Resistance to Alexander the Great'. In L. A. Tritle (ed.), *The Greek World in the Fourth Century* (London: Routledge, 1997) 189–227.

'King and Companions: Observations on the Nature of Power in the Reign of Alexander'. In J. Roisman (ed.), *Brill's Companion to Alexander the Great* (Leiden: Brill, 2003) 197–225.

'The Conquests of Alexander the Great: 336–323'. In K. H. Kinzl (ed.) *Blackwell's Companion to the Classical Greek World* (Oxford: Blackwell, 2006) 560–88.

'The Conquest of Asia'. In Waldemar Heckel and L. A. Tritle (eds), *Alexander the Great: A New History*, (Wiley-Blackwell, 2009) 26–52.

'A King and his Army'. In Waldemar Heckel and L. A. Tritle (eds), *Alexander the Great: A New History* (Wiley-Blackwell, 2009) 69–82.

'The Three Thousand: Alexander's Infantry Guard', in B. Campbell and L. A. Tritle (eds), *The Oxford Handbook of Warfare in the Classical World* (Oxford, 2013) 163–78.

Proceedings of Conferences

'Factions and Macedonian Politics: 336–323 BC', *Ancient Macedonia*, vol. 4 (Thessaloniki, 1986) 293–305.

'The Politics of Antipatros: 324–319 BC', *Ancient Macedonia* 6 (Thessaloniki, 1999) vol. 1, 489–98.

'The Politics of Distrust: Alexander and his Successors'. In Daniel Ogden (ed.), *The Hellenistic World: New Perspectives* (London: Duckworth, 2002) 81–95.

'Alexander and the Limits of the Civilized Word'. In Waldemar Heckel and Lawrence A. Tritle (eds), *Crossroads of History. The Age of Alexander.* (Claremont, CA: Regina Books, 2003) 147–74.

'The Earliest Evidence for the Plot to Poison Alexander'. In W. Heckel, L. A. Tritle and Patrick Wheatley (eds), *Alexander's Empire. Formulation to Decay* (Claremont, CA: Regina Books, 2007) 265–75.

'The asthetairoi: a closer look'. In Patrick Wheatley and Robert Hannah (eds), *Alexander and His Successors: Essays from the Antipodes* (Claremont, CA, 2009) 99–117.

'Scythed Chariots at Gaugamela'. In E. D. Carney and D. Ogden (eds), *Philip II and Alexander the Great: Father and Son, Lives and Afterlives.* (Oxford, 2010) 103–113. (with C. Willekes and G. Wrightson)

Articles

'Amyntas, Son of Andromenes', *Greek, Roman and Byzantine Studies* 16 (1975) 393–8.

'The Conspiracy against Philotas', *Phoenix* 31 (1977) 9–21. (Republished in J. Roisman, *Alexander the Great*, D. C. Heath, 1995) 154–63.

'The Flight of Harpalos and Tauriskos', *Classical Philology* 72 (1977) 133–5.

'Asandros', *American Journal of Philology* 98 (1977) 410–12.

'The Somatophylakes of Alexander the Great: Some Thoughts', *Historia* 27 (1978) 224–8.

'Kleopatra or Eurydike?' *Phoenix* 32 (1978) 155–8.

'On Attalos and Atalante', *Classical Quarterly* n.s. 28 (1978) 377–83.

'Leonnatos, Polyperchon and the Introduction of proskynesis', *American Journal of Philology* 99 (1978) 459–61.

'One More Herodotean Reminiscence in Curtius Rufus', *Hermes* 107 (1979) 122–3.

'The Somatophylax Attalos: Diodoros 16.94.4', *Liverpool Classical Monthly* 4.10 (Dec, 1979) 215–16.

'Philip II, Kleopatra and Karanos', *Rivista di Filologia e Istruzione Classica* 107 (1979) 385–93.

'Alexander at the Persian Gates', *Athenaeum* 58 (1980) 168–74.

'Kelbanos, Kebalos or Kephalon?' *Beiträge zur Namenforschung* 15 (1980) 43–5.

'IG II² 561 and the Status of Alexander IV', *Zeitschrift für Papyrologie und Epigraphik* 40 (1980) 249–50.

'Marsyas of Pella, Historian of Macedon', *Hermes* 108 (1980) 444–62.

'Some Speculations on the Prosopography of the Alexanderreich', *Liverpool Classical Monthly* 6.3 (1981) 63–9.

'Polyxena, the Mother of Alexander the Great', *Chiron* 11 (1981) 79–86.

'Two Doctors from Kos?' *Mnemosyne* 34 (1981) 396–8.

'Leonnatus and the Captive Persian Queens: A Case of Mistaken Identity', *Studi Italiani di Filologia Classica* 53 (1981) 272–4.

'Honours for Philip and Iolaos: *IG* II² 561', *Zeitschrift für Papyrologie und Epigraphik* 44 (1981) 75–7; cf. *SEG* 31 (1981) 20–1, text no. 80.

'Roman Writers and the Indian Practice of Suttee', *Philologus* 125 (1981) 305–11 (co-authored by J. C. Yardley).

'Philip II and the Quadriga', *Liverpool Classical Monthly* 7.9 (1982) 39–40.

'The Career of Antigenes', *Symbolae Osloenses* 57 (1982) 57–67.

'Who Was Hegelochos?' *Rheinisches Museum für Philologie* 125 (1982) 78–87.

'The Early Career of Lysimachos', *Klio* 64 (1982) 373–381.

'Alexandros Lynkestes and Orontas', *Eranos* 81 (1983) 139–43.

'Adea-Eurydike', *Glotta* 61 (1983) 40–2.

'Kynnane the Illyrian', *Rivista storica dell' Antichità* 13–14 (1983–84) 193–200.

'Demetrios Poliorketes and the Diadochoi', *La Parola del Passato* 219 (1984) 438–40.

'The Macedonian Veterans in Kilikia', *Liverpool Classical Monthly* 10.7 (1985) 109–10.

'Doryphorae at Curt. 3.13.15', *Rheinisches Museum für Philologie* 128 (1985) 366.

'The Boyhood Friends of Alexander the Great', *Emerita* 53 (1985) 285–9.

'Choriness and Sisimithres', *Athenaeum* 64 (1986) 223–6.

'*Somatophylakia*, a Macedonian cursus honorum?' *Phoenix* 40 (1986) 279–94.

'Fifty-two *Anonymae* in the History of Alexander', *Historia* 36 (1987) 114–19.

'*Anonymi* in the History of Alexander', *L'Antiquité Classique* 56 (1987) 130–47.

'A Grandson of Antipatros at Delos', *Zeitschrift für Papyrologie und Epigraphik* 70 (1987) 161–2.

'The Granddaughters of Iolaus', *Classicum* 15 (1989) 32–9.

'Peithon son of Agenor', *Mnemosyne* 43 (1990) 456–9.

'Q. Curtius Rufus and the Date of Cleander's Mission to the Peloponnese', *Hermes* 119 (1991) 124–5.

'Hephaistion the Athenian', *Zeitschrift für Papyrologie und Epigraphik* 87 (1991) 39–41.

'*Doryphoroe* in Curtius 3.3.15 Again', *Rheinisches Museum für Philologie* 135 (1992) 191–2.

'Kalas son of Harpalos and "Memnon's Land"', *Mnemosyne* 47 (1994), 93–5.

'Notes on Q. Curtius Rufus' *History of Alexander*', *Acta Classica* 37 (1994), 67–78.

'*Origines Veliae*: Trogus, Prologue XVIII', *AJP* 117 (1996), 309–10.

'The Case of the Missing Phrourarch: Arrian 3.16.6–9', *AHB* 16 (2002) 57–60.

'What's New in Alexander Studies', *Amphora* 3 (2004) 10–11, 19.

'*Synaspismos*, Sarissas and Wagons', *Acta Classica* 48 (2005) 189–94.

'Mazaeus, Callisthenes and the Alexander Sarcophagus', *Historia* 55 (2006) 385–96.

'Polyperchon as Brigand: Propaganda or Misunderstanding?' *Mnesmosyne* 60 (2007) 123–6.

'Nicanor son of Balacrus', *GRBS* 47 (2007) 401–12.

'The Royal Hypaspists in Battle: Macedonian *hamippoi*', *AHB* 26 (2012) 15–20

'The Sounds of Silence: A New Wife for Kassandros son of Antipatros', *Anabasis* 4 (2013) 51–60.

Reviews

G. M. Cohen, *The Seleucid Colonies* (Historia Einzelschriften, Heft 30; Wiesbaden, 1978), *Phoenix* 34 (1980) 93–5.

J. Seibert, *Das Zeitalter der Diadochen* (Darmstadt, 1983), *EMC (Classical Views)* 3 (1984) 103–5.

K. Buraselis, *Das hellenistische Makedonien und die Ägäis* (Munich, 1982) *Phoenix* 40 (1986) 458–61.

G. Walser, *Hellas und Iran* (Darmstadt, 1984) *EMC (Classical Views)* n.s. 6 (1987) 365–73.

G. Wirth, *Philipp II.* (Berlin-Stuttgart, 1985) *Gnomon* 48 (1987) 753–4.

E. N. Borza, *In the Shadow of Olympus. The Emergence of Macedon* (Princeton, 1990), *Bryn Mawr Classical Review* 2 (1991) 2–3.

R. M. Errington, *A History of Macedonia* (Berkeley and Los Angeles, 1990), *Bryn Mawr Classical Review* 2 (1991) 6–8

J. Buckler, *Philip II and the Sacred War* (Leiden, 1989) and F. L. Holt, *Alexander the Great and Bactria* (Leiden, 1988), *EMC (Classical Views)* 11 (1992) 77–82.

J. M. O'Brien, *Alexander the Great: The Invisible Enemy* (London and New York, 1992), *Bryn Mawr Classical Review* 4 (1993), 116–118, cf. *Canadian Journal of History* 28 (1993) 323–5.

A. Kuhrt and S. M. Sherwin-White, *From Samarkhand to Sardis* (Berkeley and Los Angeles, 1993), *Bryn Mawr Classical Review* 5 (1994) 142–6.

R. Ginouves (ed.), *Macedonia from Philip II to the Macedonian Conquest* (Princeton, 1994), *Bryn Mawr Classical Review* 4 (1994) 578–80.

J. Whitehorne, *Cleopatras* (London 1994), *Bryn Mawr Classical Review* 7 (1996) 456–8.

N. G. L. Hammond, *Sources for Alexander the Great: An Analysis of Plutarch's Life and Arrian's*

Anabasis Alexandrou (Cambridge 1993), *Bryn Mawr Classical Review* 8 (1997), 439–43.

A. B. Bosworth, *A Historical Commentary on Arrian's History of Alexander*, vol. 2 (Oxford 1995), *Bryn Mawr Classical Review* 8 (1997) 419–23.

Richard Stoneman, *Alexander the Great* (Routledge: New York and London, 1998), *Ancient History Bulletin* 12 (1998) 69–70.

Andrew Stewart, *Faces of Power: Alexander's Image and Hellenistic Politics* (Berkeley 1994). In *Echos du Monde Classique/Classical Views* 43 (1999) 150–4.

J. R. Hamilton, *Plutarch's Alexander* (2nd edn), *Scholia* 9 (2000) 14.

N. G. L. Hammond, *Philip II of Macedon*, *Gnomon* 72 (2000) 273–5.

Daniel Ogden, *Polygamy, Prostitutes and Death*, *BMCR* 2001.03.02.

J. E. Atkinson, *Curzio Rufo*, vol. 1, *Acta Classica* 43 (2000) 173–4 (review by W. Heckel and J. C. Yardley).

D. Hamel, *Athenian Generals, CR* 51 (2001) 107–9.

A. B. Bosworth and E. J. Baynham (eds), *Alexander the Great in Fact and Fiction* (Oxford 2000), *American Historical Review* (2002) 920–1.

J. S. Romm, *Herodotus* (Princeton, 1998), *Ariel* 32 (2001) 183–6.

A. B. Bosworth, *The Legacy of Alexander. Politics, Warfare and Propaganda under the Successors* (Oxford 2002), *International History Review* (2004) 583–6.

J. S. Romm and Pamela Mensch, *Alexander the Great. Selections from Arrian, Diodorus, Plutarch and Quintus Curtius* (2005), *Bryn Mawr Classical Review* 2005.10.25.

J. D. Grainger, *Alexander the Great Failure* in *BMCR* 2008.09.30.

M. Cosmopoulos (ed.), Experiencing War: Trauma and Society in Ancient Greece and Today, *Journal of Military History* 74.3 (2010) 908–10.

CONTRIBUTORS

Edward M. Anson is Professor of History at the University of Arkansas at Little Rock (USA).
emanson@ualr.edu

Elizabeth Baynham is Senior Lecturer in Classics and Ancient History at the University of Newcastle (Australia).
elizabeth.baynham@newcastle.edu.au

A. B. Bosworth is Professor Emeritus of Classics and Ancient History at Macquarie University (Australia).
brian.bosworth@mq.edu.au

Lee L. Brice is Professor of History at Western Illinois University (USA).
ll-brice@wiu.edu

Stanley Burstein is Professor Emeritus of History at California State University, Cal State, Los Angeles (USA).
sburste@calstatela.edu

Elizabeth Carney is Professor of Ancient History and Carol K. Brown Scholar in Humanities at Clemson University (USA).
elizab@clemson.edu

Philip de Souza is Senior Lecturer in Classics at University College, Dublin (Ireland).
philip.desouza@ucd.ie

E. Edward Garvin is Lecturer in Classics and History at the University of Alberta (Canada).
egarvin@ualberta.ca

Franca Landucci Gattinoni is Associate Professor of Greek History at the Catholic University of Milan (Italy).
franca.landucci@unicatt.it

William Greenwalt is Professor of Classics at Santa Clara University (USA).
wgreenwalt@scu.edu

Timothy Howe is Associate Professor of History and Ancient Studies at St. Olaf College (USA).
howe@stolaf.edu

Alexander Meeus is a Post-Doctoral Fellow at Katholieke Universiteit Leuven (Belgium).

Sabine Müller is Visiting Professor of Ancient History at Innsbruck University (Austria) and Lecturer of Ancient History at Christian-Albrechts University in Kiel (Germany).
smueller@email.uni-kiel.de

Daniel Ogden is Professor of Ancient History at the University of Exeter (UK) and Research Fellow at the University of South Africa.
d.ogden@exeter.ac.uk

Joseph Roisman is Professor of Classics at Colby College (USA).
jsroisma@colby.edu

Gordon Shrimpton is Professor Emeritus of Greek and Roman Studies at the University of Victoria, British Columbia (Canada).

Guiseppe Squillaci is Senior Lecturer in Ancient Greek History at the University of Calabria, Rende (Italy).
giuseppesquillace@libero.it

John Vanderspoel is Professor of Greek and Roman Studies at the University of Calgary (Canada).
vandersp@ucalgary.ca

Carolyn Willekes is a Lecturer for the Archaeological Institute of America (USA and Canada).
carolynwillekes@gmail.com

Graham Wrightson is Assistant Professor of History at South Dakota State University (USA).
graham.wrightson@sdstate.edu

FOREWORD

"So, Polybius, that's how the dream ended." Polybius thought for a moment. "Scipio," he said, "that's difficult to interpret, but I may know where to find an answer, or perhaps some help. Timaeus, that Sicilian historian I've occasionally mentioned to you, refers to Alexander's plans for a western campaign against Rome. While no soldier himself, he does get some things right from time to time. I'll see if he has anything useful to say about the Macedonian king."

No Timaeus, Waldemar Heckel in fact has many useful things to say about the great Alexander, his father Philip, and the Macedonians at war. In spite of editing three books together, Waldemar and I remain friends, or as he once put it with self-effacing humor, Timaeus to my Polybius, as we share common interests in the beast called War. So what I have to write cannot be considered objective, as I write not only about a friend, but a long-time collaborator. Yet there can be little doubt that his scholarship is no less distinguished than his friendship, that his contributions to the study of ancient Macedonia are considerable. The collection of essays offered here are testimony to both that contribution and the esteem of friends and colleagues around the world.

Those who study ancient Macedonia might nominate as standards any number of Waldemar's many publications. Certainly his *Who's Who in the Age of Alexander the Great* (Oxford: Blackwell, 2006) would take pride of place beside its antecedent, H. Berve's *Das Alexanderreich auf prosopographischer Grundlage* (1926), and explains its selection by Peter Green as among the outstanding books of 2006 noted in the *Times Literary Supplement* that year. But the *Who's Who* rests on a foundation of numerous prosopographic studies beginning in the late 1970s and which contributed in no little way to Waldemar's 1992 study, *The Marshals of Alexander's Empire* (London: Routledge).

While both studies will remain standards, innovative and challenging ideas and arguments characterize his scholarship no less. In particular I would call attention to his essay *Alexander and the 'Limits of the Civilised World'* (Heckel and Tritle 2003, 147–74) and *Mazaeus, Callisthenes, and the Alexander Sarcophagus*, (*Historia* 55 [2006], 385–96). In the first he suggests that the 'mutiny' of the Macedonian army at the Hyphasis was likely to have been carefully choreographed by Alexander to extract himself, and his army, from a difficult situation: how to return home with honor, authority, and image intact. His discussion of the so-called Alexander sarcophagus, offers not only a stimulating interpretation but one that leads to a compelling conclusion – that the sarcophagus, made *c*. 325, honors Alexander as well as its occupant, Alexander's one time enemy and new found friend and ally, the Persian Mazaeus.

There can be little question that such studies as these enliven the study of ancient history broadly and Alexander in particular. But Waldemar's contribution lies also in his editorial work, especially the founding of *The Ancient History Bulletin* (in 1986, with Brian Lavelle and John Vanderspoel), which took as its mission the speedy publication of scholarly contributions designed to stimulate debate and further discussion of received wisdoms and new ideas.

Many and varied scholarly contributions characterize the long career of Waldemar Heckel in the study of the ancient world. A genuine concern for making that study more accessible, and teaching and mentoring a new generation of young scholars, complements that scholarship and more than explains the collection of essays and the expressions of admiration and gratitude that follow.

Lawrence Tritle
Los Angeles, July 2014

INTRODUCTION
WALD

I am flattered to have been asked to provide this introduction to the Heckel Studies volume, especially since I could by no stretch of the imagination be called an Alexander scholar. I did, in fact, try to impress this fact on the proposers of the book, but was assured that I was required only to provide some memories of my nearly four decades of friendship and collaboration with our honorand and say nothing about the book's contents.

I think I can say, without fear of contradiction even from Waldemar, that the independence of thought and spirit that would characterize the scholarship of his more mature years did not in his youth make him the most popular person at the institutions at which he studied; he was, as they say in his part of the world, a burr under the saddle of a number of teachers and advisers whose minds were, unfortunately, narrower and smaller than his. His reputation for 'being awkward' often seemed to count for more than that country-wide reputation of his for courage, which he showed when, at the Canadian Classical Association annual meeting in Edmonton, Alberta, in 1975, he 'stood up to Badian' while still a lowly graduate student. It certainly did not help him when, nearly two years later, he applied for his position at the University of Calgary, where he was to have a distinguished career that spanned 35 years. It was a reputation that dogged him all the way to the job interview that started that career; and yet, paradoxically, it was also the very thing that secured him the interview. A number of colleagues at the departmental meeting for drawing up the list of candidates for interview had reservations about him, and I must confess, as I have often done to Waldemar, to having had some myself at the time; but what was to turn the tables for him was an unsolicited letter of *non*-support that arrived on the very day of our meeting and was read out to the departmental assembly. This had the opposite effect of what the writer presumably intended: the feeling now was that fair play demanded that the vilified candidate *should* be interviewed.

Waldemar's visit to Calgary a few weeks later involved a sample lecture to a class, which was memorable less for its subject matter (some Cleopatra or other, and not the Elizabeth Taylor one, which stumped most of the class) than the fact that he appeared in then-fashionable men's high-heeled shoes and an elegant suit, hand-made by a German tailor friend of his father. This was, I believe, the last time he was seen in a suit.

Any misgivings that I had were quickly dispelled after his arrival on campus, when we discovered that we had far more in common than the discipline that I call Classics and he Ancient History, and the history of Rock and Roll. But both of these being important to us, we quickly became friends.

His stellar performance as a new assistant professor, with a quick succession of articles in our best known journals plus his *Historia Einzelschrift* on the *Liber de Morte Alexandri*, soon led to an enviable CV and easy promotion through the ranks to Full Professor within a decade of his arrival in Calgary. It was largely because of his dedication to scholarship that my respect for him grew, and our friendship with it, as we competed for acceptance within our respective fields (the 'good *eris*', as we used to say, with a nod to Hesiod). And I can say (without hubris, I believe) that this led to mutual benefit, and the story of how this mutual benefit came about may be of interest to his many Alexander colleagues and former students who, I hope, will put their hands on this volume or appear in it.

In the 1970s Waldemar and I started jogging together at the end of the working day, our starting and finishing point being the University of Calgary gymnasium. This was a much more modest affair in the nineteen seventies (before its transformation for the '88 Winter Olympic Games) than it is now, but it did boast a decent-sized sauna, of which we would avail ourselves after our run. Here, in the sauna's heat, our conversations were relaxed and varied, and one day (probably in 1977 or 1978) Waldemar told me within its walls that a desideratum for his Alexander class was "a readable translation of Quintus Curtius' History of Alexander." I had to admit that, though I was classified in the department as a Latinist, that particular Roman author had eluded me at both the undergraduate and postgraduate level, but I added that I'd always been attracted by the idea of producing a readable translation of a Roman or Greek author. We exited to take our mid-sauna shower, but I returned slightly before him and on his return Waldemar by mistake – his spectacles always steamed up on entering the sauna – took his seat not next to me, but next to a rather elderly gentleman of the town (he was probably about our present age). The good man politely, but completely bemused, listened to how this annotated translation of Quintus Curtius Rufus was to proceed and why it was needed for the students ... until I, to Waldemar's acute embarrassment, addressed them both from the other side of the sauna and explained the mistake. This was the rather inauspicious inception of the Penguin Curtius.

I should add that before we were ready to commit ourselves to something that would clearly be a very time-consuming project, we decided to send off a sample of the translation and introduction/notes to several university presses in the hope of securing a contract. I think just about every university press in North America received that sample, as did Penguin Classics, in which we had really placed no hope and which I am sure would have been omitted from our list of possible publishers had we ourselves been responsible for mailing costs. The responses were, to say the least, underwhelming, and we were rejected so many times as to have brought acute depression on more sensitive souls; so we were flabbergasted when eventually a handwritten note arrived in the mail from the marvellous Betty Radice to tell us that Penguin was interested. For days we traipsed the corridors of the arts building with penguin-like waddles. And that was the start of our collaboration, which lasted many years, and which benefitted me far more than it did him, as he so often tells me, since it got me away from a field of studies that was becoming clogged with trendy rubbish and into one that I found and still find exhilarating and demanding, the translation of Greek and Latin texts.

Another interesting collaboration, some years later, was the Blackwell, *Alexander the Great: Historical Sources in Translation*, and how that started I shall let Waldemar narrate in his own words, taken from the preface of the book:

> Dan Quayle must have had a premonition when he made his famous gaffe about 'Latin' America. This book began on a country road in Guatamala, in the back of a crowded and painfully slow-moving minivan bound from Tikal to Flores, with a man too long without a bathroom break to continue his journey in comfort. For this was my predicament in June 1999, when I began sketching the outline of an 'Alexander sourcebook' in an attempt to divert my mind from what was quite literally a more pressing matter. John Yardley, wedged into the seat beside me and co-conspirator in this diversion, had come up with the idea for such a book several months before, but at that time there was no sense of urgency...

I am sure there are stories behind his many other books but, regrettably, I was not part of them.

That last paragraph indicates that our friendship went beyond the academic sphere, or perhaps it would be more correct to say embraced a rather different academic sphere, namely the colonization of Mexico and Central and Southern America, in which he still retains an interest that he occasionally claims surpasses even that of Alexander studies. This stage of our friendship began some years after I had left Calgary when he visited me 'down east' in Milton, Ontario, my present home. Pleased to see each other, I suppose, we stayed up most of the night in rather too-well-lubricated conversation, after which, to cool our heads, we took a walk at dawn through the suburban streets of Milton. It was during this that he suggested that we should that summer pay a visit to Mexico, Belize and Guatemala, and he emphasised the seriousness of his suggestion by addressing buenos diases to bemused early-rising Miltonians en route to early-morning employment. That proposed visit took place either the same or the following year, and the Flores-Tikal journey was part of it – I remember vividly his taking out a pencil and notebook from his breast pocket to jot down chapter headings for the book after the driver, half-way up a steep hill, geared down the *colectivo*, an old VW camper van, to second gear, turning Waldemar's discomfort to panic. And that trip was followed by many others that included Venezuela, Ecuador, Chile, Argentina, Uruguay and, *si memini*, all Central America save El Salvador, which a landslide had rendered a little too dangerous even for his intrepid spirit. I hope there will be more to come.

But just as memorable for me was his first – and so far only – trip to my native Wales, in 1999, and he took it less because he found Wales a more exciting destination than the Central and South American countries than because the University of Calgary was prepared to pay for it. He had been invited to a prestigious international conference to be held at Baskerville Hall in the beautiful Wye Valley – it claimed that it had once had Conan Doyle as a visitor and had been the inspiration for that dog story of his, but that the author had changed the location in it to Dartmoor in Devonshire just to prevent hordes of sight-seers invading this idyllic Welsh country house. I decided to make my annual visit coincide with Waldemar's, and even attend the conference. This did in fact happen, and our relative positions at the meeting were quickly made clear when, on our arrival, he was shown into an elegant Victorian room with a huge bed and a beautiful, functioning antique bath that actually stood in the middle of it, and I, a *paying* guest, ascended to a garret that must have once served as a part of the servants' quarters.

But we had earlier decided that we would, before the conference meet-up, spend a few days with my cousin, Patricia, in the South Wales town of Bridgend, whose fame resides in its reputation for teen-age suicides (a reputation which, I hasten to add, well post-dates Waldemar's visit). I think the part of that sojourn that Waldemar will most remember was our Saturday afternoon visit to the (now, sadly, defunct) Ogmore Club, Bridgend's last men-only club, which defended its male-chauvinism with the (actually true) claim that it had insufficient funds to install female toilets. Among the memorable occurrences there was a 'performance' by one Roger Parish who, Waldemar observed, was the closest thing he'd ever encountered to what he imagined a Homeric rhapsode to have been. Everyone knew well the jokes Roger told, because they'd heard them over beer every Saturday afternoon for years on end, but all were entranced by his performance and every week kept calling on him to tell again "the one about…." Later on, Waldemar became engaged in conversation with two friends of mine, one, my oldest friend from high school days, Colin Lewis (father of Sian Lewis, whose book *The Athenian Woman* will certainly be known to readers of this volume), and the other a very plain-talking Bridgend native by the name of Wayne Edwards. At one point Wayne observed that he and Waldemar must be roughly coeval and when Waldemar told him how old he was a surprised Wayne could only observe "Boy, you've had a hard life!"

There are, of course, many memories that could be added and expanded on: the uniformed schoolgirls singing on the bus in Venezuela as we traversed the hills before descending to Puerto Colombia; the bus in Belize where the driver stopped in a village so an apparently sick child could be examined by a doctor (fortunately the child was OK), a corpulent male passenger objecting to that and the irate mother addressing him in the local pidgin "shaddap you – you ain't nuttin but a big fat nuttin you"; the climb up Mt Chimborazo in Ecuador when our breath was labouring in the thin air and our guide pulled out a cigarette and proceeded to smoke; the three of us (Waldemar, Colin and I) sweating along the Argentinian side of the Iguazu Falls; Waldemar's fury when we then entered Chile and Colin and I, as British passport holders, paid no visa fee (thanks to Maggie Thatcher's cosy relationship in the past with General Pinochet) and he had to cough up a hundred dollars; and our Riobamba railway journey that took ten hours instead of four to get us to Alausi because the train derailed four times; and so many others, many of which, as Fordyce observed on his omitted Catullus poems, "do not lend themselves to comment." But to relate all *ante diem clauso componet Vesper Olympo*, as the bard says.

Well, pace Wayne Edwards, life for Waldemar hasn't been that hard, and certainly isn't now. Our honorand has, we hope, many more years, many more books, and many more trips before him. I am pleased and proud to have had so many years of collaboration and friendship with him. The University of Calgary was very fortunate to have had him as a member of its Classics Department for so long, and I'm sure it misses him even more than he misses it. Keep on rockin', rollin', writin', Wald (and, readers, please note that only Colin and I are permitted to call him that).

J. C. Yardley,
Milton, Ontario,
July, 2014.

DARIUS I AND THE PROBLEMS
OF (RE-)CONQUEST: RESISTANCE, FALSE
IDENTITIES AND THE IMPACT OF THE PAST

Sabine Müller[1]

After his accession in 522/21 BCE, Darius I was confronted with a problem common in ancient conquest societies: The appearance of pretenders proclaiming themselves descendants of the last independent rulers of their countries. This was as much a social as a political problem and in Darius' case it also turned out to be a military problem. The pretenders took over the identity of former local rulers or their descendants. Thus, by underpinning their claim to have a family-right to the throne of their region, they led revolts against Darius' reign. The result was that various parts of the empire rebelled, including Persis, Media, and Babylonia.

While the identity of the 'false Bardiya' who was killed by Darius and his six accomplices is a matter of debate, the phenomenon of the claims of the other rebels has rarely been discussed in its own right. This paper's objective is to analyze the rebels' strategy of taking over a false identity in order to legitimize their deeds. It will be argued that this is strictly speaking not a case of identity theft but more a kind of 'identity borrowing'. The rebels meant to revive or complete the political program their 'borrowed' figure was associated with. The paper also attempts to examine the common features of the various incidents when such imposters appeared like the false Philips, the false Neros or the false Alexanders.[2]

A swift expansion and the vast size of an empire presented great challenges.[3] This was a lesson not only the conquerors themselves but also their successors had to learn. Cases of

---

[1] It is a special pleasure and honor to contribute to the Festschrift for Waldemar Heckel. For many years his articles and books have been a source of inspiration for all scholars dealing with Macedonian history. His manifold publications always provide scholarship with new directions and perspectives. As I owe him so much, I hope that he finds interesting this study that tries to combine two of his special fields of interest: Achaemenid History and Prosopography. I would like to thank Anneli Purchase for her kind help.

[2] Pseudo-Philippos (the pretender Andriscus who revolted against the Romans in Macedonia in 151–148 BCE): Diod. 31.40a, Liv. Epit. 49.21–23. Pseudo-Nerones (three pretenders appearing in the Roman East between 68–89 BCE): Tac. Hist. 2.8–9; Dio 66.19.3; Suet. Nero 57. The first Pseudo-Alexander (Alexander Balas, Seleucid king 153/50–145 BCE, husband of Cleopatra Thea): Just. 35.1.5–36.1. The second Pseudo-Alexander (an alleged daimon of Alexander the Great appearing in Moesia following Caracalla's route in order to announce the reign of Severus Alexander in 221/22 CE): Dio 39.17.2–18.3.

[3] Cf. Van de Mieroop 2007, 290.

political discontinuity, especially, caused tension, conflict and local desires for autonomy. At the beginning of his reign, Darius I experienced exactly that, being confronted with revolts. But we should not view these rebels as a connected movement or in any way linked. Indeed, some of the rebels were not content with fighting against Darius, but intended to neutralize the whole Persian conquest since Cyrus II by trying to become autonomous again.

It is a matter of debate whether Darius was a liar himself who had killed the true Bardiya, legitimate son of Cyrus II and Cambyses' full brother, and then invented the story of a usurper named Gaumata in order to justify his bloody coup.[4] Apart from this insoluble problem, most scholars agree that Darius was a member of the extended royal Persian clan.[5] However, the multiple revolts against his rule show that he had some problems with his legitimacy and was regarded as a usurper by large parts of the population.[6] Obviously, after the last male member of Cyrus' immediate family had died, the leading clans in the empire thought they would be released from the ties of trust and obligation that had linked them to the royal house.[7] Thus, the game of thrones was on again. While the clans struggled for autonomy, Darius tried to (re)establish the clan harmony by force.

The prime source for these events is the Behistun inscription, carved on a cliff high above the road from the plains of Mesopotamia to Ecbatana.[8] Commissioned by Darius, this piece of royal propaganda contains the explanation of how he was chosen by Ahuramazda to restore divine order and the royal house:

> Saith Darius the King: There was not a man, neither a Persian nor a Mede nor anyone of our family who might make that Gaumata the Magian deprived of the kingdom (…) Not anyone dared say anything about Gaumata the Magian, until I came (…) I took the kingdom from him (DB § 13).[9]

Darius branded the rebels as liars.[10] As his definition of 'lie' (*drauga*) has religious and political connotations, it includes the meaning of 'rebellion'.[11] He also made clear that Ahuramazda had given the whole empire to him alone:

> Saith Darius the King: Ahuramazda bestowed the kingdom upon me; Ahuramazda bore me aid until I got possession of this kingdom; by the favour of Ahuramazda I hold this kingdom. (...) Saith Darius the king: This is what I did by the favor of Ahuramazda in one and the same year after that I became king. XIX battles I fought; by the favor of Ahuramazda I smote them and took prisoner IX kings (DB §§ 9, 52).

---

[4]   Cf. Jacobs 2011, 644; Kuhrt 2010, 136–8; Müller 2009, 47–8; Rollinger 2006; Brosius 2006, 17; Briant 1996, 113–14; Balcer 1987, 89; Dandamaev 1976, 108–27.

[5]   Cf. Jacobs 2011, 641–50; Kuhrt 2010, 152, n. 4; Frye 1993, 97. Contra: Brosius 2006, 17.

[6]   Cf. Jacobs 2011, 647; Wiesehöfer 2005, 33–43; Briant 1996, 180–81; Heinrichs 1987, 504–5; Balcer 1987, 50.

[7]   Cf. Müller 2009, 48.

[8]   Cf. Kuhrt 2010, 141; van de Mieroop 2007, 291; Rollinger 2006, 43; Wiesehöfer 2005, 33, 40–1; Frye 1993, 95.

[9]   Translation of all passages taken from DB: R.G. Kent.

[10] DB §§ 52, 54.

[11] Cf. Kuhrt 2010, 152, n. 15; Müller 2009, 36; Kent 1953, 192: "'the Lie', the evil force opposed to Ahuramazda."

Darius reports that several pretenders proclaimed themselves descendants of the last local rulers of their countries:

> One, Nidintu-Bel by name, a Babylonian; he lied, thus he said: "I am Nebuchadnezzar, the son of Nabonidus"; he made Babylon rebellious. (…) One, Phraortes by name, a Mede; he lied, thus he said: "I am Khshathrita, of the family of Cyaxares," he made Media rebellious. One Ciçantakhma by name, a Sagartian, he lied; thus he said: "I am king in Sagartia, of the family of Cyaxares," he made Media rebellious. (…) One, Vahyazdata by name, a Persian; he lied, thus he said: "I am Smerdis, the son of Cyrus"; he made Persia rebellious. One, Arkha by name, an Armenian; he lied; thus he said: "I am Nebuchadnezzar, the son of Nabonidus"; he made Babylon rebellious (DB § 52).

In Babylon, the pretenders Nidintu-Bel and Arkha one after the other claimed to be Nebuchadnezzar, the son of Nabonidus, the last Chaldean king of the Neo-Babylonian Empire defeated by Cyrus II in 539.[12] Interestingly, in Cyrus' time, Nabonidus had not been that popular in Babylon. He had estranged the influential priests of city-god Marduk by paying much attention to the sanctuaries of the moon god Sin in Ur and Harran.[13] Consequently, differences with the urban elite of Babylon occurred. The priests of Marduk supported Cyrus' invasion and circulated his propaganda that he was Babylon's savior selected by Marduk to restore order and justice, freeing the people from Nabonidus' tyranny.[14] However, this negative image of the last Chaldean king seems to have been forgotten by the supporters of Nidintu-Bel's and Arkha's revolts. At this stage of his afterlife, Nabonidus had become a symbol of 'good old times'. His name served as a reminder of freedom and autonomy, signifying a better way for Babylonia than to be governed by Darius. Otherwise Nidintu-Bel and Arkha would not have been able to mobilize any support. We cannot tell whether they were in fact believed to be sons of Nabonidus. However, it is probably safe to assume that their supporters agreed with the policy in relation to Babylon associated with the memory of Nabonidus' house. In addition, their choice of the throne-name Nebuchadnezzar illustrates their claim to revive ancient Mesopotamian tradition by constructing a fictitious political continuity.[15]

Media is a special case. Probably, there was no royal house of a unified empire as the Greek sources imply. Instead, the political structure of Media was a confederacy of several leading families headed by 'war-lords'.[16] In Media, two imposters named Phraortes and Ciçantakhma claimed to be descendants of Umakishta, a local heroic figure.[17] The hellenized form of his name is Cyaxares as mentioned by Herodotus.[18] Cyaxares was a successful

---

[12] DB §§ 16, 49.

[13] This does not mean that he neglected the cult of Marduk as claimed by his enemy Cyrus (Cyrus Cylinder, l. 5–9). But the priests of Marduk were obviously irritated. Cf. Müller 2012, 139–40; Van de Mieroop 2007, 280; Wiesehöfer 2005, 88; Jursa 2005, 37; Kuhrt 1992, 31.

[14] Cyrus Cylinder, l. 5–17. Cf. Müller 2012, 135–140; Van de Mieroop 2007, 278–81; Kuhrt 1992, 48–52; Balcer 1987, 27.

[15] Cf. Rollinger 2005.

[16] Cf. Kuhrt 2010, 19; 1992, 22; Van de Mieroop 2007, 273; Wiesehöfer 2003, 391–96; Rollinger 2005; 2003; Briant 1996, 132.

[17] DB §§ 24, 33.

[18] Hdt. 1.106.

warrior selected as the leader of the Medes who had attacked Assyria and destroyed that empire with Babylonian help.[19] Hence his name was associated with glorious memories of Median victories and military strength presumably preserved by oral tradition within the families involved. By claiming to be his descendants, the rebels certainly intended to associate themselves with Cyaxares' military skills and triumphs implying that they were the ones to overcome the Persian threat and bring back 'Median golden times'. Again, it is not clear whether their supporters believed their claim to be associated with Cyaxares' house. In any case, the rebels' political agenda seemingly engaged their supporters' hopes for autonomy.

In Persis, a rebel called Vahyazdata took over the identity of Bardiya, Cyrus' legitimate son, Darius' predecessor.[20] Darius calls this movement a 'second uprising in Persia' (after the usurpation of Gaumata).[21] Probably, it is different from the local uprisings in Media and Babylonia. As the local royal house that the imposter associated himself with was the dynasty of the conqueror and founder of the empire, Cyrus the Great, Vahyazdata's claim might have been to rule over the whole empire without being restricted to Persis.[22] In any case, he denied Darius' legitimacy and relied on the impact of the name of Cyrus' family branch.

In consequence, Darius had to re-conquer various parts of the empire. Like the rebels, he also made use of the power of the past by stressing his royal descent:

> Saith Darius the King: (…) From long time ago our family had been kings. Saith Darius the King: VIII of our family (there are) who were kings afore; I am the ninth. (...) The kingdom which had been taken away from our family, that I put in its place; I established it on its foundation (DB §§ 3–4, 14).[23]

However, the rebels denied his right to reign. Some even denied the validity of the political structure established under the reign of Cyrus II and Cambyses II. Thus, these false identities became the essential core of the rebels' propaganda, linking them to their local past by constructing an idea of political continuity.[24] Hence, the idealized past is the central point, while the future, as defined by the rebels, was actually a renewal of that idealized past.

Invented, idealized pasts are one common feature of an intelligible pattern against which to set appearances of imposters under false royal identities. The Syrian satirist Lucian of Samosata seems to be one of the first to recognize this kind of pattern. In *The Ignorant Book-Collector*, he writes: "… you were even persuaded that you resembled a certain royal person in looks, like the false Alexander, the false Philip, the false Nero in our grandfather's time, and whoever else has been put down under the title 'false' (pseudo)."[25]

---

[19] Cf. Van de Mieroop 2007, 273.

[20] Bardiya ruled at least for eight months (Hdt. 3.67.2: seven months). Cf. Kuhrt 2010, 152, n. 19; Rollinger 2006, 48; Wiesehöfer 1978, 55–6.

[21] DB § 42.

[22] Although his revolt was actually limited only to Persis, cf. Zawadski 1995.

[23] For the construction of his genealogy see Jacobs 2011, 636–58; Kuhrt 2009, 152, n. 4; Müller 2009, 44–5; Kent 1946, 208–11.

[24] Cf. Müller 2009, 49; Rollinger 2005; Briant 1996, 132.

[25] Luc. *Ind.* 20–21. Translation: A. M. Harmon.

In modern scholarship, Fergus Millar stated that the 'false king' phenomenon helps to illuminate the question of popular conceptions of monarchy, and reactions to individual monarchs.[26] Martin Charlesworth (1950) and Edward Champlin (2003) suggested that there were three conditions necessary for the appearance of an impostor under false identity: The historical figure he impersonates should have been popular with large parts of the population, should have died with his work incomplete, and his death should have been sudden and mysterious.[27] I would refine this somewhat so that it better fits the ancient world and suggest that there are six central elements: a deep-rooted monarchical tradition, the existence of the idea of a charismatic kingship, a situation of political discontinuity, the popularity of the dynasty with the local population, a longing for the past, and an idealization of the historical persons as benefactors and protectors.

To sum up, the picture that has emerged from this examination of evidence is that the longing for an idealized past is at the centre of these 'false king' uprisings. The persons the imposters claimed to be were local figures associated with hopes for a better future characterized as a 'return to the past'. The pretenders tried to revive and complete the political program that was associated with their doppelgängers. This does not mean that the pretenders' ideal necessarily corresponded to their real policy, merely that it seemed to do so. In the end, this phenomenon suggests that memories can be used as effective propagandistic weapons against conquerors and their successors, largely because they engage a 'time before the conquest'.

Bibliography

Balcer, J. M. (1987) *Herodotus and Bisitun*. Stuttgart.

Briant, P. (1996) *Histoire de l'Empire Perse de Cyrus à Alexandre*. Paris.

Brosius, M. (2006) *The Persians*. London and New York.

Champlin, E. (2003) *Nero*. Cambridge, MA and London.

Charlesworth, M. (1950) Nero: Some Aspects, *Journal of Roman Studies* 40, 69–76.

Dandamaev, M. A. (1976) *Persien unter den ersten Achaimeniden*. Wiesbaden.

Frye, R. N. (1993) *The Heritage of Persia*. Costa Mesa.

Heinrichs, J. (1987) 'Asiens König'. Die Inschriften des Kyrosgrabs und das achaimenidische Reichsverständnis. In W. Will and J. Heinrichs (eds) *Zu Alexander d. Gr. FS G. Wirth*, vol. I, 487–540, Amsterdam.

Kent, R. G. (1946) The Oldest Old Persian Inscription, *Journal of the American Oriental Society* 66, 202–12.

— (1953) *Old Persian*. Chicago.

Kuhrt, A. (1992) Usurpation, Conquest and Ceremonial: From Babylon to Persia. In D. Cannadine and S. Price (eds) *Rituals of Royalty*, 20–55, Cambridge.

— (2010) *The Persian Empire. A Corpus of Sources from the Achaemenid Period*. London and New York.

Jacobs, B. (2011) 'Kyros der große König, der Achämenide.' Zum verwandtschaftlichen Verhältnis und zur politischen und kulturellen Kontinuität zwischen Kyros dem Großen und Dareios I. In R. Rollinger, B. Truschnegg and R. Bichler (eds) *Herodotus and the Persian Empire*, 635–63, Wiesbaden.

Jursa, M. (2004) *Die Babylonier*. München.

Millar, F. (1964) *A Study of Cassius Dio*. Oxford.

Müller, S. (2009) Das antike Perserreich im Ausnahmezustand. Dareios I. im Kampf gegen die 'Lüge'. In O. Ruf (ed.), *Ästhetik der Ausschließung*, 21–50, Würzburg.

---

[26] Cf. Millar 1964, 218.

[27] Cf. Champlin 2003, 21–24; Charlesworth 1950, 73–4.

— (2012) Empathie, Recht und Herrschaftsausübung in der Inschrift des Kyroszylinders. In M. Gruber and S. Häußler (eds) *Normen der Empathie*, 136–49, Berlin.

Rollinger, R. (2003) The Western Expansion of the 'Median Empire'. In G. B. Lanfranchi (ed.) *Continuity of Empire: Assyria, Media, Persia*, 289–319, Padua.

— (2005) Das Phantom des 'Medischen Großreichs' und die Behistun-Inschrift. In E. Dabrova (ed.) *Ancient Iran and its Neighbours*, 11–29, Krakow.

— (2006) Ein besonderes historisches Problem. Die Thronbesteigung des Dareios und die Frage seiner Legitimität. In Historisches Museum der Pfalz Speyer (ed.) *Pracht und Prunk der Großkönige*, 41–53, Stuttgart.

Van de Mieroop, M. (2007) *A History of the Ancient Near East*. Oxford.

Wiesehöfer, J. (1978) *Der Aufstand Gaumatas und die Anfänge Dareios' I*. Bonn.

— (2003) The Medes and the Idea of the Succession of Empire in Antiquity. In Lanfranchi, 391–96.

— (2005) *Das antike Persien*. Düsseldorf.

Zawadski, S. (1995) Is there a Document dated to the Reign of Bardiya II (Vahyazdata)? *Nouvelles Assyriologiques Brèves et Utilitaires* 54.

CLAUSEWITZ
AND ANCIENT WARFARE

E. Edward Garvin[1]

In 499 Aristagoras, then Tyrant of Miletus, approached Cleomenes of Sparta requesting assistance in a planned rebellion against Persian rule over the Greeks of Asia. Cleomenes listened to Aristagoras' various incentives and then asked about the distance from the Ionian coast to the Persian capital.[2] When Cleomenes heard the answer, a three month journey, he ordered Aristagoras to leave Sparta by sunset.[3] It was not the distance to the battlefield that Cleomenes was concerned about; he did not ask where and by what means Darius would oppose the invasion. He asked about the distance to Susa, the administrative capital of the Persian Empire, which Aristagoras had suggested was the objective necessary to achieve victory.

Two issues critical to military success are in consideration here: The identification of strategic objectives, and the delivery of decisive force over a great distance. The combination of these issues recurs with some frequency in our ancient Greek historical record with more examples of spectacular failures than successes. Perhaps the most spectacular of the failures would be Xerxes' Hellenic campaign but the Sicilian Expedition certainly belongs on the list. Of successes there are fewer examples; one, in fact.[4] Alexander managed to accomplish what Cleomenes thought impossible and what any rational individual would have advised against. Even more astonishing is that rather than three months, it was over three years before Alexander entered Susa.

Various scholars and analysts over the centuries have offered insightful and often informative explanations for the failure of Xerxes and the Sicilian Expedition, the success of Alexander, and other such events, but almost without exception they fall back on the

---

[1] In 1986 I attended the University of Calgary with a plan: I would earn a BA in History focusing on Tudor-Stuart England, specifically English Common Law, and then pursue an LLB and live happily ever after. But I took a course on Alexander the Great and was bitten by a dog. The dog who bit me, Waldemar Heckel, was first my teacher, then mentor and now friend. If ever I have done it right, it is Waldemar I must thank. The errors, of course, are my own.

[2] Herodotus (5.50.2) suggests that Aristagoras should have lied.

[3] Herodotus (5.49–51) seems to combine two traditions: In the other Gorgo, the daughter of Cleomenes and future wife of Leonidas, warns her father of the corrupting power of wealth.

[4] I omit the Roman sphere only partly to adhere to the theme, but mostly for the sake of brevity.

obvious, and safe, assignation of praise and blame to the character of the leader: Xerxes was overconfident, Nicias too timid (or the Ecclesia too bold), and Alexander a genius. Few, however, turn to military theory for explanatory paradigms.[5] The reason for this is, perhaps, that the pattern is so well established in our primary sources, which are also scarce where military theory is concerned. It would be a statement nearly without contention that history, as a genre of literature and as a pragmatic examination of data, began as the study of war; more specifically, I argue, the study of leadership and character tested in the most extreme circumstances. But nowhere in our ancient sources do we find an overt, systematic, might we say Aristotelian, analysis of Grand Strategy, Polyaenus notwithstanding. I doubt that this is either an accident or a shortcoming but rather a testament to the stubborn resistance on the part of war, as an object of study, to be categorized, systematized, encoded and reduced to practical formulae.

Contemporaneous with the classical period in western history, in China, Sun Tzu composed the earliest known theoretical treatise, the *Art of War*,[6] but nothing of comparative importance emerged in the west until Carl von Clausewitz wrote *On War*.[7] Clausewitz, a veteran of the Napoleonic wars and later director of the Prussian War Academy, died of cholera in 1831 leaving an unfinished manuscript which was published by his widow in 1832.[8] The work received little attention until Moltke defeated the Austrians and French in 1871 and announced that his secret was three books: *The Bible*, Homer, and Clausewitz (Keegan 1993, 20).

Contemporary with Clausewitz, Baron Antoine Henri Jomini, also a veteran officer of the Napoleonic wars, also wrote on strategy and his work, *The Art of War* (1862), gained far more currency in the latter nineteenth and early twentieth centuries, especially in Britain and the United States through the influence of Alfred Thayer Mahan.[9] Both appear to agree that the fundamental principles of strategy exist in a dimension above tactics and therefore above technology, above context, and for that reason the same analytical paradigms, a philosophy of strategy, should be applicable across temporal and cultural expanses.[10] The difference is that while Jomini thought those timeless fundamentals could be reduced to formulae with practical and direct applicability, Clausewitz thought in the abstract.[11] Jomini's formulae were soon enough revealed to be tactical, rather than strategic, and very much a product of, and reaction to, the stand-and-shoot massed infantry warfare of the Napoleonic age. While Clausewitz's abstractions are more easily applicable to more varied

---

[5] As an example, see Barry Strauss' *Masters of Command* (2012), in which Strauss' focus, understandably, is on the personal attributes of his subjects. See also Strauss and Ober 1990.

[6] Griffith 1963, 11.

[7] Throughout, I refer to the J. J. Graham translation of Clausewitz (1874), revised by F. N. Maude for the 1997 Wordsworth edition.

[8] A succinct biography is found in Keegan 1993, 14–20.

[9] For a biography and critique see Crowl 1986.

[10] Jomini writes: "…strategy alone will remain unaltered, with its principles the same as under the Scipios and Caesars … since they are independent of the nature of the arms and the organization of the troops" (1971, 48).

[11] Of Clausewitz Paret (1992, 108) comments; "An idea is defined with extreme, one-sided clarity, to be varied, sometimes chapters later, and given a new dimension…" Beyerchen (1993, 60) suggests that Clausewitz is either too theoretical to be practical or too practical to be theoretical.

circumstances they are so only because of their ambiguity. The recent popularity of the text might have something to do with the fact that it lends itself so well to a variety of interpretations which have given rise to long standing and continued debate.

Despite interpretative disagreement, *On War* has been and continues to be employed as a pedagogical and analytical tool by militaries, military training institutions and historians of war. Individual Clausewitzian concepts have become *topoi*: Economy of Force; the Fog of War and, more specific to this paper, the Centre of Gravity (CoG) and the Culminating Point of Attack (CPA).

Clausewitz's presentation of the concept of the Culminating Point of Attack is fraught with uncertainty not because Clausewitz himself was uncertain but because his death prevented him from developing the theory – or at least recording the development – fully. It appears in the fifth section of the seventh book; an incomplete section in an unedited part of the manuscript.[12] The lack of completion is problematic enough, but Clausewitz is less than straightforward at the best of times. Alan Beyerchen (1993) brilliantly demonstrates that the theories and philosophies presented by Clausewitz are best explained in terms of 'nonlinear dynamics' and more akin to chaos theory than traditional linear thought processes. But, for the purposes of analysis, a graph is really the only way to simplify CPA theory, even at the risk of allowing the linearity of the graphic to distort the theory itself.[13] On the graph below, the CD axis represents time-space and the AC axis represents force capability. The upper, solid arc on the left side represents the attacker and can be called the Arc of Attack; while the lower, dotted arc on the left represents the defender and can be called the Arc of Defense.

According to the theory, the attacker begins with a high force capability or, to borrow Clausewitz's metaphor, a high level of capital, but as the attacker moves through space-time attrition, the increasing difficulty of supply and communication, the morale of the troops, the financial burden and a myriad other factors cause an exponential reduction in his force capability.[14] If the attacker does not achieve a favourable peace at a point in space-time before his force capability falls below that of the defender, the probability of success diminishes dramatically. That point at which the reversal of advantage occurs is Clausewitz's Culminating Point of Attack. The end of the conflict, be it decisive victory or, as Clausewitz prefers, a desirable peace, must be located somewhere to the left of the CPA for the attacker to be successful.

The theory becomes most interesting and useful, in my opinion, with the analogy Clausewitz uses to clarify it: The attacker's capital (force capability) will be *spent*, regardless of all else, so it must be spent acquiring assets. If a desirable peace can be reached without the complete destruction of the enemy, then the attack should proceed only until the attacker has acquired enough assets to trade for that peace. If, on the other hand, the

---

12 Willmot, 'introduction' to Clausewitz, *On War* (1997, xxii). The theory is explained at 324 of the 1997 edition, Book Seven, Chapter Five, but the explanation refers to arguments that have been developed throughout the manuscript.

13 Which is where Vego (2009) goes so horribly wrong. His lengthy analysis of CPA includes a number of complex graphs all and each of which only complicate the issue beyond necessity.

14 Simply because of the fact that "every reduction in strength on one side can be considered an increase on the other" the defense is always in an advantageous position (Vego 2009, vii–75).

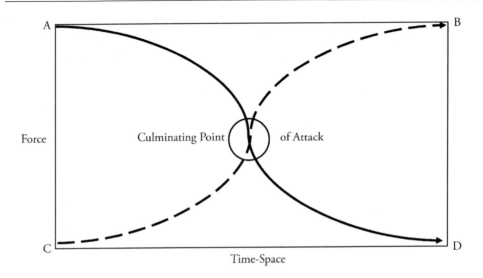

attacker passes the CPA and is unable to achieve the objective, the assets can still be used to negotiate an exit.[15]

Returning to Cleomenes and the Ionian Revolt: It would be an indefensible position to suggest that Cleomenes was a military genius. In 509 he marched to Athens in support of his friend Isagoras and attempted to occupy the Acropolis against a hostile population and with insufficient forces (Hdt. 5.70–73: *Ath. Pol.* 20). In 507 he marched to Attica once again, this time with sufficient forces but in a coalition so loose that it dissolved before a battle was fought (Hdt.5.74–5). In the end, Herodotus (5.41) insists that Cleomenes was not mentally stable; a diagnosis necessary to explain his inglorious end (Hdt. 6.74–5). Nevertheless, his decision to refuse Aristagoras in 499 may well have been based on the very considerations that the CPA predicts.[16]

It didn't require that Cleomenes be a military genius for him to recognize that the Arc of Attack might look something like an inclined plane, and a steep one, if Spartan forces attempted to march from Miletus to Susa and achieve a decisive victory without passing well beyond the CPA. But just where would the CPA have been located? How is the *point* determined? As Vego (2009, vii–74) explains, "A culminating point should not be understood too literally; it is not a 'point', but rather an area of uncertainty or nonrecognition (*sic*) in terms of space and time," which is an improvement on Clausewitz's own statement that the identification of the CPA, because of the "number of the elements of which an equation of the forces in action is composed," in the end, "hangs on the silken thread of imagination" (Clausewitz 1997, 325). Nevertheless, there are a few critical elements affecting the Arc of Attack that hang on a chain of empirical observation. Discussions of CPA often focus on

---

15 The Peace of Nicias is a very good example: Each side holding assets of value to the other so a peace was easily negotiated based on trade.

16 The Athenians, however, did agree to participate and Herodotus comments: "…it would seem that it is easier to deceive many than one, seeing that, though he did not prove able to deceive Cleomenes the Lacedaemonian by himself, yet he did this to thirty thousand Athenians" (5.98.2).

the centre of the graph, the CPA itself, but while this paper will attempt to demonstrate the usefulness of CPA (and CoG) theory as an explanatory paradigm, it will also redirect focus to the top left of the graph because, as Aristotle tells us, "the beginning is more than half of the whole" (*Nic. Eth.* 1098b).

The Ionian Revolt began in 499 and was not brought to a completion until the sack of Miletus in 494 but it would be a gross error to suggest that Ionian resistance endured for five years. Using the CPA graph, it can be explained that the Ionians began too low on the A–C axis, force capability, and that the Persians were, at the outset, very high in that regard. There should be no surprise that Darius "made no account of the Ionians, because he knew that they at all events would not escape unpunished for their revolt" (Hdt. 5.105) nor should there be any surprise that the Athenians withdrew their support after the Persian cavalry defeated the rebels near Ephesus in 498 (Hdt. 5.102). The passing of the CPA was proven by the Persian ability to operate throughout the theatre with speed, a high level of organization, and a high level of force capability.

Herodotus' account of the battle for Cyprus includes the story of Artibius' horse (5.111–12), the message being that a strategy to deal with the Persian cavalry is a necessity, and one the Ionians on the mainland lacked. The Ionian Revolt was the sack of Sardis, the rest was a Persian mop-up operation. Even more importantly, there is little in Herodotus' account that indicates just what the 'desirable peace,' the actual objective, might have been for the Ionian cities. It is unsatisfactory to say 'freedom,' regardless of how powerful that notion might be. It would have to be a freedom in which the Persian king was so depleted in force capability that he thought it no longer worth the effort or cost to regain control of Ionia.[17] Barring that, it would have to be the complete destruction of the Persian Empire, which is the only military objective described by Aristagoras to Cleomenes. It is easy enough, even for Cleomenes, to see that the objective is far towards the right of the graph.

But most importantly, according to Clausewitz's theory, there is no point in time or space between 499 and 494, between Sardis and Miletus, when the Ionians had acquired anything in the way of assets that could have been used to negotiate an end to the hostilities, and so Persian retribution continued until Athens in 480.

A more obvious candidate to test CPA theory would be the disastrous expedition that Athens launched against Syracuse in 415. In this event we find Nicias, another actor who has never been credited with genius, presented by Thucydides as the only Athenian who did see the equation and argue against the expedition.[18] In very general terms, we can say that Athenian forces had passed the CPA before they arrived at the Great Harbour or the walls of Syracuse for the very reasons Nicias enumerates in his first and second speeches to the Ecclesia (Thuc. 6.9–14). The first speech, for example, stresses the importance of the security of the home base, the point at which the Arc of Attack begins. The level of force capability is only partly determined by the combat forces themselves but largely by the strength, moral resolve (the will to fight), and security of the home base. The point

---

[17] As was the case by 449 when Persia agreed to the Peace of Callias. One might think that it was Mycale and Eurymedon that encouraged the Peace, but Persia did not come to the decision until Athens proved it was capable of operating on Cyprus and in Egypt.

[18] Plutarch's characterization (2.4) is favorable but he does admit Nicias' weaknesses.

needs no explanation, when Nicias says, "I warn you, then, that you leave many enemies behind you here even as you sail there only to bring more enemies back with you" (Thuc. 6.10.1), he is articulating a truism.[19]

Nicias' second attempt to dissuade the Athenians (Thuc. 6.20–23) recognises that the force capability of Syracuse and Selinus (identified as the military objectives) is very high and not easily disrupted, while the force capability of Athens will be extended and therefore reliant on uncertain allies. The clearest articulation of CPA theory comes at the end of the second speech (6.23.2) when Nicias offers a rare but accurate pinpoint identification of the CPA: "We must be masters of the country the very day we land … and failing this everything will be hostile to us."[20] The impossibility of such a landing meant that the CPA for Athens was actually somewhere in June of 415 in the Piraeus harbour. In addition to the security and unity of the home front, a critical element of CPA theory is the attacker's ability to operate in foreign territory.

Even more spectacular than the Athenian failure on Sicily is the Persian failure in Hellas in 480/79. The sudden withdrawal of the king and his main forces after Salamis seems a bit of an overreaction. He had, after all, possession of the city of Athens and all of Hellas from Attica north.[21] He also had an intact and undefeated army but that, of course, was the problem. Xerxes' invasion, as is well known and needs no further comment, is a lesson in Clausewitz' concept of the Economy of Force.[22] But the turning point, the Battle of Salamis, is classic CPA: Xerxes, despite his other faults, realized that he had passed the point at which his forward momentum was greater than the enemy's ability to defend, that the Arc of Attack was below the Arc of Defense, and that regardless of troop numbers or territory held, the Greeks were now able to disrupt his supply and communication and had taken the initiative in the war. Xerxes wisely withdrew.[23]

Another concept which informs the Persian Wars narrative more accurately is that of *Schwerpunk*, Centre of Gravity, a concept Clausewitz introduced in Book Six, also part of the unedited section of the manuscript. Since the sixth book was also among those he had intended to rewrite we can never be sure that Clausewitz himself was satisfied with any particular section. It is, I think, easy enough to demonstrate that his ideas on the subject are not represented in full maturity in the manuscript that has been left to us. It is, however, possible to trace Clausewitz's theoretical and logical progress and to arrive at some conclusions. Clausewitz begins with analogy:

---

[19] And, of course, it must be kept in mind that the words are Thucydides', not Nicias', and our author could insert irony because he knew the outcome.

[20] Nicias' letter to the Athenians (Thuc. 7.11– 15) in the winter of 414/13 simply affirms what the earlier speeches forewarned. A better description of a force long past the CPA could not be had.

[21] As per the speech of Mardonius following the battle (Hdt. 8.100).

[22] Artabanus, the *truth teller* in this story, articulates the Economy of Force rule as Xerxes is about to cross the Hellespont (Hdt. 7.49). But his speech at 7.10 seems to anticipate the speech by Nicias to the Athenians mentioned above.

[23] And equally wisely followed the first rule of gambling: Risk only what you are willing to lose. The force left under Mardonius was a gambler's wager. See the advice of Artemisia at Hdt. 8.102. CPA theory, if you do not have enough assets to negotiate a desirable peace – and Xerxes did not – your only option is the complete destruction of the enemy: hence Mardonius' pledge (Hdt. 8.100) to conquer all of Hellas or die trying.

As a centre of gravity is always situated where the greatest mass of matter is collected, and as a shock against the centre of gravity of a body always produces the greatest effect, and further, as the most effective blow is struck with the centre of gravity of the power used, so it is also in war.

(Clausewitz 1997, 317 = Bk 6:27)

Clausewitz has simply borrowed a principle from physics that can be used to describe the application of force. [24] At first, that was all that Clausewitz saw because that was the basis of the analogy; a concentration of force in a physical object, applied against a like concentration in another. It was easily and readily applicable to battle and to tactics. Therefore, he continues, the centre of gravity is "where the greatest bodies of troops are assembled" (Clausewitz 1997, 317). The idea, and the deployment of the term, was not new: A similar concept is described by Jomini when he lists his "fundamental principle of war" and says that it is "to throw the mass of the forces upon the decisive point...which is of the first importance to overthrow."[25] For Jomini the Decisive Point was a place on the battlefield and purely tactical.[26] From these two texts it has been deduced that war can be reduced to the simple formula of the superiority of force, that the Clausewitzian and Jominian theories are the same: Whatever the enemy's CoG, hit it with a CoG of your own that far exceeds theirs in mass. 'Centre of Gravity' and 'Decisive Point', both *Schwerpunkt* in the respective texts, are merely two translations of terms for the same, *tactical*, theory.

To accept that conclusion we have to assume that the 'greatest bodies' line was all Clausewitz had to say on the subject. But Clausewitz had already dismissed the idea of the superiority of force quite early in the treatise: "to see the whole secret of the art of war in the formula, *in a certain time, at a certain point, to bring up superior masses* – was a restriction overruled by the force of realities" (Clausewitz 1997, 84, italics mine).[27] Those forceful realities are, I believe, the historical record itself. Xerxes had a clear superiority of mass on land and sea but he failed. Alexander had a clear inferiority of mass and he succeeded, to list but two examples. Recognizing the problem but unwilling to dismiss the idea, Clausewitz postulates that "there remains nothing, therefore, where an absolute superiority is not available, but to produce a relative one at the decisive point..." (Clausewitz 1997, 167). Through Book Eight, this "collection of notes and sketches,"[28] we can see the concept expand well beyond the initial analogy and well beyond the tactical, practical and purely physical to the point where CoG becomes another nonlinear equation.[29] As the process reaches maturity, the CoG is no longer just the concentration of troops, nor even a physical object: It can be the national leader, the capital city, a 'unity of interests' among allies, or even public opinion. It is here that the most profound expression of the concept is found:

---

[24] Clausewitz developed his theory of *Schwerpunkt* (CoG) after attending a series of lectures by the physicist Paul Erman (Echevarria 2003, 110).

[25] Jomini, 1971, 70.

[26] *Ibid.*, 186

[27] See also Lidell Hart 1968, 342.

[28] Willmot 1997, xxii.

[29] Beyerchen 1993, 84.

...the great point is to keep the overruling relations of both parties in view. Out of them a certain centre of gravity, a centre of power and movement, will form itself, on which everything depends; and against this centre of gravity of the enemy, the concentrated blow of all the forces must be directed.

(Clausewitz 1997, 351 = Bk 8; 4)

Clausewitz here transcends the obvious, the superficial reality of armies on the field of battle and begins to see his CoG not as a thing at all but as an understanding of relationships. Unfortunately, it does nothing to clarify; rather, only confuses the issue further. It is easy to identify 'the greatest bodies of troops assembled' and the military is adept at delivering blows against those bodies,[30] but what of 'overruling relations'? What of a 'centre of power and movement'? It seems clear that the production of a relative superiority has to do with the identification and disruption of the 'overruling relations' where the CoG forms itself but this resides in the realm of strategy and must, therefore, precede tactics. It also seems clear that Clausewitz's theory has nothing to do with massing an infantry attack at the enemy's strongest position. We can restate: The Centre of Gravity is the strength and mobility that arises out of overriding relationships. It should not be necessary to be so pointed and overt, but the many analysts of late who have attempted to twist Clausewitz's theory into some other and strange thing have so confused the issue that an emphatic declaration of the original intent seemed appropriate.[31] We are left, then, not with two descriptions of the same theory, but two distinct concepts transcending and bridging strategy and tactics: the *Centre of Gravity* and the *Decisive Point*. The latter is a tactical consideration that may well involve a blow against massed infantry, but the former has to do with the kinds of relationships that give rise to, or produce, the ability and the will to enter the fight in the first place.

Can I suggest, then, that the centre of power and movement for the Athenian forces in 415 was their relationship with Alcibiades and the promises he made of riches and lands in Sicily?[32] Perhaps the removal of Alcibiades was the blow at the CoG and, as such, the force which put the Athenian forces off balance. I make the suggestion tentatively because the corollary is that Syracuse's greatest ally was the Athenian Ecclesia as it was the Ecclesia who delivered the blow against their own CoG![33] On the other side we can turn once again to Nicias: "From all that I hear we are going against cities that are great and not subject to one another, or in need of change, so as to be glad to pass from enforced servitude to an easier condition, or in the least likely to accept our rule in exchange for freedom" (Thuc. 6.20). Nicias has hit on the most important consideration – there were no relationships in Sicily that were easily breakable, and without an identifiable CoG there could be no

---

[30] Lidell Hart takes exception to Foch's interpretation of Clausewitz and his doctrine of the need to concentrate "all one's resources at a given moment on one spot." (1968, 342).

[31] See, as examples: Strange 1996; Echevarria 2003; Eikmeier 2004; Strange and Iron 2004; Vego 2009.

[32] Thucydides (6.24) allows that hope for financial gain was a major motivating factor, but he does not suggest, as do Plutarch (*Nicias* 12, *Alcibiades* 17) and Diodorus (13.2), that the Athenians on the expedition were also hoping for allotments of land in Sicily.

[33] One of those ideas more easily said than proven is that there was a large but cowed opposition to the Expedition inside of Athens, and that the Defamation and Profanation were contrivances designed to remove divine sanction – and therefore the people's willingness to continue.

outcome other than the complete conquest of Sicily. But since the Athenians passed the CPA and had their own CoG disrupted, success was impossible.

The misinterpretation of 'overriding relationships' might itself explain much of what occurred in the events discussed above. Aristagoras had tried to convince Cleomenes that Susa was the military objective the acquisition of which would bring down the Persian Empire. The identification of a capital city is, perhaps, the most common misapplication of CoG theory and this is certainly proven at Athens in 480. Xerxes' political objective was to punish the Athenians for their participation in the Ionian Revolt; his military objective was the Acropolis – tit-for-tat for the burning of the temple in Sardis. That much he achieved (Hdt. 8.102.3). But the city of Athens, even the Acropolis itself, was not the CoG for the Athenian people. As Xerxes approached, the goddess herself left the Acropolis (Hdt. 8.41) and the people of Athens moved first to Salamis, and then made plans to relocate their entire community to Siris, in Italy (Hdt. 8.62). The CoG of a commonwealth, a unity of citizens, is not the city but the constitution, the overriding relationship that each citizen has to the idea of commonwealth.

The same is true of the Ionian Revolt. Events played out much as Herodotus alludes to in his Scythian Logos[34] – many of the Greek tyrants were quite content under Persian governance largely due to the Persian policy of 'live and let live' adopted by Cyrus the Great and continued through much of the early empire. There was a revolt, but it was half-hearted, proven by the ease with which many of the cities came back in line. Dardanus, Abydus, Percote, Lampsacus and Paisus, all on the Hellespont, each capitulated the very day the Persian forces arrived (Hdt.5.117). The tyrants, all exiled by Aristagoras and the rebels, were serving on the side of the Persians and, as our history of *stasis* indicates, must have had oligarchic factions within these cities willing to support them again. The Persians won the Battle of Lade with bribes rather than arms (Hdt. 6.9).

As Agesilaus looked east in 396 those relationships were much different from what Cleomenes had seen. The Persian satrapal system was less effective and less loyal than it had been in 499[35] and the Spartans had inherited control of Ionia from the defunct Athenian Empire. Perhaps of equal importance, the March of the Ten Thousand had given indication of Persian military weakness, or Greek military ability. Decisive Point theory might indicate a high probability of success for Spartan forces in Asia, but CoG, as interpreted here, suggests failure.

Agesilaus went to Asia on the claim that he was protecting the Greek cities there from Persian aggression (Xen. *Hell.* 3.4.5), his pretext predicted a series of relationships in which Artaxerxes was the oppressor, the Ionians oppressed, and Agesilaus the liberator. The fact was that the Spartan *harmosts* installed by Lysander "were being driven out by the citizens (ὑπὸ τῶν πολιτῶν), and even put to death" (Plut. *Ages.* 6.1). Like Nicias in Sicily, Agesilaus was operating in territory that was less than receptive and, far from *Soter*,

---

[34] The Ionians refused to cut the bridges which allowed Darius' escape from Scythia and on this occasion Herodotus (4.142), speaking through un-named Scythians, says that the Ionians are the most perfect slaves.

[35] Those satraps appointed by Darius I knew that they held their positions at the pleasure of the king. The grandsons and great-grandsons believed that they held their lands by birthright.

he was seen as *Tyrannos*. Most of the wealthy and influential Greeks of Asia, when called upon by Agesilaus, preferred to pay mercenaries to take their place (Plut. *Ages.* 9.3–4).[36] Without the ability to correctly identify breakable relationships, and therefore the CoG of the Persian satraps, Agesilaus could not specify any political or military objective; he was just there, campaigning. But to what end? With only thirty Spartiates, two thousand helots and six thousand allied troops (Xen. *Hell.* 3.4.2; Plut. *Ages.* 6.2) he could not possibly have envisioned the conquest of the Empire.

A Persian CoG is, therefore, out of the discussion, and because of that Agesilaus' CPA loomed near. That is why Artaxerxes did so little to counter Agesilaus: he was content to let the Spartan spend too much capital acquiring too few assets before using his own capital (literally) to redirect the war itself.[37] Plutarch turns the whole affair into a series of jokes, the best coming when he quotes the line, "Ares rules: Greeks fear not gold," completely robbing Agesilaus of his "ten thousand archers" punch-line (Plut. *Ages.* 14.2–15.6). That, perhaps, is why Plutarch made so much of the comparison between Agesilaus and Agamemnon (*Ages.* 6.4–6). Both kings had made too many enemies at home as the price for crossing from Aulis.[38]

The most dangerous enemies that Agesilaus left behind him were not, however, the Thebans, but rather the same enemies that in all likelihood prevented Cleomenes from crossing in 499. Too often, when we consider Spartan martial capability, and Spartan culture as a whole, we focus on the Spartiate in hoplite battle with other Greeks, or Barbarians, and under-value the more mundane but infinitely more critical purpose of the Spartiate: In Laconia and Messenia the population of the helots must have outnumbered the Spartiates by factors of tens.[39] Helot revolt, not foreign war, was always the central issue of Spartan policy. In other words, taking the Spartan military elite *to* Susa was nothing so dangerous as taking them *from* Sparta.

Despite Clausewitz's warning that the elements which affect CPA are so numerous and complex that they 'hang on a silken thread of imagination'; and despite my claims above that CoG is no more concrete and itself hangs on similar threads, we are able to employ these theoretical concepts so long as we maintain the simplicity of the fact that success in delivering decisive force over a great distance depends on the ability to identify the enemy's CoG, and to extend the CPA.

Alexander was able to do both with startling success.

I have suggested that the key to understanding Clausewitz's CoG theory is in prioritizing his reference to relationships and there are few examples in the historical record that better illustrate his point than Philip and Alexander. Macedon had been a tribute paying subject of the Persians since 512 (Hdt.5.17–21) and we can assume that few people on the European side had better knowledge of, and contact with, Persian informants than the Macedonian court. Plutarch (*Alex.* 5.1) tells us that Alexander had opportunities to visit with and even

---

[36] As with the Ionians in 499/8, Agesilaus' problem was cavalry (Xen. *Hell.* 3.11– 15).

[37] Was Tissaphernes condemned (Xen. *Hell.* 3.4.25) for losing a battle, or for engaging in one?

[38] Compare Xen. *Hell.* 3.4.3–4, where this whole episode is given a mere two lines.

[39] Numbers are difficult to establish, but there were never more than 9,000 (Plut. *Lyc.*) Spartiate families and we know that this number had decreased significantly by the end of the Peloponnesian War.

question Persian ambassadors. Diplomatic contact between Philip and grandees inside the Empire indicates that relationships had been forged that could be exploited during the war. An exhaustive study, beyond the scope of this paper, would reveal the importance of these relationships in Alexander's campaign but one in particular deserves mention. The Great Satrap's Revolt of 362 betrayed deep rifts in the relationships between the Great King and his nobles but the revolt of Artabazus in 356 (Diod. 16.22.1–2) may well have provided Alexander with his most important friend. Artabazus sought refuge with Philip after being exiled by Ochus (Diod. 16.53.3), but he returned and became a close advisor to Darius III (Curtius 3.13.13; 5.9.1). Our sources indicate that Artabazus remained a loyal servant of the Persian cause until finally surrendering in Hyrcania in 329 but was hardly treated like a defeated adversary. Alexander lavished him with honours and offices and had even taken Barsine, Artabazus' daughter, as a concubine. Another daughter, Apame, was married to Ptolemy and another, Artonis, to Eumenes (Plut. *Eum.* 1.7).[40]

The most important relationships were, however, closer to home. Alexander's CoG was his army or, more accurately, the relationships Philip and Alexander forged not only with the Macedonian barons and soldiers, but quite literally with anyone who might be an asset. On the grand scale, the policy established by Philip was to appeal to the most basic of human motivations: Greed. Philip was able to build a national, royal, armed forces by guaranteeing a share of the kingdom, and of the prizes of conquest, with the barons (Diod. 16.75.3, 95.4).[41] But on a personal level, Philip exploited the more complex motivations of obligation and reciprocity. Fair treatment, forgiveness for wrongs done, and outright benefactions likely won more battles for Philip than force of arms (Diod. 16.60.4; 95.4).

Alexander was also able to exploit greed and reciprocity to his advantage. As he was about to set out for Asia he divided his personal property amongst his companions (Plut. *Alex.* 15.3), but this should be seen far less as an indication that he had no intention to return (as Justin 11.5.5) and far more as spending capital to purchase assets, the asset here being loyalty. Alexander's men followed him as long as the risk-reward equation looked promising – and it was promising indeed.[42] I need not make a list here; Alexander's generosity is well attested.

Alexander knew, well before he set out, that he was *hegemon* of a unified Greece in theory only, and then through compulsion, and that his home front was far from secure. He had, of course, conquered the Triballi and Illyrians so as not to leave those enemies in his rear (Arr. *Anab.* 1.1.4), and the sack of Thebes served as a warning to other Greek *poleis*. Sparta was openly hostile and Athens only awaiting opportunity, but Antipater was left in Macedon with 12,000 infantry and 1,500 cavalry as protection from a possible, indeed likely, Greek revolt.[43] The home front needed to be secure.

Leaving such a large force at home might have been a difficult decision, but the forces

---

[40] For the career of Artabazus see Heckel 2006, 55.

[41] See also Errington 1990, 41–2, 60; Austin 1993, 205. See also Hammond 1997 for speculation on Philip's debt to Thebes.

[42] Vego 2009, vii–14 correctly identifies Alexander's army as his CoG but without explanation.

[43] For a bio and source list see Heckel 2006, 35ff. A good discussion of the situation is found in Green 1974, 190–92, 212.

he did take to Asia indicate that Alexander practiced Economy of Force[44] with precision. He crossed with just over 30,000 infantry and 5,000 cavalry,[45] but the results prove that the numbers were sufficient. His force was not enough to win the war, but was exactly enough to defeat those forces that the Persians could oppose him with at that time, and it was not so large a force that he would encounter problems with supply or accommodation.[46]

Returning to CPA, as far as purchases go, Alexander could not have found a better bargain than the Battle of the Granicus River. The victory "at once made a great change in the situation to Alexander's advantage, so that he received the submission even of Sardis, the bulwark of the barbarian dominion on the sea-coast" (Plut. *Alex*. 17.1). Having lost all of their available force capability in one battle the Persians had no choice but to cede Anatolia to Alexander, and Mithrenes, the commander of Persian garrison at Sardis, handed over the city, the citadel and treasury. Alexander had not only accomplished what the Ionian rebels had failed to do, and what Nicias had failed to do in Sicily, but he had effectively repositioned the CPA – The Granicus bought Alexander both time and space and the investment paid off in cash and resources. It also made him 'master of the country', a condition he optimized by establishing and re-enforcing relationships. For example, Alexander ordered that the oligarchies be overthrown and democracies be set up in the Greek cities of Asia (Arr. *Anab*. 1.18.2). This move should not be seen as ideological in any way: The oligarchies were supported by and loyal to the Persians and Alexander was simply reversing the Persian strategy that worked so well in ending the Ionian Revolt. But the most valuable asset Alexander purchased with his losses at the Granicus were the 2000 Athenian mercenaries he took as prisoners. These were kept, as surety against Athenian participation on the side of the Persians, until Alexander was confident that there were no Persians to side with (Arr. *Anab*. 1.29.6; 3.6.2).[47]

That did not happen until Alexander took control of the Aegean and Mediterranean coastal cities and the Phoenician fleet, the final element in the safety of the home front, but even before that Alexander had an opportunity to achieve a decisive victory, at least according to his assessment of the Persian CoG, at Issus.

The identification of the enemy's CoG is, of course, of principle importance because it immediately informs and helps to determine the political objective of the war. Just what Alexander's objective was has always been a matter of debate, but the pretext, a war of retribution for the burning of the temple at Athens in 480, suggests that the burning of Persepolis itself was, at the least, the propaganda objective (Curtius 4.5.7; Arr. *Anab*. 3.18.12). Diodorus (17.17.2) and Justin (11.5.10) report that Alexander cast his spear from his ship onto the shore as he completed the crossing of the Hellespont thereby claiming

---

[44] The theory of the Economy of Force is what Clausewitz uses (1997, 324–5 = Bk 7: 5) to link CPA and CoG theory, to form a tripartite theory. Simply put: Too large a force will mean that the assets it purchases will be too expensive; *i.e.*: Xerxes.

[45] Arrian's numbers (*Anab*. 1.11.3).

[46] One wonders if those cities that welcomed Alexander would have done so had his army been 100,000 strong. The damage even of such an army passing through is well enough described by Herodotus.

[47] Aeschines (3.163) suggests that Darius would have accepted an alliance with Athens and he is critical of Demosthenes for not putting the motion forward to the Ecclesia.

Asia as spear-won territory,[48] and this symbolic gesture, if indeed it happened (it is omitted by Arrian and Plutarch), should also be seen as propaganda rather than any statement of intent. But propaganda, perception, the public message, might actually be the point here. Another, and more certain, element of Alexander's propaganda machine was the portrayal of the king as Heracles and Alexander may have taken a lesson from the ancient hero: Persia was a Hydra, a many headed beast but with only one head that really mattered. Immediately after his Granicus narrative, Plutarch (*Alex.* 17.3) says that Alexander was "eager to encounter Darius and put the whole issue to hazard…" because Alexander had identified the person of the King as the CoG of the Persian Empire. At the Battle of Issus Alexander made directly for Darius because no one else on the Persian side was fighting for anything more than obedience to the king[49] – and few would have cared one bit what the king's name was. Alexander understood that Darius III, very recently a private citizen, had not established the bonds of reciprocal obligation, the relationships, with his subordinates that Philip and Alexander had,[50] and because of that all Alexander had to do was prove his own valour by defeating Darius in battle (Justin 11.6.8), and kill Darius personally thereby claiming the right to replace him. The other heads, Artabazus for example, would continue under a new king. The strategy failed at Issus, but before Arbela Alexander was calm and confident because "Darius had freed him from all anxiety by assembling all his forces into one place" (Diod. 17.56.3).[51]

But because of the failure at Issus, and before he could face Darius at Arbela, Alexander had to deal with the problem of the CPA. The line from Plutarch cited above (*Alex.* 17.3) continues "…and many times he would make up his mind to practice himself first, as it were, and strengthen himself by acquiring the regions along the sea." Plutarch is referring, of course, to the controversial decision by Alexander not to pursue Darius after Issus, but to move south along the Levantine coast and take Egypt.[52] I have argued elsewhere that Darius was attempting to implement a rational defense much along the lines of the strategy Artaxerxes employed against Agesilaus – the culmination of which would have seen a weakened and humiliated Alexander returning home to fight a war for his own survival against Greek forces led by Sparta and financed by Persia.[53] But I also argued that there was a plan B, that Darius was equally prepared to bring Greek forces to Asia to attack Alexander in the rear as he moved east. There are two further pieces of evidence that I would like, now, to add to that argument.

Arrian (*Anab.* 2.17.1ff), has Alexander assure his troops that, "Once we have brought over Egypt, we shall have no cause of uneasiness for Greece…" and I was always fixated

---

[48] For commentary and a bibliography see Yardley and Heckel 1997, 109.

[49] Recall the advice of Demaratus to Xerxes in Herodotus 7.102–5.

[50] So much is the theme of Arrian's epitaph at *Anab.* 3.22.

[51] A similar statement is made by Justin at 11.13.3.

[52] For the argument that Alexander blundered here see: Bosworth 1988 a, 65; Bloedow 1998, 26; and Worthington 1999, 45–6. Contrary arguments are Green 1974, 190–92; Romane 1987; and Yardley and Heckel 1997, 145.

[53] Garvin 2003. For a concise summary of Spartan activities see Heckel 2006, 7–8. Many of my most cherished visits with Waldemar included 'what if' discussions about Alexander, Darius, Agis and the Levantine coast. I thank him for his advice and insight, but mostly for being so very difficult to convince.

enough on Tyre that I completely overlooked the apparent foolishness of the statement.[54] Once the Phoenician fleet was in Alexander's hands, what did he have to fear from Egypt? Egypt had no fleet to speak of and Darius himself admitted the importance of Tyre when he conceded everything west of the Euphrates and asked for terms only after Alexander had taken control of the Phoenician fleet (Arr. *Anab.* 2.25.1). Egypt seems moot.

It is, I think, no random choice that Aristotle made when presenting an example of a syllogism, his relationship with Alexander had left this strategy prominent in his thoughts:

> We must prepare for war against the king of Persia and not let him subdue Egypt. For Darius of old did not cross the Aegean until he had seized Egypt; but once he had seized it, he did cross. And Xerxes, again, did not attack us until he had seized Egypt, but once he had seized it, he did cross. If, therefore the present king seizes Egypt, he also will cross, and therefore we must not let him.
>
> *Rhetoric* 1393a.32–1393b.4

But the importance of Egypt to Alexander is best demonstrated on his return trip to Tyre, after the submission of Egypt and just before he marched east. At Tyre, in the early summer of 331, Alexander stopped to celebrate his victories. He held games which involved athletic and literary contests and he made sacrifices to Heracles (praying for more help with the Hydra?). The Paralus met him there and Alexander agreed to release the two thousand Athenians he was holding as prisoners (Arrian *Anab.* 3.6; Curtius 4.8.12–16; Plut, *Alex.* 29).[55] All of this, especially the lavish celebrations, seems to indicate that, in Alexander's mind at least, some phase had come to an end, some objective – but not the primary objective – had been realized. Waldemar Heckel (2003, 151–55) observes that sacrifices to Heracles and Zeus, games and the arrival of ambassadors became standard procedure for Alexander as he defined the boundaries of his conquests.

For all of the reasons mentioned above, I would argue that Alexander's arrival at Tyre in 331 signifies the completion of the first war and, more pertinent to this discussion, the repositioning of the CPA.

Recalling the graphic above, the theory posits that the attacker's force capability will be 'spent' as the attacker moves farther in time and space from his home base. Conversely, as the fighting moves closer to the defender's home base the defender's force capability increases. In a campaign where great distances are involved – even more so than in short distance campaigns – the attacker's ability to control the factors that affect the CPA is not only limited but unpredictable. The one thing the attacker can control is the location of home. By moving the home base closer to the defender's home the attacker can essentially relocate the CPA to the right of the CoG and dramatically increase his chances of success.

Might Cleomenes have asked himself, 'where will my home base be?' If the only possible answer was Miletus, we can easily understand his reluctance. For Xerxes the answer was Thebes, even though it did him no good; Nicias certainly hoped to establish an alliance

---

[54] Although the importance of the Levant should never be underestimated. "Since time immemorial Phoenicia-Palestine was a transit region essential for the great eastern powers" (Mildenberg 1999, 204).

[55] Diodorus and Justin omit the celebrations at Tyre, but the line, 'the earth cannot have two suns', found in both (Diod. 17.54.5 and Justin 11.12.15) indicates a common source.

in Sicily that would mimic a home base, and his failure to do so is, perhaps, the failure of the Sicilian Expedition. Agesilaus attempted to use Ephesus but he failed to establish the relationships necessary to be not only welcomed but also supported by the local population. Alexander succeeded, and the proof is in the multicultural and multiethnic forces that followed him east.

This paper has, admittedly, treated each subject with less detail than it deserves, but it was not my intent here to examine these issues exhaustively, but rather to suggest an evaluative paradigm that might serve such an exhaustive study. I am attempting to open a discussion rather than close one, to ask new questions rather than answer old ones. I will let Clausewitz make the final argument:

> If theory investigates the subjects which constitute war; if it separates more distinctly that which at first sight seems amalgamated; if it explains fully the properties of the means; if it shows their probable effects; if it makes evident the nature of objects; if it brings to bear all over the field of war the light of essentially critical investigation – then it has fulfilled the chief duties of its province.
>
> (Clausewitz 1997, 92).

Bibliography

Austin, M. (1993) Alexander and the Macedonian invasion of Asia: Aspects of the historiography of war and empire in antiquity. In J. Rich and G. Shipley (eds) *War and Society in the Greek World*, 197–223, London.

Badian, E. (1971) Alexander the Great, 1948–67, *The Classical World* 65.2, 37–83.

Beyerchen, Al. (1993) Clausewitz, Nonlinearity and the Unpredictability of War. In *International Security* 17.3, 59–90.

Bloedow, E. F. (1998) The Siege of Tyre in 332 BC, Alexander at the Crossroads of his Career, *La Parola Del Passato Rivista di Studi Antichi* 53.4, 255–293.

Bassford, C. (1994) *Clausewitz in English: The Reception of Clausewitz in Britain and America, 1815–1945*, New York.

Bosworth, A. B. (1988a) *Conquest and Empire*. Cambridge.

— (1988b) *From Arrian to Alexander: Studies in Historical Interpretation*. Oxford.

Clausewitz, C. von. (1976) *On War*. P. Paret and M. Howard trans. Princeton.

— (1997) *On War*. (1874). J. J. Graham trans. Hertfordshire.

Crowl, P. A. (1986) Alfred Thayer Mahan: The Naval Historian. In P. Paret (ed.) *Makers of Modern Strategy from Machiavelli to the Nuclear Age*, 444–77, Princeton.

Dixon, N. (1984) *On the Psychology of Military Incompetence*. (1976) London.

Echevarria, Lt. Col. A. J. II. (2003) Clausewitz's Center of Gravity, It's Not What We Thought, *Naval War College Review*. Vol LVI.1, 108–23.

Eikmeier, Col. D. C. (2004) Centre of Gravity Analysis, *Military Review*. July–August 2004, 2–5.

Errington, M. R. (1990) *A History of Macedonia*. Catherine Errington trans. Berkeley.

Fuller, Maj.-Gen. J. F. C. (1960) *The Generalship of Alexander the Great*. Newark.

Garvin, E. E. (2003) Darius III and Homeland Defense. In W. Heckel and L. A. Tritle (eds) *Crossroads of History: The Age of Alexander*, 87–112, Claremont.

Gat, A. (1988) Machiavelli and the Decline of the Classical Notion of the Lessons of History in the Study War. In *Military Affairs* 52.4, 203–05.

Green, P. (1974) *Alexander of Macedon*. New York.

Griffith, S. B. trans. (1963) *Sun Tzu, The Art of War*. Oxford.

Hammond, N. G. L. (1997) What May Philip Have Learnt as a Hostage at Thebes? *Greek Roman and Byzantine Studies* 38, 355–372.

Handel, M. I. (1996) *Masters of War, Classical Strategic Thought*. 2nd edn. Portland.

Hanson, V. D. (2000) *The Western Way of War, Infantry Battle in Classical Greece*. Berkeley.

— (2001) *Carnage and Culture, Landmark Battles in the Rise of Western Power*. New York.

Heckel, W. (1997) Commentary in *Justin, Epitome of the Philipic History of Pompeius Trogus*. Books 11–12.Yardley, J. trans. Oxford.

— (2003) Alexander the Great and the 'Limits of the Civilised World'. In W. Heckel and L. A. Tritle (eds) *Crossroads of History: The Age of Alexander*, 147–174, Claremont.

— (2006) *Who's Who in the Age of Alexander the Great*. Blackwell.

Holborn, H. (1986) The Prusso-German School: Moltke and the Rise of the General Staff. In P. Paret (ed.) *Makers of Modern Strategy from Machiavelli to the Nuclear Age*, 281–95, Princeton.

Holt, F. (1999) Alexander the Great Today: In the Interests of Historical Accuracy? *Ancient History Bulletin* 13.3, 111–117.

Jomini, Baron de (1971) *The Art of War*. Capt. G. H. Mendell and Lieut. W. P. Craighill trans. (1862) Westport CN.

Keegan, J. (1993) *A History of Warfare*. New York.

Kipp, J. W. (1992) General-Major A. A. Svechin and Modern Warfare: Military History and Military Theory. In A. A. Svechin *Strategy*. Kent D. Lee (ed.), 23–56, Minneapolis.

Liddell Hart, B. H. (1968) *Strategy*. (1954) New York.

Mildenberg, L. (1999) Artaxerxes III Ochus (358–338 BC) A Note on the Maligned King. In *Zeitschrif des Deutschen Palästina-Vereins* 115.2, 201–27.

Ober, J. (2012) *Masters of Command*. New York.

Moltke, H. von (1909) *Sur la stratégie: Mémoire de l'année 1871*. Paris. Excerpted for G. Chaliand (ed.) (1994) *The Art of War in World History*, A. M. Berrett trans., 767–69, Berkeley.

Paret, P. (1992) *Understanding War: Essays on Clausewitz and the History of Military Power*. Princeton, NJ.

Romane, J. P. (1987) Alexander's Siege of Tyre, *The Ancient World* 16, 79–90.

Shrimpton, G. (2003) Herodotus' Intellectual Context – A Review Article. In *Ancient History Bulletin* 17.3–4, 149–57.

Strange, J. L. and R. Iron, (2004) Center of Gravity: What Clausewitz Really Meant. In *Joint Forces Quarterly* 35, 20–27.

Strange, J. (1996) *Centers of Gravity and Critical Vulnerabilities*. Quantico, VA.

Strauss, B. S. and J. Ober (1990) *The Anatomy of Error: Ancient Military Disasters and Their Lessons for Modern Strategists*. New York.

Svechin, A. A. (1992) *Strategy*. Kent D. Lee (ed.) Minneapolis.

Vego, M. N. (2009) *Joint Operational Warfare: Theory and Practice*. Stockholm.

Worthington, I. (1999) How Great Was Alexander? *Ancient History Bulletin* 13.2, 39–55.

Yardley, J. C. P. Wheatley and W. Heckel (1997) *Justin: Epitome of the Philippic History of Pompeius Trogus, Books 11–12: Alexander the Great*. Oxford.

THUCYDIDES
AND THE FAILURE IN SICILY

A. B. Bosworth[1]

Thucydides has no doubt that the disaster in Sicily was the worst in Greek history. Everything, both army and navy, was destroyed and few out of many returned. It was total annihilation (πανωλεθρία Thuc. 7.87.6). But despite the magnitude of the debacle Thucydides gives no detailed explanation. The nearest he comes to it is a retrospective meditation on the effect of Pericles' death and the rise of the demagogues (2.65.11). There were many mistakes caused by the conflict for supremacy in the political life of Athens, in particular the Sicilian adventure. This, he insists, was not an error of judgement regarding the people they attacked so much as a failure on the part of the politicians who sent out the expedition. They did not subsequently vote what was appropriate[2] for the men in the field, but following their individual conflicts over the championship of the *demos* they blunted the edge of the army, and they took the first step towards the convulsion of the political life of Athens. Ultimately, on this interpretation, the responsibility for the disaster lay at the door of unscrupulous politicians, who failed to take the measures necessary for the army in the field to succeed.

Thucydides' explanation has been repeatedly and sharply criticised. It is commonly held to be a contradiction of the detailed narrative he gives in Books VI and VII. How, for instance, could it be that in the first sentence of the introductory digression on the ethnography of Sicily he states that the majority of Athenians were ignorant of the size of the island and the numbers of Greeks and non-Greeks who formed its population (6.1.1), when he has claimed that the expedition was not an error of judgment? One can, however, be excessively critical. It is clear that Nicias in particular was excellently informed about the geography and resources of Sicily (6.20.2–4), while Alcibiades is represented giving the

---

[1]   It is with much affection that I offer this essay to Waldemar Heckel, *namque tu solebas meas esse aliquid putare nugas*, from whose work I have learned so much, and whose friendship I cherish.

[2]   I differ here from Hornblower 1991–2008, 1.348, who interprets οὐ τὰ πρόσφορα (2.65.11) as 'disadvantageous decisions'. I take the negation to apply to the entire clause down to ἐπιγιγνώσκοντες ('not subsequently voting what was appropriate'). There *is* an implication that sufficient forces were not earmarked for the expedition (see above), but that is only one of several failures.

assembly a lecture on Syracusan domestic politics (6.17.2–8). After that assembly, when the arrangements for the expedition were confirmed, few Athenians, even if they had a fairly hazy idea of the geography involved, would have been in any doubt that they were faced with a formidable task. However, given the numbers of troops involved and the initial successes against the mass levy of Syracusans (6.65.2, 67.2), it could not be regarded as an over-optimistic exercise. Indeed it came within a hairsbreadth of success. When Gylippus' lieutenant Gongylus reached Syracuse, he found the populace discussing capitulation. An assembly had been scheduled, and, it was only the assurance that reinforcements were close that prevented their capitulation (7.2.1–2). The Syracusans might easily have voted for surrender.

There is another favourite argument (cf. Hornblower 1991–2008, 1.348), that the inappropriate vote was the recall of Alcibiades. Thucydides certainly sees the downfall of Alcibiades as a disaster for the expedition and for the city (6.15.4), but his emphasis is upon the political struggle within the demos. It was not so much the physical conduct of the war that mattered; it was the comparative inefficiency and venality of Alcibiades' successors. His political enemies, particularly Peisander and Charmides, were instrumental in the dissolution of the democracy in 411, and it could be argued that the loss of Alcibiades allowed them to undermine the existing constitution. Alcibiades would have been an effective counterweight. The irony was that the Athenians' fear of tyranny had resulted in the imposition of an oligarchy, which proved as murderous as any tyrant.

As far as the expedition itself was concerned, Alcibiades had little chance to prove himself in the field. His formidable powers of persuasion were on display when he talked round his fellow general Lamachus to abandon his plans for a direct assault on Syracuse in favour of a diplomatic offensive in Sicily. The aim was to create a pan-Sicilian alliance, which was to campaign against Syracuse and Selinus under Athenian hegemony (6.48–9). His success in creating the 'Argive Alliance' encouraged him to repeat the strategy. In fact his plans were over-optimistic. There was no enthusiasm for the Athenian cause. Messene, his first declared objective, resisted his oratory and excluded the Athenian expeditionary force (6.50.1). At Catana he had better fortune. His oratory there attracted the citizen body to the assembly, leaving a rickety gate unguarded. As a result the partisans of Syracuse left the city, while the remainder voted for alliance with Athens. Against this success must be balanced the failure to win over Camarina and a botched attack on Syracusan soil, where, interestingly the local cavalry dealt effectively with the light-armed Athenian skirmishers (6.52.2). It was hardly an auspicious beginning to the campaign. The Athenians had certainly not been welcomed. Naxos and Catana, which Nicias had already identified as potential allies (6.20.3), did join forces, but in the latter case only after military coercion. There was no guarantee that Alcibiades' strategy would produce concrete results. On the other hand there was the problem of the festering hatred between Nicias and Alcibiades. They had clashed repeatedly before the expedition began, and they had advocated totally incompatible strategies at Rhegium, with Nicias arguing for a minimum of risks and the quickest possible withdrawal – a far cry from Alcibiades' Sicilian confederacy and his ambition to conquer Carthage.[3] Under those circumstances Thucydides may well have thought that

---

[3] 6.15.2. In his speech at Sparta Alcibiades ascribes his own plans of conquest to the Athenian demos at large

the removal of Alcibiades was actually a benefit for the expedition, an *appropriate* vote. It removed what was at best a cause of friction, at worst a paralysis of command. Nicias and Lamachus could operate together very effectively, as the winter campaign of 415/4 was to demonstrate. Thucydides still considers the disgrace and exile of Alcibiades a devastating mistake; it was better to have him working in Athens than to be in exile working against her. However, his appointment to the Sicilian command alongside Nicias was a recipe for disaster, and the prospects for the expedition were rosier without him.

What, then, were the measures that Thucydides regarded as inappropriate (or did not regard as appropriate)? I shall set the stage with an interesting, often overlooked passage. In the winter of 416/5 a joint force of Macedonians and Athenians entered the city of Methone to begin operations against King Perdiccas. There are several anomalies in this brief note. In the first place the expeditionary force is entirely composed of cavalry; there is no suggestion of any other type of soldier. Next it is notable that Athenians and Macedonians are operating together. They could clearly understand each other and shared a language of command. It is true that the Macedonians were exiles and had perhaps spent years away from their homeland, enough time to become fluent in Attic Greek; but then again in many cases at least their exile may have begun relatively recently. But the surprise is the Athenians. As we saw, their contingent was exclusively cavalry whereas we should expect an infantry force, like the three thousand hoplites who had given support to Macedonian dissidents in 432 (Thuc. 1.61.4). It looks as though the Athenian authorities were quite happy to see a substantial number of their cavalry operating in the north without infantry support. And it is all too likely that the Athenian horsemen felt some cultural affinity with their Macedonian counterparts. They belonged to a strong aristocracy, supported by an underclass, which Thucydides contemptuously dismisses as a mob of barbarians (4.124.2). Belonging to such a culture might well have been an attractive prospect to young Athenian cavalrymen. The privileged status of the Macedonian elite would contrast sharply with the limited scope of civic life in Athens.

This is an episode that comes nicely into the context of Book VI, which contains two brilliant speeches by Alcibiades, defending his personal extravagance and stating unashamedly that the city which exiled him is no longer his city. Still more extreme are the warnings of the Syracusan demagogue Athenagoras, who addresses the ambitious and moneyed youth, and accuses them of launching a scare campaign so that they can seize power and overthrow the democratic institutions. Such men, denied access to public office by age restrictions, might envy the relative freedom of the Macedonian cavalry class.

We may now revert to the Sicilian Expedition, and focus upon Thucydides' admirably precise figures for the various components of the expeditionary force. When he describes the muster conducted by the generals at Corcyra, he gives details of the various contributions of warships and hoplites as well as light-armed and archers. At the end of the list comes a reference to a single horse transport with thirty horsemen on board.[4] Nothing is stated

---

(6.90.2–3).

[4] Thucydides (6.31.2) compares the Athenian forces at Poteidaea under Hagnon (6.31.2): There were 4,000 hoplites, 100 triremes and 300 cavalry, a quarter of the entire complement. By contrast the Syracusans could match the entire Athenian levy of 1200 (6.67.2; cf. 2.13.8).

about their nationality or why these cavalrymen appear in such small numbers.[5] The dilemma is even greater when we turn to Nicias' second speech. We find him underlining the Syracusans' abundant supply of cavalry, which gives them the advantage over Athens (6.20.4), and he raises the possibility of being denied access to the land by the superior numbers of enemy cavalry (6.21.1). However, when asked to give an estimate of the troops he requires, he gives detailed figures for the fleet and hoplite forces, but says nothing about cavalry (6.25.2). It looks as though he envisages recruiting horsemen from Segesta and other places which can be induced to join the alliance, and he adds the telling observation that it would be a disgrace to send for reinforcements later, after making an ill advised decision at the start (6.21.2).

His words were prophetic. The Athenians were at a disadvantage from the beginning of operations in Sicily. They were able to recruit cavalry from Segesta (6.62.3), but the numbers were evidently small (6.62.3), and the Athenians had made over the territory of the people of Hyccara[6] to acquire them. On their return to Catana the Athenians launched their first attack on Syracuse, and the strategy was dominated by their lack of cavalry. They could not march by land for fear of harassment by the Syracusan cavalry (6.64.1 – anticipation of the final retreat), and when they finally attack the city the position they take (by the precinct of Olympian Zeus) is determined by the need to neutralise the enemy horse (6.66.1–2): The battle site is chosen to protect the Athenian flanks, so that they cannot be outmanoeuvred by the cavalry. Even though the engagement was a brilliant Athenian success, they were unable to hold the position and suspended hostilities until they could send for cavalry from Athens "so that they would not be altogether worsted in the cavalry department" (6.71.2). The overtures to Athens proved successful. In the spring of 414, 250 cavalrymen arrived from Athens with instructions to procure horses in Sicily (6.94.4), and with allied support the Athenian cavalry force had increased to 650. The effect was immediate. The Athenian troops engaged in fortifying the high ground of Epipolae were subjected to routine harassment by Syracusan cavalry, but they retaliated. A tribal division of hoplites *together with their entire cavalry* routed the Syracusans and erected a trophy to celebrate the *hippomachia* (6.98.4). That, however, is practically the last we hear of the Athenian horse. Cavalrymen on the Athenian side appear briefly in 413, in a desultory sortie, again with hoplites. The horsemen are routed and leave 70 of their mounts in the hands of the Syracusans (7.51.2, 54).[7]

In the meantime the Syracusan cavalry had been active countering the Athenian siege work on Epipolae. After an initial setback, they engaged with the Athenians in favourable terrain and routed their left wing (7.6.3). That is precisely where we should expect to find Athenian cavalry, but there is no hint that any sizable force was operating on the high

---

[5] 6.43. Note Dover's comment (1970, 4.310): "we hear no more of these cavalry; in 64.1 the Athenians have none."

[6] Hyccara was a native Sican settlement, *c.* 20 km west of modern Palermo (modern Carini). Its destruction will hardly have endeared Athens to the indigenous population (6.2.2).

[7] These cavalrymen need not have been native Athenians. The allied forces which had mustered at Syracuse included 300 horsemen from Egesta and a hundred more from other places in Sicily. Some detachments may have stayed on and given the support that the Athenians proper could not. If that was the case, the Athenian contingent may already have left Sicily after a very short stay.

ground. At the same time Athenian foraging parties were attacked by the Syracusan cavalry (7.4.6; cf. Nicias at 7.11.4), and the Athenians seem to have been powerless to stop it. It looks as though the cavalry had largely evaporated. The allied forces had presumably returned to their home cities, leaving the Athenians outnumbered. At all events it is hard to see why their cavalry was so inactive.

The Athenians did send reinforcements, but once again cavalry were noticeably lacking. When Demosthenes arrived in Syracuse he brought with him about 5,000 hoplites, Athenian and allied, as well as javelin men, slingers and archers and an adequate supply of other armaments (7.42.1). What those other armaments comprised is not spelled out, but it would be surprising if cavalry were subsumed in such a vague expression.[8] We may conclude that the reinforcements contained neither horses nor riders. Consequently the problem of the Syracusan cavalry persisted. Even in the first flush of confidence at the arrival of Demosthenes' forces the Athenians were unable to counter hit-and-run attacks by the Syracusans (7.42.6). The disparity was all too apparent in the final tragic retreat, when the Athenian army was totally exposed to harassment by the Syracusan cavalry and javelin men. There is no record of serious resistance and no indication that any horses or horsemen were active on the Athenian side.

The dearth of Athenian cavalry must reflect the fraught political atmosphere in Athens. Immediately before the debate on Sicily there had been the tension of the ostracism, which had starkly illustrated the factional nature of the political class in Athens. The unexpected result removed a relatively insignificant player, Hyperbolus, while the rivalry between Alcibiades and Nicias continued unchecked, and Phaeax was also a competitor for power. Their factional associates were largely the young and moneyed striplings who comprised the cavalry class. To recruit them to the expedition would be to transfer the factional conflict to the front, with potentially disastrous consequences. The worries will have intensified after the mutilation of the Hermae, which was clearly perpetrated by the young elite and their political groupings.[9] Alcibiades was personally accused of staging the profanation of the Mysteries, and his accomplices were largely members of the jeunesse dorée of Athens. This was yet another reason to treat the cavalry with caution. Alcibiades might be allowed to continue his command, but it was best to leave his associates in the city. Hence there was to be no cavalry for the expedition. It was a military risk, but less dangerous than the prospect of political subversion.

By the end of 415 Alcibiades had been recalled, and the danger from rival political groups had eased. The remaining generals were not at loggerheads, and now it could be considered prudent to send out the cavalry necessary if the Syracusan harassment was to be stopped. But there is another problem. After the first successful ἱππομαχία there is, as we have seen, practically no mention of the Athenian cavalry, and it is hard to think that they were not used, if they were actually present. The most economical explanation is that

---

[8]   Compare 2.100.2, where horses are explicitly distinguished from τῇ ἄλλῃ παρασκευῇ.

[9]   Note too 6.37.1, where Athenagoras enumerates the supposed weaknesses of the Athenian forces: First the horse, then the hoplite contingent and then τήν τε ἄλλην παρασκευήν. It looks as though the expression refers to the non-military component of the army; vivandiers, sutlers and the like.

   For a useful list of accused persons see Dover, 1970, 4.276–82.

they had been recalled. Perhaps the political factions of the city had continued to affect the cavalry on campaign, and the unit had become dysfunctional. This was something Thucydides may well have felt uncomfortable with. There is the same discomfort in his treatment of the scandals of the Hermae and Mysteries. His account is terse and abbreviated, and apart from Alcibiades not a single participant is named, not even the arch informer, Andocides. The episode was too important and sensational to be ignored, but the names of the protagonists were better suppressed. They may have included his own relatives and erstwhile friends.

Indeed Thucydides had considerable sympathy for the elite classes of Athens (to which he belonged), and praised the wide based oligarchy of the Five Thousand as the best constitution in his lifetime (8.97.2). It would have been embarrassing to report antisocial behaviour among the cavalry, the class from which the Five Thousand would later be drawn. Thucydides may well have omitted their recall and the reasons the demos had for its actions. Instead he focused on its failure to vote appropriate measures. There were, no doubt, many such measures, including the refusal to replace Nicias as general in charge. But the cavalry must have featured strongly in Thucydides' thinking. The demos was at fault in not sending cavalry with the original expeditionary force, and its error was compounded by sending the wrong forces too late.

The lack of cavalry support was one of the major military problems from the start to the finish of the expedition. It gave the Syracusans the tactical initiative, and the Athenians were constantly under harassment. On the other hand, sending an adequate number of horsemen risked exporting the factional conflict of the city into the front line. Whether the demos withheld or dispatched horsemen, it was the wrong thing at the wrong time, and a major contributory cause of the disaster. In the light of this bitter experience Thucydides may well have considered that the appropriate measures were not the reinforcement of the troops in the field but the recall of the expedition. When Nicias gave the Athenian demos the choice between recalling and reinforcing (7.15.1), he clearly favoured the first alternative – and he was right.

Bibliography

Dover, K. J., A. W. Gomme and A. Andrewes (1970) *A Historical Commentary of Thucydides. Volume IV: Books V 25–VII*. Cambridge.
Hornblower, S. (1991–2008) *A Commentary on Thucydides*. 3 vols. Oxford.

WOMEN AND SYMPOSIA
IN MACEDONIA

Elizabeth Carney

The conventional view about women and symposia in the Greek world is well known. Ordinary women did not attend symposia; even female servants were not present, although *hetairai* (courtesans) and female entertainers certainly were. At family feasts occasioned by events like visits to shrines, both men and women were present, though they may have sat apart or in separate rooms. In addition, there were all female feasts and festivals involving drinking.[1] In terms of Macedonia, Herodotus' story (5.17–21) about the Macedonian court at the time of Amyntas I (end of the 6th, beginning of the 5th century BCE) has usually been understood to say that elite women did not participate in symposia at the Macedonian court. While the historicity of this Herodotean tale is doubtful,[2] we should note, however, that Herodotus actually has Amyntas assert only that their custom (*nomos*) was to separate women and men whereas the Persians expected their wives and mistresses to sit beside them (5.18). (The rest of the story seems to imply that the women may have been in another room since Amyntas has to send for them.)

Certainly, literary accounts of the Argead court dealing with later periods in history, most notably the reigns of Philip II and Alexander, never refer to the presence of women other than *hetairai* at Macedonian symposia. Neither Plutarch nor Satyrus mentions the presence of the bride herself at the symposium that followed Philip II's last marriage (Plut. *Alex.* 9.4–5; Satyr. *ap.* Ath. 13.557d). Curtius (5.7.3–7) and Diodorus (17.72) place the supposed *hetaira* Thaïs at the famous drinking party that led to the burning of the Persepolis palace. Scholars (I include myself) have usually interpreted the omission of references to royal women to signify their absence.[3] The presumption (mostly unstated) has been that the circumstance of the Argead women was much like that of Athenian women, where the presence of a woman at a symposium was regarded as proof that she was not a wife, but something less (Isaeus 3.13–14). Even if this presumption is correct, of course, it tells us only where royal women were not.

The issue of the role of royal and elite women in court symposia is simply one aspect of

---

[1] Burton 1998; see also Dalby 1993, 172–87.
[2] See Borza 1990, 102.
[3] So Carney 2000, 28, but Carney 2007, 142–44 and 2011, 48 are less certain.

a broader problem: It is hard to connect even the best-known of Macedonian royal women to a particular physical place and context and therefore difficult to determine to what degree they did or did not share in the ideal of the comparative seclusion of middle and upper class women that existed in Athens and other southern cities.[4] We should not begin with the presumption that their circumstance, at least in the fourth century, was identical to that of Athenian women. Literary and epigraphic evidence from the fourth century, in fact, demonstrates considerable difference between the two categories of women in several aspects. Royal women knew many people at court and corresponded with and spoke to prominent Macedonian and non-Macedonian public figures. Several Argead women appeared in front of armies. During the fourth century, a number exercised considerable political influence. Argead women also, however, participated in actions like those of elite women further south. In the fourth century, they functioned as patrons of shrines as well as dedicators. Probably they appeared at public religious ceremonies and festivals. Olympias played an organizing role in an all female Dionysiac ceremony or festival (Plut. *Alex.* 2.6). Elsewhere in Greece, elite women held important priesthoods and Olympias and other royal women likely did as well (Athen. 659f–660a).[5]

Given the widely acknowledged political role of a number of Argead women, the issue of their participation or lack of it in court symposia is not a trivial matter. Court symposia in Macedonia had a quasi-constitutional function: they were the context for much decision making at the Macedonian court.[6] It would be helpful to know whether Olympias and her daughter or other royal women were present at such affairs, even if they sat apart or were comparatively silent. Plutarch (*Pyrrh.* 5.5) recounts an anecdote about a brother and sister in the younger generation of Olympias' Molossian royal family (her grandson and granddaughter) in which the siblings dine, drink, and plot together, with other respectable women in attendance. Macedonian and Molossian ways, particularly in terms of the two royal dynasties, were not identical, but they were similar. Some court banquets could have been understood as family affairs, less intimate versions of the Molossian event.

What about archaeological evidence? Macedonian female burials do not typically include the sets of banqueting vessels frequently found in male burials. The woman in the antechamber of Tomb II at Vergina conforms to this conventional pattern; not even a single wine cup was found buried, let alone a banqueting set. As elsewhere in the ancient world, images of banqueting are sometimes associated with Macedonian burials. These *totenmahls* may have little to do with reality, at least in this life. Recently Tsibidou-Avloniti has plausibly argued that the central scene of the frieze of a Macedonian tomb found at Agios Athanasios in 1994 depicts a symposium scene from daily life.[7] If so, the frieze would support what literary evidence has implied: it pictures six male banqueters, entertained by a female flute player and a female cithara player (both presumably professionals and not members of the 'respectable' classes).

Material evidence does, however, sometimes associate women and drinking. Female

---

4   Carney 2010.
5   Connelly 2007, 44. See Carney 2000, 29, n. 113
6   Borza 1983.
7   Tsibidou-Avloniti 2006, 324.

burials may not have included banqueting sets (unless, the female burial is combined with that of a man) but they often do contain wine cups of various sizes[8] and *stephanoi* (these metallic crowns had, however, uses other than the sympotic).[9] It is, admittedly, one thing to drink wine and another to participate in a symposium. Some scholars have concluded that material remains do indicate that Macedonian women had some level of sympotic involvement. Rhomiopoulou[10] wondered if the scene painted in the tympanum of the pediment of the 'Palmette' tomb at Lefkadia might signify that elite Macedonian women sometimes banqueted with men. It is dated to the first half of the third century. The scene depicts what Rhomiopoulou described as "a mature couple in a reclining position."[11] She interpreted the pair as a "married couple half reclining and facing each other, as at a banquet."[12] Others[13] have identified the couple as Persephone and Hades, but the grey hair of the male, the rather matronly figure of his companion, and the key, which the male holds in his hand, often a sign of priestly office, makes the latter identification less convincing than that of Rhomiopoulou.[14] Even if, however, we concur with Rhomiopoulou that the couple in the tympanum represents the pair buried in the tomb, this may not represent daily reality. The painting does suggest, if Rhomiopoulou is correct, that the artist (and his patron) imagined some sort of banquet – in this world or the next – in which the elite pair dined, reclining, together. In many *totenmahl* scenes, however, the man reclines but the woman sits on his *kline*. This imagined celebration could, of course, have been conceived of as a private affair or as something more public.

Hoepfner used entirely different evidence to conclude that court women participated in symposia, but in single sex banquets not coed affairs. Impressed by the increasing public role of royal women and apparently unaware of the dominant view based on literary information, he suggested that the double *andron* (the room where symposia were held) pattern found in the palace at Vergina/Aegae, perhaps in private houses at Pella, and elsewhere in Macedonia, may have been intended for separate but parallel male and female symposia.[15] Much of the ground floor of the palace at Aegae was devoted to 16 banqueting rooms of varying dimension, allowing for up to 230 couches.[16] The huge courtyard may have been used for outdoor symposia, larger scale versions of the one pictured in the Agios Athanasios fresco. The varying sizes of the Vergina *andrones* have been explained as serving various elements

---

8   *E.g.* a 4th century female burial at Pydna (Makrygialos field 279, grave 1) contained six golden *fibulae*, a ring, and a silver *kylix* (cup) Pydna.

9   Vokotopoulou 2001, 732, 737, however, associates *stephanoi* and drinking.

10   Rhomiopoulou 1973, 90.

11   She compared the woman in the scene to the women in the 'Macedonian Royal Family' Boscoreale painting (Rhomiopoulou 1973, 90).

12   Rhomiopoulou 2000, 32–33.

13   Mantis 1990, 35; Brécoulaki 2006, 52.

14   Brécoulaki 2006, 52, though supporting Mantis, concedes that these are telling points.

15   Hoepfner 1996, 13–15. Etienne 2006, 113 has doubts but suggests that women could have been present, sitting rather than reclining. He cites Andronicos 1993, 150; Andronicos, however, refers only to *Totenmahls* and questions that burials consistently associate women and thrones and men and *klinai*.

16   Saatsoglou-Paliadeli 2011, 298–33, especially 327. See also Tomlinson 1970, 315; Börker 1983, 18; Kottaridi 2004, 70.

in the royal hierarchy.[17] Absolutely no evidence connects the double symposia suites to some sort of sexual segregation, but it is not easy to imagine another court grouping that would require such parallel separation. Tomlinson, for instance, calculated that the rooms in one pair of *andrones* held eleven couches.[18] If these rooms were intended for the inner circle of the king's *Hetairoi*, in which room would the king have reclined? Hoepfner's idea remains highly speculative but intriguing.

In the context of Hoepfner's theory, one might wonder whether the rest of the Vergina palace suggests anything about sexual segregation. No archaeological evidence confirms the existence of separate quarters for women (Herodotus 5.20 does have the court women retreat to a *gunaikeia*), but little is known of the upper story and the current excavator believes the palace was not residential, but used only for entertaining. Moreover, recent work on Greek domestic space has indicated that women's quarters may have been in people's heads but not in the architecture of their houses.[19] Thus the kind of sexual segregation imagined by Hoepfner at the Vergina palace is neither confirmed nor denied by other features of the *basileia*.

Kottaridi and Lilibaki-Akamati[20] believe that Argead women were priestesses who participated in public banquets and symposia, on special occasions. They base their conclusions on a cluster of elaborate female burials at Aegae – the best known of these, the 'Lady of Aegae' burials, they presume are the graves of royal women. The nine tombs range in date from the mid sixth to the mid fourth centuries and include the so-called 'tomb of Eurydice'. They cite the presence in these burials of objects connected to sacrifice and its subsequent feasting – iron spits, bowls, *oinochoai*, *pateras* – and of sympotic equipment – *kylikes*, *kantharoi*, *amphorae*, *klinai* – as reasons for their findings. They assume that these practices continued past the Archaic period and included women like Olympias and others of her era. Neither scholar, however, imagines these actions as anything other than 'royal exceptions' to what they understand as the generally male nature of Macedonian as well as Greek symposia.[21] Their views involve a number of unproven assumptions, namely that these women were priestesses, that they were royal, and that they took part in public banquets with men.

The first of these assumptions seems the most likely, given the objects found in the burials and the tendency already noted for elite women throughout the Hellenic world to hold priesthoods. I might add to this evidence a letter attributed to Olympias that implies her involvement in ritual associated with the royal house (Ath. 559f–660a). The second assumption is somewhat more problematic. Literary evidence says that the Macedonian kings were buried at Aegae; Cynnane and Adea Eurydice we know, were buried there and so, presumably, were other royal women. Not everyone interred in the city, however, was a member of the royal family and I am not certain that we can always distinguish a royal woman from a female member of the elite. Still, the location of this cluster of tombs implies a royal connection. The most problematic assumption of the three is that these women

---

[17] Lauter 1986, 346.
[18] Tomlinson 1970, 314.
[19] Kottaridi 2011b, 328–9. See Nevett 1999, 155; Etienne 2006, 113, n. 45.
[20] Kottaridi 2004a, 140; 2004b, 69; 2011, 167–68; Lilibaki-Akamati 2004, 91.
[21] Kottaridi 2004b, 69.

took part in coed symposia. The tomb goods indicate banquets, but can tell us nothing about who was present.

Kottaridi[22] offers Homeric royal women as precedents and possible models for the participation of royal Macedonian women in coed symposia. Helen, Penelope, and Arete were present while men drank and banqueted and they participated in the conversation. Literary evidence and archaeological finds confirm the Homeric nature of many aspects of Macedonian elite culture. For instance, the similarity between the practices described in epic for burial and those of the Macedonian elite are striking.[23] Olympias' Aeacid dynasty claimed descent from Achilles; she and her son made much of this genealogical identity. Long ago I suggested that the role of Homeric royal women quite possibly influenced that of Macedonian royal women.[24] If, however, Homeric precedents are genuinely relevant to the Argead court, then one must question whether Kottaridi and Lilibaki-Akamati's understanding of female participation in symposia as 'exceptional' is valid or merely the consequence of an attempt to bridge the gap between the conventionally Hellenic picture of Herodotus and the different world of Homer and, perhaps, of the Macedonians.

In light of the highly speculative and ambiguous evidence I have so far discussed, one might wonder if the role of non-royal women in Macedonia in the period of the monarchy is relevant to the practices of court women. Perhaps, but currently we do not have enough information to tell. Thanks to limited evidence, Pomeroy[25] and Tataki[26] concluded that Macedonian society in matters of gender was similar to that of Athens, but Archibald, based on the prominence of female burials,[27] thought that the role of elite women in Macedonia was less limited than that of women in southern Greece. Le Bohec-Bouhet noted indications that Macedonian women had, in terms of the disposal of property, somewhat broader rights than Athenian women, but cautions against making much of this conclusion. She examined the possibility that royal women – who demonstrably did have some income and control over property – influenced the rights and actions of ordinary women and concluded that there is no evidence that they did.[28] Thus, even if we knew more about ordinary Macedonian women, let alone their drinking habits, it is unlikely that this knowledge would illuminate the practices of royal women.

All the evidence examined thus far has neither demonstrated that Macedonian royal and elite women attended court symposia nor that they did not. Grave goods simply indicate that these women drank wine and banqueted, as elsewhere in Greece.[29] Archaeological material hints faintly that they may have done so in more public, less sexually segregated ways, but even this conclusion could easily be too generous. Unless we find some elite female burials that contain entire collections of sympotic vessels, it is unlikely that specific material evidence will take us any further.

---

[22] Kottaridi 2004b, 65, 69. Pownall 2010.
[23] Andronicos 1984, 170, citing *Od.* 24.40ff and *Il.* 24.788ff.
[24] Carney 1993, 315–16.
[25] Pomeroy 1984, 3.
[26] Tataki 1988, 433.
[27] Archibald 2005, 24; see also Hammond 1989, 5.
[28] Le Bohec-Bouhet 2006, 193–96.
[29] Dalby 1993, 171–87 gives a review of the general Hellenic evidence.

There is another kind of evidence relevant to the issue of women and sympotic activity in Macedonia that has not been addressed: the role of women in the presentation of Macedonian monarchy in the fourth century. This was a period during which an elaboration of the visible signs of dynastic ideology took place, an elaboration utilizing various forms, including that of the royal palace itself.[30] Philip II, in particular, consciously shaped a dynastic image by means of monuments like the Philippeum, public actions and festivals, and patronage. Women played a prominent part in this dynastic image he was creating: his seven marriages symbolized his power to control and centralize; his mother apparently funded a shrine to the goddess Eucleia (a shrine in which her portrait may have appeared) and made dedications elsewhere somehow associated with women citizens; the godlike images of his mother and the mother of his son appeared in the Philippeum and, quite possibly (in the case of Eurydice), elsewhere in Macedonia as well; some of his daughters' names commemorated his victories; and he turned his daughter Cleopatra's wedding into an international festival.

In the cities of southern Greece, the line between public and private, *oikos* and *polis*, was clearly drawn though hardly unbridgeable, but it barely existed in the Argead monarchy. Kottaridi has said about the Macedonian king that as "a symbolic persona, the monarch himself was essentially deprived of a private life."[31] It would be more accurate to say that one could not easily distinguish his public and private life. The same might be said about the lives of the women of the dynasty. Unlike other Greek women of their class, these women were referred to in public by their personal names. In inscriptions, royal women appeared with their personal names and patronymics but made no reference to their husbands. Their dedications and even their shopping trips became matters of public discussion.[32]

The Vergina palace reflects this lack of division between public and private in the Argead monarchy. The palace was imbedded in the city, placed near tombs and other structures. The palace was apparently built or rebuilt at the same time as the theater immediately below it, presumably as part of a ceremonial whole. It is likely that those who stood or sat on the palaces' veranda or stoa – perhaps royal women – could view events in the theater. Indeed, the very existence of palace stoa confirms the shadowy line between public and private in the palace. Women were associated with the *oikos* in many ways and this particular *oikos* was open to the world. In effect, the palace and the dynastic image generated by Philip and maintained to some degree by Alexander and certainly by the Successors, did confirm Plutarch's complaint: the *basileia* really was contaminated by the world of women (Plut. *Alex.* 9.3).

If we apply this general circumstance to the topic of royal women and symposia, it begins to seem more likely that royal women did, in some sense, participate in court symposia. Ordinary women and men dined together on family occasions and court events, at least many of them, would fit that description. Women may have sat apart, perhaps in separate rooms as Hoepfner imagined, or they may have attended only briefly, like Penelope, but it

---

[30]   Etienne 2006, 107.

[31]   Kottaridi 2004, 69.

[32]   Savalli-Lestrade 2003, 61 describes the situation of Hellenistic royal women as "semi-private, semi public" and rightly (2003, 65–66) notes how "ambivalent" a royal wife's status remained.

is likely that they were present, witnesses, apparently silent ones (or silent to our sources), to many of the contests and controversies played out at court symposia. Their role in these events may never have been systematized or regular, or their burials would also contain the sets of sympotic table ware that distinguish the burials of the male elite. Nonetheless, despite the absence of specific evidence, it is likely that Eurydice and Olympias appeared on some occasions at court banquets and those elite women, in their own homes and perhaps elsewhere, may have done the same.

Bibliography

Andronicos, M. (1994) The 'Macedonian tombs'. In R. Ginouvès (ed.) *Macedonia from Philip II to the Roman Conquest*, 144–191, Princeton.

Archibald, Z. H. (2005) Officers and Gentlemen (or Gentlewomen): Exploring Macedonian Elites in the Classical and Early Hellenistic Periods, *Antiquitas* 28, 13–25.

Borza, E. N. (1983) The Symposium at Alexander's Court, *Ancient Macedonia* 3, 45–55.

Brécoulaki, H. (2006) La Peinture funéraire en Macédoine. In A. M. Guimier-Sorbets, M. B. Hatzopoulos and Y. Morizot (eds) *Rois, Cites, Necropoles: Institutions, Rites Et Monuments En Macédoine*, Meletemata 45, 47–61, Athens.

Burton, J. (1998) Women's Commensality in the Ancient Greek World, *Greece & Rome* 14, 2, 143–65.

Carney, E. D. (1993) Foreign Influence and the Changing role of royal Macedonian Women, *Ancient Macedonia* 5, 1, 313–23.

Carney, E. D. (2000) *Women and Monarchy in Macedonia.* Norman, OK.

— (2007) Symposia and the Macedonian Elite: The Unmixed Life, *Syllecta Classica* 18, 129–81.

— (2010) Putting Women in Their Place: Women in Public under Philip II and Alexander III and the Last Argeads. In E. D. Carney and D. Ogden (eds.) *Philip II, Alexander III: Father and Son, Lives and Afterlives*, 43–54, Oxford.

Carney, E. D. and D. Ogden (eds) (2010) *Philip II, Alexander III: Father and Son, Lives and Afterlives.* Oxford.

Connellly, J. B. (2007) *Portrait of a Priestess: Women and Ritual in Ancient Greece.* Princeton.

Dalby, A. (1993) *Siren Feasts: A History of Food and Gastronomy in Greece.* London and New York.

Etienne, R. (2006) Architecture palatiale et architecture privée en Macédoine, IVe–IIe s. av. J.-C. in A. M. Guimier-Sorbets, M. B. Hatzopoulos and Y. Morizot (eds), 106–115.

Faklaris, P. (2011) Les symposia des Macédoniens. In S. Descamps-Leguime and K. Charatzopoulou (eds) *Au royaume d'Alexandre le Grand: La Macédoine antique*, 388–407, Paris.

Guimier-Sorbets, A. M., M. B. Hatzopoulos and Y. Morizot (eds) (2006) *Rois, Cites, Necropoles: Institutions, Rites Et Monuments En Macédoine*, Meletemata 45. Athens.

Hammond, N. G. L. (1989) *The Macedonian State: Origins, Institutions and History.* Oxford.

Hoepfner, W. (1996) Zum typus der Basileia und Der königlichen Androns. In W. Hoepfner and G. Brands (eds) *Basileia. Die Paläste Der Hellenistischen Könige*, 1–43, Mainz.

Hoepfner, W. and G. Brands (eds) (1996) *Basileia. Die Paläste Der Hellenistischen Könige.* Mainz.

Kottaridi, A. (2002) Discovering Aegae, the old Macedonian capital. In M. Stamatopoulou and M. Yeroulanou (eds) *Excavating Classical Culture: Recent archaeological discoveries in Greece*, 75–81, Oxford.

— (2004) The Symposium. In D. Pandermalis (ed.) *Alexander the Great: Treasures from an epic era of Hellenism*, 65–88, New York.

— (2011a) The Royal banquet: a capital institution. In A. Kottaridi (ed.) *Heracles to Alexander the Great: Treasures from the royal Capital of Macedon, a Hellenic Kingdom in the Age of Democracy*, 167–80, Oxford.

— (2011b) The Palace of Aegae. In R. Lane Fox (ed.) *Brill's Companion to Ancient Macedon: Studies in the Archaeology and History of Macedon, 650 BC–300 AD*, 297–334, Leiden and Boston.

Lauter, H. (1986) *Die Architektur des Hellenismus.* Darmstadt.

Le Bohec-Bouhet, S. (2006) Réflexions sur la place de la femme dans la Macédoine antique. In A. M. Guimier-Sorbets, M. B. Hatzopoulos and Y. Morizot (eds), 187–98.

Lilibaki-Akamati, M. (2004) Women in Macedonia. In D. Pandermalis (ed.) *Alexander the Great: Treasures from an epic era of Hellenism*, 139–48, New York.

Mantis, A. G. (1990) *Problemata tes eikonographias ton iereion kai ton iereon sten archaia ellenike techne* (Deltion suppl. 42).

Nevett, L. C. (1999) *House and Society in the Ancient Greek World*. Cambridge University Press, New Studies in Archaeology series, Cambridge.

Pomeroy, S. B. (1984) *Women in Hellenistic Egypt*. New York.

Pownall, F. (2010) The Symposia of Philip II and Alexander III of Macedon: The View from Greece. In Carney, E. D. and D. Ogden (eds) 55–65.

Rhomiopoulou, K. (1973) A New Monumental Chamber Tomb with Paintings of the Hellenistic Period near Leukadia (West Macedonia), *Athens Annals of Archaeology* 6, 87–92.

— (2000) *Lefkadia: Ancient Mieza*. Athens. 2nd edn.

Roller, M. (2005) Horizontal Women: Posture and Sex in the Roman *Convivium*. In B. Gold and J. F. Donahue (eds) *Roman Dining*, 49–94, Baltimore.

Saatsoglou-Paliadeli, C. (2001) The Palace of Vergina-Aegae and its Surroundings. In I. Nielsen (ed.) *The Royal Palace Institution in the First Millennium BC*, 201–14, Aarhus.

— (2011) The Palace of Aegae. In R. Lane Fox (ed.) *Brill's Companion to Ancient Macedon*, 297–33, Leiden.

Savalli-Lestrade, I. (2003) Remarques sur les elites dans les *poleis* Hellenistique. In M. Cebeillac-Gervasoni and L. Lamoine (eds) *Les elites et leurs facettes. Les elites locales dans le monde hellenistique et romain*, 51–64, Rome-Clermont-Ferrand.

Tataki, A. B. (1988) *Ancient Beroea: Prosopography and Society*. Athens.

Tsibidou-Avloniti, M. (2002) Excavating a painted Macedonian tomb near Thessaloniki. An astonishing Discovery. In M. Stamatopoulou and M. Yeroulanou (eds) *Excavating Classical Culture: Recent archaeological discoveries in Greece*, 91–97, Oxford.

Tsibidou-Avloniti, M. (2006) La tombe macédonienne d'Hagios Athanasios près de Thessalonique. In A. M. Guimier-Sorbets, M. B. Hatzopoulos and Y. Morizot (eds), 321–31.

Vokotopoulou, J. (2001) Makedonika Symposia. In J. Vokotopoulou (ed.) *Studies on Epirus and Macedonia*, II, The Archaeological Society at Athens Library No. 199, 729–38, Athens.

INFANTRY AND THE EVOLUTION
OF ARGEAD MACEDONIA

William Greenwalt[1]

The development of the Argead army and the nature of the Argead state have long generated conversations among scholars. What follows is an outline of what I believe blended the two together, and set the stage for the Hellenistic era. Once the Argeads were no more (except through Cassander's wife, Thessalonike), a new era in Macedonian history began, and not just with the change in dynasty.

Until the reign of Archelaus (*c.* 413–399), Argead Macedonia had no organized infantry to speak of. This was made manifest in 424 when Archelaus' predecessor, Perdiccas II in the midst of the Peloponnesian war, agreed to help pay the expenses of a Spartan army under Brasidas (including 1,700 hoplites) which was meant to raise havoc amongst Athenian interests in the north. Perdiccas' primary interests were not those of Brasidas. The Argead king intended his contribution to buy Brasidas' help in subjecting Arrhabaeus of Lyncus, a goal that had little direct influence on the larger conflict between Sparta and Athens (Thuc. 4.79.2–83).[2] After Perdiccas' initial attempt to lure Brasidas into his conflict failed (Brasidas suggested arbitration instead of war), circumstances allowed Perdiccas a second opportunity in 423 (Thuc. 4.124–128). For the campaign of 423 against Arrhabaeus, Brasidas had at his disposal about 3000 hoplites, composed of elements of the force he had led north, reinforced mostly by the Chalcidians and Acanthians. Also mentioned was a 'crowd' of native troops and a cavalry of Macedonians and Chalcidians numbering almost 1,000. Since the war against Arrhabaeus was important to Perdiccas, and since Thucydides omitted any specific reference to Argead infantry, we can only conclude that Perdiccas did not have access to significant hoplite resources at the time (at least Thucydides, who was well informed, did not think so), and that whatever infantry accompanied the king was

---

[1] Whether or not Waldemar Heckel agrees with the conclusions I have drawn over the years concerning the development of the Macedonian infantry and the evolution of the Macedonian state, I offer the following paper with great respect for his scholarship and past kindnesses. What follows here contains little new scholarship. I hope, however, that in bringing together disperse arguments, I can set the stage for an eventual interpretation of Macedonian kingship during the reign of Cassander, and, help to bring some clarity to the discussion of the Macedonian 'constitution' under the Argeads.

[2] Greenwalt 2007, 89–90; Roisman 2010, 150–152.

of inferior quality and poorly organized. This conclusion is made all the more certain by the disarray amongst Perdiccas' troops, which occurred when some Illyrian mercenaries originally procured by Perdiccas, turned and supported Arrhabaeus instead. Thucydides notes that the discipline of Brasidas' hoplites allowed the general to extricate the core of his army from the difficulties that ensued after Perdiccas' Macedonians abandoned Brasidas and retreated pell-mell before the Illyrian foot then allied with the forces of Arrhabaeus. Thucydides makes no other mention of Perdiccas' army, but it seems unlikely that major military reforms were undertaken as long as he remained engaged on the periphery of the Peloponnesian War. This assumption seems certain: Hoplite infantrymen could not be conjured out of thin air and their existence in the Greece of the polis was largely dependent upon the existence of a class of farmers, who both constituted the backbone of the polis' army and the city-state's political structure. Macedonia appears neither to have yet experienced the socio-economic evolution that allowed for the drafting of hoplite armies, nor the financial wherewithal to maintain a force of mercenary hoplites.

The situation of Perdiccas in 423 should be contrasted with what Thucydides wrote about Archelaus' reforms (2.100.2), where amid praise for the latter's military efforts, the historian mentioned the development of an Argead infantry (pointedly superior to anything Perdiccas commanded). This is not the place to rehash Archelaus' reforms, the foundation of Pella, or the hellenization of Archelaus' realm.[3] What is clear from the evidence, however, is that Archelaus took advantage of Athens' waning fortunes in the north and the Peloponnesian War itself, to reorganize and centralize his realm, not only reconfiguring both its infantry and cavalry, but also fortifying the realm for greater security against invasion and linking the new infrastructure with a network of military roads. In addition, Archelaus maximized his profits from the harvesting of timber and completely revolutionized the realm's coinage.[4] This latter point is important, for a royal coinage of substance gave Archelaus the wherewithal to trade (especially forest products, as Athens' control of Amphipolis was lost) and to spend in his own interests with less deference to landed interests, especially those of the *hetairoi*, from which class he and his predecessors derived the realm's cavalry. Of course, relying heavily on cavalry empowered the aristocratic class politically, limiting the scope of any early Argead king's freedom of rule. Therefore, Thucydides' brief comment about infantry with up-graded training and weaponry is important, not only from a military perspective (who else would man the new fortifications?), but also from a political one. Any Argead with access to infantry as well as cavalry would have a stronger realm against foreign incursion (which is Thucydides' point), but to some extent, an improved infantry would also have counter-balanced the political influence of the Companions.

So, where did Archelaus' infantry come from? Some were probably culled from the Greeks within his realm, others were probably mercenaries paid with the larger coin denominations he issued. Others might well have been cultivated from a growing class of native Macedonians, who would have had to procure land if they were going to be drafted along the lines of a polis' infantry (there is no mention of Archelaus outfitting his troops, so we can assume soldiers in Macedonia also fitted the Greek norm, that is, that

[3]   Borza 1992, 171–177; Borza 1993; Borza 1987; Greenwalt 1999; Greenwalt 2003.
[4]   Greenwalt 1994.

the individual provided his own panoply).[5] If such a class was cultivated, it is unlikely that Archelaus intended to grant many political rights to those who composed his infantry, at least in its infancy. Nevertheless, over time a reliable infantry would have understood its value to the king and demanded some consideration beyond the battlefield.

Regardless of how many of these sources were actually exploited in the creation of an infantry, the resulting rise of an infantry class in Argead Macedonia had the effect of lessening the military importance of the *Hetairoi* class, from which Argead kings had traditionally drafted the bulk of their military strength. To repeat for emphasis, any growth in the military importance of an Argead infantry would also have had a political dimension, if only to the degree of mitigating the influence of those families who had traditionally provided Argead kings with their horse troops. This could not have pleased members of the Hetairoi – it is little wonder that Archelaus was assassinated.[6] Our sources note that the murder of Archelaus during a royal hunt came about as a result of a personal insult, ultimately tied to broken marriage promises (Arist. *Pol.* 1311b.11–2–; 30–34). The royal hunt, however, was a political act, as was marriage in Argead Macedonia.[7] There is no reason to doubt the expressed motive for Archelaus' assassination, insofar as it goes. In the larger context, however, it is myopic to disassociate Archelaus' death entirely from his reforms and the seismic shift in Argead society they boded to both his own kingdom and the polities surrounding it. A partial support for this latter conclusion is found in the seven year civil war which followed Archelaus' death.[8] Archelaus' policies had disturbed the status quo.

The realm was stabilized by Amyntas III (393–371/0), an Argead from a different line than Archelaus. Stability, however, was not strength.[9] Amyntas was driven from his realm at least once, and probably twice by Illyrians (thereafter paying tribute to an Illyrian chieftain for probably the 13 years of his life), and, for a time the eastern portion of his realm was occupied by the Chalcidic League. A testament to Amyntas' military weakness is seen in 382 when a 3,000 man Spartan army ejected the Chalcidians from Argead lands, while using Derdas of Elimea as a primary local contact, not Amyntas (Diod. 15.20.2; Xen. *Hell.* 5.2.24). Yet, it is notable that despite these challenges to Amyntas' rule, he is the only Argead king who is known to have died of natural causes at a relatively old age, and to be succeeded by a son who faced no trouble from existing rivals (Diod. 15.60.3; Just. 7.4.8; Isoc. 6.46; Aeschines 2.26). Next to nothing is known of Amyntas' domestic policies (yet see Xen, *Hell.* 6.1.11; Diod.15.60.2), but the quality of his coinage strongly suggests that the relative prosperity under Archelaus did not return during his reign.[10]

The stigma of his father's weakness seems to have spurred Alexander II (Amyntas' son and successor) to more vigorous actions. For instance, we know of a failed gambit in Thessaly (Diod. 15.61.3–5).[11] Somewhat more controversial is a fragment from Anaximenes (*FgrH* 72 F4) which attributes to an Alexander the organization of an infantry which was

---

5   Greenwalt 1999, 170–172.
6   Greenwalt 1999, 181–183.
7   Carney 2002; Greenwalt 1989.
8   Hammond and Griffith 1979, 167–180.
9   Hammond and Griffith 1979, 167–180.
10 Greenwalt 1994.
11 Graninger 2010, esp. 312.

subsequently known as the "...Foot-Companions, in order that both [the cavalry and the infantry], sharing the royal Companionship, should always be most zealous."[12] Although not all scholars accept that the Alexander appearing in Anaximenes was the second of that name, Anaximenes could not have been referring to Alexander I, because his successor Perdiccas II had no infantry, and it is extremely unlikely that such a reform could have come as late as Alexander III (and, there is no reason to think that Anaximenes misnamed the king to whom he is referring). Moreover, attributing the move to Alexander II fits what little we know about his reign.

We know that Archelaus was assassinated during a hunt at least partially for personal reasons, but if he truly consolidated his realm along the lines which Thucydides' mentions, then he could not have been terribly popular among the Hetairoi who may have appreciated the increased security Archelaus brought to the kingdom, but who could not have been pleased by an increased reliance upon an infantry class. All the more would have been the case if Alexander II had appropriated the coveted title 'Companion' and given it to a re-organized infantry. Alexander must have been busy immediately after coming to the throne, because he too was assassinated less than two years after his accession. It seems more than coincidence that these two kings, who appear to have developed infantry resources, were assassinated. As with the murder of Archelaus, the slaying of Alexander II brought on political instability within Argead Macedonia. Since Alexander was diplomatically and militarily active during his short reign, and thus had to have been aggressive soon after his accession, it appears most likely that he envisioned manipulating greater power than had his father. If he coined the phrase 'Foot-Companion' this could only be seen as a challenge to the established aristocratic Companions. Empowering an infantry would strengthen the realm militarily, but it should also be interpreted as an attempt to lessen the influence of the aristocracy. Alexander II, of course, overshot his mark, and he paid for it with his life, being replaced by a regent named Ptolemy, until Ptolemy himself was assassinated by Perdiccas III, Alexander II's next younger brother.

After a tumultuous interregnum of three years, the accession of Perdiccas III (365–360/59) revived the spirits of Archelaus and Alexander II.[13] Leaving aside anecdotal evidence about the improvement of revenue collection and the slight numismatic evidence (*e.g.* [Arist.], *Oec.* 2.1350a16–22), there is one telling piece of evidence which suggests the kingdom was rebounding under Perdiccas III and that an infantry had become institutionalized under the second of Amyntas III's sons. In 360, a massive Illyrian invasion of Macedonia occurred, probably largely stimulated by the rapid development of Perdiccas' kingdom. Perdiccas mobilized a desperate, but in the end futile, defense of his realm. Diodorus (16.2.4–5) cites that in the war's decisive battle, Perdiccas was killed along with 4,000 of his men (Polyaenus 4.10.1). The size of Perdiccas' army is not known (we know that not all of his military resources were on the scene, because Philip II was not present along with whatever military contingent he commanded, Athen. 11.506e), but two things appear evident: 1) that the gravity of the situation demanded as large an army as Perdiccas could muster; and 2) that the size of the loss meant that Perdiccas had employed significant infantry levies.

---

[12]   Greenwalt 1999, 182–183.
[13]   Roisman 2010, esp. 161–164.

In light of Thucydides' praise of Archelaus, Alexander II's probable association with Foot-Companions, and Arrian's Opis speech (7.9.2–3, qualified by Montgomery),[14] it seems that a substantial number of Perdiccas' infantry were hoplites.

As cruel as it is to state, perhaps the best thing to happen to Macedonia moving forward was the death of Perdiccas and the totality of his loss.[15] This was so, because it brought to the throne the incomparable Philip II at a time when those who survived the Illyrian onslaught were desperate to try something new for the sake of security, and after the established aristocratic Companion class had been decimated. Certainly many of those who died with Perdiccas must have been from the cavalry, and the deaths removed them from the political calculus of the realm. Philip put his own men in their place and worked both deftly and quickly to re-create a viable infantry.

Of course, Philip's phalanx was not the traditional Greek phalanx. Philip, however, had access to the Macedonian forests, from which he could harvest the sarissa, both an offensive and a defensive weapon. By providing the harvest of cornel wood to his troops, Philip greatly increased the size of the Macedonian infantry and made the Argead army a very formidable entity. With success after success, Philip accrued a personal charisma far more potent than that long associated with his dynasty and created a realm far larger than had been ruled by any Argead predecessor.[16] Nor did it hurt Philip that so many of his victories were diplomatic, thereby winning even greater loyalty from among the vast majority of his subjects. Nevertheless, threats existed from just about every point of the compass, forcing Philip to maintain Argead Macedonia on an extended military alert which precluded any significant reform of the political structure of his realm.[17] Philip's assassination had a political dimension (what murder of a king has not had one?),[18] but that act did not result from a Companion disgruntled over the growing importance of an infantry class – that group was ensconced for good by Philip's day.

I have argued elsewhere that Aristotle (*Pol.* 3.10.2; 3.11.11–13) posited that Macedonian kingship was of an absolutist type, with the king essentially acting as the head of a royal household that was one and the same as his realm.[19] Neither Philip II nor Alexander III changed this, and both did act in totalitarian ways at times. What had changed during their extraordinary reigns was the scope of their kingdoms, and the magnitude of their charismas, now greatly enhanced religiously.[20] No monarch, however, could afford to ignore absolutely the concerns and even the voices of those whom they led into battle, especially with it becoming necessary to detach significant numbers of units for significant amounts of time from their royal persons. Just as any head of a household is traditionally bound to consider the rightful concerns of those under his authority, any Argead king, no matter how powerful, could simply not have been deaf to those upon whom his power rested. This

---

[14] Montgomery 1985 rightly argues that the condensed version of Macedonian history reported in Arrian should not be attributed to Philip alone.

[15] Greenwalt 2010, esp. 160–161.

[16] Greenwalt 2010, esp. 160–161; Markle 1977; Markle 1979.

[17] Greenwalt 2010, 162–163.

[18] Hammond and Griffith 1979, 676–679.

[19] Greenwalt 2010, 158–163.

[20] Greenwalt 2011.

would have been true of the infantry as well as the cavalry. This is where, I surmise, the so called 'traditional' rights of things like free speech as argued by some modern scholars came from the need to hold the *oikos* together. Family dinner tables may be dominated by a strong-willed tyrant of a father or a mother, but woe to the head-of-the-household who completely shuts out those who have personal access and are wielding knives. Such common sense became even more prevalent after the Argeads, with their long established religious charisma, had been swept away.

Bibliography

Borza, E. N. (1987) Timber and Politics in the Ancient World: Macedon and the Greeks, *Proceedings of the American Philosophical Association* 131, 32–52.

— (1992) *In the Shadow of Olympus: The Emergence of Macedon* (revised paperback edn). Princeton.

— (1993) The Philhellenism of Archelaus, *Ancient Macedonia* 5, 237–244, reprinted in C. G. Thomas (ed.) *Makedonika*, (Regina, 1995), 125–133.

Carney, E. D. (2002) Hunting and the Macedonian Elite: Sharing the Rivalry of the Chase. In D. Odgen (ed.) *The Hellenistic World. New Perspectives*, 59–80, London.

Graninger, D. (2010) Macedonia and Thessaly. In I. Worthington and J. Roisman (eds) *A Companion to Ancient Macedonia*, 306–341, Malden, MA.

Greenwalt, W. S. (1989) Polygamy and Succession in Argead Macedonia, *Arethusa* 22, 19–45.

— (1994) The production of coinage from Archelaus to Perdiccas III and the Evolution of Argead Macedonia. In I. Worthington (ed.) *Ventures into Greek History*, 105–133, Oxford.

— (1999) Why Pella? *Historia* 58, 158–183.

— (2003) Archelaus the Philhellene, *The Ancient World* 34, 131–153.

— (2007) The Development of a Middle Class in Macedonia, *Ancient Macedonia* 7, 89–90.

— (2010) Argead *Dunasteia* during the Reigns of Philip II and Alexander III. In E. D. Carney and D. Ogden (eds) *Philip II and Alexander the Great: Father and Son, Lives and Afterlives*, 151–163, Oxford.

— (2011) Royal Charisma and the Evolution of Macedonia during the Reigns of Philip and Alexander, *The Ancient World* 42, 148–156.

Hammond, N. G. L., and G. T. Griffith. (1979) *A History of Macedonia*. II. Oxford.

Markle, M. M. (1977) The Macedonian Sarissa, Spear and Related Armor, *American Journal of Archaeology* 81, 323–39.

— (1979) Use of the Sarissa by Philip and Alexander of Macedon, *American Journal of Archaeology* 82, 483–97.

Montgomery, H. (1985) The Economic Revolution of Philip II – Myth or Reality? *SymbOslo* 60, 37–47.

Roisman, J. (2010) Classical Macedonia to Perdiccas III. In J. Roisman, and I. Worthington, (eds) *A Companion to Ancient Macedonia*, 145–165, Malden, MA.

EQUINE ASPECTS OF ALEXANDER THE GREAT'S MACEDONIAN CAVALRY

Carolyn Willekes

Greek warfare of the Archaic and Early Classical periods was dominated by the hoplite.[1] The primary function of the horse was to serve as transportation and status symbol for the aristocratic classes.[2] This was due in large part to the limited availability of equines in Greece and the expense involved in *hippotrophia*.[3] The horse evolved to be a grazing, plains-dwelling herd animal and outside of regions like Thessaly, Sparta, and Macedonia, the topography and vegetation of the Greek Peninsula was better suited to the husbandry of goats and sheep than equines.[4] The toll this environment can take on the equine body is evident from Thucydides' reference to the Athenian cavalry at Decelea: "…and as the cavalry rode out daily upon excursions to Decelea and to guard the country, their horses were either lamed by being constantly worked upon rocky ground, or wounded by the enemy."[5] As a result of these topographical conditions, the horse became a luxury item that was not disposed of readily on the battlefield. Before 480 this lack of cavalry power did not hinder the Greek armies, as horses were not an essential component of combat tactics.[6] Battles were fought primarily on a local scale and not for the purpose of large-scale

---

[1] For an introduction to the evolution of the hoplite see van Wees 2004, 47–57.

[2] See van Wees 2004, 57–59. The horses of antiquity were rarely used for any kind of heavy work; agricultural jobs such as ploughing and transporting weighty loads were the provenance of donkeys, mules and oxen. This was due in part to the hardiness of these animals in comparison to the horse – they required less food and management. Another limiting factor was the horse collar; the yokes used in antiquity were not suitable for the horse as they placed a great amount of pressure on the throat and prevented the animal from being able to pull heavy loads properly. The true horse collar did not appear until the middle ages. Isager and Sydsgaard 1992, 86.

[3] In the *Clouds*, Aristophanes provides us with a vivid picture of the potentially crippling expenses involved in *hippotrophia*, particularly lines 12–78. See also Griffith 2006, 200; for details on the cost of purchasing and maintaining a horse see Hyland 2003, 141–143; Spence 1993, 272–286; for the horse as a status symbol see Howe 2008, 108–118.

[4] Griffith 2006, 197. For a detailed analysis of Greek husbandry practices see Howe 2011, 4–25, especially 15–16 for the requirements of specific animal species.

[5] Thuc. *Pelop* 7.27.5 (all quotations from Xenophon, *Anabasis* are from the Landmark Thucydides, Richard Crawley translation).

[6] Gaebel 2002, 53, 67–70.

conquest.[7] Only during the Persian Wars of 480–78 did the Greeks begin to realize that an army deficient in cavalry could be a liability, particularly when Greek infantry were faced with Persian cavalry.[8]

> The horsemen rode out and attacked, inflicting injuries on the entire Greek army with their javelins and arrows, for they were mounted archers and it was impossible for the Hellenes to close with them. They also blocked and destroyed the Spring of Gargaphia, which had been the source of water for the whole Greek army.[9]

The Peloponnesian War introduced a new style of warfare to Greece and with this came a greater respect for the potential uses of cavalry. Throughout the Peloponnesian War and the later ascendancy of Thebes, cavalry performed a variety of essential combative and non-combative roles, indicating a growing awareness of mounted combat in Greece; but even then its use as a major striking force was not considered.[10] Greek cavalry did not reach its full potential until the reign of Alexander the Great, both in its deployment with infantry for a combined attack, as well as in the actual use of the horse in combat. This came about in part because Alexander was heir to Macedonia's rich equestrian heritage; but more importantly, Alexander was able to revolutionize the use of the military horse by incorporating an understanding of equine behaviour and physiology into training and tactics. Alexander utilized the natural herd mentality and hierarchical structure of equine society to overcome the prey instincts of the horse. In doing this, Alexander made his cavalry a primary striking force on the battlefield in which the horse served as important a role as his rider.

Until the mid-4th century BCE, Greek cavalry traditionally operated independently from infantry on the battlefield, serving as a supporting arm to the hoplite. It was only with the ascendancy of Macedonia that the full potential of a combined attack was realized and it subsequently became a mainstay of Alexander's combat strategy. The advantage of this style of fighting was made clear when Alexander marched against the Triballians:

> Alexander ... ordered Philotas to take the cavalry of upper Macedonia and charge their right wing, where they had advanced farthest in their outward rush. Heracleides and Sopolis were ordered to lead the cavalry from Bottiaea and Amphipolis against the left wing. The infantry phalanx and the remaining cavalry, which he deployed in advance of the phalanx, he led against the center. While the battle was still at long range, the Triballians did not have the worst of it, but when the phalanx in close formation charged them in full force and the cavalry, no

---

[7]   Hanson 1989, 27–39; van Wees 2004, 27–30. One obvious exception to this pattern is the Spartan conquest of Messenia.

[8]   Cawkwell 2005, 112–115; Gaebel 2002, 71–80.

[9]   Herod. *Hist.* 9.49.2 (all quotations from Herodotus are from the *Landmark Herodotus*, tr. Andrea Purvis); cf. the lack of Athenian cavalry during the Sicilian campaign Thuc. *Pelop.* 6.63.3; 6.66.1; 6.70.3; 6.74.2; 6.94.4; 6.98.1–4; 6.101.5; 7.4.6; 7.6.3; 7.11.4; 7.13.2; 7.43.6; 7.44.8; 7.51.2; 7.78.3; 7.84.2–7.85.1. Xenophon sums up the predicament of an army without cavalry nicely when he writes "... and they had been left all alone, without a single horseman in their army, which, they were sure, meant that even if they won a battle they would not kill any of the enemy, while if they lost, not one of them would survive." Xen. *Anab.* 3.1 cf Xen. *Anab.* 2.4 (all quotations from Xenophon, *Anabasis* are from the Robin Waterfield translation).

[10] Gaebel 2002, 90–109; Spence 1993, 102–117; van Wees 2004, 65–68.

longer shooting, but actually thrusting them with their horses, fell on them here, there and everywhere, they turned in flight...[11]

Alexander's basic strategy in battle relied upon speed: a hard, rapid attack, giving his opponents no chance to gather themselves and retaliate. The potential success of this strategy depended upon the ability of cavalry and infantry to work in unison, something easier said than done. Alexander's line effectively functioned like a giant bullwhip. The Greek cavalry on the left held the defences, moving forward to take up a pursuit only at the end of the battle. The sarissa-phalanx in the center held their ground and slowly moved forward to push through any gaps in the enemy line. The key attack came from the right, where the Macedonian cavalry surged forward to engage the horsemen, supported by the hypaspists who moved amongst the horses pulling down enemy cavalrymen.[12]

Before Alexander commanders were aware of the potential benefits of a joint cavalry-infantry attack and had experimented with the combined formations. In his *Cavalry Commander* Xenophon alludes to the greater strength of cavalry when used in conjunction with infantry. He suggests that:

> Both divisions should have an infantry contingent; and if the infantry hidden away behind the cavalry, came out suddenly and went for the enemy, I think they would prove an important factor in making the victory decisive.[13]

The usefulness of Xenophon's recommendation can be seen in accounts of such a combined attack. While performing a reconnaissance of the Piraeus, Pausanias was surprised by enemy troops. In retaliation he "ordered the cavalry to charge them at the gallop and the infantry in the age group 20–30 to follow the cavalry. He himself came in support of them with the rest of the infantry."[14] Likewise, the Philasians successfully deployed a combined attack against the Sicyonians in 366 when Chares:

> ...set out on the march and the Philasian cavalry and infantry went ahead. They led the way at a great pace from the start, and then they began to run, and in the end the cavalry were riding at a full gallop and the infantry were running as fast as men in line can run, and then came Chares following eagerly behind.[15]

We occasionally come across mention of a unit of foot soldiers called *hamippoi*. The first reference to them is found in Xenophon's *Cavalry Commander* in which he states

> Another duty of the cavalry commander is to demonstrate to the city the weakness of cavalry destitute of infantry as compared with cavalry that has infantry attached to it. Further, having got his infantry, a cavalry commander should make use of it.[16]

---

[11] Arr. *Anab.* 1.2.5–7 (all quotations from Arrian, *Anabasis* are from the *Landmark Arrian*, Pamela Mensch translation).

[12] Heckel 2008, 25–28.

[13] Xen. *Eq. mag.* 8.19 (all quotations from Xenophon, *Eq* and *Eq.Mag* are from the Loeb edition, E. C. Marchant translation).

[14] Xen. *Hell.* 2.4.31–32 (all quotations from Xenophon, *Hellenica* are from the Penguin edition, Rex Warner translation).

[15] Xen. *Hell.* 7.2.21–22.

[16] Xen. *Eq. mag.* 5.13

Men who must have acted as *hamippoi* are recorded as taking part in the annual *dokimasia* which evaluated cavalrymen and their mounts as well as "the foot-soldiers that fight in the ranks of the cavalry, and anyone it votes against is thereby stopped from drawing his pay."[17] A possible *hamippos* is seen in a 4th-century stele at the Louvre.[18] The stele depicts a light-armed infantryman running alongside a horse while holding onto the tail,[19] this follows with literary evidence which suggests that the *hamippoi* fought interspersed among the cavalry. At the Granicus, the Persian cavalry "were suffering heavily from the light troops, who had intermingled with the cavalry…"[20] The primary function of the *hamippos* was probably to pull enemy cavalrymen off their horses and dispatch them once they were on the ground. A cavalryman who fell from his horse was placed at great risk. Being thrown from a horse is disorienting even at the best of times, at the worst it can result in serious injury or death. Even taking a mild tumble would cause a cavalryman to experience a momentary loss of spatial awareness, making him vulnerable to an attack by a light-armed *hamippos*. It is logical to assume that anyone serving as a *hamippos* was familiar with equine behaviour and movement; this knowledge would have been essential for a *hamippos* to fight safely and effectively alongside cavalry. A horse savvy *hamippos* could also jump on a riderless horse if necessary, either to take part in a skirmish or to round up loose animals on the battlefield.

This concept of horsemen and infantry working together on the battlefield presents us with a much different picture of how a cavalry charge worked. It certainly was not the mad hell for leather gallop frequently portrayed in film and fiction. Considering that a galloping horse can reach speeds in excess of 35 miles per hour, it is absurd to imagine that even the fittest of light infantry could keep up with them, especially for any length of time. The cavalry must have maintained a pace that the infantry were easily capable of matching.[21] When Alexander made his customary use of a combined attack at Issus his advance towards the Persian lines was clearly an organized, controlled movement:

> He continued to lead on in line, at marching pace at first, though he now had Darius' force in view, to avoid any part of the phalanx fluctuating in a more rapid advance and so breaking apart.[22]

To better understand the mechanics of a cavalry charge, we need to look at the horse himself. The effectiveness of the mounted charge lay, as with the phalanx, in maintaining formation. If it is difficult for running men to maintain a cohesive unit, it is even more so for cavalry. The faster a horse moves the more challenging it becomes to maintain control over him. Horses can be very competitive and will speed up if they hear another horse approaching behind them. Thus, the greater the number of horses moving at speed, the

---

[17] Arist. *[Ath. Pol.]* 49.1 (all quotations from Aristotle, *Ath. Pol.* are from the Loeb edition, H. Rackham translation).

[18] Hamiaux and Pasquier 2002, 223.

[19] Spence 1995, 58–9.

[20] Arr. *Anab.* 1.16.1.

[21] At full stretch a galloping horse reaches speeds from 30 to 45 miles per hour, and covers a distance of 7–8 meters with each stride. Harris 1993, 49; cf. Kiley-Worthington 1993, 174.

[22] Arr. *Anab.* 2.10.3.

harder it becomes to maintain a unified formation. This is not to say that cavalry never attacked from a gallop, but it was a controlled pace, not a flat out sprint.[23]

In Greek art, the horse is typically depicted in a collected state. 'Collection' refers to a way of moving in which the horse shifts his weight onto his hindquarters, lightening his forehand to carry himself in a balanced, upright manner.[24] Collection is,

> ...necessary in order to ride the horse in shortened gaits and tight corners and to execute smooth and flowing half-halts. Collection allows a higher degree of flexion of the haunches and thus enables a superior level of athleticism, at the same time preventing early wear on the joints of the horse.[25]

This is the natural way of movement for a horse, as can be seen by watching a horse playing at liberty in his field. The higher head carriage of the collected horse does not allow the animal to bolt forwards or sideways. Any uncontrolled rapid movement requires a full extension of the horse's body, including a lowered head and extended neck.[26] Thus, the collected horse is a controlled horse. Collection would have been essential in all cavalry manoeuvres. The collected gallop used in a cavalry charge allowed the rider to sit up and remain centered on his horse in a position well suited to fighting. The cavalryman could use the power of his horse's movement to add force to his blows, while his centered seat gave him a much stronger base of support, making it more difficult to unhorse him. The racing gallop not only led to an out of control animal, it also required the rider to bend forward at his hips into the crouched position portrayed by the Artemision jockey. This allowed the rider to stay balanced over the horse's center of gravity, but would have been close to impossible to fight from with any accuracy or security.[27]

The importance of training and maintaining a collected cavalry horse is a notion that runs throughout Xenophon's two treatises on cavalry and horsemanship. Xenophon's preference for collection is clear from the outset when he states that the ideal horse should have a naturally upright head carriage:

> His neck should not hang downwards from the chest like a boar's, but stand straight up to the crest, like a cock's; but it should be flexible at the bend ... a horse of such a mould will have least power of running away, be he never so high-spirited, for horses do not arch the neck and head, but stretch them out when they try to run away.[28]

For Xenophon, the ultimate goal was to produce a horse capable of carrying his rider with the same amount of balance, power and expression displayed when showing off at liberty, when "he raises his neck highest and arches his head most, looking fierce; he lifts his legs

---

[23] As opposed to the racing gallop, charging cavalry must have used something akin to our 'hand gallop' which is an upright, balanced gait of 18 miles per hour that a fit horse can easily maintain over long distances. Harris 1993, 174.

[24] The horse naturally carries 60% of his weight on his forehand and 40% on his hind end when standing at rest. The challenge for any rider is to shift the weight back to his hindquarters so the horse moves in an 'uphill' manner, as opposed to 'downhill'. Harris 1993, 75–76.

[25] Dietz 2004, 41.

[26] Gaebel 2002, 30.

[27] Gaebel 2002, 30–31.

[28] Xen. *Eq.* 1.8.

freely off the ground and tosses his tail up."[29] Here Xenophon is describing a specific state of collected forward movement – the *passage*. This is a compressed, powerful trot with high, supple leg action. It is the most cadenced and measured gait a horse can produce. The *passage* along with the *piaffe* – an elevated trot on the spot – serve to maintain impulsion and rhythm, while also allowing the horse to burst forward rapidly, but in balance.[30] Impulsion and rhythm were essential elements on the battlefield. A cavalryman could not allow his horse to come to a halt while he was engaged in combat. Just as a runner will not stop dead at a traffic light, but instead jogs on the spot to keep his muscles warm, the cavalry horse would likewise need to stay engaged under his rider at all times. This is the advantage of the *passage* and *piaffe*: the horse remained balanced enough for his rider to fight securely, but also maintains enough power and impulsion to respond to any sudden command for forward or lateral movement. Collection was essential for the style of cavalry combat favoured by Alexander.

The greatest contribution Alexander made to cavalry in the ancient world was with its actual use in combat. This change is first seen at Chaeronea in 338 when an 18-year-old Alexander made his dramatic military debut as a cavalry commander. He was assigned the formidable task of defeating the Sacred Band with his cavalry. The Thebans did not deploy any horsemen against Alexander, as they assumed that the heavily armed hoplites of the Sacred Band would easily stop him. In this they were very wrong and Alexander's cavalry broke through the phalanx. Alexander's attack at Chaeronea was revolutionary not because he dared to attack heavily armed infantry, but on account of what he did once he broke through their ranks:

> Then Alexander, his heart set on showing his father his prowess and yielding to none in will to win, ably seconded by his men, first succeeded in rupturing the solid front of the enemy line and striking down many he bore heavily on the troops opposite him. As the same success was won by his companions, gaps in the front were constantly opened. Corpses piled up, until finally Alexander forced his way through the line and put his opponents to flight.[31]

Alexander's horsemen engaged the hoplites in hand-to-hand combat, fighting an infantry style battle on horseback. The standard tradition for cavalry was to fight from a distance using long-range weapons like javelins and bows or as skirmishers making rapid attacks and retreats.[32] This made sense as it took advantage of the inherent benefits offered by the horse: the cavalryman could use the power and impulsion of his horse to add distance and force to his throw while also utilising equine manoeuvrability and speed to harass the enemy with projectiles before wheeling away to safety. Alexander introduced an entirely new style of mounted combat at Chaeronea by seeing the horse not just as an aid to javelins and arrows, but as a weapon in his own right. In the close-order fighting he preferred and perfected,

---

29 Xen. *Eq.* 10.4.
30 Anderson 1961, 118–119; Morris 1993, 67.
31 Diod. 16.86.3 (all quotations from Diodorus are from the Loeb edition, C. Bradford Welles translation).
32 See for example Thuc. 2.79.1–6; 5.10.9; 5.58.4; 6.70.3; Xen. *Hell*, 3.2.3; 3.4.13–14; 4.3.4–5; 4.8.18; 5.4.39; 5.4.52–53; 7.2.10.

the horse could do just as much damage as spears and swords by wheeling, crushing and ramming enemy men and horses.[33] At the Granicus Arrian reports:

> Though the fighting was on horseback, it was more like an infantry battle, horse entangled with horse, man with man in the struggle, the Macedonians trying to push the Persians once and for all from the bank and force them on to the level ground, the Persians trying to bar their landing and thrust them back again into the river.[34]

These tactics required a new approach to training. The horse is both a prey and herd animal; factors that heavily influenced the training of a cavalry mount, particularly with respect to close-order fighting. As a prey animal, the horse prefers to avoid danger by following a 'flight' rather than 'fight' reaction.[35] A horses' sense of hearing, sight and smell are extremely acute as he depends on them to perceive danger. The equine ear can detect a vast range of sounds at high and low frequency. Their ears are very mobile as they are controlled by sixteen muscles that allow them to rotate one hundred and eighty degrees, picking up sounds from all sides of the animal. What might be an unpleasantly loud noise for a person would be an unbearable racket for a horse.[36] The horse also has one of the largest eyes in the animal world, with a three hundred and forty degree range of vision; the only blind spots lie directly in front of and behind the body. These large eyes provide the equine brain with one-third of its sensory input. The placement of the eyes on the side of his head allows the horse to see the world through a panoramic view. This wide range of vision permits the horse to see what is happening on either side of him without turning his head. This means that the horse sees an entirely different view of the battlefield than the cavalryman.[37] Smell is one of the most important senses for equines: it allows them to scent a hidden predator, find food and water, and recognize individuals as friend or foe.[38] By entering into hand-to-hand combat, the cavalryman is asking his mount to ignore his senses and override basic instinctual reactions. The influence of the equine flight reaction on strategy can be seen at the Hydaspes, where Alexander clearly had to take into account the reaction his horses would have to Porus' elephants.

> He realized that he would be unable to cross where Porus himself had made camp by the bank of the Hydaspes, for in addition to Porus' large number of elephants, a vast army, drawn up and armed to the teeth, would attack his men as they emerged from the river. Also, he

---

[33] Spence 1993, 113–114; For the potential trained aggressiveness of a warhorse see Hdt. 5.111 "Now Artybios was riding a horse that had been trained to rear up on its hind legs when directly in front of a hoplite; and Onesilos, when he learned of this, said to his shield bearer – a Carian by race who was quite distinguished in warfare and daring in other respects as well – 'I hear that the horse of Artybios stands on its hind legs and with its hooves and its mouth destroys anyone in front of it. So think for a moment and then tell me which of the two do you want to watch for and strike, the horse or Artybios himself?'"

[34] Arr. *Anab.* 1.15.4

[35] This is not to say that a horse will never fight – if cornered or unable to find any means of flight a horse will lash out in defence; but his preference is to avoid combat if possible. The desire to avoid a full on fight is regularly seen among wild horses where combat, even between rival stallions, is rare. Hubert and Klein 2007, 68–74; Kiley-Worthington 2005, 203.

[36] Morris 1997, 21.

[37] Morris 1997, 46; Warren 2013, 58–59.

[38] Morris 1997, 43; Kiley-Worthington 2005, 69–72.

imagined that his horses would refuse to set foot on the opposite bank, since the elephants would immediately charge and the sight and sound of the beasts would terrify them; even before that point, he realized, his horses would not remain on the hide floats ferrying them across but would panic and leap into the water when they caught sight of the elephants on the other side.[39]

The frantic or violent reaction a horse produces in response to fear can be seen in the 'taming' of Bucephalus by Alexander, who recognized that the horse was not naturally aggressive, but actually scared of his shadow. According to Plutarch:

> The king and his friends went down to the plain to watch the horse's trials, and came to the conclusion that he was wild and quite unmanageable, for he would allow no one to mount him, nor would he endure the shouts of Philip's grooms, but reared up against anyone who approached him…. Alexander went quickly up to Bucephalus, took hold of his bridle, and turned him towards the sun, for he had noticed that the horse was shying at the sight of his own shadow, as it fell in front of him and constantly moved away whenever he did. He ran alongside the animal for a little way, calming him down by stroking him, and then, when he saw he was full of spirit and courage, he quietly threw aside his cloak and with a light spring vaulted safely on his back. For a little while he kept feeling the bit with the reins, without jarring or tearing his mouth, and got him collected. Finally, when he saw that the horse was free of his fears and impatient to show his speed, he gave him his head and urged him forward, using a commanding voice and a touch of the foot.[40]

Bucephalus strikes out at his handlers not because he is a violent or aggressive horse, but rather an animal who is frightened and cornered with no option of flight. The flight instinct causes the horses to react negatively to pain. Unlike predatory animals, the horse will try to avoid or flee from a source of pain, as opposed to facing it down or fighting it.[41] When fighting in close quarters, the risk of injury was great and the cavalryman had to depend on training to override the flight response to pain. Again at the Granicus, we read that:

> The Persians were now being roughly handled from all quarters; they and their horses were struck in the face with lances, they were being pushed back by the cavalry…[42]

If the horse registers a painful or bad experience with combat, it could be difficult to coerce him into a similar situation again.[43] To overcome these inherent instincts, correct training was of utmost importance. Obedience had to be instilled in the horse through regular drills

---

[39] Arr. *Anab.* 5.10.1–2.

[40] Plut. *Alex.* 6 (all quotations from Plutarch, *Alexander* are from the Penguin, *Age of Alexander* edition, Ian Scott-Kilvert translation).

[41] This is the premise behind using a whip to make the horse go forwards. A rider will tap or smack the horse on the flank to urge him forward – in the case of horse racing, it is to ask for a burst of speed, while a jumper might use it to push a hesitant or lazy horse towards a fence; similarly, a rider can use a whip to his horse's shoulders for directional control, as the horse will automatically move away from the whip and straighten out.

[42] Arr. *Anab.* 1.15.8.

[43] Horses have particularly good episodic memories and can remember a bad experience for their entire life. Kiley-Worthington 2005, 129. A horse I knew as a child had an overwhelming fear of cows. As a foal she had been caught in a stampede, and even ten years later, the mere sight/sound/smell of a cow would cause her to bolt in terror.

and schooling in an arena, but also work across country and out hunting.[44] The horse had to learn to follow his rider's commands without question and the only way to accomplish this was by exposing the horse to potentially stressful or frightening situations to de-sensitize him. Once this was accomplished, the cavalryman could begin to use equine behaviour to his favour, channelling body language and the herd mentality towards combat.

A horse suitable for the type of cavalry combat favoured by Alexander needed to be bold and dominant. This certainly explains Alexander's preference for riding stallions in battle rather than mares or geldings. Stallions are physically more developed, territorial by nature and always the most alpha member of a herd because it is their responsibility to guard the harem from any potential dangers. Alexander's horses needed this bold nature, but they could not display excess violence or aggression. Their dominance had to be trainable so they remained brave but obedient. The overly aggressive horse was as much a liability to his rider as the enemy; he was just as likely to lash out at another horse in his own unit as he was to attack an opponent. In close order combat a cavalryman needed an animal that would not back down from a challenge because this type of fighting was more psychological than physical: an enemy horse could be psychologically defeated by playing on innate herd mentality. Horse herds are strictly hierarchical: animals achieve and maintain their position through physical intimidation, particularly posturing. Even in encounters between rival harem stallions, conflict rarely results in outright physical violence. One stallion will attempt to 'psych out' his opponent with aggressive body language. Only if neither horse backs down will the situation become physically violent. When the situation escalates to this level, the confrontation continues until one horse overwhelms the other.[45] It is easy to see how this type of equine psychological warfare can be advantageous in close-combat: If an opponent's horse submits to yours, the rider is rendered useless as no amount of force will make that animal stand up to his aggressor. This is because of the overwhelming influence herd behaviour has on any horse: in the herd, a submissive horse will try his best to avoid any contact with a more dominant animal by staying as far away from them as possible.[46]

There are several characteristic equine body signals that can be exploited by a cavalryman in close combat. The body check is used by a dominant horse to restrict the movements of a rival – the aggressor aligns his body across the front of his opponent, preventing him from advancing. The checked horse can either submit or try to force his way forward; if he gives ground at all, he is admitting defeat. A more aggressive variation of the body check is the shoulder barge. This is a dominant action in which one horse rams another out of the way with his shoulder.[47] A cavalryman can accomplish this by riding in the same direction as his opponent and approaching him from the side, pushing his horse laterally into the enemy and shoving him out of the way. When done at speed, this move can throw the

---

[44] See Xen. *Eq.* 8.10 "Since it is necessary that the rider should have a firm seat when riding at top speed over all sorts of country, and should be able to use his weapons properly on horseback, the practice of horsemanship by hunting is to be recommended where the country is suitable and big game to be found."

[45] Bourman 1986, 9–10.

[46] Budiansky 1997, 90. The hierarchy of an equine herd is remarkably stable, and aggression within a herd is displayed predominantly by lower-ranking animals towards new herd members. Boyd 1991, 305–308.

[47] Morris 1997, 35–37.

rival equine off balance and even knock him down, causing serious issues for his rider.[48] The *levade* is a highly collected and controlled rear, in which the horse rocks back on his haunches while raising his forehand off the ground at a 45-degree angle.[49] Rearing is a classic form of posturing used by rival stallions; the *levade* allows the cavalryman to use the same principle while keeping a balanced, secure seat and gaining a greater degree of leverage for hand-to-hand fighting. A more extreme version of the *levade* is the *courbette* in which the horse rears straight up and launches himself forward in a series of jumps. If the *levade* is a controlled form of posturing, the *courbette* is intended to mentally overwhelm and terrify both equine and human opponents, and could be used to break up small clusters of fighters.[50]

Not all horses are suited to this manner of fighting. Docile or submissive equines will make no attempt to approach, let alone face down, a potentially more dominant opponent. This is dangerous for the cavalryman because he cannot trust his horse to respond to commands. Thus, there is no point in attempting to use this type of horse for close-order fighting. Likewise, a nervous or flighty horse is more of a hazard than a help in battle as he is far more likely to overreact and spook or panic, creating a major problem. Herd behaviour can work to the advantage of a cavalry unit: if a bold horse is placed at the head of a formation, the other animals will follow without much question. If, however, one horse in a formation panics, the same herd instinct will spread the anxiety throughout the group, causing it to fall into disorder. The physical and psychological toll this manner of close-order fighting had on man and horse can be seen in Arrian's description of the cavalry engagement at Gaugamela:

> This proved the fiercest cavalry engagement of the whole action. The barbarians, who were drawn up in depth, since they were in squadrons, rallied, and clashed with Alexander's troops front to front: there was no more javelin-throwing and no manoeuvring of horses, as usual in a cavalry engagement, but each strove hard to break his own way through; they kept on giving and taking blows unsparingly, treating this as the one hope for safety, inasmuch as they were men now no longer fighting for another's victory, but for their own very lives.[51]

This highlights the importance of the horse-human relationship. To ride a horse to war, both man and animal had to trust each other implicitly. The horse had to believe that his rider would not intentionally put him at risk, while the cavalryman needed to know that his mount would obey commands without question. The absence of trust led to miscommunication, which could be fatal. This level of trust came in part from training, but also from a human understanding of equine behaviour and physiology. This understanding was the crux of Alexander's success. The story of Alexander and Bucephalus is not just an apocryphal tale predicting Alexander's greatness; it is much more important than that. It shows Alexander's fascination with equine behaviour – a fascination that grew into a new way of using cavalry.

---

48 The shoulder barge at speed is a common tactic used in polo; a sport that originated in Persia as a tool for training horses and men for combat.

49 The Dexilios stele and Alexander Sarcophagus both show excellent examples of the *levade*.

50 Loch 1990, 37.

51 Arr. *Anab.* 3.15.2.

Why did Alexander go to the trouble of changing traditional cavalry combat? It could not have been a simple task. It required a complete overhaul of standard training methods for horse and rider. It also necessitated a greater emotional investment due to the bond that developed between the cavalryman and his mount. The relationship between Alexander and Bucephalus may be an extreme example of this bond, but it nonetheless highlights the fact that the Macedonian cavalryman did not see his horse merely as a tool for combat.[52] The answer lies in the nature of his enemy. Persia and the Persian Empire were home to some of the most celebrated horse cultures in the ancient world. Alexander could not hope to defeat Darius with infantry alone; even the superiority of the sarissa-phalanx could not promise success against the horsemen of Asia. Nor could Alexander hope to out-do the Persians with regards to sheer horsepower. Medea was home to the Nesaean horse – a powerful animal, with considerably greater muscle mass than other horses of the period due to his alfalfa-rich diet, while the steppe-lands of the Near East provided Darius with a massive supply of nimble, hardy horses and the nomads to ride them. Thus, the only way Alexander could out-horse Darius was to make use of a new form of combat. The psychological basis of Alexander's cavalry tactics negated the physical superiority of the Nesaean horse, while the hand-to-hand fighting overwhelmed the lighter armed horse archers and javelin-men from the steppe.

Bibliography

Anderson, J. K. (1961) *Ancient Greek Horsemanship.* Berkley.

Bouman, J. (1986) *Particulars About the Przewalski Horse.* Klaaswaal.

Boyd, L. (1991) The Behaviour of Przewalski's Horses and its Importance to their Management, *Applied Animal Behaviour Science* 29, 301–318.

Budiansky, S. (1997) *The Nature of Horses: Exploring Equine Evolution, Intelligence, and Behaviour.* New York.

Cawkwell, G. (2005) *The Greek Wars: The Failure of Persia.* New York.

Dietz, A. J. (2004). *Training the Horse in Hand: the Classical Iberian Principles.* Guildford.

Gaebel, R. E. (2002) *Cavalry Operations in the Ancient World.* Norman.

Griffith, M. (2006) Horsepower and Donkeywork: Equids in the Ancient Greek Imagination, *Classical Philology* 101, 184–246.

Hamiaux, M. and A. Pasquier (2002) *Les Scupltures Greques I. Des origines à la fin du IV siècle avant J-C.* Paris.

Hanson, V. D. (1989) *The Western Way of War: Infantry Battle in Classical Greece.* Berkley.

Harris, S. (1993) *Horse gaits, Balance and Body Movement: The Natural Mechanics of Movement Common to all Breeds.* Hoboken.

Heckel, W. (2008) *The Conquests of Alexander the Great.* New York.

Howe, T. (2008) *Pastoral Politics: Animals, Agriculture and Society in Ancient Greece.* Claremont.

— (2011) Good Breeding: Making Sense of Elite Animal Production in Ancient Greece, *Scholia* 20, 4–25

Hubert, M. L. and J. L. Klein (2007) *Mustangs: Wild Horses of the West.* Buffalo.

Isager, S and J. E. Skydsgaard (1992) *Ancient Greek Agriculture: An Introduction.* New York.

Kiley-Worthington, M. (2005) *Horse Watch: What it is to be Equine.* London.

---

[52] For example, Arrian tells us that "In the Uxian country Alexander once lost him [Bucephalas], and issued a proclamation throughout the country that he would kill every Uxian unless they brought him back is horse; he was brought back immediately after this proclamation. Such was Alexander's devotion to him…" Arr. *Anab.* 5.19.6.

Loch, S. (1990) *Dressage: The Art of Classical Riding*. North Pomfret.

Morris, D. (1997) *Illustrated Horsewatching*. Ottawa.

Morris, G. H, (1993) *The American Jumping Style*. New York.

Smythe, R. H. and P. Grey (1993) *Horse Structure and Movement*. London.

Spence, I. (1995) *The Cavalry of Classical Greece: A Social and Political History*. Oxford.

Van Wees, H. (2004) *Greek Warfare: Myths and Realities*. London.

Warren, N. (2013) Planet Horse, *Horse and Rider* July, 58–62.

MACEDONIAN ARMIES, ELEPHANTS, AND THE PERFECTION OF COMBINED ARMS

Graham Wrightson[1]

> The concept of combined arms in ground combat has existed for centuries, but the nature
> of that combination and the organizational level at which it occurred have varied greatly....
> Since then twentieth-century warfare ... developed to the point where some form of combined
> arms is essential for survival, let alone victory.
>
> (House 2001, 3)

The term 'combined arms' is relatively modern in military theory,[2] but although the
specific term is new in its use it is not new in practice.[3] Gradually, use of the theory of
combined arms is coming to define scholarly discussions of Greek warfare, in particular
with regards to the armies of Philip and Alexander.[4] However, elephants became integral
only after Alexander, in the armies of the Successors, and it took time for them to be
fully integrated tactically allowing for their best use in battle. In this paper I will show
that it was only in the armies of the Successors of Alexander, in particular at Ipsus, that
combined arms warfare was perfected by successfully, and correctly, integrating all types of
units available.[5] Indeed, the best tactical use of elephants in battle was not achieved until
the battle of Ipsus in 301.

Before analyzing the use of elephants in Macedonian warfare it is necessary to outline
what is meant by combined arms. The theory of combined arms, simply put, is the tactical

---

[1] I am delighted to be able to present this paper in this festschrift for Waldemar Heckel. He has been my
academic supervisor throughout my MA and PhD and without his constant support and advice I would
not be where I am today. His publication and teaching records speak for themselves and it has been a
privilege to work (and play) so closely for so long alongside such an esteemed academic.

[2] See House 1984; Spiller 1992 and in particular House 2001. As House 2001, 5 aptly summarizes, the
application of combined arms tactics in battle "is the area that is of most concern to professional soldiers,
yet it is precisely this area where historical records and tactical manuals often neglect important details."

[3] My PhD, as yet unpublished, deals more fully with the developments of combined arms in Greek and Near
Eastern warfare: Wrightson 2012.

[4] Pederson 1998; Jones 1987; Lonsdale 2004; and 2007, who all discuss combined arms in the armies of
Philip and Alexander but add little context or detailed analysis.

[5] As Bar Kochva (1976, 203) observes, the achievements in battle tactics of Hellenistic generals are often
ignored by scholars in favour of Philip II and Alexander.

integration of two or more units in battle. The goal of combined arms is to enable a coordination of action in a battle that brings each unit into offensive or defensive action to mutually support the rest of the army, "working in concert towards a common objective to destroy or disrupt the enemy forces."[6] A successful complete use of combined arms must integrate fully *all* the diverse units available into a successful tactical plan on the battlefield. All the units "must be used in concert to maximize the survival and combat effectiveness of the others. The strengths of one system must be used to compensate for the weaknesses of others."[7] Combined arms in battle is intended "to achieve an effect on the enemy that is greater than if each arm was used against the enemy independently."[8] Units must work efficiently in concert from the outset in order to overcome the enemy as easily as possible. A battle plan that principally relies on one type of unit, such as the hoplite phalanx, is not utilizing combined arms and can often be exposed as a result.

The nature of ancient warfare led to many instances of the use of combined arms in battle, but at very different levels of sophistication. The simple use of infantry and cavalry together was common. However, the Macedonian army after the accession of Philip II was the first in the ancient world to design battle plans that made full use of combined arms in every engagement regardless of terrain, fully integrating every type of unit available from sarissa phalanx to archers and cavalry:[9]

> [This army] in many ways represented the culmination of classical trends. The Macedonian army was powerful, not only because of the phalangite who replaced the hoplite as the mainstay of the infantry, but also because of the coordinated use of different types of military forces: cavalry of different types, peltasts, slingers and archers.
>
> (Hunt 2007, 145)

Philip is criticised by Demosthenes (9.47–52) for instilling into his professional army the discipline and ability to fight year round. Yet it is this professionalism that allowed Philip's army to become so proficient in battle and expert at the use of combined arms.

Philip II's overwhelming victory at the first battle after his accession to the throne of Macedon – at Heraclea Lyncestis in 358 – was brought about by his coordinated use of infantry and cavalry in attack.[10] Philip continued to develop his army throughout his reign so that by the time he defeated the Greeks at Chaeronea his army was experienced in and effective at the use of combined arms.[11]

---

6   Pederson 1998, xii.

7   House 2001, 4.

8   Pederson 1998, xii.

9   Philip fought four major battles (Heraclea Lyncestis; against Onomarchus; the Crocus Field; Chaeronea). At all four Philip led an army of cavalry, missile troops and phalangites. The last of these are discussed in more detail below. For secondary accounts of the army of Philip II see: Griffith 1992; Ashley 1998, 22–54, 111–164; Worthington 2008, esp. 23–37. For an excellent discussion of the training and armaments of Philip's (and Alexander's) army see Karunanithy 2013. For fuller discussions of Philip's use of combined arms see Pederson 1998; and Wrightson 2012, 210–212.

10   Diod.16.4–8; Front. *Strat.* 2.3.2.

11   Diod. 16.85–86; Polyaen. *Strat.* 4.2.2; Plut. *Alex.* 12 and *Dem.* 20 (all references to Plutarch's *Lives* use the Loeb edition section numbers). There is only one detailed account of the battle from Polyaenus, who is the only source to mention the feigned withdrawal, though others gloss over the actual events. For secondary

At Chaeronea the Greeks had drawn up their battle line on an angle, probably so that they had an escape route through the mountains behind them. The Theban Sacred Band was placed on the Greek right wing by the river Cephisus, the traditional place for the elite infantry. Philip's right wing, led personally by him, was closest to Chaeronea and his left, where Alexander was with the heavy cavalry, was refused. Philip had posted his light infantry and missile troops on his right flank in the foothills to prevent a flanking maneuver. Philip advanced on the Macedonian right but Alexander remained stationary on the left. The sarissa phalanx held the Greek hoplites in place, protected by light infantry on the flank, and then pretended to withdraw up the hill. The Athenians thought that the Macedonians were retreating and pressed forwards at speed and without concern for maintaining their own formation. The Sacred Band remained where they were, unwilling to expose their flank resting on the river in the face of Alexander's cavalry, with the result that the Greek line was stretched and their formation disrupted. Alexander then attacked the Sacred Band leading the Companion cavalry. Philip, once his retreating phalanx had got onto a slight rise in the ground, attacked the disordered Athenian hoplites and defeated them easily. The whole Greek line broke and fled, except for the Sacred Band who fought to the last man.

The victory at Chaeronea was due to Philip's novel battle plan relying on the perfect execution of the feigned retreat from an oblique battle line, and the effective combination of his different units, in particular the sarissa phalanx and the heavy Companion cavalry. It was the discipline, and steadiness, of the heavy infantry phalanx coupled with the offensive rapid attack of the heavy cavalry that was so effective. The tactics of a feigned withdrawal and the oblique battle line were not vital to the use of combined arms; rather they were the demonstration of tactics that could be used to allow the principles of combined arms to succeed. The former tactic is one of the most difficult maneuvers to accomplish in the chaos of an ancient battle and Philip's reliance on it, and its perfect execution in the battle, reveals both his own tactical genius and the superb training of the Macedonian army. The annihilation of the Sacred Band by the Macedonian cavalry finally ended the hoplite era in Greece and forced the advanced use of combined arms in Greek warfare.

Under Alexander the Macedonian army was practiced at using combined arms in battle and achieved an even greater level of tactical integration of units.[12] As Hammond (1981, 33) states:

> The remarkable feature of the European army which Alexander inherited from his father and led into Asia was its composite nature and the specialized expertise of each part. Alexander had at his disposal almost every known variety of cavalry and infantry, heavy or light, regular or irregular, as well as experts in siegecraft, artillery, road making, bridge-building, surveying and so on. Each unit was the best of its kind, properly equipped and highly trained.

---

discussions of the battle see Hammond 1938; Rahe 1981; Buckler and Beck 2008, 254–8 (213–276 for the battle in context of the campaign in Greece); Wrightson 2012, 238–240. For the battle in the context of the other battles of the Macedonians see Pietrykowski 2009, 19–33. For Philip in Thrace see Badian 1983; Adams 1997.

[12] There is much scholarship on the army of Alexander. The fullest analyses are: Fuller 1960; Milns 1976; Bosworth 1989, 259–277; Ashley 1998, 165–360. For fuller discussions of Alexander's use of combined arms see Jones 1987, 21–26; Pederson 1998; and Wrightson 2012, 212–214.

Alexander's use of the hypaspists as a link between the slow attack of the sarissa phalanx and the rapid charge of the heavy cavalry units was an important improvement on Philip's combined arms tactics.[13] The hypaspists were positioned to protect the exposed right flank of the phalanx and attacked at a rapid pace, alongside Alexander and the Companion cavalry. This mobile heavy infantry unit gave the cavalry the freedom to attack wherever the enemy was weak, while allowing the phalanx to continue to advance slowly, without having to worry about its flanks.

The battle of Gaugamela is the best example of this.[14] The Persian line was significantly longer than the Macedonian on both sides.[15] Alexander drew both his wings back to compensate and placed the Greek allied infantry in his rear as a last line of defence. Darius had leveled the plain so that his scythed chariots could be unimpeded as they attacked the Macedonian lines. Alexander edged his whole line to the right so that his right flank extended beyond the flattened area and beyond the Persian left. The Persians sent a cavalry squadron to their left so that they were not outflanked and Alexander attacked the resultant hole in the Persian line with the Companions and hypaspists. Darius fled and the retreat spread to the whole Persian line. Gaugamela demonstrates the Macedonian expertise at using combined arms in battle and reinforces this system's effectiveness against less adept armies.

Thus, Philip and Alexander had laid the groundwork for the integrated armies of the Successors, and had demonstrated to subsequent generals how to employ the system of combined arms at a great level of sophistication; however, the armies of Alexander's Successors also required the coordinated use of elephants in battle in order to maintain an advanced use of combined arms fully utilizing every unit available. The most successful tactical use of elephants in combined arms warfare was achieved at the battle of Ipsus.[16] By 301 the Macedonian style armies of the Successor kingdoms had successfully managed to tactically incorporate all styles of unit available in the army and each unit was at its peak level of martial efficiency.

The normal use of elephants in battle was primarily as flank guards held in echelon, as part of an oblique formation. This was the tactic used by both Antigonus and Eumenes at the battles of Paraetacene (Diod. 19.26–31) and Gabiene (Diod. 19.39–43; Plut. *Eum.*

---

[13] Because the Macedonian battle plan under Alexander used a rapid charge of heavy cavalry to press for victory this often left a hole in the battle line where the enemy could expose and attack the weak flanks of the phalanx. The hypaspists, a unit of heavy infantry who were not armed with the sarissa and could move at a faster speed, were used, and maybe even created, by Alexander to bridge this gap. The most notable instance of their use in this role is at Gaugamela (Arr. *Anab.* 3.8–15; Curt. 4.9; Diod. 17.56–61). For the hypaspists see in particular: Fuller 1960, 49–50; Milns 1967; Milns 1971; Ellis 1975; Milns 1976; Markle 1978; Anson 1981; Markle 1982; Anson 1985; Bosworth 1989, 259–270; Hammond 1991; Foulon 1996; Heckel 2005. For a recent (but under referenced) discussion see English 2009, 28–35, though I disagree with his analysis of their armament.

[14] Arr. *Anab.* 3.8–15; Curt. 4.9; Diod. 17.56–61. For a detailed discussion of the battle see Griffith 1947; Cawkwell 1962; Marsden 1964; Devine 1975; Welwei 1979; Devine 1986; Bosworth 1989, 74–84; Charles 2008; English 2011, 110–157. For the battle in the context of the other battles of the Macedonians see Pietrykowski 2009, 60–72.

[15] Arr. *Anab.* 3.8–15; Curt. 4.9.9–10 and 12–16; Diod.17.56.61; Plut. *Alex.* 32–33. See Devine 1989.

[16] Plut. *Dem.* 28–29; App. *Syr.* 55.

16).[17] At the latter battle, Eumenes' hand was forced into this defensive deployment since a number of his elephants had lost their mahouts in a previous skirmish with Antigonus (Diod. 19.39).[18] Elephants were very able to hold a flank defensively, especially against cavalry unused to pachyderms:[19]

> As a screen from behind which to charge with one's cavalry, elephants had proved useful at Paraitakene and Gabiene...but as an attacking force in themselves, elephants were effective in ancient warfare only against enemies who had not encountered them before and were overawed by their size and strength.[20]

This serves to add an extra defensive element to the battle formation but does not make sufficient use of the offensive power of elephants. Eumenes' fate at Gabiene demonstrates that it was very difficult to change the tactical deployment of elephants during battle, or to use them offensively once the oblique screen had been formed.[21] Eumenes sought to kill Antigonus and end the war and so decided to charge with his more numerous elephants instead of holding them back defensively. Since they had already been drawn up en echelon in the customary flank guard, Eumenes' elephants arrived into the attack at intervals, thus minimizing their impact (Diod. 19.42). The elephant-on-elephant battle that ensued went well for Eumenes until his lead elephant was killed. Despite enjoying a significant numerical superiority in elephants, once the lead animal fell the others behind fled.[22] It was often quite easy to defeat a force of elephants by killing the lead animal or forcing it to flee. This is the one large drawback of using elephants offensively and is the main reason why they were often used in a defensive manner.

Macedonian generals were normally reluctant to use elephants offensively because of the possibility that they could be goaded into turning on their own troops. For example, at the battle of the Hydaspes, Porus, the Indian king, stationed elephants across the front of his whole battle line, intermingled with light infantry.[23] This was intended to break the formation of the Macedonian phalanx and prevent it from reaching his inferior infantry. Instead the Macedonians were able to use their sarissas to goad the elephants into turning on their own army causing significant carnage.

Another peril of using elephants in battle was losing them entirely. In 312, Demetrius intended to win the battle of Gaza, against Ptolemy and Seleucus, using his elephants to defeat the phalanx (Diod. 19.80–84; Plut. *Dem.* 5). Unfortunately for Demetrius, Ptolemy wanted to capture the animals, since he had few of his own, and devised easily movable chains of iron spikes to trap the elephants in position. This device proved so successful

---

[17] For the fullest secondary discussion of these battles see Devine 1985a; and 1985b. See also Pietrykowski 2009, 91–112.

[18] For the time required to train new mahouts see Kistler 2007, 51. See also Kruse 1972, 76.

[19] Bar Kochva 1976, 137 states that elephants usually panic horses even if they are used to elephants.

[20] Billows 1990, 127.

[21] This is an important fact to bear in mind when examining Seleucus' deployment of his elephant reserve at Ipsus, as discussed below.

[22] Elephants are by nature herd animals and usually follow the lead female: Scullard 1974, 21.

[23] Arr. *Anab.* 5.8–19; Curt. 8.13–14; Diod. 17.87–89; Plut. *Alex.* 60–62.

that Ptolemy was able to capture all forty-three of Demetrius' elephants, and as a result easily won the battle.[24]

Pyrrhus' victory over the Romans at Asculum, where his elephants tore through the infantry legions, demonstrates the effectiveness of elephants against an infantry armed with swords rather than spears.[25] But Pyrrhus was successful for the most part because of the Roman soldiers' (and their horses') fear of the unfamiliar beasts (Plut. *Pyr.* 21.7). At the final battle of the campaign at Beneventum, Pyrrhus' elephants were initially successful against the Roman legions until they fell afoul of the Romans' anti-elephant devices.[26] The defeat of his elephant charge cost Pyrrhus the battle. His defeat demonstrates that elephants are most effective against an enemy that has not seen them before. Once the enemy devises plans to deal with them, elephants alone cannot bring victory.[27]

Tarn suggests that it was the very frightening experience of facing elephants at the Hydaspes that prompted Seleucus to exchange territory in India for 500 war elephants (Plut. *Alex.* 62; Strab. 15.2–9, 16.2–10).[28] Even if this is the case, elephants were not normally used to charge Macedonian infantry phalanxes directly, as Bosworth (2002, 166–7) summarises adeptly:

> There is no evidence of the beasts attacking enemy infantry, as Porus' elephants had done at the Hydaspes. Perhaps the dangers of their being wounded in the eyes or trunk were too acute.... Accordingly, elephants tended to be used against each other or to keep cavalry at bay. Their usefulness was limited, but they clearly had a mystique, a psychological advantage for their army.

In general, elephants are much more effective against cavalry than infantry, since horses that are unused to elephants are terrified of them (Scullard 1974, 67; Kistler 2007, 20, 67). The victories of Pyrrhus over the Romans at Heraclea,[29] and of Antiochus over the Galatians (Luc. *Zeux.* 8–12), were both a result of sending elephants against cavalry. However, both kings fought against an enemy that was unused to elephants, and so could rely on the psychological effect of an elephant charge to disrupt the enemy formation and precipitate a rout. Armies and generals unused to elephants were vulnerable to them but cavalry whose horses grew up around elephants,[30] and infantry who had opposed the animals before, were able to counter any offensive actions of elephants.

Fuller mistakenly believed that the adoption of war elephants as a 'shock arm' was the 'greatest innovation of all' in Hellenistic warfare.[31] Ducrey even goes so far as to blame the demise of Macedonian cavalry on the increased reliance on war elephants.[32] This is

---

[24] Kistler (2007, 61) summarizes the effectiveness of this device well.

[25] Plut. *Pyr.* 21; Dion. Hal. 20.1–3; Zonaras 8.5; Orosius 4.1.19–23.

[26] Plut. *Pyr.* 24–25; Dion. Hal. 20.10–11; Orosius 4.2.3–6.

[27] Another notable use of anti-elephant devices was against the army of Polyperchon at the siege of Megalopolis where the elephants ran amok after their feet had become impaled upon caltrops (Diod. 18.71.2–3).

[28] Tarn 1975, 94. See also Tarn 1940.

[29] Plut. *Pyr.* 16–17; Zonaras 8.3; Orosius 4.1.8–15.

[30] It is for this reason that the Seleucid Empire set up the national cavalry training facility at Apamea in Syria alongside the elephants (Strab. 16.2.10).

[31] Fuller 1945, 32.

[32] Ducrey 1986, 183.

certainly going too far. The Successor kingdoms could not produce elephants in significant numbers to replace cavalry. Elephants rarely breed in captivity, even with today's methods of artificial insemination (Kistler 2007, 68–69). With the exception of Egypt's elephant capture program,[33] and the Seleucid Empire's limited breeding program at Apamea,[34] Hellenistic kingdoms had to rely upon captured elephants, and once those used by Alexander's immediate Successors died, very few were found to replace them.

In view of this discussion of earlier examples of the use of elephants in battle I will now move on to a brief analysis of the battle of Ipsus in 301 as a case study to demonstrate the most efficient tactical use of elephants in a combined arms system. At this battle Cassander, Lysimachus and Seleucus opposed Demetrius and Antigonus (Diod. 21.1.2). The Antigonids had 70,000 infantry, 10,000 cavalry and 75 elephants and the allies had 64,000 infantry,[35] 10,500 cavalry,[36] and 120 chariots,[37] but significantly more elephants to the sum of 400 (Plut. *Dem.* 28.3).[38] Both sides used the standard deployment of elephants along the front of the whole line mixed in with peltasts and missile troops. However, Seleucus remained behind the allied line with a reserve force of elephants.[39]

The usual skirmish of the elephants and light troops began the battle while the cavalry of each side engaged one another on each wing. Demetrius routed the allied left and pursued them too far (Plut. *Dem.* 29.3). Seleucus deployed his elephant reserve to block Demetrius and hold him fast. Seleucus then, instead of charging the Antigonid phalanx, which was now unprotected by cavalry, threatened to do so in order to encourage the infantry to change sides. Lysimachus sent more missile troops to the centre, while he continued the cavalry battle on the right. The missile troops in the centre were so numerous that their volleys forced the Antigonid phalanx to retreat in disorder. Antigonus died fighting in the phalanx, and to the end believed Demetrius would ride in and save the day.

At Ipsus both armies fielded varied units that were fully integrated into the battle plan. The allied army's strength lay in its huge force of elephants. As a result the generals had to ensure they got the best use out of these animals in order to make the most of their advantage. As discussed above, the previous use of elephants in battle was as a static flank

---

[33] Casson 1993.

[34] Bar Kochva 1976, 79 argues that the Seleucid elephants in Apamea, and those used in battle, were nearly all bulls and so could not produce a large new herd.

[35] Bar Kochva 1976, 82 argues that of this force the 20,000 brought by Seleucus were predominantly light infantry.

[36] Bar Kochva 1976, 247 n. 11 argues that this is a textual corruption and the allied cavalry total should be 15,000.

[37] These chariots probably did not feature in the battle. Seleucus unsuccessfully used chariots against Demetrius shortly before the battle of Ipsus (Plut. *Dem.* 48.2).

[38] Seleucus, after a failed invasion of India, gave up a significant amount of territory to the Indian king Chandragupta in exchange for 500 elephants (Plut. *Alex.* 62; Strab. 15.2–9, 16.2–10). Seleucus brought most of these with him to Ipsus. Diodorus (20.113.4) states that Seleucus brought through Cappadocia 480 elephants, 12,000 cavalry, 20,000 infantry and over a hundred chariots and these figures fit well into the allied troops totals given by Plutarch. Bar Kochva 1976, 76 suggests that Seleucus lost twenty elephants in crossing through Cappadocia and afterwards another eighty were unfit for battle. Ipsus, then, is the only battle in Greek warfare where so many elephants were deployed.

[39] Tarn 1940. Bar Kochva 1976, 108 argues that there was no elephant reserve behind the army.

guard to shield the phalanx. However, the main problem with this deployment was that the slow elephants could not be moved if and when the phalanx advanced beyond the protection the animals afforded to its flank. At Ipsus the allies had enough elephants to post them opposite Antigonus' animals and still keep hundreds for use elsewhere. It is Seleucus' use of these other elephants as a screen against Demetrius' isolated cavalry that was the catalyst for Antigonus' defeat and demonstrates the most effective tactic of elephants in battle.

Tarn argued that Seleucus planned this all along and ordered his son Antiochus, commanding the left wing cavalry of the allies, to fall back at the assault of Demetrius in order to draw him away from the battle so that Seleucus could deploy his elephants to block his return.[40] There is no evidence for this in the sources but the details of the battle are scarcely recorded as it is and Seleucus' speed of action in successfully redeploying so many slow moving elephants is more understandable if it was pre-planned. The tactic of the fake retreat was probably used by Seleucid armies at the later battle of Elasa, suggesting that it was a tactic known to Seleucus and his successors.[41] Moreover all the allied generals, and the Antigonids, would have recalled Philip II's effective use of the feigned withdrawal at Chaeronea, as discussed above.[42]

Seleucus' trap for Demetrius shows that the best use for elephants is as a flank screen against heavy cavalry, as long as their immovability does not expose the flank of the phalanx (Plut. *Dem.* 29.3). Heavy cavalry, used to close-quarter combat, are largely ineffective against elephants. Without missiles or sarissas to harass and turn the elephants, or kill their mahouts, they could achieve little success. It was Demetrius' inability to return to the battle that cost Antigonus both the victory and his life (Plut. *Dem.* 29).

At Ipsus both sides deployed elephants in front of their phalanx (Plut. *Dem.* 28–29; App. *BS* 55). This is the most confusing aspect of the use of elephants by fourth century generals. Porus' defeat at the Hydaspes demonstrated the ineffectiveness of elephants against a sarissa phalanx disciplined enough to face the beasts and use sarissas to blind them or kill their mahouts.[43] Moreover, the elephants would disrupt the formation of the phalanx and reduce its effectiveness at opposing the enemy infantry. Perhaps Kistler (2007, 66) is right when he states that, faced with Lysimachus' 100 elephants in the centre, "Antigonus had no choice but to put his seventy-five beasts in front of his infantry, lest his own men

---

[40] Tarn 1940, 87 n. 1; 1975, 68–9. Bar Kochva 1976, 109–110 argues that the terrain behind the allied battle line at Ipsus was such that it took significant effort and time for Seleucus to post enough elephants to prevent Demetrius' return. As a result it must have been a pre-planned tactic induced by a fake retreat of Antiochus' cavalry. Since Antiochus was Seleucus' son the two commanders could easily have organized this together. Bar Kochva 1976, 109 also suggests Demetrius may have been attempting to capture the allied baggage camp after routing Antiochus' cavalry.

[41] For this battle see Bar Kochva 1976, 184–200. It is only described in I Maccabees 9.1–22 but this account does not mention the fake withdrawal which Bar Kochva believes occurred. Bar Kochva believes that surprise tactics were commonly used in other Seleucid battles, in particular Cyrrhestica (Plut. *Dem.* 48–49, see Bar Kochva 1976, 111–6); against Molon (Polyb. 5.48.17–54, see Bar Kochva 1976, 117–123); and against the Galatians (Luc. *Zeux.* 9). In every case the ancient source for the battle, just as at Ipsus, does not specifically describe such tactics.

[42] On the possible use of this tactic in sieges by Alexander see now: Antela-Bernardez 2015.

[43] Arr. *Anab.* 5.8–19; Curt. 8.13–14; Diod. 17.87–89; Plut. *Alex.* 60–62. For full discussions of the battle see Hamilton 1956; Devine 1987.

panic." Certainly the sight of a hundred elephants charging would frighten even the most disciplined army. But had Antigonus adopted Ptolemy's method of defending against an elephant charge at Ipsus using caltrops, he could have used his elephants elsewhere with much more effectiveness.

The allied generals' execution of the battle plan at Ipsus was perfect in its use of combined arms, employing elephants, infantry, cavalry and missile troops in harmony to attack the enemy's weaknesses while eliminating their own. It is clear that "At Ipsus, the elephants played a decisive role," (Kistler 2007, 67) and Gaebel (2002, 226) is perhaps right when he argues that the battle of Ipsus was "the greatest achievement of war elephants in Hellenistic military history."

Elephants briefly transformed warfare in the Hellenistic World but it took time for generals to understand how best to make use of the animals and to overcome their deficiencies – an integral part of the theory of combined arms. It was not until the battle of Ipsus that the allied generals got the best out of every unit, including elephants, while simultaneously protecting the weaknesses of each and thus perfected the use of combined arms.

Bibliography

Adams, W. L. (1997) Philip and the Thracian Frontier, *Actes 2e Symposium international des études thraciennes. Thrace ancienne*, vol. 1. Komotini, 81–88.
Anson, E. M. (1981) Alexander's Hypaspists and the Argyraspids, *Historia* 30, 117–20.
— (1985) The Hypaspists: Macedonia's Professional Citizen-Soldiers, *Historia* 34, 246–8.
Antela-Bernardez, B. (2015) Furious Wrath: Alexander's campaign and siege against Thebes. In G. Lee, H. Whittaker and G. Wrightson (eds), *An Introduction to Current Research in Ancient Warfare*, Cambridge.
Ashley, J. R. (1998) *The Macedonian Empire: The Era of Warfare Under Philip II and Alexander the Great, 359–323 BC.* Jefferson, NC.
Badian, E. (1983) Philip II and Thrace, *Pulpudeva* 4, 51–71.
Bar Kochva, B. (1976) *The Seleucid Army.* Cambridge.
Buckler, J. and H. Beck. (2008) *Central Greece and the Politics of Power in the Fourth Century BC.* Cambridge.
Billows, R. A. (1990) *Antigonos the One-Eyed and the Creation of the Hellenistic State.* Berkeley and Los Angeles.
Bosworth, A. B. (1989) *Conquest and Empire. The Reign of Alexander the Great.* Cambridge.
— (2002) *The Legacy of Alexander. Politics, Warfare and Propaganda under the Successors.* Oxford.
Casson, L. (1993) Ptolemy II and the Hunting of African Elephants, *Transactions of the American Philological Association* 123, 247–260.
Cawkwell, G. L. (1965) Gaugamela Reconsidered, *The Classical Review* 15, 203–205.
Charles, M. B. (2008) Alexander, Elephants and Gaugamela, *Mouseion*, Series III, vol. 8, 9–23.
Devine, A. M. (1975) Grand tactics at Guagamela, *Phoenix* 29, 374–85.
— (1985a) Diodorus' Account of the Battle of Paraitacene (317 BC), *Ancient World* 12, 75–86.
— (1985b) Diodorus' Account of the Battle of Gabiene, *Ancient World* 12, 87–96.
— (1986) The battle of Guagamela: a tactical and source critical study, *Ancient World* 13, 87–115.
— (1987) The Battle of the Hydaspes: A Tactical and Source-Critical Study, *Ancient World* 16, 91–113.
— (1989) The Macedonian army at Gaugamela: its strength and the length of its battle line, *Ancient World* 19, 77–80.
Ducrey, P. (1986) *Warfare in Ancient Greece.* New York.
Ellis, J. R. (1975) Alexander's Hypaspists Again, *Historia* 24, 617–18.
English, S. (2009) *The Army of Alexander the Great.* Barnsley.

— (2011) *The Field Campaigns of Alexander the Great.* Barnsley.

Foulon, E. (1996) Hypaspistes, peltastes, chrysaspides, argyraspides, chalcaspides, *Revue des Études Anciennes* 98, 53–63.

Fuller, J. F. C. (1945) *The Influence of Armament on History from the Dawn of Classical Warfare to the End of the Second World War.* New York.

— (1960) *The Generalship of Alexander the Great.* New Brunswick, NJ.

Gaebel, R. (2002) *Cavalry Operations in the Ancient Greek World.* Norman, OK.

Griffith, G. (1947) Alexander's generalship at Guagamela, *Journal of Hellenic Studies* 67, 77–89.

— (1992) Philip as a general and the Macedonian army. In M. Andronikos, M. B. Hatzopoulos, M. Sakellariou and L. D. Loukopoulos (eds) *Philip of Macedon*, 58–77, Athens.

Hamilton, J. R. (1956) The Cavalry Battle at the Hydaspes, *Journal of Hellenic Studies* 76, 26–31.

Hammond, N. G. L. (1938) *The two battles of Chaeronea: 338 BC and 86 BC.* Leipzig.

— (1981) *Alexander the Great. King, Commander and Statesman.* London.

— (1991) The various guards of Philip II and Alexander III, *Historia* 40, 396–418.

Heckel, W. (2005) Synaspismos, Sarissas and Wagons, *Acta Classica* 48, 189–94.

House, J. M. (1984) *Toward Combined Arms Warfare: A Survey of 20th-Century Tactics, Doctrine, and Organization.* Lawrence, KA.

— (2001) *Combined Arms Warfare in the Twentieth Century.* Lawrence, KS

Hunt, P. (2007) Military Forces. In P. Sabin, H. van Wees and M. Whitby (eds) *The Cambridge History of Greek and Roman Warfare.* vol. 1, 108–46, Cambridge.

Jones, A. (1987) *The Art of War in the Western World.* Chicago.

Karunanithy, D. (2013) *The Macedonian War Machine: Neglected aspects of the Armies of Philip, Alexander and the Successors 359–281 BC.* Barnsley.

Kistler, J. M. (2007) *War Elephants.* Lincoln.

Kruse, G. (1972) *Trunk call.* London.

Lonsdale, D. J. (2004) *Alexander the Great, Killer of Men.* New York.

— (2007) *Alexander the Great: Lessons in Strategy (Strategy and History).* London.

Markle, M. M. (1978) Use of the Sarissa by Philip and Alexander of Macedon, *American Journal of Archaeology* 82, 483–97.

— (1982) Macedonian Arms and Tactics under Alexander the Great. In B. Barr-Sharrar and E. Borza (eds) *Macedonia and Greece in Late Classical and Early Hellenistic Times,* 87–111, Washington, DC.

Marsden, E. W. (1964) *The campaign of Gaugamela.* Liverpool.

Milns, R. D. (1967) Philip II and the Hypaspists, *Historia* 16, 509–12.

— (1971) The Hypaspists of Alexander III – Some Problems, *Historia* 20, 186–95.

— (1976) The army of Alexander the Great. In *Entretiens Hardt* 22, 87–136, Geneva.

Pederson, R. B. (1998) *A Study of Combined Arms Warfare by Alexander the Great.* MA Dissertation, Fort Leavenworth, Kansas.

Pietrykowski, J. (2009) *Great Battles of the Hellenistic World.* Barnsley.

Rahe, P. A. (1981) The annihilation of the Sacred Band at Chaeronea, *American Journal of Archaeology* 85, 84–7.

Scullard, H. H. (1974) *The Elephant in the Greek and Roman World.* Ithaca.

Spiller, R. J. (1992) *Combined Arms in Battle Since 1939.* Leavenworth.

Tarn, W. W. (1940) Two Notes on Seleucid History: 1. Seleucus' 500 Elephants, *Journal of Hellenic Studies* 60, 84–89.

— (1975) *Hellenistic Military and Naval Developments.* Chicago.

Welwei, K. W. (1979) Der Kampf um das makedonische Lager bei Gaugamela, *Rheinisches Museum* 122, 222–8.

Worthington, I. (2008) *Philip II of Macedonia.* New Haven.

Wrightson, G. (2012) *Greek and Near Eastern warfare 3000 to 301: the development and perfection of combined arms.* PhD Dissertation University of Calgary.

MILITARY UNREST IN THE AGE OF PHILIP AND ALEXANDER OF MACEDON: DEFINING THE TERMS OF DEBATE

Lee L. Brice[1]

The armies created and employed by Philip II and Alexander III of Macedon were undeniably superior implements of conquest.[2] Despite the military successes they enjoyed, both kings occasionally had disciplinary trouble with their soldiers, including several significant outbreaks of collective unrest. The famous incidents at the Hyphasis and Opis remain the best-known examples of such episodes. Other, smaller episodes abounded but have received limited attention from historians. Waldemar Heckel devoted much more attention to the Hyphasis mutiny in his recent work,[3] so it is only fitting to honor him by refining the terms necessary to debate and discuss what actually occurred at the Hyphasis River in 326.

Military unrest is a topic that, until recently, seemed beyond the interests of historians of the pre-modern world. However, unrest in the military, both of individuals and collectively in groups, was a problem with which every officer had to contend at some point. Incidents large and small occurred in every army. While limited primary sources have been an impediment to studies of ancient military unrest, an even greater basic stumbling block has been establishing the vocabulary for discussing military unrest. This chapter addresses that dilemma by refining the terms necessary to identify and discuss military unrest, especially in regard to ancient soldiers.

Military discipline need not be defined by formal rules, or brutality, (or both), nor be maintained by the same in order to be effective. When modern readers think of discipline, it is often in terms of punishments and regulations, especially the necessity of following commands. It is important to recognize that military discipline, ancient and modern, is more complex than adherence to orders or punishment for infractions; it is a means of control that includes physical, mental, and social components reinforced with positive as well as negative sanctions.[4] This discipline could, as C. Julius Caesar recognized, be

---

[1]   I am grateful to Frank L. Holt and W. Lindsay Adams for reading over drafts of this article and providing helpful comments. Any errors that remain are my own.
[2]   See most recently, Sekunda 2010, 446–71; and Brice 2011, 137–47.
[3]   Heckel 2003, 165–73. I thank the editors for inviting me to honor Waldemar in this way.
[4]   For recent discussions of discipline in ancient armies see Phang 2008; Lendon 2005, 177–231; and Carney 1996, 20–31. On classical Greek military discipline see Pritchett 1974, 232–45.

enforced effectively through willing compliance and maintaining morale in combination with clear expectations and regulations.[5] No such laws that promoted discipline survive from Alexander's period, although Elizabeth Carney's examination of Philip's and Alexander's disciplinary practices and punishments demonstrates that there were certainly explicit expectations, and probably also regulations.[6] Training soldiers to maintain ranks, maneuver collectively, and even remain in battle requires that they learn and are accustomed to a certain level of discipline. Military discipline is acquired and reinforced through various parts of service including training and learning how the unit works in battle, getting to know one's comrades in arms, and getting accustomed to the society of the army.[7] That the Macedonian army under Philip II and Alexander III was generally a well-disciplined army is beyond doubt (*e.g.*, Arr. *Anab.* 1.1.8–9, 6.1–3; Polyaen. *Strat.* 4.2.2).

Examinations of military unrest in Macedonian armies have referred to all such incidents as either 'mutiny' or something nebulous, as if mutiny was the only form of unrest.[8] Privileging the modern term 'mutiny', or the Latin *seditio,* or even the Greek *ataxia,* has hamstrung the debate. Not every incident was a mutiny. Ancient authors in all periods used an array of terms in Greek and Latin to describe varieties of military unrest and so must modern historians examining those events. Military-sociologists and modern military historians have developed a varied and useful vocabulary for treating unrest by soldiers.[9] This vocabulary provides a level of distinction and standardization that allows differentiation of scale and significance which is currently lacking from many discussions of unrest in ancient armies.

Military unrest emerged in one of several forms including military conspiracy, mutiny, expression of grievances, and insubordination.[10] The first two categories are the more serious manifestations of indiscipline. The other categories are not necessarily threatening in and of themselves and are, thus, not well attested in the sources, but they do reflect problems within the military and the complexities of unrest. Additionally, historians recognize that military leaders usually treated sleeping on duty and panicked flight in battle as serious forms of military unrest. Listed in roughly descending order of size and seriousness, these terms permit a more nuanced and realistic discussion of unrest in any military context, including that of the ancient world. What follows is a brief discussion of the terms 'military conspiracy', 'mutiny', 'expression of grievances', and 'insubordination'. What will become

---

[5] Wheeler 2011, 70–71.

[6] Carney 1996, 24–31. The Antigonid inscriptions recording military regulations regarding discipline and punishments are products of a later period and cannot be assumed to derive from any regulations or laws in effect in the fourth century; they may derive from earlier precedents, but to date there is no epigraphic evidence that they do; see Hatzopoulos 2001, esp. 151–67.

[7] MacMullen 1984, 440–456; Phang 2008, 37–73. Although both discussions focus on the Roman army, aspects of their discussion can apply to other ancient militaries including the Macedonian.

[8] Carney 1996; Holt 1982, 33–59; Bosworth 1988, 160; contra, Brice 2015, forthcoming.

[9] Kaegi 1981; Rose 1982; Brice 2003, 65–76; and idem 2014. Cornelis Lammers's work (1969; 2003) on strikes and mutinies is important to understanding how a mutiny can progress, but because his research is limited to modern naval mutinies some of his conclusions do not apply to incidents in ancient armies. For example, the type of mutiny/strike he called (1969) a "promotion of interest protest" would lump together most mutinies and all expressions of grievances in ancient militaries and so is too imprecise to use effectively.

[10] Discussed and defined in Brice 2003, 65–76, esp. n.203 (currently under revision for publication).

clear is that the definitions are sufficient to cover all instances of indiscipline and are consistent with modern military history and military-sociology.

Military conspiracy

Conspiracy was, from a leader's perspective, the most dangerous manifestation of military unrest. Other forms of unrest may have threatened discipline in the camp or in a battle in exchange for achieving a limited goal, but conspiracies were intended to result in a leader's (or king's or officer's) removal or death, or both. When Kaegi defined 'military conspiracy' as "the conscious combination of [military] men, often generals or their subordinate officers, for a *coup d'etat* or revolt in the field," he had the entirety of the Byzantine Empire in mind.[11] If one accepts that a revolt in the field could include a plot by subordinates to remove a superior officer lower in rank than the king or emperor, then Kaegi's definition is broad enough to encompass plots of all sizes and targets. Military institutions in Macedon were structurally conducive to conspiracies due to the autocratic nature of the monarchy, the hierarchical distribution of power among officers, and the importance of the army in society. Even where the death of a king was not the goal, the potential for broader disruption of the kingdom was clear.

Various commanders faced such conspiracies among their officers. Reports that Alexander III was the victim of conspiracy by several of his generals have been discounted (Diod. 17.117.5–118.2; Arr. *Anab.* 7.27; and Plut. *Alex.* 77), but the longevity of the reports arises from the plausibility of military conspiracy and its later effectiveness. Kings were not the only persons who needed to be concerned about conspiracy in the army: the much-debated, alleged conspiracy against Philotas, seems to have been a military conspiracy by men seeking his position or power;[12] and Perdiccas was not the last of the Diadochoi to fall victim to a military conspiracy by his subordinates (Diod. 18.33–37; Arr. *Succ.* 1.28; Plut. *Eum.* 8.2–3).

Mutiny

Of the terms employed to describe resistance within the military, 'mutiny' is perhaps the most problematic. Although 'mutiny' evokes a wealth of vivid images of insubordination or violence by lower ranks against commanders, no broad consensus exists among ancient historians for its historical definition and specific usage. On the basis that it is a modern term and potentially anachronistic, some authors question application of the word 'mutiny' to any type of unrest in ancient armies.[13]

Refusal to employ 'mutiny' in this context, however, is neither necessary nor appropriate. There is no simple alternative in the English language that can easily be substituted if 'mutiny' is abandoned. Indeed, without the word 'mutiny', the Latin term *seditio* is difficult to translate with any reasonable and consistent sense, for the use of 'sedition' will not work for *seditio*, because it now carries for readers a connotation of overthrowing or undermining

---

[11] Kaegi 1981, 4.

[12] For discussions and historiography see Badian 2012, 434–39; and Heckel 1992, 23–33.

[13] Carney 1996, 19–21, esp. 20; and Chrissanthos 1999, 4, 7–12.

the established constitutional authority.[14] Additionally, if historians of any period find that an event meets all the criteria for a modern term, then the modern term should be employed, especially if it is not something that is chronologically dependent. No one would suggest that the word 'government' or 'marriage' should be rejected outright just because it is a modern word. Neither these words nor 'mutiny' are chronologically dependent in the same way as are terms like 'radar' or 'margin call'. In the end the term 'mutiny' can be defined broadly enough to be chronologically open, while remaining sufficiently narrow to be useful in delineating the scale of particular incidents.

A 'mutiny' is defined here as collective, violent (actual, potential, or threatened) opposition to established military authority. Events included in this variety of unrest are riots, tumults, disturbances, and similar incidents, as well as the incitement of these outbreaks. In this definition, 'mutiny' is always a collective action and nearly always refers to actions by regular soldiers – although some low-level officers might participate in special cases. Mutiny was merely one type of military unrest and was not even the most common or most dangerous variety, but because of its occasional notoriety and potential for damage, it merits attention. Because soldiers were trained to fight, were usually armed, and were accustomed to working together, they represented a much greater threat to stability when they engaged in collective dissent than did typical crowds of non-soldiers. In addition to its potential for violence, because a mutiny damaged military order in the units where it occurred and could undermine discipline among military units that did not even participate, it was obviously a great threat to military stability.

Through use of this definition, it becomes easier to identify certain incidents of military unrest and discuss them with more precision. The so-called mutiny at the Hyphasis has been recognized previously as not having reached the stage of a mutiny, but since no agreed upon definition existed, debate has continued.[15] This definition will settle the debate, allowing historians to focus on other aspects of the event. The unrest at Opis in 324 and at Babylon after Alexander's death can now be discussed in terms of mutinies, just as various other events and close-calls during the Hellenistic period.[16] Macedonian leaders' responses to mutiny are also easier to investigate and understand when the examination is made on the basis of consistent and coherent definitions. The king or commander had authority to deal swiftly with such events.[17] Although mutiny does not appear to have been a genuine threat to the Macedonian kingdom during Philip's and Alexander's reigns, it did become a problem for the Diadochic kingdoms.

Expression of grievances

Not every form of unrest by soldiers was violent, or threatened the use of violence. Although the surviving sources distinguish military conspiracies and mutinies as 'greater'

---

[14] Kaegi 1981, 4; Chrissanthos 1999, 8.

[15] Badian 2012, 445; Holt 1982, 33; Spann 1999, 67 and n. 38.

[16] Arguing that Opis is not a mutiny see Carney 1996, 40–42; and Bosworth 1998, 160; contra, Roisman 2012; Brice 2015. On events at Babylon see Bosworth 2002, 29–57 and Brice 2015, both of whom agree it was a mutiny.

[17] Brice 2015.

forms of unrest, there were other types of indiscipline that were usually non-violent. Among these 'lesser' forms of unrest, an expression of grievances was the most peaceful. These less notorious varieties were often agitated, but non-violent, vocal confrontations or communications in which soldiers, often acting collectively, sought to protest various grievances, real and illusory, and to protect their interests.

The expression of grievances was distinct from mutiny and insubordination, even if there were only shades of difference between this type of episode and some other forms of insubordination. Like a mutiny, an expression of grievances was collective, but the latter could include both soldiers and officers, whereas a mutiny was nearly always confined to non-officers. Also, in addition to being peaceful, an expression of grievances did not include a total resistance to authority through a refusal to follow orders or engage in combat. An expression of grievances could emerge in an assembly, but was not limited to such gatherings.[18] Such peaceful forms of unrest were important because they could be larger in breadth and scale than any other manifestation of indiscipline, and were most likely to be successful without resulting in punishment or retribution for their participants. They were important because they could be broader in breadth and scale than any other manifestation of unrest, and were most likely to be successful.

Compared with their Roman counterparts, Macedonian soldiers seem to have been less inclined to employ this peaceful form of unrest, but it did occur. The most famous Macedonian example of an expression of grievances is the unrest in Alexander's army at the Hyphasis River in 326.[19] A careful examination of our sources will reveal several more examples during the period after Alexander's death. The limited number of episodes is probably as much a function of the few extant sources as of the nature of Macedonian leadership.[20]

Insubordination

The most common type of unrest, insubordination, includes a variety of lesser crimes and misdemeanors by individuals and groups. Officers and soldiers alike could take part in all these lesser forms of unrest. Chief among these crimes were disobedience or failure to follow orders, defection, desertion, and dereliction of duty.[21]

Disobedience could include an act of purposeful intent to commit unrest, similar to

---

[18] On expressions of grievances in general, see Kaegi 1981, 4; and MacMullen 1984, 449–50 and 454–56.

[19] Roisman 2012, 32–40. Contra Howe and Müller 2012, who argue that there never was any mutiny, unrest, or expression of grievances at the Hyphasis, and that Alexander did not in fact ever cross the river. Though Howe and Müller's argument benefitted greatly from responding to an earlier version of the present paper, given at two 2012 conferences in Calgary and Athens, Greece, space here does not permit a rebuttal of their conclusions. A full response and a detailed study of the unrest at the Hyphasis is forthcoming by the author.

[20] The language in the Antigonid military regulation (Hatzopoulos 2001, 151–67) suggests that by the time of Philip V there were official mechanisms through which soldiers could protest, but the evidence for such practices during the Argead dynasty is still a matter of debate, see Adams 1986, 48–50; and Anson 1991, 233–34.

[21] All the forms of insubordination have seldom been treated together as a single category of unrest, although some have been recognized (Carney 1996, 22–24) as indiscipline; see Brice 2015. On these offenses in classical Greece see Pritchett 1974.

mutiny, but by an individual, or it could be as simple as a man leaving his post. One could argue that in the event that an officer exercised his own initiative without intending to commit disobedience and it turned out badly, he could be charged with a lesser crime, but it was still considered to be insubordination. There were many possible reasons for disobedience, including a desire to assert one's own judgment or an excess of caution, as well as negligence or basic incompetence; in all the cases the offender made a choice of commission or omission. Although individuals often engaged in these actions, they could involve groups of men and units. Desertion is a form of insubordination usually conceived of as an individual action and is more typical of soldiers than of sailors. Desertion was certainly considered to be unrest and was treated accordingly, but it actually provided soldiers with an alternative to more serious forms of unrest. Soldiers could walk away from growing tensions, if they could get away unseen. Sailors, however, were stuck aboard ship or in lands far from home and so usually had to mutiny to achieve relief from onerous service. Defection could be by an individual or include entire units.[22] During the Diadoch wars entire armies occasionally defected. Since sources more readily report details of these large-scale actions, defections dominate the record of lesser forms of unrest.

Furthermore, there were some incidents that ancient leaders treated as insubordination even though these actions did not really involve a rational choice and action on the part of the offender. When a man panicked in battle, it might have an impact only on the individual or it could contribute to a larger unit panic. Although some soldiers do make a calculated decision to flee, other soldiers are not necessarily making a rational choice to panic. Neuroscientists have now shown, that military panic is in large part caused by neurophysiological responses to perceived stimuli on the battlefield and that the way these are manifested for one man may be different for others.[23] That physiological fact does not make panic any less of a problem for armies, but at least it explains why some men panic when others do not. Similarly, for some men, sleeping at a post was a physiological response rather than a choice. Regardless, they all faced the insubordination charges because their act was contrary to good discipline and ancient commanders assumed that the men had made rational choices. Punishment set an example, but was not going to stop a physiological response.

Examples of insubordination in the Macedonian army of Philip II and Alexander III do survive. During his battle against Onomarchos in 353, parts of Philip's army panicked and fled (16.35.2). Diodorus does not report the punishment, if there was any. Alexander had some troubles but the best examples of insubordination were: the 'indisciplined company' following Parmenio's execution (Diod. 17.81.1; Curt. 7.2.35–38; Just.12.5.4–8); the execution of Menander in Bactria for deserting his post (Plut. *Alex.* 57.2); and Alexander's punishment of malingerers at the assault on Aornus in 326 (Arr. *Anab.* 4.29.7). Despite the problems in our sources we do learn about enough incidents of insubordination and about some punishments to draw some conclusions about discipline in the Macedonian army. The importance of this unrest by soldiers lay in the potential for unexpectedly broad consequences despite what seemed like minor insubordination.

---

[22] Brice 2015.

[23] Heidenreich and Roth 2014, forthcoming.

We can visualize the types of military unrest along a matrix:

Types of Military Unrest	Aims	Participants	Collective	Violence
Military Conspiracy	Removal or death (or both) of leader(s) or superior officer(s)	Officers	Initiated by a small nuclear group	Yes
Mutiny	Opposition to established military authority	Soldiers, and sometimes low-ranking officers	Always	Yes
Expression of Grievances	Protest grievances (real and illusory)	Soldiers, and sometimes officers in support	Always	No
Insubordination	Disobedience, cowardice, defection, desertion, and dereliction of duty	Any military personnel	Not necessarily	Not necessarily

Conclusion

Armies are more than battles, discipline, weapons, and wounds. They are made up of men who must work together as required both in and out of battle for the duration of their service. In many armies, discipline contributed to keeping men in good order in stressful circumstances and increased unit efficiency and lethality. Discipline was a key element in the success of fourth-century Macedonian armies and later Roman legions. No matter how good their discipline, however, conditions of service could reach a point where soldiers were prepared to 'act out' against authority, individually or collectively, in a variety of ways. All of these acts were (and are) forms of military unrest.

Just as there is more to warfare than combat, army life is more than discipline. Unrest was (and remains) a normal element in all militaries. Some armies were more inclined to outbreaks of unrest than others, but it has long been a normal quality of military activity. Historians now appreciate that in order to understand military history we must study the men who made up the military. Doing so permits a better understanding of not only the army, but also the society of which it was a part and the way these interacted at many levels. Focusing on unrest is part of examining the soldiers' society.

A fundamental problem in trying to examine and discuss military unrest has been the lack of a broadly accepted language with which to discuss unrest by soldiers. Elizabeth Carney recognized its importance for understanding Macedonian army leadership, but lacked the tools with which to explore the topic fully. In this article I have provided a vocabulary for discussing military unrest. Grounded in modern military-sociology and historical studies of armies and societies it is consistent with modern concepts of unrest and yet works well for describing an element of ancient military activity.

A consideration of military unrest will not diminish the history of any army. Rather, a careful study of the manner in which these events occurred and how militaries responded to them reveals why some armies were more stable and successful institutions than others. Waldemar Heckel has, in his treatments of the unrest at the Hyphasis, highlighted the importance of understanding such incidents and the men who were behind them. No military historical treatment of Philip II or Alexander III or both can be complete without a consideration of military unrest.

Bibliography

Adams, W. L. (1986) Macedonian Kingship and the Right of Petition, *Ancient Macedonia* 4, 43–52.

Anson, E. (1991) The Evolution of the Macedonian Army Assembly 330–315 BC, *Historia* 40.2, 230–47.

Badian, E. (2012) Conspiracies. In R. Stoneman (ed.) *Collected Papers on Alexander the Great*, 434–39, New York.

Bosworth, A. B. (1988) *Conquest and Empire*. Cambridge.

— (2002) *The Legacy of Alexander: Politics, Warfare, and Propaganda under the Successors*. Oxford.

Brice, L. L. (2003) Holding a Wolf by the Ears: Mutiny and Unrest in the Roman Military, 44 BC–AD 68. PhD Dissertation, University of North Carolina at Chapel Hill.

— (2011) Philip II, Alexander the Great, and the Question of a Macedonian Revolution in Military Affairs (RMA), *Ancient World* 42.2, 137–47.

— (2015) Seleucus I and Military Unrest in the Army of Alexander the Great. In R. Oetjen and F. Ryan (eds) *Seleukeia: Studies in Seleucid History, Archaeology and Numismatics in Honor of Getzel M. Cohen*, Berlin.

Carney, E. (1996) Macedonians and Mutiny: Discipline and Indiscipline in the Army of Philip and Alexander, *Classical Philology* 91.1, 20–31.

Chrissanthos, S. (1999) *Seditio*: mutiny in the Roman army, 90–40 BC. PhD Dissertation, University of Southern California.

Hatzopoulos, M. B. (2001) *L'organisation de l'armée macédonienne sous les Antigonides: problèmes anciens et documents nouveaux*. Μελετήματα vol. 30. Athens.

Heckel, W. (1992) *The Marshals of Alexander's Empire*. New York.

— (2003) Alexander the Great and the 'Limits of the Civilised World'. In W. Heckel and L. Tritle (eds) *Crossroads of History: The Age of Alexander*, 165–73, Claremont, CA.

Heidenreich, S. and J. Roth (forthcoming) Neurophysiology of Panic on the Ancient Battlefield. In L. L. Brice (ed.) *New Approaches to Greco-Roman Warfare*, Malden, MA.

Holt, F. (1982) The Hyphasis Mutiny: A Source Study, *Ancient World* 5, 33–59.

Howe, T., and S. Mueller (2012) Mission Accomplished: Alexander at the Hyphasis, *Ancient History Bulletin* 26, 21–38.

Kaegi, W. E. (1981) *Byzantine Military Unrest 471–843. An Interpretation*. Amsterdam.

Lammers, C. J. (1969) Strikes and Mutinies: A Comparative Study of Organizational Conflicts between Rulers and Ruled, *Administrative Science Quarterly* 14.4, 558–72.

— (2003) Mutiny in Comparative Perspective, *International Review of Social History* 48, 473–82.

Lendon, J. E. (2005) *Soldiers and Ghosts*. New Haven.

MacMullen, R. (1984) The Legion as a Society, *Historia* 33, 440–456.

Phang, S. E. (2008) *Roman Military Service*. Cambridge.

Pritchett, W. K. (1974) *The Greek State at War*. vol. 2. Berkeley and Los Angeles.

Roisman, J. (2012) *Alexander's Veterans*. Austin.

Rose, E. (1982) The Anatomy of Mutiny, *Armed Forces and Society* 8.4, 561–74.

Sekunda, N. V. (2010) The Macedonian Army. In J. Roisman and I. Worthington (eds) *A Companion to Ancient Macedonia*, 446–71, Malden, MA.

Spann, P. O. (1999) Alexandr at the Beas: Fox in a Lion's Skin. In F. B. Titchener and R. F. Moorton, Jr. (eds) *The Eye Expanded. Life and the Arts in Graeco-Roman Antiquity*, 62–74, Berkeley and Los Angeles.

Wheeler, E. (2011) Greece: Mad Hatters and March Hares. In L. L. Brice and J. T. Roberts (eds) *Recent Directions in Ancient Military History*, 53–104, Claremont, CA.

OPPOSITION TO MACEDONIAN KINGS: RIOTS FOR REWARDS AND VERBAL PROTESTS

Joseph Roisman

Vigorous historical investigation of the character of Macedonian monarchy for the last two centuries has produced two distinct scholarly camps, with the inevitable middle position. The main division is between the 'constitutional' school, which notes significant checks on royal power, and those who see that power as largely autocratic.[1] It is not my intention to join a debate that since its inception has produced many interpretations but little new evidence. In full awareness of the practical and cultural constraints on Macedonian royal power, I am closer to the 'autocratic' school. This study, however, aims to broaden our perspective of the nature of this monarchy by showing how it reacted to two forms of opposition. Generally, opposition to Macedonian monarchy ranged from assassination attempts to subversive disobedience, with historians paying particular attention to conspiracies against the kings and to mutinies in their armies. The scholar honored in this book, and who has left such an indelible imprint on Alexander studies, has also offered his characteristic insightful interpretations of the evidence regarding plots against Alexander or his dealing with the army's opposition to his wish to continue the campaign deeper into India.[2] In this paper I hope to show how different Macedonian kings negotiated two other forms of opposition involving riots for rewards and verbal protests, and how the conduct of both parties in the dispute was dictated by the overwhelming power of the Macedonian monarchy.

Rioting for rewards due

As employer and benefactor, the Macedonian king was expected to reward his troops for their service. Failure to meet this expectation could result in riots, although the record shows only four instances of troops protesting on this account. The small number may be due to our deficient evidence, or even to the good record of kings as paymasters, but it

---

[1] For useful recent surveys of views of Macedonian monarchy, including references to earlier literature, see Borza 1990, 231–52; Müller 2003, 17–21; King 2010. Middle position: *e.g.*, Griffith in Hammond and Griffith 1979, 2:385–386; Mooren 1983.

[2] Plots: Heckel 2003 (with which I am in agreement); Mutiny on the Hyphasis: Heckel 2008, 120–5 (which I respectfully view differently).

may also serve as a warning against the tendency to readily correlate loyalty and discipline of royal troops to their compensation.[3]

But before commencing the investigation, something should be said about historical anecdotes, one of which comprises the evidence for our first case of riots for pay. Scarcity of sources forces scholars to use such stories, whose reliability has been quite persuasively assailed by Richard Saller.[4] My position on the historical validity of anecdotes is less universally negative, especially when there is no other evidence that contradicts or questions their contents, when additional evidence seems to support it, and when the purpose of telling the anecdote by the extant source does not make the story suspect. But I also share Sallers' view that anecdotes are valuable illustrations of people's expectations of, or disappointments with, a ruler. Thus even if the details of the anecdotes are uncertain, the ideas that informed them and even the context in which they are set can be assumed to be authentic.

A tale from Polyaenus' book of stratagems describes how Philip II resorted to trickery in dealing with troops who demanded payment. The Macedonians surrounded Philip when he was wrestling with an athlete in the palaestra and clamored for their wages. The king, who had no money, conceded the justice of their demand but also claimed that he was practicing and sweating so that he could greatly increase their reward in the future. He then played the buffoon. He ran through their midst and jumped into a pool, provoking their laughter, and continued a diving competition with the athlete until the troops gave up and left. Philip was fond of telling in parties how he elegantly avoided paying the soldiers (Polyaen. *Strat.* 4.2.6).

The anecdote might have originated in sympotic stories designed to amuse the participants more than to record history, and yet it suggests circumstances familiar from other situations.[5] Complaints against kings tended to be aggressive in the absence of peaceable or formal mechanisms of forcing the king to fulfill his duty. The king, on his part, invoked the image of the ruler toiling for his people's benefit, which was in line with a common expectation of monarchs, but also one that kings used to reproach their subjects in conflict situations. Thus, both Alexander, in the course of the mutiny at Opis in 324, and Antigonus Doson, when he was facing Macedonian rebels at Pella or Aegae in 229, hoped to shame the mutineers into submission by claims of toiling harder and facing greater danger than they for their sake.[6] In the case of Philip, the attempt failed, and according to the story, he clowned his way out of the predicament. His dismissal of the troops' demand was well within the code of ethics of generals in distress, which allowed and even encouraged them to trick troops

---

[3]   *E.g.*, Rostovtzeff 1941, 1, 144; Austin 1986, 463; Serrati 2007, 481.

[4]   Saller 1980, who deals with Roman material but his methodology and conclusions can be applicable to our case. Cf. also Gleason 2011, 77–78.

[5]   For sympotic anecdotes and history in a Roman context, see Saller 1980, 70–71. Adams 1984, 48–49 uses the story to illustrate the Macedonians' freedom of speech.

[6]   Doson: Just. 28.3.9–16. Alexander: Arr. 7.9.9–10.4. Bosworth (1988b, esp. 104–5), however, thinks that Arrian's main inspiration for Alexander's complaint is Xenophon's speech to the returnees in Xen. *Anab.* 7.6, as well as borrowings from his own narrative.

out of their just reward.[7] The troops, who left the scene empty-handed, suggested how a king could shirk his responsibility with impunity.

Two additional incidents of riots, or mutinies, for pay took place in the troubled times that followed Alexander's death. I shall deal with them only briefly both because I have discussed them extensively elsewhere and because the soldiers protested not against the king but his more powerful guardians, whose authority was outwardly lesser. The first mutiny took place in 320 in Triparadeisus when the veterans demanded payments promised or due since Alexander's time. Their complaints were directed against the regent Antipater, with the queen, Eurydice-Adea, who presumably spoke for her husband, Philip III, and actually stood by their side or even at their head. It was a highly unusual case of a royalt personage encouraging the army to riot in order to advance its power. Antipater used trickery and force to restore order, and the sources' silence about the veterans' compensation suggests that they received none.[8] About a year later, and just before Antipater was about to cross from Asia to Europe, his troops rioted again for pay. The regent promised to reward them in a few days, but then sneaked away to Europe with the kings. The veterans followed him there with nothing to show for their insubordination. Antipater's conduct, thus, was in line with Philip II's of the anecdote, when commanders got away with tricking the soldiers out of their wages.

The troops of Philip V appear to have fared better. In 218 he was engaged in a campaign in Greece, and Polybius, who depicts Apelles, Leontius, and other prominent Macedonians as fellow conspirators against the king, claims that they incited the royal troops camping in and around Corinth to riot. They hoped in this way to intimidate Philip and to recover from their earlier failure in a conflict with the king and his trusted adviser, Aratus. The historian alleges that the 'conspirators' suggested to the elite military units of the hypaspists and the *agema* that they received none of their due rights and failed to get their customary share of the booty, even though they risked their lives on behalf of all. The agitation moved the younger troops to get together, plunder the tents of Philip's leading friends, and break into the royal residence. Soon chaos reigned in the streets of Corinth.[9]

Before discussing the rest of the episode, it would be useful to dispense with the role of the so-called conspirators in the affair. Our interest is in the relationship between the troops and their king, from which Polybius's biased depiction of the plotters is a distraction. I agree with scholars who view the charges of incitement by Leontius and his friends as a later fabrication, but what matters is that the troops believed that they were wronged, regardless of who told them so.[10] That the complaints might not have been groundless is suggested

---

7   See below for Antipater's tricking his unpaid troops. Eumenes of Cardia used a stratagem to keep his companions from seizing the enemy baggage: Plut. *Eum.* 9. For both incidents, see Roisman 2012, 1–2, 157–158, 162–170.

8   Riots in Tripradeisus: Arr. *Succ.* 1.31–33, 38; Diod. 18.39.2–4; Polyaen. 4.6.4; Roisman 2012, 136–12. Antipater's tricking of his troops: Arr. *Succ.* 1.45; Roisman 2012, 157–158.

9   For the peltasts and the agema of the hypaspists, see conveniently Le Bohec 1993, 293–295; Foulon 1996; Hatzopoulos 2001, 56–66. For the bellicosity of young warriors in Hellenistic armies, see Chaniotis 2005, 44–46.

10 Polyb. 5.25.1–4. Walbank 1940, 58–61, trusts Polybius on the incitement but is undecided about the existence of Apelles' conspiracy. Errington (1967, esp. 30–35) regards the charges as a later fabrication

by the fact that Polybius (or Philip in his later address to the soldiers, which focused on their behavior) failed to contest them, at least explicitly. Scholars, indeed, have suggested that the troops were shortchanged by Philip when he used much of the considerable booty he had seized in Aetolia, Oeantheia, and Laconia on a buildup of a naval power, or when he sold booty just before their outburst.[11]

As probable as these conjectures are, Polybius nowhere suggests that any of these royal actions was responsible for, or even linked to, the riots. Moreover, the exclusive scholarly focus on the booty as the issue may be too narrow. Polybius mentions the soldiers' getting less than their due share of the plunder, but this does not mean that it was their only grievance or that their raiding of the nobles' and the king's living quarters is sure proof of it. The similar raiding and destruction of the camp and the royal tent of Demetrius Poliorcetes in 287 following his escape from his mutinous army (Plut. *Demetr.* 44), or even the veterans' plundering of the royal treasury in Babylon during the controversy over Alexander's succession in 323 (Curt. 10.6.23–24), had nothing to do with economic loss but suggest that raiding and political dissent were inseparable. The troops at Corinth were upset with Philip for what they considered his and his friends' unfair and disrespectful treatment of them, including the distribution of the booty, and their reaction resembled other forms of opposition to the king in response to perceived injustice and damaged honor.[12] Their plundering combined acquisitiveness with defense of their rights, of their preferred status, and of the prestige that came with them. The alleged violation of the unwritten understanding between them and the government, according to which greater risk brought greater honor and reward, legitimized their taking the law into their hands.

Philip was in the Corinthian port of Lechaeum when he heard of the disturbances. He rushed to the city and called the Macedonians to a meeting in the city theater, where he both exhorted and reproached them. The meeting became tumultuous and confused, with some calling for the arrest and punishment of the culprits and others advising reconciliation and pardon. Philip left pretending (as he often does in Polybius) to be convinced by the advocates of leniency and not to know who provoked the crisis (Polyb. 5.25.4–7).

Philip's success in getting the rioters into the theater and even to discuss punitive measures there suggests that their displays of indiscipline were not as uncontrolled as Polybius would have us believe. Apparently, the soldiers were as interested as their king in repairing their relationship after showing him that wronging them had consequences. As in other mutinies, the main issue became their conduct rather than its causes. Polybius does not identify the authors of the different suggestions offered, but in other army assemblies in the time of Alexander and his immediate Successors, assembly speakers tended to come from the military elite, and the audience rarely did more than indicate their approval

---

originating in the king's court. Hammond in Hammond and Walbank 1988 3:382n1 is also skeptical of the generals' involvement, but his view of Philip is more charitable.

11 Philip's successful plundering: 5.7.6, 8.4, 8.8, 13.1, and see also 5.17.8, 17.10. Selling the booty: Polyb. 5.24.10, and see Loreto 1990, 343–44. Spending it on naval preparations: Walbank 1940, 58–59. Upset with the sale of booty: Errington 1967, 30–35.

12 Several Macedonian kings were killed by men of the elite they had insulted: Arist. *Pol.* 5.8.9–11 1310a37–b17, but even the masses could react in indignation: the mutiny at Opis against Alexander had much to do with the veterans' wounded pride: Roisman 2012, 44–50.

or opposition.[13] The king's refusal to take action worked in his own interest and in the troops'. It allowed him to ignore not only the question of who incited the troops, but also the causes of their discontent, thus escaping the need to yield to popular pressure by reversing a royal decision or action about their rewards. The troops, for their part, showed the authorities that changing the rules regulating their rewards and status could be costly. They also succeeded in keeping what they had plundered.[14]

Philip's response is significant also because it stands in contrast to the way Alexander and Antigonus Doson handled insubordination (above). For all three kings, mass punishment was out of the question, yet Alexander and Antigonus insisted on punishing the ringleaders (Arr. 7.8.3; Just. 28.3.16). Philip chose not to follow this course for the reasons discussed above and especially because inaction accorded with his desire not to win the conflict but to defuse it. It was the king's prerogative to decide when a show of opposition deserved retributive action.

Verbal protests

Action against a royal decision, deed, or policy was usually accompanied by remonstrative words as in the case of mutinies, but words alone were rarely effective. There were of course exceptions. Macedonians' criticisms of Philip II's and Demetrius Poliorcetes' miscarriage of justice made the kings reconsider their actions, but the protesters in these cases appeared to be individuals who were nonthreatening or easy to satisfy.[15] By contrast, mass complaints or outcry were normally ineffective. Because of the ampler information on protests in Alexander's army, I shall discuss his handling of them only after dealing with other Macedonian kings.

The Macedonians' celebrated freedom of speech, if unaccompanied by action, could always be trumped by the royal prerogative not to listen.[16] When Philip V arrested his general Leontius, and Leontius' peltasts protested, their protest actually led the king to execute their commander (Polyb 5.26.4–8). In contrast, Alexander's troops who combined verbal protests with displays of indiscipline in Opis, and Demetrius's soldiers who did the same and forced him to flee the country, both saw gains.[17] Coenus, who successfully spoke against Alexander's march deeper into India, is not truly an exception, because he

---

[13] *Pace* O'Neil (1999, 43) who identifies the speakers as soldiers. For speakers in the army assemblies, see Roisman 2012, esp. 23–25, 34–40.

[14] Hatzopoulos (2001, 144–145) thinks that the Amphipolis diagramma (*ISE* 114) that includes royal regulations concerning booty was issued in response to the riots at Corinth. Yet the date of the inscription is uncertain and the possibilities that it was significantly later or even earlier than the crisis cannot be excluded: see Juhel 2002, 412 (later) and Faraguna 1998, 385 (earlier). The surviving lines suggest no reaction to insurrection but a royal attempt to control booty revenues tightly. For the text and its interpretation, see also Loreto 1990; Hatzopoulos 1996, 2: no. 12; Juhel 2002.

[15] Philip: Plut. *Moral.* 177d–e; cf. Front. *Strat.* 4.7.37. Demetrius: Diod. 21.9.

[16] See Adams 1986, 52. Freedom of speech and protest: Griffith in Hammond and Griffith 1979, 2, 392, and above.

[17] Demetrius' troops got rid of an unpopular ruler and availed themselves to his possessions: Plut. *Demtr.* 44. Alexander's veterans who wanted to go home left Opis with a large bonus and in a greater number than Alexander had originally planned: Roisman 2012, 55–57.

resorted to persuasion, not protest, and the troops largely followed his example with their fairly passive resistance.

Other examples of verbal protests support this pattern. Probably around 345, Philip II initiated a large transfer of population, settling people on the Macedonian frontiers and in cities, largely as a security measure and in preparation for future campaigns. Justin's description of the people's reaction is overwrought with drama. He says they lamented their own fate and their children's, regretting the loss of their native homes and the tombs of their ancestors. He then adds, probably in an attempt to make their suffering more poignant, "... there was silent, forlorn dejection, as men feared that even their tears might be taken to signify opposition," and goes on to suggest that concealment made their grief even more painful (Just. 8.5.8–6.2, Yardley translation).

It is hard to accept Justin's depiction of the silently suffering Macedonians at face value, not because it contradicts their alleged right to a frank speech, but because their fear of crying in public seems exaggerated: by all accounts Philip did not share Stalin's obsessive suspicion of all opposition. Justin also fails to mention the rewards that may have been used as inducements to the colonists, or the advantages that awaited them in their new abodes. Years later (323), Alexander is said to have reminded the Macedonians of his father's benefactions, including their life as city dwellers and other civilizing benefits (Arr. 7.9.2). We can assume, then, that those who were upset with Philip said so, though perhaps they were afraid of doing more. Whether they protested or merely grieved, however, they achieved nothing.[18]

The reaction of those transplanted by Philip V was more vociferous but had identical results. According to Polybius, Philip prepared for his war with Rome by transplanting families from Macedonian cities to the country in Emathia, (formerly Paeonia), repopulating the cities with barbarians more loyal to him (183). Those affected raised a general clamor, crying out in lament and cursed the king. In an effort to eliminate future opposition, Philip ordered governors of the cities to imprison the children of prominent Macedonians he had executed, whose misfortune and humiliation evoked general pity (Polyb. 23.10.4–7; Livy 40.3.5). Similar to the case of the Peltasts' protesting the treatment of their leader (above), the vocal opposition of the transplanted led to a punitive action rather than royal concessions. Philip's action suggests his concern about attempts to exploit the discontent, perhaps by those who had personal motives for getting even with him.[19] Instead of bringing about a change, the verbal protests and lamentations led to the tightening of his grip over the population.

Other expressions of anger at perceived royal wrongs were equally ineffective. In 274 Pyrrhus returned to Macedonia to plunder the country and to resume his claim to the Macedonian throne. When he reached the Macedonian capital of Aegae, he left there a Gallic garrison that robbed the royal tombs nearby and scattered the bones of their occupants. Pyrrhus did nothing about this insolent sacrilege (he clearly needed the Gauls'

---

[18] Ellis (1969, 13) thinks that Justin describes an authentic experience but not necessarily in this case. Fear factor: Worthington 2008, 109–10, 199.

[19] Walbank 1940, 243–45; 1957–1979, 3:230–232, speculates that there is a (hard-to-prove) link between the discontent and the opposition to Philip's anti–Roman policy.

services). The Macedonians harshly criticized the king, and the philosopher Teles remarked, perhaps in reference to the outrage, that it was better for a king to be poor than to rob graves. By all signs, this was the only price Pyrrhus paid for his troops' crime or his inaction. He did nothing to correct the wrong, and shortly thereafter, he left Macedonia for southern Greece, where he was killed in action. No source, however, linked his departure to Macedonian dissatisfaction.[20]

Livy, probably using Polybius as his source, recounts a dramatic story about royal injustice that involves a woman who killed herself and her stepchildren before Philip V could lay his murderous hands on them (c. 182). Their fate so reignited the people's hatred for the king that they cursed him and his children. Livy adds that when the gods heard the curses they drove Philip to the cruel murder of his own children, and he goes on to relate the demise of Prince Demetrius. It is significant that, according to the historian, retribution came from heaven and not from any opposition movement. Ever since Hesiod, people who were impotent in the face of royal power sought solace in divine justice.[21]

Opposition to Alexander the Great came in many forms, but because it has been treated in numerous publications, I shall focus just on verbal protests and in relative brevity. The evidence shows that verbal protests in Alexander's camp were no more successful than those against other Macedonian kings. This is true for events whose historicity is not in doubt and even for those whose authenticity is debated. For example, Curtius reports that an eclipse of the moon on September 21, 331, caused panic in the army before the battle of Gaugamela. The men complained that the gods were against them, that many were dying for the sake of the king's ambition, and that he disowned Philip. (It was common for discontent to attract unrelated grievances.) Alexander sent for Egyptian seers, who convinced the superstitious troops that the eclipse was a good omen, and the army resumed its march (Curt. 4.10.1–8). The story of this near-mutiny is unique to Curtius and has been questioned by scholars, but even if historical, it illustrates that the king did not have to confront the opposition in order to quiet it.[22] The troops' willingness to meet the enemy after being assured that they would win the battle also showed that fear, rather than unhappiness with Alexander's ambition and claim of divine birth, was at the core of their protest: none of their complaints were addressed.

Some protests required greater or subtler efforts of Alexander. According to Curtius, the execution of Philotas made the troops change their attitude from resentment of Philotas to pity for him and his father, Parmenion, and their mutinous sentiments were conveyed to the king. In response, Alexander called an army assembly to try Alexander of Lyncestis and the sons of Andromenes for treason. The Macedonians found the former guilty but the latter innocent. It appears that the trials were intended to remind the army of the

[20] Plut. *Pyrrhus* 26; Diod. 22.12. Teles: *Teletis Reliquiae* Hense, 43; Tarn 1913, 237; Lévèque 1957, 569. Walbank (1957–79, 3:261–3) suggests that Pyrrhus was hurt by the Macedonians' refusal to join his army and by their support of Antigonus Gonatas, but neither form of opposition is attested.

[21] Livy 40.5.1–2; Hesiod *WD* 213–73. Polybius as Livy's likely source and his depiction of Philip's last years as a moralizing tragedy: Walbank 1938, 62–64; 1940, 245; cf. Eckstein 1995, 242.

[22] Doubts about Curtius's account: Atkinson 1980, 1:388, but Bosworth 1980a, 1:287–288 appears to set a greater value on the report. Cf. also Curt. 9.4.15–23.

danger to Alexander's life and thus undercut the sympathy for those he had eliminated.[23] Parmenion's execution invoked greater antagonism in the army, which led Alexander to take precautionary measures, when he grouped the malcontents in one unit. If Curtius's claim that these men turned out to be among the most valorous in Alexander's army is correct, the irony is double. Alexander got away with killing his most senior and respected general and then motivated those who resented him for it to sacrifice their lives for him. The gap between protest and its outcome could not be wider.[24]

The failure of the verbal protest and complaints to dissuade the king is evident even in regard to Alexander's most controversial steps, namely, his claim to be the son of the god Ammon and his adoption of Asian institutions and traditions, which in the eyes of the Macedonians amounted to trading his Macedonian identity and kingship for a foreign one and perhaps as an affront to the gods. The most vocal critics of his policies and leadership style were arguably the old general Cleitus and the young noble Hermolaus, the former during a drunken quarrel with the king and the latter in his defense speech on conspiracy charges. It is common to view both as speaking for other Macedonians, but is no less significant that Alexander did not yield an inch to any of their criticisms.[25]

Less confrontational criticism or protest produced similarly futile results, with the exception of Alexander's attempt to have Europeans do *proskynesis* to him. There were more than one reason for the opposition's success or failure in these conflicts but one of them had to do with the type of challenge it presented to Alexander's authority. Unlike the Macedonians who protested the population transfer under Philip II and Philip V, those who criticized Alexander's claim to a divine father or his wish to be accorded obeisance did not go against a royal command. The king might have ordered adding 'Ammon's son' to his titles (Curt. 4.7.30–31, 8.5.5), but he never tried the impossible, which was to compel his people to acknowledge his divine origin or status. This restraint on Alexander's part allowed the Macedonians to vocalize repeatedly their disapproval of his claim to divine descent, but it also allowed the king to persist in making that claim. He similarly did not command the Macedonians to do obeisance, or *proskynesis*, to him. In spite of Justin's assertion that the king ordered that he be thus saluted or worshipped, all other sources describe elaborate schemes of exerting informal pressure on royal guests to perform the ritual.[26] Seeing the Macedonians' negative response, the king decided not to press the issue.

In the matter of *proskynesis*, then, the opposition triumphed over the king, but with two

---

[23] Curt. 7.1.1–2.7; cf. Arr. 3.27.1 for the timing of these trials. Bosworth (1988, 1:103), however, thinks that Alexander exploited the army's hysteria, and that he got the verdicts he aimed for; cf. Anson 2008, 147. Yet, the sources suggest that successful pleading and even the question of guilt or innocence mattered; see also Heckel 2003, 213–216.

[24] For the unit and in support of its historicity, see Curt. 7.2.35–38; Diod. 17.80.4; Just. 12.5.5–8; Badian 1960, 335; Heckel 1997, 213.

[25] For selected bibliography, see Roisman 2011.

[26] Justin 12.7.1 as opposed to Arr. 4.10.1–12.7; Curt. 8.5.5–6.1; Plut. *Alex.* 54–55. The different versions of how the pressure was exerted do not necessarily contradict each other. See Badian 1981, 48–54. Jeep's emendation of Curtius's text in 8.5.5 from *atque* to *iussitque*, as if Alexander ordered the practice, is as unnecessary as it is wrong. For the relatively narrow range of the opposition to the custom: Heckel 2009, 79–80.

significant qualifications. As in the case of his descent from Ammon, or even the 'mutiny' in India, the resistance was to royal aspirations, and a king's wish was not necessarily his command. Although the line between the two could be blurred, it was easier for a king to yield in a matter of mere desire, which did not raise issues of indiscipline and irrevocable decrees. Secondly, the way the monarch was challenged mattered. Alexander could afford conceding to urgings, because they implied no contest that the king must win to preserve his authority. With that said, and in spite of the Macedonians' opposition, criticism, or derision, Alexander continued to regard and call himself the son of Ammon and have the Asians perform obeisance to him.

Alexander also provoked suspicion and anger with his adoption of royal Persian protocols, his befriending and promoting of Asian men of distinction, and especially his incorporation of Asian recruits into the army. Rather than give up, the king only intensified the process of Asianizing his administration, the army, the court, and his monarchy.[27]

In sum, opposition to kings in Macedonia was very much shaped by the fact that its political system lacked institutional mechanisms of appeal against royalty and that the king was unaccountable to his decisions and actions. The result was that dissent against the king tended to be confrontational in nature. In dealing with dissatisfied, protesting Macedonians, the king might prefer not to confront them, and even to tolerate their conduct, as long as their words did not lead to action. But he was also unyielding, and, as the cases of riots for reward and verbal protests show, only when the opposition took matters to its own hand it could hope for a positive result.

Bibliography

Adams, W. L. (1986) Macedonian Kingship and the Right of Petition, *Ancient Macedonia* 4, 43–52.

Anson, E. M. (2008) Macedonian Judicial Assemblies, *Classical Philology* 103, 135–149.

Atkinson, J. E. (1980) *A Commentary on Q. Curtius Rufus'* Historiae Alexandri Magni, *Book 3 and 4*. Vol. 1. Amsterdam.

Austin, M. M. (1986) Hellenistic Kings, War, and the Economy, *Classical Quarterly* 36.2, 450–466.

Badian. E. (1960) The Death of Parmenio, *Transaction of the American Philological Association* 91, 324–338.

— (1981) The Deification of Alexander the Great. In J. Dell (ed.) *Ancient Macedonian Studies in Honor of Charles E. Edson*, 27–71. Thessaloniki.

Borza, E. (1990) *In the Shadow of Olympus: The Emergence of Macedon*. Princeton.

Bosworth, A. B. (1980a) *A Historical Commentary on Arrian's History of Alexander*. Vol. 1. Oxford.

— (1980b) Alexander and the Iranians, *Journal of Hellenic Studies* 100, 1–21.

— (1988a) *Conquest and Empire: The Reign of Alexander the Great*. Cambridge.

— (1988b) *From Arrian to Alexander: Studies in Historical Interpretation*. Oxford.

Chaniotis, A. (2005) *War in the Hellenistic World: A Social and Cultural History*. Oxford.

Eckstein, A. M. (1995) *Moral Vision in the Histories of Polybius*. Berkeley.

Ellis, J. R. (1969) Population-Transplants by Philip II, *Makedonika* 9, 9–17.

Errington, R. M. (1967) Philip V, Aratus, and the 'Conspiracy of Apelles', *Historia* 16.1, 19–36.

Faraguna, M. (1998) Aspetti amministrativi e finanziari della monarchia macedone tra IV e III secolo a. C., *Athenaeum* 86, 349–395.

Foulon, É. (1996) Hypaspites, Peltastes, Chrysaspides, Argyraspides, Chalcaspides, *Revue D'Etudes antiques* 98.1–2, 53–63.

---

[27] For Alexander and the Asians, see, *e.g.* Bosworth 1980b, but also Olbrycht 2010, 351–368.

Gleason, M. (2011) Identity Theft: Doubles and Masquerades in Cassius Dio's Contemporary History, *Classical Antiquity* 30.1, 33–86.

Hammond, N. G. L. and G.T. Griffith. (1979) *A History of Macedonia*. Vol. 2. Oxford.

Hammond, N. G. L. and F.W. Walbank. (1988) *A History of Macedonia*. Vol. 3. Oxford.

Hatzopoulos. M. B. (1996) *Macedonian Institutions under the Kings*. 2 vols. Athens.

— (2001) *L'organisation de l'armée macédonienne sous les Antigonides. Problèmes anciens et documents nouveaux*. Athens.

Heckel W. (1997) *Justin Epitome of the Philippic History of Pompeius Trogus, Books 11–12 Alexander the Great*. J. C. Yardley, trans. Oxford.

— (2003) King and Companions: Observations on the Nature of Power in the Reign of Alexander. In J. Roisman (ed.) *Brill's Companion to Alexander the Great*, 197–225, Leiden.

— (2008) *The Conquests of Alexander the Great*. Cambridge.

— (2009) A King and His Army. In W. Heckel. and L. A. Tritle (eds) *Alexander the Great. A New History*, 69–82, Malden, MA.

Juhel, P. (2002) 'On Orderliness with Respect to the Prizes of War': the Amphipolis Regulation and the Management of Booty in the Army of the Last Antigonids, *Annals of the British School at Athens* 97, 401–412.

King, C. J. (2010) Macedonian Kingship and Other Political Institutions. In J. Roisman, and I. Worthington (eds) *A Companion to Ancient Macedonia*, 373–391, Malden, MA.

Le Bohec, S. (1993) *Antigone Dôsôn. Roi de Macédoine*. Nancy.

Lévèque, P. (1957) *Pyrrhos*. Paris.

Loreto, L. (1990) Polyb.10.17.1–5 e il regolamento militare macedone. Norme ellenistiche in materia di saccheggio e di bottino di Guerra, *Index* 18, 331–366.

Mooren, L. (1983) The Nature of the Hellenistic Monarchy. In E. van't Dack, P. Van Dessel and W. Van Gucht (eds) *Egypt and the Hellenistic world. Proceedings of the international colloquium, Leuven 24–26 may 1982*, 205–240, Louvain.

Müller, S. (2003) *Massnahmen der Herrschaftssicherung gegnüber der makedonischen Opposition bei Alexander dem Grossen*. Frankfurt am Main.

Olbrycht, M. J. (2010) Macedonia and Persia. In J. Roisman, and I. Worthington (eds) *A Companion to Ancient Macedonia*, 342–369, Malden, MA.

O'Neil, J. L. (1999) Political Trials under Alexander the Great and His Successors, *Antichthon* 33.1, 28–47.

Roisman, J. (2011) Alexander the Great, *Oxford Bibliography Online*.

— (2012) *Alexander's Veterans and the Early Wars of the Successors*. Austin, TX.

Rostovtzeff, M. I. (1941) *The Social and Economic History of the Hellenistic World*. 3 vols. Oxford.

Saller. R. (1980) Anecdotes as Historical Evidence for the Principate, *Greece & Rome* 27.1, 69–83.

Serrati, J. (2007) Warfare and the State. In P. Sabin, H. van Wees and M. Whitby (eds) *The Cambridge History of Greek and Roman Warfare*, 461–497, Cambridge.

Tarn, W. W. (1913) *Antigonus Gonatas*. Oxford.

Walbank, F. W. (1938) *ΦΙΛΙΠΠΟΣ ΤΡΑΓΩΙΔΟΥΜΕΝΟΣ*: A Polybian Experiment, *Journal of Hellenic Studies* 58.1, 55–68.

— (1940) *Philip V of Macedon*. Cambridge.

— (1957–1979) *A Historical Commentary on Polybius*. 3 vols. Oxford.

Worthington, I. (2008) *Philip II of Macedonia*. New Haven.

ARRIAN AND 'ROMAN' MILITARY TACTICS. ALEXANDER'S CAMPAIGN AGAINST THE AUTONOMOUS THRACIANS

Timothy Howe[1]

In the spring of 335, after his accession to the Macedonian throne and confirmation as Ἡγημών of the League of Corinth, Alexander was compelled to deal with the developing unrest among Macedonia's tribal neighbors to the north, northwest and east. In the words of Arrian, "since they were neighbors, it did not seem good to [Alexander] to leave them behind, when going on an expedition so far from home, unless they were wholly subdued."[2] Alexander's Balkan campaign, then, was designed to thoroughly humble any rebellions tribes.[3] And it seems to have been quite successful since the Odrysians, Triballians and Illyrians contributed 7,000 men to Alexander's army when he invaded Persia.[4] Although there is some debate over the route,[5] we know that Alexander first marched against those Thracians who had not been conquered by his father, what Arrian chooses to call the 'Autonomous Thracians'.[6] In the ensuing confrontation, approximately 1500 of them were killed, and all of the women and children who had accompanied the men captured and enslaved.[7]

And so we might leave the 'Event with the Autonomous Thracians', were it not for the unusual tactics that Alexander employs. Unfortunately for modern scholars, this minor episode in Alexander's military career against a rather insignificant (and soon extinct)

---

[1] It is my great honor and privilege to offer this short study on Arrian to my dear friend Waldemar Heckel, not least because the thesis of the paper derived from a late night, 'what if?' conversation at his home in Calgary.

[2] καὶ ἅμα ὁμόρους ὄντας οὐκ ἐδόκει ὑπολείπεσθαι ὅτι μὴ πάντῃ ταπεινωθέντας οὕτω μακρὰν ἀπὸ τῆς οἰκείας στελλόμενον. All Arrian passages, including *Tactica* and *Acies contra Alanos* are from Roos and Wirth's 1967 Teubner edition. For a text and translation of *Tactica* and *Acies contra Alanos* see DeVoto 1993.

[3] For the wider historical context of Alexander's Thracian campaign see Bosworth 1988, 28–30; Ashley 1998, 166–175; Lonsdale 2004, 56–7.

[4] Heckel 2008, 158.

[5] For a discussion of the debate over Alexander's route see Seibert 1972, 78; Bosworth 1980, 51–56.

[6] Hammond 1980a, 456, n. 4, argues that Philip II had conquered all of Thrace up to the Danube River, but Bosworth, 1980, 54, is likely correct that, while Macedonian influence was present, this area's subjugation to Macedonian rule was at best incomplete.

[7] Arr. *Anab.* 1.1.13.

Thracian hill people, which only Arrian reports,[8] has caused no end of trouble among the scholarly community because of the *testudo*-like shield wall Arrian has Alexander using.[9] Indeed, so contentious has the issue become that many military and biographical surveys of the period choose to skip over the details (*e.g.* Lonsdale 2004, 56–7; Engels 2006, 46) or report Arrian's description of events without comment or analysis (*e.g.* Green 1970, 125–6; Lane Fox 1974, 81–2; Bosworth 1988, 29; Ashley 1998, 168–169). The result has been a skewed understanding of both Alexander's military strategy *and* Arrian as a source for it. In 2004 Waldemar Heckel attempted to resolve the first part, Alexander's military strategy, by returning to Arrian's narrative, offering a close reading of the text and proposing an ingenious solution: Alexander armed his hypaspists as hoplites and ordered them to form a shield wall with their larger shields, while the phalangites fought off the Thracians along the flanking edges of the shield wall.[10] In what follows, I hope to complement Heckel's work by analyzing the second part, Arrian as the unique source for Alexander's campaign against the Autonomous Thracians.

Flavius Arrianus (Xenophon), to give the historian Arrian his full name, was not inexperienced in the military maneuvers such as those employed in Thrace by Alexander, including the shield wall. In 135 CE Arrian himself campaigned along the Black Sea coast near Trebizond against a recalcitrant, autonomous barbarian group, the Alanoi.[11] Like Alexander's forces Arrian's legionaries were a mix of pikemen and spearmen, and according to his own account of the campaign, these groups formed a composite phalanx very similar to that used by Alexander against the Autonomous Thracians.[12] Moreover, just like Alexander in Thrace, Arrian used the more heavily armed portion of his phalanx to break the charge of the Alan attack and form a defensive wall so the rest of the army could strike out along the flanks:[13]

> If [the Skythians][14] indeed approach, let [the pikemen] fall with shields pressed with their shoulders to receive the projectiles as powerfully as possible. Let the first three formations press together in a very dense interlocking [of shields] as strongly as possible. Let the fourth thrust [hurl?] spears.
>
> (Arrian *Acies contra Alanos* 26).[15]

---

8   Bosworth 1980, 51. Polyainos *Strat.* 4.3.11 also reports the event but I follow Bosworth 1980, 55 and Hammond 1996, 37–38 that he is using Arrian as his source. Cf. Melber 1885, 616; Buraselis 1995, 121–140.

9   Fuller 1960, 221; Hammond 1980b, 59; Bosworth 1980, 51–56; Bloedow 1996, 120–122; Worthington 2004, 39; Heckel 2004, 189–94.

10 Heckel 2004, 194, n. 13.

11 Bosworth 1977, 217–55; Stadter 1980, 1–18, 45–49; Syme 1982, 181–211; Bosworth 1994, 230–1; and esp. 269 for an analysis of Arrian's role in this battle.

12 So Bosworth 1994, 256.

13 Arr. *Acies contra Alanos* 26; Bosworth 1994, 257.

14 Throughout the *Acies contra Alanos* Arrian refers to the Alans as Skythians and Sarmatians. Bosworth 1994, 256–7.

15 εἰ δὲ δὴ πελάζοιεν, ἐγχρίμψαντας ταῖς ἀσπίσι καὶ τοῖς ὤμοις ἀντερείσαντας δέχεσθαι τὴν προσβολὴν ὡς καρτερώτατα καὶ τῇ συγκλείσει πυκνοτάτῃ τὰς πρώτας τρεῖς τάξεις ξυνερειδούσας σφίσιν ὡς βιαιότατον οἷόν τε. τὴν τετάρτην δὲ ὑπερακοντίζειν τὰς λόγχας.

Arrian (27–31) then has his flanks capitalize on the fact that the Alans' main advance is engaged by the center's interlocking shields by bringing cavalry and light infantry to harry the enemy flanks. Unfortunately the text breaks off there; however, enough remains of Arrian's maneuver against the Alans to note that it has much in common with Alexander's battle with the Thracians in 335. Compare Arrian *Anab.* 1.1.7–10:

> They collected carts and set them up in their front as a stockade from which to put up a defense, if they were pressed; but it was also in their mind to launch the carts at the Macedonian phalanx as the troops mounted the slope just where the mountain was most precipitous. Their idea was that the denser the phalanx when the descending carts charged it, the more violent descent would scatter it. Alexander consulted how he could most safely cross the ridge; and since he saw that the risk must be run, for there was no way round, he sent an order to his hoplites that whenever the carts tumbled down the slope, those who were on level ground and could break formation were to part to the right and left leaving an avenue for the carts; those caught in the narrows were to draw close together; and some were actually to fall to the ground and link their shields closely together so that when the carts came at them they were likely to bound over them by their gathered impetus and pass without doing harm. The event corresponded to Alexander's advice and conjecture. Part of the phalanx divided, while the carts sliding over the shields of the others did little harm; not one man perished beneath them.[16]

Notice that in Alexander's battle the enemy charges, though here with carts, not the horses Arrian faced when fighting the Alans. Then, Alexander's center forms a shield wall συγκλεῖσαι ἐς ἀκριβὲς τὰς ἀσπίδας. Arrian's forces do as well. Indeed, Arrian uses similar language in the *Acies contra Alanos* to describe the way in which his soldiers came together, τῇ συγκλείσει πυκνοτάτῃ 'in a dense interlocking'. Moreover, Arrian's use of ξυννεύειν 'to learn together'[17] in *Anabasis* 1.1.9 is unique in Arrian's writings[18] but seems to echo ξυνερειδεῖν 'to pack together', also unique, in *Acies contra Alanos* 26. Thus, it is reasonable that Arrian's own experience with the Alans informed the language he used to describe Alexander's battle with the Autonomous Thracians. Bosworth (1994, 267) however, sees this as the other way round, that Arrian has borrowed from his readings in the Alexander historians for *Acies contra Alanos* 26. There is no evidence either way, but since no other work but Arrian uses the ξυννεύειν it seems unlikely that Arrian 'borrowed' it from anywhere. In the end, I see

---

[16] Trans. Brunt 1976, 5–9. ξυναγαγόντες δὲ ἁμάξας καὶ προβαλόμενοι πρὸ σφῶν ἅμα μὲν χάρακι ἐχρῶντο ταῖς ἁμάξαις ἐς τὸ ἀπομάχεσθαι ἀπ' αὐτῶν, εἰ βιάζοιντο, ἅμα δὲ ἐν νῷ εἶχον ἐπαφιέναι ἀνιοῦσιν ᾗ ἀποτομώτατον τοῦ ὄρους ἐπὶ τὴν φάλαγγα τῶν Μακεδόνων τὰς ἁμάξας. γνώμην δὲ πεποίηντο ὅτι ὅσῳ πυκνοτέρα τῇ φάλαγγι καταφερόμεναι συμμίξουσιν αἱ ἅμαξαι, τοσῷδε μᾶλλόν τι διασκεδάσουσιν αὐτὴν βίᾳ ἐμπεσοῦσαι. (8.) Ἀλεξάνδρῳ δὲ βουλὴ γίγνεται ὅπως ἀσφαλέστατα ὑπερβαλεῖ τὸ ὄρος καὶ ἐπειδὴ ἐδόκει διακινδυνευτέα, οὐ γὰρ εἶναι ἄλλην τὴν πάροδον, παραγγέλλει τοῖς ὁπλίταις, ὁπότε καταφέροιντο κατὰ τοῦ ὀρθίου αἱ ἅμαξαι, ὅσοις μὲν ὁδὸς πλατεῖα οὖσα παρέχοι λῦσαι τὴν τάξιν, τούτους δὲ διαχωρῆσαι, ὡς δι' αὐτῶν (9.) ἐκπεσεῖν τὰς ἁμάξας ὅσοι δὲ περικαταλαμβάνοιντο, ξυννεύσαντας, τοὺς δὲ καὶ πεσόντας ἐς γῆν, συγκλεῖσαι ἐς ἀκριβὲς τὰς ἀσπίδας, τοῦ κατ' αὐτῶν φερομένας τὰς ἁμάξας καὶ τῇ ῥύμῃ κατὰ τὸ εἰκὸς ὑπερπηδώσας ἀβλαβῶς ἐπελθεῖν. καὶ οὕτω ξυνέβη ὅπως παρῄνεσέ (10.) τε Ἀλέξανδρος καὶ εἴκασεν. οἱ μὲν γὰρ διέσχον τὴν φάλαγγα, αἱ δ' ὑπὲρ τῶν ἀσπίδων ἐπικυλισθεῖσαι ὀλίγα ἔβλαψαν ἀπέθανε δὲ οὐδεὶς ὑπὸ ταῖς ἁμάξαις. ἔνθα δὴ οἱ Μακεδόνες θαρσήσαντες, ὅτι ἀβλαβεῖς αὐτοῖς, ἃς μάλιστα ἐδεδίεσαν, αἱ ἅμαξαι ἐγένοντο, σὺν (11.) βοῇ ἐς τοὺς Θρᾷκας ἐνέβαλον.

[17] So Heckel 2004, 190 n. 2.

[18] Bosworth 1980, 55.

no reason to doubt that Arrian had in mind his own experiences with the Alans when he wrote this passage.

But we need not leave the argument there, as simply a strong plausible solution. The fact that Polyainos relied on Arrian for his source of information about Alexander's campaign against the Autonomous Thracians, coupled with the fact that none of the other Alexander sources seem inclined to mention this unusual battle involving wagons, suggests that something unique is at work here in Arrian's *Anabasis*. Three observations can be made, none of which need be mutually exclusive: (1) the *first generation* authors for the battle with the Autonomous Thracians gave it little attention, perhaps simply mentioning in passing, as they moved to the main battles against the Triballi and Getai; or (2) the *first generation* authors gave a terse and confusing description of the wagon-dominated fight against the Autonomous Thracians; or (3) the first generation authors did not mention the Autonomous Thracians by name at all and consequently these Thracians are rather an addition by later writers. The reality is that Diodorus, Justin and Plutarch do not mention the battle with the Autonomous Thracians (the Curtius manuscript is missing for this part of Alexander's campaign) but for some reason Arrian does. In addition, Arrian seems to know stylistically unique, and seemingly anachronistic details, hence the modern confusion. But this fact need not result in scholarly gridlock; we can move the discussion forward if we look more closely at Arrian and his literary methods and linguistic style as a whole.

Most work on the subject of Alexander and the Autonomous Thracians has tended to view Arrian's *Anabasis Alexandri* in isolation.[19] However, if we look at the *Anabasis* in context with the *Tactica* and, as above, with the *Acies contra Alanos,* some interesting patterns emerge. Arrian has a tendency to use his own military experiences to fill in what he seems to perceive as gaps in his sources.[20] For example, in *Anabasis* 5.28.3, Arrian engages his own command experience to observe that Alexander took to his tent after killing Kleitos, so that he could give the men a chance to change their minds, "as is often the way of a crowd of soldiers."[21] In the *Tactica*, Arrian's use of his own experience is even more pronounced. As Bosworth and Devine have convincingly demonstrated for the *Tactica*, Arrian used his Hellenistic tactical source, which he has in common with Aelian and Asklepiodotos[22] and has elaborated on it with his own eyewitness experience. As Devine 1994, 326, puts it, "Arrian, who had first-hand experience of the Alani and Armenians as governor of Cappadocia, and also probably of the Parthians earlier during Trajan's Parthian War, expands on Aelian's definitions, doubtless on the basis of autopsy." Hence, Arrian's inclusion of the Sarmatians in *Tactica* 4.3, 4.7–9, 11. While I see no reason to doubt these conclusions, since the beginning of the *Tactica* is missing we can only begin to guess what Arrian meant to achieve by such 'blending'. Kiechle (1964, 109–14) and Wheeler (1979, 303–18) have made a convincing start, however, arguing that Arrian included old and new

---

[19] Bosworth 1980, 51–56, is the notable exception.

[20] See Howe and Muller 2012, 34–37, for Arrian using both his own experience and near-contemporary military narratives, such as those of Tacitus, to make sense of what his often sparse sources reported him.

[21] οἷα δὴ ἐν ὄχλῳ στρατιωτῶν τὰ πολλὰ φιλεῖ γίγνεσθαι.

[22] Devine 1994, 323–4. Bosworth 1994, 255, "the contemporary eye-witness material is coupled with Hellenistic material which is for the most part of antiquarian interest."

material because even the so-called phalanx sections were highly relevant to the Roman legions that Arrian had commanded.[23]

To return to the problem at hand, that of Alexander's shield wall and the wagons of the Autonomous Thracians, it is useful to examine the section of the *Tactica* that explains the shield wall in more detail.[24]

> A phalanx is deployed by depth ... if it is necessary to thrust back those charging, as it is necessary to deploy against Sauromatai and Skyths. Assembling from a thinner to a thicker [phalanx] by comrade and by rear chief is densification, that is, by length and depth. Interlocking of shields is whenever you increase density in the phalanx to the extent that the formation no longer allows a continuous slant in either direction. From this shield interlocking the Romans make a tortoise, most often square, but sometimes rounded or oblong, whatever is convenient. Everything is thus accurately protected so that projectiles are received just as on a roof. Even wagon stones do not break the interlocking; rather, rolling off, they fall to the ground
>
> (Arrian, *Tactica* 11.2–6).[25]

Here, Arrian treats the interlocking (σύγκλεισις) of shields in detail and in characteristic fashion by adding in Saurmatians and Skythians, as well as contemporary Roman legionary contexts. Notice in particular Arrian's use of tense: χρὴ τάττειν, ποιοῦνται, διαλύειν are all present tense. Bosworth has demonstrated that Arrian only uses the present tense when he wishes to insert his own eyewitness information.[26] Notice also Arrian's use of πύκνωσις 'density', 'denseness', when referring to the quality of the maneuver. While Asklepiodotos (*Tact.* 4.1, 3) and Aelian (*Tact.* 11.3) use πύκνωσις in exactly the same way,[27] Arrian goes farther and adds a digression about the Roman *testudo*, χελών in Greek. In doing this, Arrian seems to expand on his source's narrative in order to offer the reader a practical image for the effectiveness of interlocking shields (συνασπισμός). Here, he also introduces uniquely new vocabulary to the *Tactica*, σύγκλεισις 'dense interlocking', which seemingly can protect an army from anything, even stones so large they need to be transported by

---

23 Cf. Bosworth 1977, 242–4.

24 For the Arrian's *Tactica* see Kiechle 1964, 87–129; Stadter 1978, 117–28; Wheeler 1978, 351–65; Devine 1994, 312–337.

25 εἰ αὐτῇ τῇ (2.) πυκνότητι καὶ τῇ ῥύμῃ τοὺς πολεμίους ἐξῶσαι δέοι ... ἢ αὖ εἰ δέοι τοὺς ἐπελαύνοντας ἀποκρούσασθαι, καθάπερ πρὸς τοὺς Σαυρομάτας τε καὶ (3.) τοὺς Σκύθας χρὴ τάττειν. καὶ ἔστι πύκνωσις μὲν ἡ ἐκ τοῦ ἀραιοτέρου ἐς τὸ πυκνότερον συναγωγὴ κατὰ παραστάτην τε καὶ ἐπιστάτην, ὅπερ ἔστι κατὰ μῆκός τε καὶ (4.) βάθος· συνασπισμὸς δὲ ἐπὰν εἰς τοσόνδε πυκνώσῃς τὴν φάλαγγα ὡς διὰ τὴν συνέχειαν μηδὲ κλίσιν τὴν ἐφ' ἑκάτερα ἔτ' ἐγχωρεῖν τὴν τάξιν. καὶ ἀπὸ τοῦδε τοῦ συνασπισμοῦ τὴν χελώνην Ῥωμαῖοι ποιοῦνται, τὸ πολὺ μὲν τετράγωνον, ἔστιν δὲ ὅπου καὶ στρογγύλην ἢ ἑτερομήκη (5.) ἢ ὅπως ἂν προχωρῇ. οἱ μὲν ἐν κύκλῳ τοῦ πλινθίου ἢ τοῦ κύκλου ἑστηκότες τοὺς θυρεοὺς προβέβληνται πρὸ σφῶν, οἱ δ' ἐφεστηκότες αὐτοῖς ὑπὲρ τῶν κεφαλῶν ἄλλος ὑπὲρ τοῦ ἄλλου ὑπεραιωρήσας προβάλλεται. (6.) καὶ τὸ πᾶν οὕτω ἀκριβῶς φράττεται, ὥστε καὶ ἀκοντιστὰς ἄνωθεν καθάπερ ἐπὶ στέγης διαθέοντας δέχεσθαι, καὶ λίθους ἁμαξιαίους μὴ διαλύειν τὴν σύγκλεισιν, ἀλλὰ κατακυλιομένους τῇ ῥύμῃ ὑπερπίπτειν εἰς τὸ δάπεδον.

26 Bosworth 1994, 258. Indeed, section 11 is the only passage where the present tense is used. The rest of the book up to section 33 is clearly, as Bosworth, 1994, 258, puts it, "an antiquarian exercise," conducted in the past tenses.

27 See n. 29, below for a comparison of Arrian's *Tactica* 11 and Aelian's *Tactica* 11.

wagon (λίθους ἁμαξιαίους).[28] Because of *Anabasis* 1.1.7–10, one is tempted to read a great deal into λίθους ἁμαξιαίους, and while doing so might be interesting it is not necessary for the present argument. It is necessary, however, to underscore the fact that Arrian has taken a mundane description of interlocking of shields – συνασπισμός in his source as we see from Asklepiodotos and Aelian – and has embellished and refined the presentation, going so far as to add new vocabulary, σύγκλεισις. Significantly, the only other times Arrian uses σύγκλεισις is when describing his own military experiences against the Alans and Alexander's actions against the Autonomous Thracians.[29]

At this point, it is important to bring the strands of the argument together. Arrian's *Tactica* has provided a window into Arrian's method: He seems to begin a section of his works by paraphrasing from his Hellenistic source, then he seems to embellish the narrative from his own military experience.[30] Returning to *Anabasis* 1.1 (see text above), I suggest we view Alexander's battle in Thrace in this way, understanding section 7 as a paraphrase from the original source, most likely Ptolemy, as Bosworth (1980, 51) argues, and sections 8–10 as Arrian's exegesis of his original source, embellished with his own experience.[31] The similarities in word choice and subject with *Acies contra Alanos* 26 and even *Tactica* 11.4–6 suggest Arrian's own hand at work here. Thus, it seems clear that Arrian chose to embellish Alexander's encounter with the Autonomous Thracians and in so doing has confounded generations seeking to understand Alexander's military. But we need not be permanently confounded, since the outline of events seem plain enough: Alexander used interlocked shields, συνασπισμός, to fight the Autonomous Thracians, probably much as Heckel has reconstructed, with the hypaspists forming the bulk of the shield wall (2004, 194). Beyond that, much of the passage, especially Alexander's thought processes and prediction of how events would ultimately play out (*Anab.* 1.1.8 and 10) seems to be Arrian's own interpolation. But should we blame Arrian for being creative? We forget that these ancient historiographers were themselves literary craftsmen, not merely slavish

---

[28] Askl. 4.1 (1.) Τοῦτον δὴ τὸν τρόπον ἐξομοιωθέντων τῷ ὅλῳ τῶν μορίων ἑξῆς ἂν εἴη ῥητέον περὶ διαστημάτωνκατά τε μῆκος καὶ βάθος τριττὰ γὰρ ἐξηύρηται πρὸς τὰς τῶν πολεμίων χρείας, τό τε ἀραιότατον, καθ' ὃ ἀλλήλων ἀπέχουσι κατά τε μῆκος καὶ βάθος ἕκαστοι πήχεις τέσσαρας, καὶ τὸ πυκνότατον, καθ' ὃ συνησπικὼς ἕκαστος ἀπὸ τῶν ἄλλων πανταχόθεν διέστηκεν πηχυαῖον διάστημα, τό τε μέσον, ὃ καὶ πύκνωσιν ἐπονομάζουσιν, ᾧ διεστήκασι πανταχόθεν δύο πήχεις ἀπ' ἀλλήλων.

[29] *Acies contra Alanos* 26 and *Anabasis* 1.1.6–9, respectively. Cf *Anab.* 5.17.7.

[30] Both Arrian and Aelian begin their sections on interlocking shields with the same vocabulary and syntax, but then where Aelian moves on to the next subject, Arrian embellishes with his own experiences: Arrian *Tact.* 11.3–4. ἔστι πύκνωσις μὲν ἡ ἐκ τοῦ ἀραιοτέρου ἐς τὸ πυκνότερον συναγωγὴ κατὰ παραστάτην τε καὶ ἐπιστάτην, ὅπερ ἔστι κατὰ μῆκός τε καὶ (4.) βάθος· συνασπισμὸς δὲ ἐπὰν εἰς τοσόνδε πυκνώσῃς τὴν φάλαγγα ὡς διὰ τὴν συνέχειαν μηδὲ κλίσιν τὴν ἐφ' ἑκάτερα ἔτ' ἐγχωρεῖν τὴν τάξιν. καὶ ἀπὸ τοῦδε τοῦ συνασπισμοῦ τὴν χελώνην Ῥωμαῖοι ποιοῦνται, τὸ πολὺ μὲν τετράγωνον, ἔστιν δὲ ὅπου καὶ στρογγύλην ἢ ἑτερομήκη (5.) ἢ ὅπως ἂν προχωρῇ. But Aelian *Tact.* 11.3–4. ἔστι δὲ πύκνωσις, ὅταν ἐκ τῶν ἀραιοτέρων διαστημάτων ἐλάσσονα τὰ διαστήματα ποιήσας πυκνώσῃς κατὰ παραστάτην καὶ ἐπιστάτην, τοῦτ' ἔστι κατὰ μῆκος καὶ κατὰ βάθος, οὕτως μέντοι, ὥστε ἔτι δέχεσθαι μεταβολήν. (4.) συνασπισμὸς δέ ἐστιν, ὅταν τῆς προειρημένης πυκνώσεως ἔτι μᾶλλον ἡ φάλαγξ πυκνωθῇ κατὰ παραστάτην καὶ ἐπιστάτην, ὥστε διὰ τὴν συνέχειαν τοῦ στρατοῦ μὴ χωρεῖν κλίσιν μήτε ἐπὶ τὰ δεξιά, μήτε ἐπὶ τὰ εὐώνυμα.

[31] Cf. Bosworth 1980, 51, who argues that "the entire campaign narrative is taken directly from Ptolemy, who is avowedly Arrian's principle source."

copiers of Hellenistic originals. We so desperately want to read Ptolemy's original text that we gloss over the fact that Arrian, however much he is indebted to Ptolemy's history, is not simply a conduit for Ptolemy, but a stylist and historian in his own right. Indeed that creative element seems to be the difference between historiographers who also happen to write tactical manuals, like Arrian, and cataloguers of tactics and collectors of facts like Asklepiodotos, Aelian and Polyainos.

Bibliography

Ashley, J. R. (1998) *The Macedonian Empire: The Era of Warfare Under Philip II and Alexander the Great, 359–323 BC.* Jefferson, NC.

Bosworth, A. B. (1977) Arrian and the Alani, *Harvard Studies in Classical Philology* 81, 217–55.

— (1980) *A Historical Commentary on Arrian's History of Alexander. Vol I.* Oxford.

— (1988) *Conquest and Empire.* Cambridge.

— (1994) Arrian and Rome: the Minor Works, *Aufitieg und Niedergang der romischen Welt* 2.34.1, 226–275.

Bloedow, E. F. (1996) On 'Wagons' and 'Shields': Alexander's Crossing of Mount Haemus in 335 BC, *Ancient History Bulletin* 10, 110–130.

Brunt, P. A. (1976) *Arrian: Anabasis of Alexander, Books I–IV (Loeb Classical Library No. 236).* Cambridge, MA.

Buraselis, K. (1995) The Roman World of Polyaenos. Aspects of a Macedonian career between past and provincial present, Ἀρχαιογνωσία 8, 121–140.

Devine, A. M. (1994) Arrian's *Tactica*," *Aufitieg und Niedergang der romischen Welt* 2.34.1, 312–337.

DeVoto, J. (1993) *Flavius Arrianus. Techne Tactica and Extaxis kata Alanos.* Chicago.

Engels, J. (2006) *Philipp II. und Alexander der Große.* Darmstadt.

Fuller, J. F. C. (1960) *The Generalship of Alexander the Great.* Brunswick, NJ.

Green, P. (1970) *Alexander of Macedon.* Harmondsworth.

Hammond, N. G. L. (1980a) Some Passages in Arrian concerning Alexander, *Classical Quarterly* 30, 455–76.

— (1980b) Training in the use of a sarissa and its effect in battle, 359–333 BC, *Antichthon* 14, 53–63.

— (1996) Some Passages in Polyaenus *Stratagems* concerning Alexander, *Greek Roman and Byzantine Studies* 37.1, 23–53.

Heckel, W. (2005) Synaspismos, Sarissas and Thracian Wagons, *Acta Classica* 48, 189–194.

— (2008) *The Conquests of Alexander the Great.* Cambridge.

Howe, T. and S. Müller (2012) Mission Accomplished: Alexander at the Hyphasis, *Ancient History Bulletin* 26, 21–38.

Kiechle, F. (1964) Die 'Taktik' des Flavius Arrianus, *Bericht der römisch-germanischen Kommission* 45, 87–129.

Krentz, P. and E. L. Wheeler (1994) *Polyaenus: Stratagems of War, Books I–V.* Chicago.

Lane Fox, R. (1974) *Alexander the Great.* New York.

Lonsdale, D. J. (2004) *Alexander the Great, Killer of Men.* New York.

Melber, J. (1885) Über die Quellen und den Wert der Strategemensammlung Polyäns, *Jahrbücher für classische Philologie (NJPhP) Suppl.* 14, 418–688.

Roos, A. G. and G. Wirth (1967) *Flavii Arriani quae exstant omnia.* Leipzig.

Seibert, J. (1972) *Alexander der Große.* Darmstadt.

Stadter, P. A. (1978) The Ars Tactica of Arrian: tradition and originality, *Classical Philology* 73, 117–28.

— (1980) *Arrian of Nicomedia.* Chapel Hill.

Syme, R. (1982) The Career of Arrian, *Harvard Studies in Classical Philology* 86, 181–211.

Wheeler, E. L. (1978) The Occasion of Arrian's Tactica, *Greek Roman and Byzantine Studies* 19, 351–65.

— (1979) The Legion as Phalanx, *Chiron* 9, 303–18.

Worthington, I. (2004) *Alexander the Great: Man and God.* London.

COUNTER-INSURGENCY:
THE LESSON OF ALEXANDER THE GREAT

Edward M. Anson[1]

During Alexander the Great's conquest of what had been the Persian Empire, which took him from Greece to Egypt to the Punjab and back to Babylon, he only endured one serious insurrection against his once established authority.[2] This paper will examine his strategies for dealing with conquered populations and his methods for managing his one great insurgency. Briefly these were the retention of the basic political, cultural, and religious institutions of the acquired lands, establishing close bonds with local elites, and crushing with the utmost brutality any resistance to his authority.

Part of understanding Alexander's success in conquering and holding such a vast empire is to realize that Alexander's ultimate goal was personal glory achieved, as in the case of his ancestor Achilles and his father Philip, through warfare. While he became a catalyst for change and the progenitor of what became the Hellenistic Age, such a transformation was not his intention. He was not out to change the world, he was out to conquer it. His leadership was such that after thousands of miles of marching across every conceivable landscape and environment, battling so many different nations, it took the Indian monsoon finally to sap the army's will to continue. On the Beas in what is today north-western Pakistan, the army, in a sense, went on strike (Faure 1982, 155).[3] This time Alexander's entreaties and promises were met with silence and even he knew the march east was over.[4] After his return to Babylon, he began preparations for new conquests in the West all the way to the Pillars of Heracles (Diod. 18.4.2–4).[5]

---

[1] I have known Waldemar for more than thirty years. He has been a great friend and colleague, and I certainly wish him the best in retirement. His contributions to the profession are well known to all, so I will not go into great detail, only to say that of the books that I keep always near to hand while doing my research and writing, his make up half. Congratulations on a great career and may it continue for a long time.

[2] There was the brief insurrection by the satrap of Areia, Satibarzanes, but this was quickly ended (Diod. 17.78.2; Curt. 6.6.22–3).

[3] This incident is often called a 'mutiny', but the use of the term has long been questioned (Carney 1996, 19–44; Brice, this volume). No order to advance was ever given, so no order was ever refused.

[4] It has been argued that Alexander staged the mutiny that led to his withdrawal from the Indian campaign (Spann 1999, 62–74; Heckel 2003, 147–74; Howe and Müller 2012, 21–38), but the arguments are unconvincing (see Anson forthcoming 2014).

[5] While the authenticity of these 'last plans' has been questioned, and there may be some question about

Moreover, he was not a Macedonian nationalist, as his father had been (Anson 2013, 185–6), but conceived of an empire centered in Asia and in the Asian metropolis of Babylon (Str. 15.3.9–10; cf. Diod. 17.108.4), nor did he regard Hellenic civilization as the only civilization worthy of emulation, or Greeks, as the only truly civilized people. He was not, consequently, like so many of his Greek and Macedonian colleagues, and his teacher Aristotle (*Pol.* 1255a3, 1327b 23–28, 1333b37), a racist. While his propaganda to the Greek community claimed that he had come to liberate the Greeks of Asia from Persian rule and to wreak revenge on the Persians for their interference in Greek affairs going all the way back to the sixth century (Diod. 17.24.1), this was a piece of propaganda borrowed from his father's original justification for the expedition, and, as with Philip, was designed to encourage the Greeks to support him (see Squillace 2004, 60–71). By the same token he was not a starry-eyed idealist aiming in the words of one of the great Alexander scholars of the past century, W. W. Tarn, at creating a brotherhood of all humanity (1958, 27; 1950, 399–449). He was Alexander and all others were hence inferior and his subjects. It is within this context that Alexander's operations in Asia and northeast Africa must be understood.

One result of his pursuit of glory was his desire not to spend time on administration, but to move to the next arena as quickly as possible. Alexander typically left the basic governments he found in place, on occasion even leaving the same officials in charge. That he was in a hurry did not obfuscate his shrewdness. When he 'liberated' Greek cities from Persian rule, he recognized the traditional Greek city-state governments of voting assemblies, but whereas the Persians had favored oligarchies, Alexander created democracies (*e.g.* Tod, II, 192). The Greek world had been convulsed for centuries by the struggle between oligarchs and democrats within virtually every Greek community. By favoring democracy in Asia, the Macedonian autocrat, created loyal allies in the 'freed' cities; the democrats had been 'oppressed' by the Persian supported oligarchies. In mainland Greece, where democratic city-states, such as Athens, had most often opposed the Macedonians, Alexander favored oligarchies or even tyrannies. However, 'liberation' of the Greek cities of Asia did not mean sovereignty (Badian 1965, 167; Hatzopoulos 1996, 1, 66–7, 69); they only enjoyed the same limited autonomy that had existed under the Persians. Certain communities were required to accept garrisons and all were subject to the whims of Alexander.[6]

With respect to non-Greeks, he continued the basic Persian government where that was in effect, even calling the districts after the Persian terms satrapies and the governors, most often, satraps. In Egypt, he followed Egyptian practice and became pharaoh,[7] leaving in place the traditional system of local governors (nomarchs), apparently without replacing

---

the specifics of such ambitions, the evidence would indicate that Alexander had no intention of stopping his pursuit of further conquest (see Bosworth 1988B, 185–212).

[6] These cities were free in their internal affairs only and even that was subject to Alexander's dictates (Bickerman 1934, 346–7).

[7] While there is a debate over whether Alexander ever underwent an official coronation ceremony (see in particular Burstein 1991, 139–145), he was clearly recognized as pharaoh as shown by inscriptions discovered in Luxor in Thebes. Here Alexander is described as 'Horus', 'the beloved of Ammon', but most typically as the 'son of Amon-Ra' or the 'son of Ra' (Abdullah el-Rasiq 1984; Lepsius 1972–73, III, pls 32, 82–3; IV, pls 3–5).

any of the current holders of those positions (Arr. *Anab.* 3.5.4; Curt. 4.7.5). However, the military aspect was kept in the hands of members of Alexander's military entourage (Briant 1982, 75). Belacrus and Peucestas were given supreme military command in Egypt, and the cities of Memphis and Pelusium received independent garrisons under Macedonian commanders (Arr. *Anab.* 3.5.5).

It has been argued that Alexander diverged from Persian practice by dividing control of civil, military, and financial functions among different, autonomous officials, whereas Persian satraps possessed virtual control of all civil and military functions in their satrapies (Cook 1983, 85, 173–5; cf. Briant 2002, 66–7). The evidence, however, suggests that these Persian royal officials may have had more independence than is commonly recognized and that Alexander's changes may not have been as dramatic as some have thought. Xenophon, in his description of Persian administration (*Oec.* 4.9; *Cyr.* 8.6.1), distinguished three sets of officials in charge respectively of administration, finance, and the military, with garrison commanders being specially mentioned as separate from the satraps and directly under the authority of the king. When Alexander was approaching Babylon in 331, the Persian citadel commander Bagophanes, 'not to be outdone' by the satrap of Babylonia in showing his respects to Alexander, had flowers and garlands spread on the road and personally brought the Macedonian king many gifts (Curt. 5.1.20–1). In Persepolis, the garrison commander and the 'guardian of the royal moneys' both refused to aid the satrap of Persis, Ariobarzanes, and surrendered to Alexander (Curt. 5.4.33–4, 5.2; cf. Arr. *Anab.* 3.16.2). These incidents suggest that these separate commanders may have enjoyed more independence than is generally assumed, thus making Alexander's divisions of authority simply another adoption of Persian practice. An example of Alexander's policy is seen in the case of Lydia. Alexander assigned the satrapy to Asander, while Pausanias was left in charge of the citadel of Sardis with a garrison, and Nicias was to supervise the finances and the collection of tribute; all three were theoretically independent of one another (Arr. *Anab.* 1.17.7–8).[8] This practice of divided responsibilities is also found in the satrapy of Persis, the Persian heartland, where the twin capitals of Persepolis and Susa were garrisoned under commanders whose authority was separate from that of the satrap (Arr. *Anab.* 3.16.9; Curt. 5.2.16, 6.11).

Initially most governors were Greeks and Macedonians, but later prominent Persians and others were also given these responsibilities (Arr. *Anab.* 3.16.9, 20.3). In Caria in southeastern Asia Minor, Ada, the one-time native ruler of Caria, had been turned out of office by her brother Pixodarus, but had remained in control of the fortress of Alinda.[9] On Alexander's approach, she immediately surrendered the fortress to him and adopted him as her son (Arr. *Anab.* 1.23.7–8). She was then given "the rule of the whole country." In Phoenicia, the principal cities had been ruled by their own line of kings, but subject to Persian oversight. Alexander continued the institution of local monarchy in these cities (Arr. *Anab.* 2.13.7–8; Curt. 4.1.16–26; Diod. 17.47; Just. 11.10.7–9; Grainger 1991, 36–8, 59). While these kings were, then, reconfirmed in the roles they had enjoyed during Persian administration, their authority was curtailed by the presence in some fashion of Macedonian and Greek

---

[8]   On the origin and status of these individuals, see Heckel 2006, 56–7, 179, 193.
[9]   For a study of the role of women in Carian rule, see Carney 2005, 65–91.

authorities and troops. In the case of Caria, the Macedonian Ptolemaeus had independent authority over the chief city of Halicarnassus with a garrison of 3200 (Arr. *Anab.* 1.23.6), and in Phoenicia, while all but Tyre retained their traditional form of government without the imposition of garrisons, rulers on occasion were replaced, and in the case of Tyre, the area was placed under Macedonian authority and garrisoned. The city of Sidon remained a monarchy, but a new king was chosen (Curt. 4.1.16–26; Diod. 17.47.1; Just. 11.10.7–9), while with respect to Tyre Alexander left Philotas to guard the area about the city (Curt. 4.5.9). Even though the other Phoenician cities were left without garrisons or Macedonian officials, all were under the control of Macedonian satraps for the region (Bosworth 1974, 53–6), and Coeranus of Beroea was in charge of the collection of the tribute of Phoenicia (Arr. *Anab.* 3.6.4). However, in India, Porus, a defeated monarch, was confirmed as king of his dominions and left without any Macedonian presence (Arr. *Anab.* 5.19.2–3).

In Babylonia, the first Persian to be appointed satrap was Mazaeus, but Apollodorous was general, Asclepiodorus collected the taxes (Arr. *Anab.* 3.16.4–5), and Agathon with 1000 troops commanded the citadel of Babylon (Curt. 5.1.43). The latter three were likely all Macedonians.[10] Once Alexander left Babylon and headed east into lands with sizable Persian and Persian-related populations, apparently the newly appointed satraps were given wider authority with control over finance, although treasuries and garrisons still retained independent commanders. One reason offered for the lack of separate financial officials in the East is connected with the presence of Persian administrators. Paying taxes is always burdensome, but paying it to 'foreign' invaders might be seen as too much for a former imperial people. Consequently, Alexander, ever looking for ways to accomplish his goals with as little effort as possible, only used independent financial officials in the Greek and Phoenician West where the inhabitants were used to paying their taxes to distant rulers (Griffith 1964, 38).

Much of Alexander's success was tied to establishing close bonds with local elites within the non-Greek populations. As Pierre Briant (2002, 870) relates, "Alexander was able to create the conditions for a balance between his own ambition and the [indigenous] nobility's desire not to perish in the turmoil." In general, Alexander was adept at accommodating the previous elites by maintaining their economic and political status (Briant 2002, 842–4, 1046–60). He also readily responded to acts of brutality or malfeasance by his officials or soldiers. It was on account of his desire to ensure different peoples were content with his rule that Alexander initiated what has been called his 'reign of terror' when he returned from India not the king's fear of rebellion and assassination (as Badian 1961, 21–4).[11] The King exhibited anger at the extensive abuses of those he had trusted, and, after the rebellion in Bactria and the disappointment of the Hyphasis, he was far less forgiving than in the past, but fear is not apparent. He was heading west and these areas needed to remain pacified. This was especially the case now that Alexander had begun to change the very face of his army.

---

[10] Asclepiodorus may have been a Greek (See Heckel 2006, 58).

[11] In 324, after returning from his journey down the Indus and his crossing of the Gedrosian desert, he executed two of his Macedonian generals stationed in Media for crimes against the populace (Arr. *Anab.* 6.27.4). Additionally, 600 common soldiers were also condemned for participating in these crimes.

As part of his plan of amalgamation, Alexander's court ceremony had acquired many Persian touches, such as wearing a diadem and Median costume (Arr. *Anab.* 4.7.4, 9.9; Curt. 6.6.4–8; Diod. 17.77.5; Just. 12.3.8; Plut. *Alex.* 45.1–2). In the latter stages of his campaign, he began to incorporate Persians and other Asians extensively into his army. In Susa he was joined by 30,000 Iranian young men, the '*Epigoni*', who at Alexander's command had been taught Greek and trained in Macedonian warfare (Arr. *Anab.* 7.6.1; Curt. 8.5.1; Diod. 17.108.1–2; Plut. *Alex.* 47.3, 71.1). Also present in Babylon at the time of Alexander's death were a force of 20,000 Persian infantry and units of Cossaeans and Tapurians (Arr. *Anab.* 7.23.1). These soldiers retained their traditional arms and were used to complement the Macedonian and Iranian phalanxes (Arr. *Anab.* 7.23.3–4). Earlier in the year, at Opis, the king had created Persian units bearing Macedonian titles and Macedonian equipment (Arr. *Anab.* 7.11.3; Diod. 17.110.1–2; Just. 12.12.3–4). It was also at Opis that Alexander had dismissed roughly 10,000 of his Macedonian veterans (Arr. *Anab.* 7.12.1; Diod. 17.109.2; 18.4.1), retaining only 2000 cavalry and 13,000 infantry (Curt. 10.2.8).[12] While Antipater was to bring new Macedonian recruits to Asia as replacements for those departing, at the time of Alexander's death the Macedonian regent and his forces were still in their homeland (Arr. *Anab.* 7.12.4; Just. 12.12.9). As Brian Bosworth (1988, 161) has noted, the army in Babylon was now primarily Asiatic. These actions are at the heart of Tarn's claim that Alexander wished to create an amalgamation of races. The truth is much closer to Bosworth's assertion that Alexander sought to become the common employer and master of all (Bosworth 1988, 273). The only union of Europe and Asia was to be universal allegiance to Alexander.

Alexander's actions with respect to conquered peoples, often referred to in recent military parlance as 'the Inner Front', has recently been compared to the American 'Operation Iraqi Freedom' during the command of General David Petraeus (Smith 2007). Alexander was successful in securing his inner front, or what J. F. C. Fuller (1960, 267) called "the goodwill of the civil[ian] population," by using many of the techniques currently espoused in the current U.S. Army and Marine Corps *Counterinsurgency Field Manual* (United States Department of the Army and the United States Marine Corps 2007), and most often associated with General Petraeus (Smith 2007). These include 'stability operations'; restoring security and infrastructure; the incorporation of local leaders;[13] recognizing and supporting local institutions; and establishing the legitimacy of the new order (Petraeus 2006, 46–53). As part of his attempt to win the loyalty of the conquered, Alexander, almost without fail, recognized local cultural and religious traditions, practicing religious toleration throughout his dominions (so Fredricksmeyer 2003, 260). He honored the Egyptian and Babylonian gods (Arr. *Anab.* 3.1.4, 16.3–4). Indeed, just as among the Greek communities in Asia, so in many other areas of the former Persian Empire, such as Egypt and Babylonia, Alexander was viewed as a liberator and a respecter of native deities (Arr. *Anab.* 3.1.2, 16.3–4; Curt. 4.7.1–4; 5.1.19). Polybius (5.10.8) comments, "when [Alexander] crossed into Asia to take

---

[12] Hammond estimates the number at less than 10,000 (1980, 245), and Bosworth (1988, 267) suggests maybe as few as 8000.

[13] In the words of General Petraeus, "ultimate success depends upon local leaders" and "increasing the number of stakeholders is critical to success" (Petraeus 2006, 46, 48, 52).

vengeance on the Persians the impious outrages which they had inflicted on the Greeks, he did his best to exact the full penalty from men, but refrained from injuring places dedicated to the gods; though it was in precisely such that the injuries of the Persians in Greece had been most conspicuous." When Alexander left Babylon he was accompanied by a number of Babylonian priests who were present on the expedition to perform various rites (Plut. *Alex.* 57.4). His entourage also included Egyptian astrologers (Curt. 4.10.4).

While it is claimed that Alexander repressed Persian Zoroastrianism (Shahbazi 2003, 5–38), the evidence comes from late sources in the Sassanid period, and is contested (Boyce and Grenet 1991, 3–17).[14] Persian priests are associated with Alexander's reconciliation banquet at Opis (Arr. *Anab.* 7.11.8), and Darius' wife was buried according to 'Persian custom' (Curt. 3.12.13; 4.10.23). Once in Persia itself, where liberation could not be used as a propaganda tool with the local population, Alexander included Persians in his personal entourage, began to adopt Persian dress, court procedure, advisors, and, as noted above, increasingly incorporated oriental units into his ever growing army and administration (Carney 1996, 19–44; Anson 2004, 355–7). He would even marry three eastern princesses, two of whom were Persian (Plut. *Alex.* 47.7–8; Diod. 17.107.6; Arr. *Anab.* 7.4.4),[15] and oversee the mixed marriages of a wide assortment of officers and soldiers (Arr. *Anab.* 7.4.4–8). These marriages were performed according to Persian ceremony and more than 10,000 such unions were solemnized (Arr. *Anab.* 7.4.7–8).

The only substantive evidence for Alexander's suppression of Zoroastrianism found in our admittedly western sources comes from his burning of the palace in Persepolis (Arr. *Anab.* 3.18.12; Diod. 17.70, 72.6; Curt. 5.6.1–8; Str. 15.3.6). The later Sassanid claims that he killed magi and other members of the intelligentsia likely refer to the actual period of conquest itself, not to its aftermath, although in later tradition Alexander is called 'the accursed' (Boyce 1979, 78). Many of these died in the battles and many more in the atrocities so often connected to conquest, but these deaths are not related to any attempt to eradicate the religion. With respect to the burning of the palace, it is very doubtful that Alexander's intent in the destruction had anything whatsoever to do with religion (as Friedricksmeyer 2000, 144–9). The burning was a deliberate act designed to end his war of revenge and to begin his new rule as 'Lord of Asia' (Arr. *Anab.* 3.18.12; Str. 15.3.6; Anson 2013, 153–8). Persepolis was "the city from which troops without number had poured forth, from which first Darius and then Xerxes had waged an unholy war on Europe" (Curt. 5.6.1), and it was Persepolis alone of the Persian capitals that suffered the brutality of a sack by Alexander's army (Curt. 5.6.1–8; Diod. 17.70), which was followed subsequently by the burning of part of the palace. The other claimed example of religious oppression has more substance. In India in 325, Alexander savagely repressed the Brahmans, but this was prompted by their resistance to his authority (Arr. *Anab.* 6.7.4–6, 16, 5; Diod. 17.102.6–7; see Bosworth1996, 94–7).

Throughout his military operations, Alexander also followed a policy of rewarding those who surrendered quickly and punishing severely those who resisted. The latter is a policy

---

[14] Much of the opposition to Macedonian rule occurred during the Seleucid Empire (Sherwin-White and Kuhrt 1993, 29–30).

[15] On the polygamy of Macedonian kings, see Greenwalt 1989, 19–45.

decried by the proponents of the new counter-insurgency warfare. "The moral purpose of combat operations is to secure peace" (United States Department of the Army and the United States Marine Corps 2007, 246), and ethical standards must be maintained to achieve success (United States Department of the Army and the United States Marine Corps 2007, 237–8). This last proposition has been challenged. One modern commentator refers to intimidation and terror as 'proven methods' to defeat insurgents (Luttwak 2007, 40).[16] It would appear that Alexander would have agreed. The classic example of Alexander's policy was his destruction of the rebellious city of Thebes, one of the great cities of Hellenic civilization. After being taken by assault the city itself was destroyed, except for the temples and the house of a noted poet; the survivors were sold into slavery (Arr. *Anab.* 1.7.4–8.4).[17] The brutality was decried by most Greeks, but Alexander was able to proceed to Asia without further trouble.[18] Only after his death became widely known did a widespread rebellion against Macedonian hegemony break out in the Greek peninsula.[19] This brutality was again demonstrated in the later sieges of Tyre (Arr. *Anab.* 2.24.3–6; Curt. 4.4.13–17) and Gaza (Arr. *Anab.* 2.27.7; Curt. 4.6.26–30). In both cases after the conclusion of difficult sieges the survivors were dealt with brutally. When the Uxian tribesmen, who controlled the mountainous passage between the twin Persian capitals of Susa and Persepolis, demanded that Alexander pay them for the right to cross their lands, a payment routinely made by the Persians, Alexander attacked them. So brutal and persistent was this assault that in the end, the Uxians agreed to pay a yearly tribute to Alexander for the right to retain their lands (Arr. *Anab.* 3.17.1–6). Similarly, Alexander attacked the recalcitrant Cossaeans and forced their submission (Arr. *Anab.* 7.15.2–3; Diod. 17.111.4–6; Plut. *Alex.* 72.4). One of his most brutal attacks on those who failed to submit occurred against the Malli during his voyage down the Indus (Bosworth 1997, 28, 73–4, 136–41). In this slaughter no one was spared including women and children (Arr. *Anab.* 6.11.1; Curt. 9.5.19–20; Diod. 17.99.4). Bosworth (1996, 142) correctly calls this both conquest and deterrence through terror.

The last general aspect of Alexander's campaign was his preference for the conquest of 'civilized' lands. Alexander made demonstrations against tribal nomadic groups, but seldom did he attempt to subject them to his authority through formal annexation. Even though early in his reign he led an expedition against the tribes living across the Danube, a natural barrier, he did not acquire any territory (Arr. *Anab.* 1.3.1–4.6). Likewise, Alexander crossed the Tanais (Jaxartes) and attacked the Scythians who lived north of the river purely as a demonstration of his power (Arr. *Anab.* 4.4.4–5.1; Curt. 7.9), but he did not acquire any territory here either. The results of both of these expeditions were alliances and some submissions only (Curt. 7.9.17–19), but no magistrates were assigned, nor garrisons placed. With respect to the Scythians across the Tanais, Alexander established on the southern side of the river a city, Alexandria Eschate, in the province of Sogdiana, primarily to

---

[16]   Edward Luttwak is senior fellow in the Center for Strategic and International Studies, Washington, DC.

[17]   On the destruction and Alexander's intent, see Worthington 2003, 65–86.

[18]   Greece remained at peace until 329, when the Spartans led a revolt against Macedonian hegemony and were crushed by Alexander's regent, Antipater (Diod. 17.62.6–63.3; Curt. 6.1.1–21). It should be noted that the Spartans had never been brought under the control of either Macedonia or the League of Corinth.

[19]   It does appear that a war was likely even prior to Alexander's death, but his death did trigger its start (Ashton 1983, 47–63).

protect the more settled region south of the river from nomadic marauders (Arr. *Anab.* 4.1.3, 4.1; Curt. 7.6.13; Holt 1988, 30–2, 55–9). Even though Arrian (*Anab.* 4.1.3) lists one of the reasons for the founding of this city on the Tanais as being "well placed for a future invasion of Scythia," no such expedition was ever carried out or formally planned. In the cases of the Cossaeans and Uxians, Alexander did conquer these tribal areas (Arr. *Anab.* 3.17; 7.15.2–3; Diod. 17.111.4–6; Plut. *Alex.* 72.3), but these involved different circumstances. These mountain peoples controlled the lands and the communication routes between Persis and Media, and Susa and Persepolis, respectively. Much of Alexander's hesitancy with respect to tribal lands may have been the difficulty in pursuing peoples who were primarily nomads. To make certain that they would be permanently pacified would entail a major transformation of their society into one of settled agriculture. Alexander was not interested in such long-term projects. With the exception of his planned invasion of India, Alexander also avoided crossing into areas outside the boundaries of the Persian Empire (Heckel 2003, 147–74; Howe and Müller 2012, 26–31). India itself, however, was known to Alexander as a populous and highly settled land (Arr. *Anab.* 5.25.1). With its conquest, Alexander could claim, indeed, to have conquered the civilized world of which he then knew, at least in the East.

With the Asiatic Greeks, with the Egyptians, and with the conquered peoples of west Asia and the Persian heartland, Alexander experienced few problems.[20] The one great exception occurred in the satrapies of Bactria and Sogdiana, the former roughly corresponding to the territory of modern Afghanistan, the latter, mostly the modern country of Uzbekistan, but also including part of Tajikistan. These regions, while possessed of cities, also included wide areas of tribal pastoral societies. This invasion was one of the few exceptions to Alexander's avoidance of tribal areas, but then Bactria and Sogdiana were part of the Persian Empire, now Alexander's empire, and, a Bactrian, Bessus, had murdered Darius, the previous Persian king, and was gathering forces in Bactria, proclaiming himself Artaxerxes V, the true king of Persia (Curt. 6.6.13; Diod. 17.74.2). Finally, these lands were between Persia and Alexander's goal, India. Alexander, therefore, had to acquire and pacify this territory to travel on.

In 329, when Alexander first crossed the Hindu Kush into Bactria, he encountered little resistance. Bessus had been unable to unite the Bactrian nobility behind his authority. The Bactrian cavalry abandoned him as Alexander approached, and Alexander was able to enter the satrapal capital, Bactra, without striking a blow (Arr. *Anab.* 3.28.8–29.7; Curt. 7.4.20–22, 32–40, 5.1–18). In fact, Bessus was surrendered to Alexander by his former supporters (Arr. *Anab.* 3.30. 3–5; Curt. 7.5.19–26). Earlier, Alexander had proclaimed that his quarrel was with Bessus and rewarded all those who had surrendered the self-proclaimed King of Kings. Alexander now left what he assumed was a pacified province and proceeded onto India. As Brian Bosworth (1988, 107) has noted, the conquest "had been deceptively easy."

---

[20] There were minor revolts that did break out in India, but these were quickly suppressed (Diod. 17.105.8; Arr. *Anab.* 6.27.1; Curt. 9.10.19), and two Persian noblemen, who had been fomenting revolt, were captured without any consequences (Curt. 9.10.19; Arr. *Anab.* 6.27.3). These incidents took place after Alexander had traveled on to India, had sailed down the Indus, and while he was crossing the Gedrosian desert, certainly out-of-sight, but also virtually out of mind.

However, within weeks of Bessus's capture a revolt erupted with the massacre of Macedonian garrisons scattered throughout the country (Arr. *Anab.* 3.30.10–11; Curt. 7.6.1–9). The causes of this insurrection are multiple. First, Bactria and Sogdiana were closely associated with the Persians and did not see Alexander as a liberator. The satraps of Bactria, who in the Achaemenid period also controlled Sogdiana (Briant 2002, 746), had often been members of the royal family, who typically operated with great autonomy and popularity. The land had frequently supplied royal pretenders to the Persian throne, backed by the forces of the province (Holt 1995, 39–43; Briant 2002, 76). Even though the satrap appointed by Alexander was Persian, he was not one of those who had surrendered Bessus, but rather a Persian with no previous connection to Bactria (Arr. *Anab.* 3.29.1; Curt. 7.5.1). Of course, Alexander may have been leery of trusting such individuals after the revolt of Satibarzanes in Areia (Diod. 17.78.2; Curt. 6.6.22–3). He had been the Persian satrap of that region, but had surrendered himself and his satrapy to Alexander, and been confirmed in his former position (Arr. *Anab.* 3.25.1; Curt. 6.6.20).[21] His revolt was short lived.

Alexander was also imposing greater control than had been the case with the Persians (Smith 2009/10, 64). While it has long been a truism in the 'classical' study of insurgencies that these typically involve a 'struggle for government' (Kilcullen 2010, 149; United States Department of the Army and the United States Marine Corps 2007, 2), and 'a struggle to control a contested political space' (Kilcullen 2006/07, 112), this does not appear to be the case in Bactria and Sogdiana, nor, perhaps in modern day Afghanistan either. What does appear to be the case both then and now is that these 'insurgencies' are not contests of opposing systems of government, but rather examples of what is often called 'resistance warfare' (Kilcullen 2006/07, 112–14). What is being fought for by the insurgents is a return to the status quo, which in this case is a dispersed system of political power with little centralization of authority. Alexander represented significant change from this traditional pattern of control. As in other provinces, Alexander established a city, the aforementioned Alexandria Eschate, on the border of Sogdiana across the river from the Scythian tribes. He had already garrisoned many of the 'cities' in the area (Arr. *Anab.* 4.1.4). The presence of the city in particular meant a permanent military settlement of outsiders and the annexation of prime agricultural land for these new residents (Holt 1988, 54–6; Bosworth 1990, 257). Many of the indigenous population may even have acquired the status of serfs in this settlement, similar to the status of the *laoi* in the later Hellenistic kingdoms (Briant 1978, 77–8; Holt 1988, 58, 63–4; Billows 1995, 122, 171). As Frank Holt (1995, 58) states, "they were likely to have been a segregated, second-class group serving the discharged Macedonians and Greek mercenaries who controlled this and other colonies in the king's name." Alexander's cities always possessed military cores of mercenaries and veterans unfit for battle, along with natives and volunteers.[22] For example, between Alexandria of the Caucasus and Bactria the Macedonian king founded communities containing 7000 natives, 3000 camp followers, discharged soldiers, and mercenaries (Diod. 17.83.2; Curt. 7.3.23). As Holt (1988, 54–6) points out most of the rebels were Sogdians, not Bactrians. Sogdiana was a land where the Persian imprint was barely noticeable outside a few urban centers.

---

[21] He was soon captured and beheaded (see Heckel 2006, 245).

[22] Arr. *Anab.* 3.25.1–7, 28.2–3; Curt. 6.6.20–34; 7.3.2, 4.33–7; Diod. 17.81.3.

The Persians had concentrated their attention on the cities in the fertile areas of Bactria (Briant 1978, 70; Holt 1988, 58–9).

Where Alexander had been deft in his handling of other regions, accounting for local customs and traditions, and associating members of the local elite in his rule, he appears to have lost his way in Bactria and Sogdiana. This revolt took two years to suppress. When it erupted, Alexander's first reaction was, given his previous history, predictable. Near Maracanda, the capital of Sogdiana, after an attack on a Macedonian foraging party, Alexander demonstrated how he dealt with defiance by massacring 22,000 of those associated with the attackers (Arr. *Anab.* 3.30.10–11; Curt. 7.6.1–10). Later, he destroyed a number of rebel fortresses, slaughtering the male survivors and enslaving the women and children (Arr. *Anab.* 4.2.4–3.5; Curt. 7.6.16–27). Some captured 'rebels' were whipped and then crucified (Curt. 7.11.28). This policy of terror continued until 328, when a new approach was begun.

Alexander began to recruit Bactrian and Sogdian cavalry into his forces (Arr. *Anab.* 4.17.3), and large numbers are later found in Alexander's army in India (Arr. *Anab.* 5.11.3, 12.2).[23] In the spring of 327, after taking the fortress, called 'the Rock of Sogdiana', (Arr. *Anab.* 4.17.4–5), those who surrendered were not slaughtered but spared (Arr. *Anab.* 4.21.4), as were those subsequently captured at the 'Rock of Chorienes' (Arr. *Anab.* 4.21.1–9; Curt. 8.2.19–33). One of the captives from the Sogdian Rock was Roxane the daughter of a prominent Sogdian nobleman, Oxyartes (Arr. *Anab.* 4.19.5, 20.4). Alexander subsequently married the princess (Arr. *Anab.* 4.19.5), forming an alliance with her father. Oxyartes would later be made satrap of Parapamisadae, in what is today northwest Pakistan (Arr. *Anab.*6.15.3; Curt. 9.8.9). After almost two years of brutal repression, these alliances with many of the nobles brought the revolt to an end. The costs, however, were horrific. When Alexander left for India it is estimated that over 100,000 Bactrians and Sogdians, including women and children, were dead (Holt 2005, 107). Seven thousand Macedonians also died, a total that was greater than that suffered in any previous campaign (Holt 2003, 14; 2005, 107). Additionally, when Alexander withdrew from Bactria he left a garrison of 10,000 infantry and 3500 cavalry behind with the satrap likely stationed in the capital Bactra (Arr. *Anab.* 4.22.3), what Bosworth has called, "the largest defense force in the empire" (Bosworth 1988, 238); but it is clear that additional troops were positioned in other communities. Overall the occupying force was well over 20,000. Modern American policy with respect to insurgency warfare presents a far different strategy, but then it has far different aims. "Everyone must do nation building." So says General Petraeus in his fourteen observations regarding 'soldiering' (2006, 46),[24] and the *Manual* (2007, 152–4) speaks of a final transition to local control. Alexander, of course, had no intention of relinquishing control of his empire to others or building independent nations.

While it is claimed that Bactria and Sogdiana continued to experience 'military and political unrest' from the indigenous population, the evidence is virtually nonexistent

---

[23] Curtius (8.5.1) states that Alexander recruited natives into his army "to serve simultaneously as hostages and soldiers." Having them with him also meant that they would not be available for any subsequent rebellions in their homeland.

[24] For a hostile review of this entire concept, see Luttwak 2006, 33–42.

(Holt 2005, 108–9; Brosius 2003, 189). The only actual support for unrest among the population after the suppression of the great revolt comes from 326 in the border region between Bactria and the Punjab, the province of Assacenia (the Swat valley) (Arr. *Anab.* 5.20.7), but the rebellion was quickly put down (Bosworth 1983, 37–38), and the rebels are described in our sources as Indians, not Bactrians, or Sogdians (Arr. *Anab.* 4.25.5, 26.4.27.2). Rebellions in the area came in 325 and again in 323 from the primarily Greek colonists who wished to leave their new homes for Greece (Schober 1981, 27–36; Holt 1989[1995], 84–5, 87–91).

What is clear concerning the post-revolt history is that after the death of Alexander and the wars that erupted on that event, this area became part of the Hellenistic Seleucid Empire and remained so until the middle of the third century BCE, when an independent 'Greek' regime was established and flourished well into the following century (Green 1990, 331–2). Moreover, Macedonian dynasties dominated the Near East for almost three centuries. The Ptolemaic dynasty of Egypt endured until it was finally overthrown in 30 BCE by the future Roman emperor Augustus.

In the final analysis, Alexander was successful in controlling a territory that stretched eastward from Macedonia across approximately 4000 miles and included a myriad of different peoples. Much of his success was due to his maintaining the governmental and cultural patterns of the subject populations. Moreover, he incorporated much of the existing power structure into his government. With the exception of the new urban foundations and the occasional garrison, his footprint on the local populations was light, but then his view of glory came from the submission not from the oppression of populations. In the one situation where a major insurrection did occur, that in Bactria and Sogdiana, it was suppressed. But his methods for dealing with resistance were brutal in the extreme. Indeed, part of his success in avoiding such conflicts came from this realization on the part of his potential opponents. This was especially the case when surrender to Alexander would often be followed by demonstrations of largesse, and resistance most often meant death and destruction.

Bibliography

Abdullah el-Rasiq, M. (1984) *Die Darstellungen und Texte des Sanktuars Alexanders des Grossen im Tempel von Luxor.* Mainz.
Anson, E. M. (2004) *Eumenes of Cardia: A Greek Among Macedonians.* Leiden and Boston.
— (2013) *Alexander the Great: Themes and Issues.* London and New York.
— (forthcoming 2014). Alexander the Beas. In E. Baynham and P. Wheatley (eds.) *East and West in the Empire of Alexander.* Oxford.
Ashton, N. G. (1983) The Lamian War. A false start? *Antichthon* 17, 47–63.
Badian, E. (1958) Alexander the Great and the unity of Mankind, *Historia* 7, 225–449.
— (1965) The Administration of the Empire, *Greece & Rome* 12, 166–82.
Bickerman, E. J. (1934) Alexandre le Grand et les villes d'Asie, *Revue des Études Grecques* 47, 346–74.
Billows, R. A. (1995) *Kings and Colonists: Aspects of Macedonian Imperialism.* Leiden.
Bosworth, A. B. (1983) The Indian satrapies under Alexander the Great, *Antichthon* 17, 37–46.
— (1988) *Conquest and Empire: The reign of Alexander the Great.* Cambridge and New York.
— (1990) Review: F. L. Holt, Alexander the Great and Bactria, *Journal of Hellenic Studies* 110, 256–8.

— (1996) *Alexander and the East: The Tragedy of Triumph.* Oxford and New York.

Boyce, M. (1978) *Zoroastrians: Their Religious Beliefs and Practices.* London.

Boyce, M. and F. Grenet (1991) *A History of Zoroastrianism: Zoroastrianism under Macedonian and Roman Rule.* Leiden.

Briant, P. (1978) Colonisation hellenistique et peuples indigenes. La phase d'installation, *Klio* 60, 57–92.

— (1982) *Rois, tributs et paysans: Etudes sur les formations tributaires du Moyen-Orient ancien (Annales litteraires de l'Universite de Besancon).* Paris.

— (2002) Trans. by P. T. Daniels. *From Cyrus to Alexander: A History of the Persian Empire.* Winona Lake, IN.

Brosius, M. (2003) Alexander and the Persians. In J. Roisman (ed.) *Brill's Companion to Alexander the Great*, 169–93, Leiden.

Burstein, S. M. (1991) Pharaoh Alexander: A Scholarly Myth, *Ancient Society* 22, 139–45.

Carney, E. (1996) Macedonians and Mutiny: Discipline and Indiscipline in the Army of Philip and Alexander, *Classical Philology* 91, 19–44.

— (2005) Women and *Dunasteia* in Caria, *American Journal of Philology* 126, 67–91.

Cook, J. M. (1983) *The Persian Empire.* New York.

Faure, P. (1982) *La Vie quotidienne des armées d'Alexandre.* Paris.

Fraser, P. M. (1996) *Cities of Alexander the Great.* Oxford and New York.

Fredricksmeyer, E. (2003) Alexander's Religion and Divinity. In J. Roisman (ed.) *Brill's Companion to Alexander the Great*, 253–78, Leiden.

Fuller, J. F. C. (1960) *The Generalship of Alexander the Great.* New Brunswick, NJ.

Green, P. (1990) *Alexander to Actium: The Historical Evolution of the Hellenistic Age.* Berkeley and Los Angeles.

Greenwalt, W. (1989) Polygamy and Succession in Argead Macedonia, *Arethusa* 22, 19–45.

Griffith, G. T. (1964) Alexander the Great and an Experiment in Government, *Proceedings of the Cambridge Philological Association* 10, 23–39.

Hammond, N. G. L. (1980) *Alexander the Great, King, Commander and Statesman.* Park Ridge, NJ.

Hatzopoulos, M. B. (1996) *Macedonian Institutions under the Kings.* Athens and Paris.

Heckel, W. (2003) Alexander and the 'Limits of the Civilised World'. In W. Heckel and L. Tritle (eds) *Crossroads of History: The Age of Alexander*, 147–74, Claremont, CA.

— (2006) *Who's Who in the Age of Alexander the Great.* Malden, MA.

Heckel, W. and L. Tritle (eds) (2003) *Crossroads of History: The Age of Alexander.* Claremont, CA.

Holt, F. L. (1989[1995]) *Alexander the Great and Bactria. The Formation of a Greek Frontier in Central Asia. Mnemosyne* 104. *Supplementum.* Leiden and New York.

— (1999) *Thundering Zeus: The making of Hellenistic Bactria.* Berkeley and Los Angeles.

— (2003) *Alexander the Great and the Mystery of the Elephant Medallions.* Berkeley and Los Angeles.

— (2005) *Into the Land of Bones: Alexander the Great in Afghanistan.* Berkeley and Los Angeles.

Howe, T. and S. Müller (2012) Mission Accomplished: Alexander at the Hyphasis, *Ancient History Bulletin* 26, 21–38.

Kilcullen, D. (2006/07) Counter-insurgency Redux, *Survival* 48, 111–30.

— (2010) *Counterinsurgency.* Oxford and New York.

Lepsius, C. F. (1972–3) *Denkmaeler aus Aegypten und Aethiopien.* Genève.

Luttwak, E. N. (2006) Dead End: Counterinsurgency Warfare as Military Malpractice, *Harpers Magazine* 314, 33–42.

Petraeus, D. H. (2006) Learning Counterinsurgency: Observations from Soldiering in Iraq, *Military Review. Special Edition Counterinsurgency Reader.* Combined Arms Center. Leavenworth, Kansas.

Roisman, J. (ed.) *Brill's Companion to Alexander the Great.* Leiden.

Schober, L. (1981) *Untersuchungen zur Geschichte Babyloniens und der Oberen Satrapien von 323–303 v. Chr.* Frankfurt and Bern.

Shahbazi, A. S. (2003) Iranians and Alexander, *American Journal of Ancient History* 2, 5–38.

Sherwin-White, S. and A. Kuhrt (1993) *From Samarkhand to Sardis: A new approach to the Seleucid empire.* Berkeley and Los Angeles.

Smith, M. (2009/10) The Failure of Alexander's Conquest and Administration of Bactria-Sogdiana, *Hirundo, the McGill Journal of Classical Studies* 8, 64–72.

Smith, P. P. (2007) Eating Soup with a Sarissa: 10 Insurgency Prevention and Counterinsurgency Lessons From a Comparative Analysis of Operation Iraqi Freedom and Alexander the Great's Inner Front Strategies, *A research report submitted to the faculty of the Air Command and Staff College Air University in partial fulfillment of the graduation requirements.* Maxwell Air Force Base.

Spann, P. O. (1999) Alexander at the Beas: Fox in a Lion's Skin. In F. B. Titchener and R. F. Moorton (eds) *The Eye Expanded: Life and the Arts in Greco-Roman Antiquity*, 62–74, Berkeley, Los Angeles and London.

Squillace, G. (2004) *Basileis e tyranno: Filippo II e Alessandro Magno tra opposizione e Consenso.* Rubbettino.

Tarn, W. W. (1950) *Alexander the Great. Vol. 2. Sources and Studies.* Cambridge.

Tod, N. M. (1948) *Greek Historical Inscriptions.* 2 vols. Oxford.

United States Department of the Army and the United States Marine Corps (2007) *Counterinsurgency Field Manual.* Chicago.

Worthington, I. (2003) Alexander's Destruction of Thebes. In W. Heckel and L. Tritle (eds) *Crossroads of History: The Age of Alexander*, 65–86, Claremont, CA.

THE COMPARISON BETWEEN ALEXANDER AND PHILIP. USE AND METAMORPHOSIS OF AN IDEOLOGICAL THEME

Giuseppe Squillace[1]

The comparison between Alexander and Philip is a recurrent theme in literary sources on ancient Macedonia, such as Diodorus, Curtius Rufus, Plutarch and Arrian. It assumes also a rhetorical character in writings such as Lucian's *Dialogues of the Death*, where Philip is depicted as an ideal and perfect Macedonian king while, on the contrary, Alexander is a despotic ruler and tyrant who demands divine honours while neglecting his father.[2] Beside this rhetorical adaptation found in authors such as Lucian, the Philip comparison seems to find its origin in Alexander, who first introduced it in his own political speeches for ideological and propagandistic purposes.

Philip's death in 336[3] was a dramatic event for the Macedonian monarchy. It happened at a crucial moment following his victory against Athens and Thebes at Chaeronea in 338 and the foundation of Hellenic League at Corinth in 337, when Philip was ready for a more ambitious project: the war against the Persian Empire. His unexpected death caused instability in Macedonia and many Greek communities were ready to rise up in the name of freedom. Moreover, Alexander's accession to the throne may not have been universally accepted, because he was son of the Epirot princess Olympias, and because, in 337, Philip had married Cleopatra, the niece of Attalus, a prominent Macedonian, perhaps in order to have a Macedonian heir.[4] These were the difficult political circumstances when, shortly after Philip's death, Alexander killed his father's murderers and honoured him with a solemn

---

[1] Over the last 40 years, Waldemar Heckel's studies have made a fundamental contribution to the investigation of Ancient Macedonia. In particular, Heckel's recent book *Who's Who in the Age of Alexander the Great. Prosopography of Alexander's Empire* (2006) – only one of his many monographs – has updated Berve's *Das Alexanderreich auf prosopographischer Grundlage* (1926) with new data and bibliography and today is the necessary starting point for all new investigation on these themes. This paper aims to investigate an ideological theme used during Alexander' reign. It is my personal homage to Waldemar Heckel, a great academic, who, by studying Philip and Alexander's reigns from different and original perspectives, has been for me – and for many scholars – a guide and a master.

[2] Luc., *D.M.* 13.

[3] All the dates are BCE.

[4] Satyrus, Fr. 5; Plut., *Alex.* 9.7ff.; Justin. 9.7.3; Ps. Callisthenes 1.20.1. On Philip's polygamy: Prestianni Giallombardo 1976–1977, 81–110; Tronson 1984, 116–126; Carney 1992, 169–189; Heckel 1992, 4–5; Heckel 2006, 62; 89–90; Squillace 2009, 13–15.

burial.[5] The filial gesture and act of family vengeance demonstrated Alexander's loyalty to Philip in a hard moment for the Macedonian reign.

Alexander's succession was not taken for granted. Many Macedonians thought Alexander was too young to rule, and some even believed he was responsible for Philip's death.[6] The Greeks were ready to rise up against Macedonia: the Athenians did not recognize Alexander as leader (*hegemon*) and invited other communities to revolt in the name of freedom.[7] Aetolia, Acarnania, Ambracia, Thebes, Argos, Elis, and Sparta rose against the king.[8] Alexander reacted to this dangerous situation by invoking Philip in his speeches, in order to obtain the consent of both the Macedonians and the Greeks. According to Diodorus, after avenging Philip's death, Alexander stated in conciliatory speeches that only the name of the king had changed, but not the policy. Through this assurance he obtained the consent of his people, who acclaimed him the new king.[9] According to Justin, Alexander made promises and gave grants to the Macedonians, thereby convincing them that only the body of the king had changed while his virtues remained the same. For these reasons, the Macedonians gave their consent to the new king.[10]

His accession was the first time Alexander invoked the comparison to Philip, yet he would subsequently employ the same theme at other moments: In 336 he obtained the consent of the Thessalians, who recognized that his hegemony over Greece was inherited from Philip;[11] in 335 at Dion, on the eve of the war against the Persians, he referred to his army as 'Philip's army';[12] in 333, before the battle of Issus, he reminded his contingents of their victories in Greece under Philip;[13] in 332, in his letter to Darius, he charged the Persian king with Philip's murder;[14] and at Siwah, in Egypt, he was referred to as 'Philip's avenger' by the priest of the oracle of Zeus Ammon.[15]

It was Alexander who, at these various occasions between 336 and 332, first introduced and exploited the Philip theme that appears in different manifestations in later sources like Diodorus, Curtius Rufus, Plutarch, Arrian, and Justin. Alexander employed the comparison in speeches addressed to the Macedonian nobles, the army, and the Greeks. He aimed to be recognized as Philip's successor and king of Macedonia, to obtain the *hegemonia* over the Greeks, and to reinforce and consolidate the loyalty of officials, soldiers and allies during the Asiatic expedition.

---

[5] Diod. 17.2.1; Plut. *Alex.* 10.7; Pap. Ox. 1798 = *FGrH* 148.1. According to Justin (11.2.1–3), Alexander killed the murderers on his father's grave.

[6] Diod. 17.2.2; Plut., *Alex.* 10.5–6; Justin. 11.7.1 ff. See: Badian 1963, 244–250; Badian 2000, 54; Squillace 2004, 19. Demosthenes, recalling that Alexander was young and not so able as Philip, also exhorted the Greeks to revolt against Macedonia: Aeschin., *C. Ctes.* (III) 160; Plut., *Alex.* 11.6; Plut., *Demosth.* 23.2: see Gunderson 1981, 188; Lane Fox 1981, 223.

[7] Diod. 17.3.2; Justin. 11.1.2.

[8] Diod. 17.3.3.6.

[9] Diod. 17.2.2;

[10] Justin. 11.1.10–2.1.

[11] Diod. 17.2.2.6, 4.1; but also Justin 11.2.5–6, 3.1.

[12] Diod. 17.16.

[13] Curt. 3.10.4–10.

[14] Arr. *Anab.* 2.14.5–9; Curt. 4.1.7–14.

[15] Diod. 17.51; Justin 11.1.1–11.

'Alexander vs. Philip'

The ideological nature of the Philip theme evolves after Alexander's third great victory against the Persians at Gaugamela, in 331, where he decisively defeated Darius III. This battle essentially ended the war, which he had led as the *hegemon* of the Greeks, and which he had depicted as a freedom and revenge war against the barbarians in the name of the Greeks.[16] Now Alexander planned to conquer the entire Persian Empire. His political and military aims changed, and so too the ideological themes useful for justifying them evolved. After the victory of Gaugamela and the destruction of the Achaemenid palace at Persepolis in 330, Alexander dismissed the Greek army.[17] This was the first step of his new project. The slogans of revenge and freedom remained but Alexander (and his supporters) adapted to the new military aims. Whereas in 336 the theme of revenge was addressed to the Greeks, now, since he had dismissed the Greek army, Alexander directed the revenge theme to the Macedonians and, above all, to the Persian nobles. The war was no longer justified as a war to avenge the Greeks against the Persians and Darius III, successor of Xerxes, but rather to avenge the name of Darius III against Bessus, who had murdered the Persian king.[18]

So too the Philip theme transformed after Gaugamela. It was no longer important to Alexander, who ceased to invoke the image of Philip. Instead the theme was picked up by Macedonian officers, soldiers and intellectuals. Reference to Philip became the signal for and/or the mirror of opposition among the army, and thus the theme appears in several situations where, according to the ancient sources, there was a conflict between Alexander and his generals, soldiers and intellectuals.

In 330, after dismissing the Greek contingents and continuing the expedition, Alexander – says Plutarch – was informed that charges against him were circulating among his officers and soldiers, who would no longer tolerate marches and military expeditions.[19] Plutarch does not specify the nature of these accusations. One of them – perhaps the most incisive – was the comparison between Philip and Alexander. It emerges clearly in 330 during the Philotas conspiracy. According to Curtius, Philotas, Parmenion's son and one of the most important generals of Alexander,[20] was involved in a plot to murder the king. Philotas was arrested and confessed that Hegelochus had devised the plot because Alexander had proclaimed himself the son of Ammon rather than Philip's son, and ruled not as a Macedonian king but as a tyrant.[21]

The same accusation emerges two years later in the Cleitus episode. According to the

---

[16] On these themes: Squillace 2004a, 60–71.

[17] Diod. 17.74.3–5; but also Arr. *Anab.* 3.19.5–7.

[18] Diod. 17.73.1–3; Arr. *Anab.* 3.18.11–12. According to Diodorus (17.73.4), when Darius was at death's door, he prayed to Alexander to avenge him.

[19] Plut. *Alex.* 42.3–4.

[20] See: Berve 2, 1926, 393–397; Heckel 1977, 9–21; Heckel 1992, 6, 19–27; Heckel 2006, 216–219.

[21] Curt. 6.11.21–24, see also Arr. *Anab.* 3.26.1. According to Plutarch (*Alex.* 48–49; *De fort. Alex.* 2.7 = *Mor.* 339e–f) and Diodorus (17.79.1) the plot against Alexander was devised by the *hetairos* Limnos/Dimnos of Chalaestra. On the Hegelocus plot and the Philotas cospiracy: Berve 2, 1926, 142–143, 164–165; Badian 1960, 332; Heckel 1977, 9–21; Rubinsohn 1977, 409–420; Heckel 1992, 6; Adams 2003, 113–126; Heckel 2006, 112, 131–132.

sources, Alexander and Cleitus had a quarrel during a banquet, and the king, drunk and angry, murdered the Macedonian officer.[22] Curtius and Arrian, who offer the two more detailed versions, reference the Philip theme in this circumstance. According to Curtius, Alexander devalued his father's deeds by taking credit for the victory at Chaeronea: he said that he had won the battle but Philip had assumed all of the glory. Alexander also asserted that he had saved his father during a battle and that he obtained victories in many battles in the name of Philip: battles in which Philip had not participated, such as the struggle against the Illyrians. Alexander's words angered Cleitus. Cleitus, who had been an officer under Philip, responded by praising the wars and the virtues and merits of his first king, whom he believed better than Alexander. He also blamed Alexander for the deaths of Parmenion and Attalus. Alexander was enraged by this speech and murdered Cleitus, reportedly inviting him to join Philip, Parmenion and Attalus.[23] According to Arrian, it was other guests at the banquet who downplayed Philip's deeds, thus provoking Cleitus to react by praising Philip and denigrating Alexander.[24]

The Philip theme emerges again in the same year. According to Arrian, Alexander called a meeting of Persian and Macedonian nobles in order to obtain from them all the Persian ritual of prostration (*proskynesis*). The philosopher Anaxarchus made a speech inviting all to concede this honour to the king. On the contrary, Callisthenes, Aristotle's nephew, opposed it, reminding the listeners that Alexander was not a Persian king, heir of Cambyses and Xerxes, but rather a Macedonian king, the son of Philip.[25] Callisthenes, who in his histories celebrated Alexander's deeds in Asia against the Persians, authoritatively used the Philip theme against Alexander in front of the Persians and, more importantly, the Macedonians. In his speech he praised Philip and the Macedonian traditions and attacked Alexander's orientalizing policy. The great influence of Callisthenes on the Macedonian officers and soldiers made his speech very dangerous: this compelled Alexander to renounce his invitation for the men to perform the prostration.[26] Callisthenes' words did not remain isolated but had an immediate effect. Some months later, Alexander discovered a plot against him and put to death many royal pages. He also charged that Callisthenes was involved in, and possibly the leader of, this conspiracy.[27] Curtius reports the words of Hermolaus, one of the pages. According to Hermolaus, Alexander had caused the death of Attalus, Philotas, Parmenion, Alexander of Lyncestis and Cleitus and had refused to recognize Philip as his father.[28] Alexander put Callisthenes to death, but the historian's death did not totally eliminate the Philip theme from the army. There remained opposition to Alexander

---

[22] Curt. 8.1.23–52; Arr. *Anab.* 4.8.6–9; Plut. *Alex.* 50–51; see: Berve, 2, 1926, 206–208; Heckel 1992, 34–37; Carney 1981, 149–160; Tritle 2003, 127–146; Heckel 2006, 86–87.

[23] Curt. 8.1.20–52.

[24] Arr., *Anab.* 4.8. The Philip theme is also present in Plutarch. According to Cleitus' charges, Alexander was a coward during the battle at Granicus, and he proclaimed himself Ammon's son, thus denying Philip: Plut., *Alex.* 50.10–11. On this episode: Carney 1981, 157–159; Worthington 2003, 97; Squillace 2004a, 21–28; Heckel 2008, 101–102; Müller 2010, 30.

[25] Arr. *Anab.* 4.10.5–11.

[26] Arr. *Anab.* 4.12.1.

[27] Arr. *Anab.* 4.14.1, but also Curt. 8.6.25, 7.3–10; Plut. *Alex.* 55.3–4.

[28] Curt. 8.7.3–13; see: Müller 2010, 25–32.

among the soldiers, who, disapproving of Alexander's orientalizing policy, continued to see in Philip the model of the ancient Macedonian traditions.

Again 'Alexander as Philip'

The Philip theme emerges again at Opis in 324, when Alexander decided to dismiss old and ill soldiers and send them back to Macedonia. The Macedonian soldiers felt insulted and betrayed and protested the order. Alexander sentenced the leaders of the mutiny, and then addressed his army in a speech.[29] On this occasion, he brought back the theme that he had personally introduced in 336 after the death of his father in order to become king of Macedonia and obtain the consent of Macedonians and Greeks. Even if Arrian's version of Alexander's speech (which is also found in Curtius) contains some structural and rhetorical adaptations,[30] nevertheless the occasion and the themes employed in the speech seem genuine. According to Arrian, the speech begins in this way:

> First then I shall begin my speech with my father Philip, as is right and proper. For Philip found you vagabonds and helpless, most of you clothed with sheepskins, pasturing a few sheep on the mountain sides, and fighting for these, with ill success, against Illyrians and Triballians and the Thracians on your borders; Philip gave you cloaks to wear, in place of sheepskins, brought you down from the hills to the plains, made you doughty opponents of your neighbouring enemies, so that you trusted now not so much to the natural strength of your villages as to your own courage. Nay, he made you dwellers of cities, and civilized you with good laws and customs. Then of those very tribes to whom you submitted, and by whom you and your goods were harried, he made you masters, no longer slaves and subjects; and he added most of Thrace to Macedonia, and seizing the most convenient coast towns, opened up commerce to your country, and enabled you to work your mines in peace. Then he made you overlords of the Thessalians, before whom you had long died of terror, and humbling the Phocians, made the highroad into Greece broad and easy for you, whereas it had been narrow and difficult. Athens and Thebes, always watching their chance to destroy Macedon, he so completely humbled – ourselves by this time sharing these his labours – that instead of our paying tribute to Athens and obeying Thebes, they had to win from us in part their right to exist. Then he passed into the Peloponnese, and put all in due order there; and now being declared overlord of all the rest of Greece for the expedition against Persia, he won this new prestige not so much for himself as for all the Macedonian people.[31]

Then Alexander mentions his deeds, comparing himself to his father, and promoting his Asiatic expedition as the execution of his father's Asiatic project. Alexander recognizes not only the greatness of Philip's deeds, but also the superiority of his actions. He juxtaposes the limited resources inherited by Philip (few gold and silver cups, less than sixty talents in his treasure, and many debts) with his own great conquests in Asia (from Ionia to Susa) and with the treasures that the Macedonians plundered ("the wealth of Lydia, the treasures of Persia, the good things of India, the outer ocean, all are yours"). He thus underscores

---

[29] Curt. 10.2.12–13; Arr. *Anab.* 7.8–10; but see also Diod. 17.108.3, 109.2; Plut. *Alex.* 71.5; Justin. 12.11.

[30] The authenticity of Arrian's version of Alexander's speech: Tarn 1948, 286, 290–296; Bosworth 1988, 133; Hammond 1993, 228; Nagle 1996, 152; Hammond 1999, 249; Squillace 2004b, 217–234; *contra* Wüst 1953, 187–188; Brunt 1983, 532–533; Carney 1996, 29, 33, 38.

[31] Arr., *Anab.* 7.9.2–5 (translation Robson 1983).

how all that he had done benefitted his soldiers: they were honored in many ways and had become powerful and rich.[32]

Conclusion

Therefore, the Philip theme evolved in connection with Alexander's Asiatic expedition, mirroring the relationship between the king and his army. If, in 336, Alexander created and used it to his advantage in order to obtain consent and power, during the Asiatic expedition after Gaugamela, Philotas, Cleitus Callisthenes and many soldiers, who now opposed Alexander's orientalising policy, adopted the theme and proposed a new reading of it: reference to Philip no longer highlighted in terms of 'Alexander as Philip', but rather 'Alexander *vs.* Philip'. In 324, after the army's mutiny, Alexander once again employed the Philip theme in its original, positive version, yet with a new variation. After his expedition in Asia – he said – he had created an empire and had made his people rich and powerful. Alexander could thus draw a distinction between himself and his father not by making accusations against Philip, as he apparently did in front of Cleitus in 328, but rather by calling attention to incontestable and concrete achievements such as conquests, power over foreign peoples, and wealth and plunder. In this way, Alexander, in front of his army, finally and decisively superseded the myth and memory of Philip. Thanks to these incontrovertible data he could now promote himself no longer as the king only of a little state like Macedonia, as Philip was, but instead as the king of a great empire that he personally had created.

Bibliography

Adams W. L. (2003) The Episode of Philotas: an Insight. In W. Heckel and L. A. Tritle (eds) *Crossroads of History: the Age of Alexander*, 113–126, Claremont, CA.
Badian E. (1960) The Death of Parmenio, *Transactions of the American Philological Association* 91, 324–338.
— (1963) The death of Philip II, *Phoenix* 17, 244–250.
— (2000) Conspiracies. In A. B. Bosworth and E. Baynham (eds) *Alexander the Great in Fact and Fiction*, 54–95, Oxford.
Berve H. (1926) Das Alexanderreich *auf prosopographischer Grundlage*, 2 vols. München.
Bosworth A. B. (1988) *From Arrian to Alexander. Studies in Historical Interpretation.* Oxford.
Brunt P. A. (1983) *Arrian. History of Alexander and Indica*, 2, Cambridge, MA and London.
Carney E. D. (1981) The Death of Clitus, *Greek Roman and Byzantine Studies* 22, 149–160
— (1992) The Politics of Polygamy: Olympias, Alexander, and the Murder of Philip, *Historia* 41, 169–189.
— (1996) Macedonian and Mutiny: Discipline and Indiscipline in the Army of Philip and Alexander, *Classical Philology* 91.1, 19–44.
Gunderson L. L. (1981) Alexander and the Attic Orators. In H. J. Dell (ed.) *Ancient Macedonian Studies in Honour of C.F. Edson*, 183–192, Thessaloniki.
Hammond N. G. L. (1993) *Sources for Alexander the Great. An Analysis of Plutarch's* Life *and Arrian's* Anabasis Alexandrou. Cambridge.
— (1999) The Speeches in Arrian's *Indica* and *Anabasis*, *Classical Questions* 49.1, 238–253.
Heckel W. (1977) The Conspiracy *against* Philotas, *Phoenix* 31, 9–21.
— (1992) *The Marshals of Alexander's Empire.* London.
— (2006) *Who's Who in the Age of Alexander the Great: Prosography of Alexander's Empire.* Malden, MA.

---

[32] Arr., *Anab.* 7.9.6–10 (translation Robson 1983).

— (2008) *The Conquests of Alexander the Great.* Cambridge.

Lane Fox R. (1981) *Alessandro Magno.* (London 1973) Torino.

Müller S. (2010) In the Shadow of His Father: Alexander, Hermolaus, and the Legend of Philip. In E. Carney, and D. Ogden (eds) *Philip II and Alexander the Great. Father and Son, Lives and Afterlives*, 25–32, Oxford.

Nagle D. B. (1996) The Cultural Context of Alexander's Speech at Opis, *Transactions of the American Philological Association* 126, 151–172.

Prestianni Giallombardo A. M. (1976–1977) 'Diritto matrimoniale' ereditario e dinastico nella Macedonia di Filippo II, *Rivista storica dell' Antichità* 6–7, 81–110.

Robson E. I. (1983) *Arrian. Anabasis Alexandri (books 4–7) and Indika.* Cambridge.

Rubinsohn Z. (1977) The 'Philotas Affair' – A Reconsideration. In *Ancient Macedonia*, 2, 409–420.

Squillace G. (2004a) Basileis o tyrannoi. *Filippo II e Alessandro Magno tra opposizione e consenso.* Soveria Mannelli.

— (2004b) Propaganda macedone e spedizione asiatica. Gli *oikeioi logoi* di Alessandro alle truppe, *LEC* 72, 217–234.

— (2009) *Filippo il Macedone.* Roma–Bari.

Tarn W. W. (1948) *Alexander the Great*, 2. Cambridge.

Tronson A. (1984) Satyrus the Peripatetic and the Marriages of Philip II, *Journal of Hellenic Studies* 104, 116–126.

Tritle L. (2003) Alexander the Great and the Killing of Cleitus the Black. In Heckel and Tritle, 127–146

Worthington I. (2003) Alexander, Philip, and the Macedonian Background. In J. Roisman (ed.) *Brill's Companion to Alexander the Great*, 69–98, Malden, MA.

Wüst F. R. (1953) Die Rede Alexanders des Großen in Opis (Arrian VII 9–10), *Historia* 2, 177–188.

THE CALLISTHENES ENIGMA

Gordon Shrimpton[1]

Callisthenes' *Deeds of Alexander*, written in the entourage of Alexander the Great, covered events at least to 330 and had a strong eulogistic trait, glorifying the military achievements and propagating the king's claim to divine paternity. In early 327 he alienated Alexander by his opposition to *proskynesis*, was falsely implicated in the Pages' Conspiracy, and summarily executed.

(Bosworth, 1996, 278)

This is an odd picture: a man writes a eulogistic history, propagates his subject's claims to divine paternity, then refuses to perform acts of respect to him (*proskynesis*). The enigma is made more profound if we believe that Callisthenes promoted the actual divinity of Alexander as Pearson suggests (below), and not simply the 'divine paternity' as Bosworth describes it. For Badian, in his review of Pearson (1961), the distinction makes all the difference. If Callisthenes propagated the idea that Alexander was *son* of a god and nothing more, then Callisthenes, "[f]ar from being an unprincipled fool, as he appears in most of our literature from Timaeus to Tarn, ... faced death for his principles..." (1961, 661). On the other hand, if Alexander did seek recognition as a god, Callisthenes as the court historian and publicist, would be expected to comply with his patron's demands.

"Later critics constantly complain," says Pearson, "that the book was written in a spirit of flattery, that it represented Alexander as a god, and treated events in a sensational and melodramatic way" (1961, 33). But Badian thought that Pearson had pushed the evidence too far, perhaps under the influence of Tarn. From Jacoby's *testimonia* and fragments Pearson's 'later critics' turn out to be Timaeus (Jacoby [1929] #124, T 20), Philodemus *On Flattery* (T 21), and Strabo's (and Plutarch's) description of the visit to Siwah (F 14). 'Constantly complain' looks like an overstatement.

If, however, Callisthenes did make out Alexander to be a god in his narrative of the king's exploits, the arguments attributed to him by Arrian (*Anab.* 4.11) at the time of the *proskynesis* incident are remarkable to say the least. In that passage, Callisthenes stands up to Anaxarchus, who had undertaken first to speak openly in support of the gesture. After

---

[1] For Waldemar: brilliant scholar, loyal friend.

Anaxarchus had spoken, Callisthenes is made to marshal every imaginable reason for not insulting the gods by seeking to elevate a mere mortal, however great, to their status.

Badian complained that the scholarly opinion of Callisthenes made him an 'unprincipled fool'. Unprincipled, presumably, because he declined to worship the god he had helped to create, even arguing very strongly against the idea of deifying a living mortal, and a fool because he could not be discreet. When asked to deliver a eulogy of the Macedonians, Callisthenes reportedly delivered a rousing panegyric of them, then spoke only too well when asked to argue the opposite case. Challenged by Alexander that he had revealed his true feelings toward the Macedonians in the second speech, it is reported that he replied to Alexander: "Patroclus died a better man than you by far" (Pearson 1961, 24). Badian thought that Pearson was wrong to believe these reports. The problems arise from the interpretation of our all too scant evidence, if 'evidence' is the right word for what we have.

I propose to set aside Badian's concern about alleged unprincipled behaviour and turn to the less judgmental '[in]consistency'. True, Emerson referred to "a foolish consistency as the hobgoblin of little minds", but still, a foolish *in*consistency is probably worse. Is it possible to re-examine our evidence in search of a more consistent pattern in Callisthenes' life and career? Two places catch my eye. One is late in Callisthenes' life when the reports of his words and actions are almost certainly distorted by malice. After his conviction for conspiracy in the matter of the pages, people are not likely to have remembered much to his credit in the events leading up to his denunciation. The second is in the two 'miracles' that occurred before the battle of Gaugamela: the escape of the army from drowning in the sea by Mt. Climax in Pamphylia and the delivery from the desert on the way to Siwah. Pearson (1961, 33–37) argues that these two events established Alexander's divinity in Callisthenes' narrative.

Callisthenes' boorishness is amply evident in the narratives of Plutarch (*Alex.* 53–55) and, particularly, Arrian (*Anab.* 4. 10–14). It would be useful if we could gain some sense of the extent to which it is faithfully reported or the product of malice propagated by his detractors. There were two versions of his demise: tortured and hanged, or held incarcerated for seven months until he died bloated and infested with lice (Plut. *Alex.* 55.9). Bosworth (above), like most scholars, accepted the former. It is hard to see how keeping him alive would benefit Alexander. Plutarch attributes the second alternative to Chares, and Badian (2003) goes on to explain that Chares' intention in reporting (or inventing) this version was to exonerate Alexander, but he does not say from what. It is not clear why Alexander would need to be exonerated from accusations arising from his punishment of a convicted conspirator, and the slow death Chares described could scarcely be called more merciful than its alternative.

If we accept the standard version of Callisthenes' death, someone has invented a prolonged and wretched demise for Callisthenes and the most likely motivation for telling such a story is sheer spite. 'Where there is smoke, there is fire', as the saying goes, and Callisthenes will scarcely have inspired this much hatred by being a model of discrete diplomacy, but there is no denying that Callisthenes' reputation ended up in the hands of his most vicious detractors. We should make allowances.

The alleged deification is problematic. The first item chronologically was the passage along the Pamphylian coast (Plut. *Alex.* 17, Arrian *Anab.* 1.26.2, and F31, Pearson 1961, 36–7). A comment of Eustathius (F31) that refers to the sea withdrawing before Alexander (thanks to a fortunate change of wind) and apparently performing *proskynesis* is our only clue to Callisthenes' treatment of the event, and Pearson admits that it is not clear how much is really Eustathius and how much Callisthenes. Brown, however, in his review (1961, 53) simply points out that F31 is better seen as a direct echo of Cyrus' crossing of the Euphrates (Xen. *Anab.* 1.4.18). Nevertheless, it does appear that Callisthenes recorded an unexpected event (the change in the wind's direction?) that saved the army from drowning: divine assistance, but not deification.

There is only one other fragment of Callisthenes that may be taken to support the claim that he promoted Alexander's deity. It concerns the visit to the oracle at Siwah (Hamilton 1969, 66–73). Arrian (*Anab.* 3. 4–6) describes the difficulties of the desert passage and says that Alexander was guided to the oracle by two talking snakes according to Ptolemy, but, he goes on, Aristobulus gives the more widespread (*pleon*) version that two crows flew ahead of the army to guide it. Plutarch (*Alex.* 27.4, see also Strabo 17.1.43) cites Callisthenes to say that the army was guided by ravens (an unspecified number) who persisted night and day and kept the stragglers moving toward the oracle. More information comes from Polybius' attack on Timaeus (T 20 = Polyb. 12.12b). In the quotation Timaeus attacks Callisthenes: "justly put to death for abandoning philosophy for ravens and 'corybantic women', … praising Demosthenes and others for speaking against divine honours for Alexander, then bestowing the aegis and thunderbolt on a mere mortal."

So what did Callisthenes really say? From Plutarch, Strabo, and Arrian one would conclude that he got Alexander to the oracle with some miraculous help involving (two) blackbirds, and that the oracle hailed Alexander as son of Ammon. Callisthenes probably intended the reader to understand that this was the same as hailing him as son of Zeus because the oracles of Ammon and of Zeus at Dodona were sister foundations. Herodotus had described the founding of these oracles in book two (2.54–55): "The *promanties* at Dodona say that two black ravens flew from Thebes in Egypt. One came to Libya and the other to Dodona." (The Egyptians referred to these 'ravens' as women captured by Phoenicians.) They each, birds or women, founded oracles to Zeus/Ammon in those places. The two blackbirds that guided Alexander in Callisthenes clearly evoke the Herodotean story. Did Callisthenes actually relate a version of it? If so, that might explain Timaeus' remark about corybantic women. But making Alexander expressly son of Zeus does not bestow on him an 'aegis and thunderbolt'. Timaeus may have seen something more in Callisthenes' story, or he has over reacted. Unless we are persuaded by Timaeus, therefore, it appears that Callisthenes did much the same as in F31: bring out the miraculous result thanks to divine assistance. This tends to heroize Alexander but not deify him.

In sum, it seems safe to conclude that Callisthenes was churlish, but the extreme boorishness that was remembered to his discredit is almost certainly an exaggeration. The unequivocal 'evidence' that Callisthenes actually deified Alexander is reduced to one remark of Timaeus that could be hyperbolic.[2]

---

[2] Robert D. Milns (2006/07) argues that the 'flattery' of Alexander in the fragments is really irony. He

Bibliography

Badian, E. (1961) Review of Pearson, *Lost Histories of Alexander*, *Gnomon* 33, 660–667.

— (2003) Callisthenes. In *Brill's New Pauly*. First published (German) 1996–. http://referenceworks.brillonline. com/browse/brill-s-new-pauly.

Bosworth, A. B. (1996) Callisthenes. In S. Hornblower and A. Spawforth (eds) *The Oxford Classical Dictionary*. Third edn, Oxford.

Brown, T. (1961) Review of Pearson, *Lost Histories of Alexander*, *Phoenix* 15, 52–53.

Hamilton, J. R. (1969) *Plutarch. Alexander. A Commentary*. Oxford.

Jacoby, F. (1962 [1929]) *Die Fragmente der griechischen Historiker*. Vol. 2. Leiden.

Milns, R. D. (2006/07) Callisthenes on Alexander, *Mediterranean Archaeology* 19/20, 233–237.

Pearson, L. (1960) *Lost Histories of Alexander the Great*. Oxford (*APA Monographs* 20).

Pédech, P. (1984) *Historiens compagnions d'Alexandre*. Paris. Not available to me.

doubts that Callisthenes really was appointed by Alexander to be the court historian. Furthermore, he is not convinced that all the 'fragments' in Jacoby's collection have been assigned to the correct works by Callisthenes. His arguments are sobering but not always convincing.

ALEXANDER'S UNINTENDED LEGACY: BORDERS

Stanley M. Burstein[1]

Apropos of Alexander's plans to conquer Arabia, Strabo remarked that Alexander desired to be "master of everything"; and Arrian agreed, noting that Alexander "always wanted to gain possession of more."[2] Whatever the truth of these assessments of Alexander's ultimate goals, his death and the cancellation of his 'final plans' at Babylon put paid to ideas of further expansion. As a result, without it being intended, the limits of Alexander's conquests became the borders of the empire beyond which lay other powers with which the Diadochi would have to deal. Although this development affected all of the Diadochi, space permits consideration of only one such border: the southern border of Egypt during the reign of Ptolemy I in the light of a unique document, the Satrap Stela.

The Satrap Stela[3] is the earliest extant example of the long line of royal style hieroglyphic inscriptions honoring the Ptolemies.[4] Issued in November 311,[5] it celebrates the restoration to the temples of Horus of Pe and Dep at Buto of land granted them during the early 330s BCE by Khababash, the last native king of a united Egypt, and confiscated by the Persians after his suppression. Not surprisingly, scholarship on the Satrap Stela has largely focused on the evidence it provides for the little known reign of Khababash.[6] Much less attention has been given to the fact that the Satrap Stela also contains the only contemporary account of any of Ptolemy I's military campaigns. Thus, after an elaborate dating formula (lines 1–2) and a passage celebrating Ptolemy in traditional terms as a strong and vigorous defender of Egypt against its enemies (lines 3–4), the text continues with descriptions of two of his military successes (lines 5–6):[7]

---

[1] I would like to thank Professor Jacco Dieleman of the University of California, Los Angeles and Professor Christelle Fischer-Bovet of the University of Southern California for their advice. Needless to say, I am responsible for any shortcomings in the argument.

[2] Strabo 16.1.11, C 741; Arr. *Anab.* 7.19.6.

[3] Sethe 1904, II 11–22.

[4] For a list see Huss 1991. For their characteristics see Quack 2009.

[5] For much of the twentieth century the Satrap Stela was erroneously dated to 319 BCE; cf. Fraser 1972, 11–12 n. 28 for details.

[6] The most recent discussion of the reign of Khababash is Burstein 2000.

[7] Translated by Robert K. Ritner in Simpson *et al.* 2003, 393–94.

As he [*sc.* Ptolemy] brought back the sacred images of the gods which were found within Asia, together with all the ritual implements and all the sacred scrolls of the temples of Upper and Lower Egypt, so he restored them in their proper places. As he made his residence [*sc.* in Alexandria]…, so he assembled many Greeks with their horses and many ships with their troops. He then went with his armies to the land of the Syrians, with the result that they fought with him and he entered among them with his heart strong like a raptor in pursuit of small birds, seizing them in a single instant. To Egypt he brought away their princes, their horses, their ships, and all their wonders. Afterward, he made an expedition to the territory of Irem, seizing them in a single moment. In retaliation for what they had done against Egypt, he brought away their people, both male and female, together with their gods. He then returned to Egypt with his heart happy at these things that he had done.

Identification of the first campaign is not in doubt. It has long been recognized that the reference is to the Syrian campaign of spring 312[8] during which Ptolemy defeated Demetrius at Gaza. Identification of the second campaign, however, is contentious. A few scholars[9] have suggested that it refers to a campaign in Nubia conducted by Ptolemy probably sometime in late 312 or, more likely, in early 311, but that suggestion has not been generally accepted for reasons explained below.

As a result, both histories of Ptolemaic activity south of Egypt and of ancient Nubia ignore the evidence of the Satrap Stela. Nor is it included in the comprehensive collection of sources for ancient Nubian history, *Fontes Historiae Nubiorum (FHN)*.[10] Most accounts of Ptolemaic relations with Nubia instead begin in the late 270s with the Nubian campaign of Ptolemy II and the foundation of the first of the Ptolemaic elephant hunting stations at Ptolemais of the Hunts on the Red Sea coast of central Sudan. A corollary of this reconstruction is that it presupposes that fully two thirds of a century intervened between Alexander's conquest of Egypt in 332 and the beginning of Ptolemaic activity south of Egypt. This long interval, particularly when it involves ignoring a contemporary source that might fill the gap, is, to say the least, puzzling, all the more so because throughout the long history of Pharaonic Egypt Nubia was the primary focus of Egyptian foreign activity.

Egypt and Nubia

Egyptian interest in Nubia is understandable. The region offered Egypt important opportunities while at the same time being the source of very real dangers. As the title of William Y. Adam's magisterial history of Nubia puts it,[11] Nubia was Egypt's "corridor to Africa." Through Nubia Egypt received a variety of Sub-Saharan African goods including gold, slaves, exotic woods, and ivory and other animal products that were essential to the life style of the Egyptian elite and to the performance of religious cult. At the same time, the potential for danger to Upper Egypt and for conflict further south in Nubia itself was equally real and often realized. This was particularly true during the first millennium BCE, when the rulers of Egypt faced for the first time in almost a thousand years a powerful

---

[8]   For the date of the Battle of Gaza see now Bosworth 2002, 225–28.
[9]   E.g. Kaplony 1971, 256–57; Huss 2001, 136; Burstein 2008, 136.
[10] Eide *et al.* 1994–2000.
[11] Adams 1977.

state located in central Sudan, which not only could pose a serious threat to Egyptian interests in Lower Nubia but also enjoyed considerable support in southern Egypt: The Kingdom of Kush.

While tension between Egypt and the various states designated by the term 'Kush' can be traced back to the early second millennium, relations became particularly tense after the mid-seventh century, when the Assyrians drove back into Nubia the Kushite kings of the 25th dynasty, who had conquered Egypt in the late eighth century and ruled it for half a century.[12] Despite being henceforth confined to the Upper Nile valley, their successors viewed themselves as the heirs of their great ancestors of the 25th dynasty. Like them, they styled themselves Kings of Upper and Lower Egypt. More importantly, they sought to restore their ancestors' preeminence in Lower Nubia whenever the opportunity presented itself, as it did in the fourth century BCE, when the threat from Persia forced the Pharaohs of dynasties 28–30 to focus their attention on their Asian frontier. Even our limited evidence reveals that at least twice during the century kings of Kush took advantage of Egyptian weakness to extend their power in lower Nubia. So, sometime in the first half of the century the Kushite king Harsiyotef (*c.* 404–369) campaigned as far as Syene and forced local chieftains in lower Nubia to recognize Kushite authority.[13] Again, shortly before or, possibly, during the reign of Alexander, Nastasen (*c.* 335–315) repeated Harsiyotef's campaign, imposing his authority on local chieftains as far north as Abu Simbel.[14]

Kings of Kush did not confine their activity to Nubia, however. Given the opportunity, they did not hesitate to interfere also in Egyptian politics. So, a Kushite king, probably Akhratan (*c.* 353–340), gave sanctuary to Nectanebo II following his defeat by Artaxerxes III in the late 340s, an action that may have fanned hopes during the reign of Alexander among at least some Egyptian intellectuals that a savior king from the south would free them from Macedonian rule.[15] According to Agatharchides of Knidos, it was also Kushite pretensions to Egyptian territory that provoked Ptolemy II's Nubian campaign in the 270s;[16] and at the end of the century Kushite kings intervened in Egyptian affairs on a large scale. Not only did they actively support the great native rebellion that severed most of Upper Egypt from Ptolemaic rule for two decades from 207 to 186, but they took advantage of the confusion caused by that revolt to occupy all of lower Nubia including even Philae.[17]

In this situation, it is surely worth asking if the apparent hiatus of two thirds of a century between Alexander's conquest of Egypt in 332 and the first signs of Ptolemaic concern for Nubian affairs in the late 270s is real or only a mirage. As is so often the case, the problem is the sources. In this instance, however, it is not so much the lack of sources as much as the bias of the sources that we have. A survey of the relevant texts strongly suggests that modern historians are essentially repeating official propaganda when they date the beginning of Ptolemaic activity in Nubia to the 270s.

---

[12] For relations between Egypt and Kush see Redford 2004; and Török 2009.

[13] *FHN*, Nr. 78.

[14] *FHN*, Nr. 84.

[15] Burstein 1995a.

[16] Agatharchides of Cnidus, *On the Erythraean Sea*, S. M. Burstein (ed. and trans.) ff 12–13 with the comments on p. 25.

[17] *FHN* Nrs. 128–34. Cf. Kormysheva 1997.

The sources for Ptolemy II and Nubia

It is clear that the view of Nubian affairs that is reflected in modern scholarship took shape during the reign of Ptolemy II and was intended to magnify the achievements of that king. Traces of this official version of the history of Ptolemaic activity in Nubia are still evident even in the sources. Theocritus listed the Nubian campaign as one of the key events of the first decade of the king's reign.[18] Similarly, in describing the beginning of Ptolemy II's elephant hunting initiative, the Pithom Stela highlights the novelty of the king's achievement by describing it with the traditional Pharaonic formula, "never had the same been done by any king of the whole land."[19] A generation later the claim was repeated in the Adulis inscription of Ptolemy III, which asserts that "his father and he first hunted [sc. elephants] in these countries"; and it was still alive in the early first century CE, when Juba II noted that "Ptolemy Philadelphus was the first to explore Trogodytike."[20]

The fullest expression of the official version of the significance of the reign of Ptolemy II for relations with Nubia is found, however, in the works of the second century BCE Ptolemaic official and historian Agatharchides of Knidos. Agatharchides began his account of Ptolemaic activity south of Egypt in the first book of his *On the Erythraean Sea* with Ptolemy II's Nubian campaign,[21] and summed up the significance of this campaign for Greek knowledge of Nubia in the second book of his *On Affairs in Asia* as follows:[22]

> For from ancient times until the reign of Ptolemy Philadelphus Greeks not only did not cross into Aithiopia, but they did not even travel as far as the borders of Egypt. Conditions in these regions were completely hostile to foreigners and extremely dangerous. Ptolemy Philadelphus, however, was the first to campaign in Aithiopia with a Greek army and from his time the facts concerning that country have become more accurately known.

It is not surprising, therefore, that historians have tended to discount the possibility that the Satrap Stela might document a Nubian campaign of Ptolemy I *c.* 311, when our other sources for Ptolemaic activity in Nubia seem to exclude it. Indeed, the Egyptologist Hans Goedicke went so far as to categorically assert that the idea "is, of course, not tenable because Ptolemy [*sc.* I] did not campaign in Africa."[23]

But is the idea actually untenable? The official version of the origin of Ptolemaic activity in Nubia proves on examination to be both oversimplified and exaggerated. Ptolemy II's Nubian campaign unquestionably marked the beginning of sustained Ptolemaic activity in Nubia, but it is not true that before his reign "Greeks not only did not cross into Aithiopia, but they did not even travel as far as the borders of Egypt."[24] Exceptions to this

---

[18] Theocritus, *Idyll* 17, line 87.

[19] Based on the translation of Roeder 1959, 125–26. For the emphasis on unique achievement in the Egyptian inscriptions of Ptolemy II see Quack 2009, 283.

[20] apud Pliny, *HN* 6.167.

[21] For the subject of the first book of Agatharchides's *On the Erythraean Sea* see Burstein 1995b.

[22] Diodorus 1.37.5 (=Agatharchides, *FGrH* 86 F 19).

[23] Goedicke 1984, 34.

[24] Cf. the similarly exaggerated claim made by Cornelius Gallus, the first prefect of Egypt, to enhance the significance of his Nubian raid in 30 BCE (*IPhilae* 128, lines 6–7) : *exercitu ulta Nili cataracte[n transd]ucto, in quem locum (sc.* Lower Nubia) *neque populo Romano neque regibus Aegypti [arma ante s]unt prolata....*

blanket assertion are easy to find. Most obvious, of course, are the Greek mercenaries who served in the garrisons at Aswan during the 26th dynasty and participated in Psamtek II's Nubian campaign in 593 leaving graffiti celebrating their exploits on the colossal statues of Ramses II at Abu Simbel,[25] and Herodotus, who visited the first cataract region in the fifth century.[26] In addition, both Alexander and Ptolemy I were active on Egypt's southern frontier and possibly even beyond it.

In one of my first articles[27] I argued that new and more accurate information about the hydrography of the upper Nile valley during the reign of Alexander, documented in the fragments of Aristobulus,[28] provided strong circumstantial evidence supporting the tradition that Alexander dispatched an expedition to explore Nubia during his stay in Egypt in late 332 or early 331. If he did, however, the demands of his campaign against Darius III prevented Alexander from taking further action in Nubia at that time. He did, however, garrison Elephantine[29] and that garrison continued in place during the reign of Ptolemy I.[30] Again, probably late in the reign of Ptolemy I or early in that of Ptolemy II, a Ptolemaic official named Philo traveled as far south of Egypt as Meroe where he seems to have stayed for at least a year and made astronomical observations that later were used by Eratosthenes in his *Geography*.[31] Clearly, the idea that Ptolemy I could have campaigned in Nubia in 311 and that that campaign is mentioned in the Satrap Stela is hardly 'untenable'. While, therefore, Ptolemy could have conducted such a campaign, the question is did he? The answer is to be found in the text of the Satrap Stela itself.

Evidence of the Satrap Stela

The most striking feature of the Satrap Stela's account of Ptolemy's two campaigns is their unevenness. While the account of the Syrian campaign is relatively full with both its preparations and results being described in detail, that of the second campaign is brief and vague, indicating only that it resulted in prisoners and divine images being brought back to Egypt and that it was "in retaliation for what they had done against Egypt." There is general agreement that the most likely explanation for this discrepancy is that, unlike the Syrian campaign, the second campaign was relatively small in scale, essentially a punitive raid undertaken in reprisal for an attack on Egyptian territory. Equally important, it is the sketchiness of the account of the second campaign that has made it so difficult to determine against whom it was directed. Understandably, therefore, scholars have focused their attention on the one seemingly concrete fact about Ptolemy's second campaign in the Satrap Stela: the name of the country that was its target.

According to the most obvious interpretation of the hieroglyphs, the goal of the campaign was 'the land of Irem (*p3 t3š 'Irm*)'. Since Irem is a Nubian toponym known since the second

---

[25] Meiggs and Lewis, *GHI* 7.
[26] Hdt. 2.29.1.
[27] Burstein 1995c.
[28] *FGrH* 139 F 35.19.
[29] Arr. *Anab.* 3.2.7.
[30] *P. Eleph.* 1 (311 BCE).
[31] Philo, *FGrH* 670 F 2 with my comments *ad loc.* in *BNJ* 670 F 2.

millennium BCE,[32] this should mean that the author of the Satrap Stela located Ptolemy's second campaign in Nubia, but commentators have largely rejected that interpretation. Instead, relying on the fact that multiple vocalizations of the same hieroglyphs are possible, they have proposed alternative identifications of the region or people designated by the term.[33] Arabs in Palestine,[34] Aramaeans,[35] Jews in Palestine,[36] Arab tribes in the Sinai Peninsula,[37] and, more vaguely, an 'African desert people'[38] have all been suggested.[39]

All these suggestions, however, suffer from the same fundamental flaw: They are not based on the text of the Satrap Stela but on the classical accounts of Ptolemy's reign. The pattern of argument is simple and circular. The classical accounts are scrutinized for a suitable historical context for the second campaign and then, after having identified such a context, as theoretically possible – but unattested – vocalization of the toponym is proposed. For the sake of brevity, one example will have to suffice. In an important 1991 article on Ptolemy I's activities in Syria, J. K. Winnicki[40] argued that the second campaign was a punitive expedition against Arab tribes in the Sinai Peninsula directed by Ptolemy after his victory at Gaza for the purpose of preparing the way for Seleucus' invasion of Babylonia in 311 BCE. Having identified Ptolemy's objective as Arab tribes in the Sinai peninsula, Winnicki then suggested that this reconstruction could be reconciled with the text of the Satrap Stela if the toponym were read as *p3 t3š 'Irm3'i*, 'the land of the Arabs', instead of *p3 t3š 'Irm*, 'the land of Irem'.

The same sort of argumentation underlies the other suggested identifications also. If one ignores the classical accounts and focuses on the context of the accounts of Ptolemy's two campaigns in the Satrap Stela, however, a different location for the second campaign becomes likely, namely a location in Nubia and not northeast of Egypt as is the case with the interpretations already mentioned. Specifically, I suggest that lines 5–6 of the Satrap Stela continue the theme of lines 3–4 in which Ptolemy is described as a brave fighter and champion of Egypt by providing concrete examples of Ptolemy fulfilling one of a king's most traditional and fundamental obligations: Defending Egypt against her northern and southern enemies, the former Asia, here identified with Syria, and the latter, as usual, Nubia.[41] Most familiar, of course, are examples of this *topos* from the New Kingdom, but the same list of foreign enemies is also attested during Ptolemy I's reign in the curses in the colophon of the *Bremner Rhind Papyrus* of 305, which are directed against "anyone of any

---

[32] Cf. Priese 1974; and O'Connor 1987.

[33] This approach seems to have been first formally suggested by the Egyptologist J. Yoyotte in a letter cited by Fraser 1972, 11–12 n. 28. Yoyotte indicated that three transcriptions were possible but with the important *caveat* that none of the possible readings could be identified with particular peoples.

[34] Giveon 1973, 181. He suggests a connection with the city of Elath.

[35] Goedicke 1984, 34.

[36] Schäfer 2011, 123–132.

[37] See below.

[38] Bosworth 2002, 241–42.

[39] For identifications with Cyrene or the Blemmyes proposed in the late nineteenth century but based on now discarded interpretations of the hieroglyphs see Priese 1974, 13–14.

[40] Winnicki 1991, 164–85.

[41] For this theme see Valbelle 1990, 14 and *passim*.

country of Ethiopia, Kush, or Syria."[42] More important, this interpretation is supported by four features of the text of the Satrap Stela itself.

The first is that, although the two campaigns clearly differed in scale, they are treated as similar events, each ending with the victorious return of Ptolemaic forces to Egypt accompanied by enemy prisoners and divine images. This is incompatible with interpretations that assume that the second campaign was either a part of the Syrian campaign or a mopping up operation conducted immediately after it. The second point confirms this, namely, that the two campaigns are clearly indicated as being distinct and separate events through the use of the compound preposition *m-ḫt* plus the demonstrative pronoun *nn*, 'after these things', to introduce the account of the second campaign. Since *m-ḫt nn* carries the connotation that 'these things' – the Syrian campaign – had been completed before the second campaign began,[43] the second campaign cannot have been a part of the first campaign. Third, the determinatives used with Irem – foreignness (throw stick), foreign land (three hills), and watered land (canal symbol) – are all appropriate for a location in Nubia but not in Palestine or the Sinai Peninsula.[44] Fourth, and most important, however, is the hieroglyphic spelling of the toponym *'Irm* itself.

As already mentioned, previous discussions of the term have focused on the possible phonetic values of the hieroglyphs, not the hieroglyphs themselves. Robert Ritner, the most recent translator of the Satrap Stela, however, noted that "the spelling corresponds to the Nubian site of Irem,"[45] but there is more to be said about the writing. The spelling not only corresponds to that of Irem, but it is a deliberately archaic spelling of Irem. As the Egyptologist K. H. Priese[46] demonstrated in his comprehensive study of Egyptian references to Irem, this spelling occurs frequently in New Kingdom lists of African lands and in New Kingdom royal inscriptions dealing with campaigns in Nubia, but after the end of the New Kingdom it is found only once: in the Satrap Stela. Priese rightly, therefore, characterized the use of this spelling of Irem as an example of *"der Gelehrsamkeit des Verfassers des Textes."*[47] In this situation, it is difficult to believe that the author of the Satrap Stela, having employed an archaic hieroglyphic spelling that explicitly recalled Egypt's New Kingdom empire in Nubia, would then have expected it to be understood as referring to one of Egypt's Asiatic neighbors and not to a location in Nubia.

Taken together, these considerations indicate that the Satrap Stela does, in fact, document a punitive campaign in Nubia conducted by Ptolemy I in late 312 or early 311 BCE in reprisal for a Kushite intervention somewhere near the southern border of Egypt. Unfortunately, nothing specific can be said about the course of the campaign beyond the fact that the reference to prisoners and divine images being brought back to Egypt suggests that Nubian settlements were raided. Not even how far the campaign penetrated into Nubia can be determined. While it is clear that in the New Kingdom Irem referred to territory south of the third cataract of the Nile in Upper Nubia, there is no way to determine if

---

[42] Translated by Faulkner 1937, 11.

[43] Gardiner 1957, 133, 178.

[44] For the significance of determinatives in Egyptian geographical descriptions see Loprieno 2003, 31–32.

[45] Ritner in Simpson *et al.* 2003, 393–94, n. 4.

[46] Priese 1974, 26.

[47] Priese 1974, 27.

that was still true in the late first millennium BCE or if Priese was correct in suggesting that Irem had lost its specific reference and, like Greek Αἰθιοπία, it had become a general term for lands south of Egypt.[48]

Conclusion

We do not know if Alexander had plans to deal with the kingdom of Kush, but Ptolemy's need to rush to his southern border immediately after his victory at Gaza illustrates well the consequences of failing to do so. It also probably explains one of the puzzles of this period: the absence of a representative of Ptolemy in the peace negotiations in spring 311 BCE between Antigonus, Cassander, and Lysimachus.[49] Sometimes the simplest explanations are the best. Quite simply, it is likely that Ptolemy was not represented in the negotiations because he only learned of them on his return from Nubia, at which point he made sure that he was included in the final treaty. Be that as it may, the Satrap Stela also allows no doubt that the long-term implications of Alexander's failure to find a solution to Egypt's border problems with Kush were more serious than a temporary diplomatic embarrassment.

The classical sources' focus on Ptolemy's involvement in the affairs of the eastern Mediterranean and Aegean and the struggles of Alexander's successors obscure the fact that he ruled a state located in northeast Africa and also had to deal with its particular local problems. That meant that Ptolemy's concentration on the northern and northeastern theaters of war created the same potential for danger on Egypt's southern frontier that had faced his fourth century Pharaonic predecessors,[50] and the Satrap Stela's reference to his raid being "in retaliation, for what they (sc. Kushites) had done against Egypt" indicates that the kings of Kush tried to take advantage of that opportunity just as they had done before. The Satrap Stela also suggests that Ptolemy's response was limited. He demonstrated that he would respond forcefully to Kushite provocations, but at the same time he did not attempt to extend Egyptian power in lower Nubia. How successful this policy was cannot now be determined,[51] but, if Philo's expedition to Meroe belongs to his reign, Ptolemy probably maintained at least occasional diplomatic contact with Kush. While it is true, therefore, that Ptolemy II's Nubian campaign and the beginning of his elephant hunting project in the late 270s marked the beginning of sustained Ptolemaic engagement with Nubian affairs, it was not the beginning of his dynasty's problems with Nubia;[52] they had already begun during the reign of his father if not earlier and would continue after his reign.

---

[48] Priese 1974, 27. Hence, the suggestion that the area near Meroe (Kaplony 1971, 257 n. 1; Huss 2008, 136) was intended is unlikely.

[49] *RC* 1, lines 29–31. For the date of the negotiations see Bosworth 2002, 284.

[50] The dynamic continued into the Roman period; cf. Strabo 17.53–4, C 819–20, who notes that the Kushites took advantage of the withdrawal of troops from the Roman garrison at Syene to support Aelius Gallus's Arabian campaign in the mid-20s BCE to raid the first cataract region.

[51] Small scale raids and counter raids certainly continued into the third century BCE; cf. *FHN* 97 for an example from the first half of the third century BCE.

[52] Burstein 2008.

Bibliography

Adams, W. Y. (1977) *Nubia: Corridor to Africa*. Princeton.

Bosworth, A. B. (2002) *The Legacy of Alexander: Politics, Warfare, and Propaganda under the Successors*. Oxford.

Burstein, S. M. (1995a) Alexander in Egypt: Continuity or Change. In S. M. Burstein (ed.) *Graeco-Africana: Studies in the History of Greek Relations with Egypt and Nubia*, 43–52, New Rochelle.

— (1995b) The Aithiopian War of Ptolemy V: An Historical Myth? In Burstein, 97–104.

— (1995c) Alexander, Callisthenes and the Sources of the Nile. In Burstein, 63–76.

— (1995d) *Graeco-Africana: Studies in the History of Greek Relations with Egypt and Nubia*. New Rochelle

— (2000) Prelude to Alexander: The Reign of Khababash, *The Ancient History Bulletin* 14, 149–154.

— (2008) Elephants for Ptolemy II: Ptolemaic Policy in Nubia in the Third Century BC. In P. McKechnie and P. Guillaume (eds) *Ptolemy Philadelphus and his World*, 135–148. Leiden.

Eide, T., T. Hägg, R. H. Pierce, and L. Török (1994–2000) *Fontes Historiae Nubiorum*. 4 vols. Bergen.

Faulkner, R. O. (1937) The Bremner Rhind Papyrus II, *Journal of Egyptian Archaeology* 23: 166–185.

Fraser, P. M. (1972) *Ptolemaic Alexandria* 2. Oxford.

Gardiner, A. (1957) *Egyptian Grammar: Being an Introduction to the Study of Hieroglyphs,* 3rd edn. Oxford.

Giveon, R. (1971) *Les Bédouins Shosou des documents Égyptiens*. Leiden.

Goedicke, H. (1984) Comments on the Satrap Stela, *Bulletin of the Egyptological Seminar* 6, 33–54.

Huss, W. (1991) Die in Ptolemaischer Zeit verfassten Synodal-Dekrete der ägyptischen Priester, *Zeitschrift für Papyrologie und Epigraphik* 88, 189–208.

— (2008) *Ägypten in hellenistischer Zeit 332–30 v. Chr*. Munich.

Kaplony, P. (1971) Bemerkungen zur ägyptischen Königtum, vor allem in der Spätzeit, *Chronique d'Égypte* 46, 250–74.

Kormysheva, K. (1997) Arkamani's inscription from Dakke and its historical background, *Warsaw Egyptological Studies I*, 353–61, Warsaw.

Loprieno, A. (2003) Travel and Fiction in Egyptian Literature. In D. O'Connor and S. Quirke (eds) *Mysterious Lands*, 31–52, London.

McKechnie, P. and P. Guillaume (eds) (2008) *Ptolemy Philadelphus and his World*. Leiden.

Meiggs, R. and D. M. Lewis (1969) *A Selection of Greek Historical Inscriptions to the End of the Fifth Century BC*. Oxford.

O'Connor, D. (1987) The Location of Irem, *Journal of Egyptian Archaeology* 73, 99–136.

Priese, K. H. (1974) '*rm* und '*3m*, das Land Irame. Ein Beitrag zur Topographie des Sudan in Altertum, *Altorientalische Forschungen I*, 7–41, Berlin.

Redford, D. B. (2004) *From Slave to Pharaoh: The Black Experience of Ancient Egypt*. Baltimore.

Roeder, G. (1959) *Die Ägyptische Gotterwelt*. Zürich and Stuttgart.

Quack, J. F. (2009) Innovations in Ancient Garb? Hieroglyphic Texts from the Time of Ptolemy Philadelphus. In P. McKechnie and P. Guillaume (eds) *Ptolemy Philadelphus and his World*, 275–290, Leiden.

Schäfer, D. (2011) *Makedonische Pharaonen und Hieroglyphische Stelen: Historische Untersuchungen und verwandten Denkmälern*. Studia Hellenistica 50. Leuven.

Sethe, K. (ed.) (1904) *Hieroglyphische Urkunden der Griecisch-Römischen Zeit*. 2 vols. Leipzig.

Simpson, W. K., R. O. Faulkner, and E. F. Wente, Jr. (2003) *The Literature of Ancient Egypt: An Anthology of Stories, Instructions, Stelae, Autobiographies, and Poetry*. 3rd edn. New Haven.

Török, L. (2009) *Between Two Worlds: The Frontier Region between Ancient Nubia and Egypt 3700 BC–500 AD*. Leiden.

Valbelle, D. (1990) *Les Neuf Arcs: L'Égyptien et les Étrangers de la préhistoire à la conquéte d'Alexandre*. Paris.

Winnicki, J. (1991) Militäroperationen von Ptolemaios I. und Seleukos I. in Syrien in den Jahren 312–311 v. Chr. (II), *Ancient Society* 22, 164–85.

CLEOMENES OF NAUCRATIS, VILLAIN OR VICTIM?

Elizabeth Baynham[1]

According to that great universal reference work of the Internet, *Wikipedia,* a classic humorous paradigm of inductive reasoning is the so-called 'duck test'; *i.e.* 'If it looks like a duck, swims like a duck, and quacks like a duck, then it probably is a duck.'

This aphorism has been attributed to several individuals, but Richard Immerman notes in his book on the CIA a rather interesting and sinister instance of pernicious labelling associated with the saying in the United States during the Cold War, when fear of Communist aggression drove American foreign policy and highly placed officials who had themselves suffered from Senator McCarthy's indictments applied the same highly subjective processes and criteria for discrimination to a foreign arena. The American diplomat Richard Cunningham Patterson Jr., ambassador to Guatemala in 1950 openly boasted that he could spot a Guatemalan Communist merely by projecting his own understanding of Communism to the local context.[2]

In the case of Cleomenes of Naucratis, Ptolemy's hyparch in Egypt and Alexander's former satrap (if Stanley Burstein is right),[3] we might substitute 'villain' for 'duck'; if Cleomenes seems to have behaved like a crook, and several of our ancient writers condemn him as such, then should we do the same? Well, we shall see.

Arrian (7.23.6), no doubt influenced by Ptolemy Soter's history, explicitly describes Cleomenes as a "bad man" – an *aner kakos* – who had "perpetrated many acts of injustice in Egypt." It is comparatively uncommon for Arrian to express personal judgements; elsewhere (3.6.7), as Bosworth notes, he uses the same description of Tauriscus,[4] a Greek

[1] I should like to thank Professor Waldemar Heckel for his unfailing guidance, inspiration and warm friendship over many years. It is with some trepidation that I offer a paper which touches upon an individual figure, but I have to say that scholars like Berve and Heckel have made navigating the sea of Alexander prosopography a lot easier. I should also like to acknowledge Brian Bosworth's contribution to my essay; firstly for generously sharing the third volume of his forthcoming commentary on Arrian, which is now nearing completion, and secondly for his comments. And, finally, I am grateful to Associate Professor Tim Howe and Dr Sabine Müller for their careful scrutiny and additional references; any remaining errors are my own.
[2] Immerman 1982, 102; Patterson Jr made the claim during a speech at a Rotary dinner.
[3] Burstein 2008, 183–194. See also Jacobs 1994, 58, 62; Hölbl 1994, 12.
[4] Bosworth, forthcoming, *ad loc.*

like Cleomenes, and a man who convinces Alexander's treasurer and boyhood friend Harpalus to abscond (the first time) just prior to the battle of Issus. Although theft could have been a possible reason for their flight,[5] the most likely explanation is Harpalus and Tauriscus thought that Alexander was going to be annihilated by the Persians.[6] There is also a certain implication that both Cleomenes and Tauriscus were disloyal cowards, if we take *kakos* in that sense.[7]

However, Arrian also censures Alexander the Great for what appears to be an infamous *carte blanche* in a letter that the king wrote to Cleomenes; to the effect that he, Alexander will overlook any misdeeds on his governor's part, provided that Cleomenes carried out the construction of a shrine to Hephaestion and the establishment of his cult. I shall return to Alexander's special directive and the context of the correspondence that Arrian cites shortly.

Justin (13.4.11) describes Cleomenes outright as "the man who had built Alexandria".[8] There is a fairly substantial modern bibliography on Cleomenes, as one might expect for a man who was so strongly associated with the foundation and early construction of one of the great showcase cities of the ancient world, and his role in the transformation of Egypt. Most of the scholarly literature has focussed on Alexander's elaborate administrative arrangements for Egypt and Cleomenes' initial appointment including the question of whether he usurped his position as satrap, as well as his financial acumen, particularly grain speculation and his subsequent massive accumulation of revenue. In any event, Alexander's organisation of Egypt was complicated. Arrian (3.5.2–5) states that Alexander initially appointed two Egyptians, Doloaspis and Petisis as nomarchs (a term that Herodotus also uses of rulers in Egypt).[9] As Burstein has shown (see above, n. 3), a fragmentary ostrakon names a certain 'Pediese' as the satrap under Alexander, who undoubtedly must be the 'Petisis' named by Arrian as nomarch; it is likely that Ptolemy wanted to appropriate the term 'satrap' for himself. Arrian also notes that Petisis declined the appointment, and Doloaspis took it all. Cleomenes was initially appointed as governor of the area around Heroonpolis (in the Nile Delta on the Eastern side), with instructions to extract tribute from the nomarchs. We do not know how long Doloaspis was in power; Burstein has suggested that Cleomenes seems to have assumed full control by 328/27 BCE. Whether he had 'usurped' the position as such is not known; another complication is the date of Khababash's rebellion. He was an Egyptian dynast who led an uprising against the Persians, claiming the monarchy of upper

---

5   Heckel 2006, 260.

6   Bosworth 1980, 284. Cf. Jaschinski 1981, 15–18 (accepted by Müller 2006, 72–73), that Harpalus was sent by Alexander to make clear that one of his faction, his brother-in-law, Alexander of Epirus, would succeed if he had died in Cilicia. Alexander was seriously ill, his death seemed to have been close at hand, and so concerns about succession were relevant. And Harpalus was a likely emissary since he seems to have been a relative of the Molossian dynasty and like Tauriscus, ended up in Epirus.

7   Cf. Liddell and Scott, 764; *kakos* used in the context of war is the opposite of *agathos* or *esthlos* and can mean craven or cowardly; so *Il.* 2.365, 6.489.

8   See Howe 2014 for the scholarly debate surrounding Alexander's foundation of Alexandria and Ptolemy and Cleomenes' roles therein; see also Wheatley's discussion of Cleomenes' contribution, Heckel and Yardley 2011, 90–91, and also Justin's omission of Ptolemy's removal of his *hyparch*, 150–51.

9   On that system in Persian times see Wiesehöfer 1991, 305–309.

and lower Egypt. Most scholars have previously placed Khababash's revolt in the mid 330s – around the accession of Darius III.[10]

However, Cleomenes' revenue-raising activity has been another area of interest. There is a virtual wealth of evidence in a treatise attributed to Aristotle (book 2 of the *Oeconomica*), which supplies important details relevant to fiscal exploitation.[11] According to Pseudo-Aristotle (*Oecon*. 2.1352 b19) Cleomenes bought grain directly from the growers, at 10 drachmae per measure – which is what they were getting from the merchants – and then sold it for 32. The same is true of his profiteering during the great famine of the 320s, caused by extensive drought;[12] Egypt was also affected, but not as badly as other areas of the Mediterranean world. Cleomenes held off on the export of grain until the situation became acute before allowing wheat to be shipped with a heavy excise (Oecon.2.1352 a20). Arrian does not say what the 'many injustices' (*polla aidikemata*) that Cleomenes was supposed to have committed were, but a speech preserved in the Demosthenic corpus (*Against Dionysodorus*) which was apparently delivered not long after Cleomenes' death, claims that the satrap manipulated the price of grain to the detriment of Athens and other cities (Ps. Dem. 56.7).

Unlike some satraps Cleomenes appears not to have minted coins, although scholars are divided on this issue. A paper published in 1997 by the great Georges Le Rider has suggested that Cleomenes sold grain at a high price to traders who in turn used his information on shortages – from what seems to have been a well organised network of efficient commercial spies in Cleomenes' pay – to ship grain where it was needed most; the traders could then sell the commodity at an even more inflated price. This type of speculation, which of course carried its own risks,[13] was not new; Xenophon (*Oecon*. 20.28) had also observed that grain merchants would take their produce to the places where they would be likely to get the highest value. But Cleomenes was good at it – and evidently better than his Athenian rivals, who complained about fraudulent and underhand practices. By the time of Alexander's death the treasuries of Egypt were bulging with no less than 8,000 talents in store, and the satrapy offered enviable financial reserves.[14] Moreover Cleomenes ensured the ongoing commercial viability of Alexandria by transplanting both population and the market at Canopus in the Nile Delta – about 21 kilometres from the site of Alexandria – to Alexander's new city (Ps. Arist. *Oecon*. 2.1352 a30–35).[15]

As Le Rider observed, modern historians' assessments of Cleomenes tend to fall into three groups; those who openly condemn him; those who recognise the merits of his

---

[10] Burstein 2000, 149–154.

[11] Basileios and Christos 2013.

[12] On the great drought and widespread famine of 328/27 BCE see Garnsey 1988, 161; Rhodes and Osborne 2003, 485–6. On the food supply politics that the drought inspired see Oliver 2007, 175–6; Howe 2013, 58–61.

[13] Traders risked losing money if rivals brought shipments in from elsewhere and then undersold; the skill lay in obtaining reliable information about demand and shipping produce there quickly; see Kloft 1988, 207–15; Le Rider 1997, 79–83; Collins 2012, 237–242.

[14] Bosworth forthcoming, 7.23.6 *ad loc.*

[15] Collins 2012, 237–242. But see Howe 2013, who argues persuasively that Pseudo-Aristotle was likely mistaken here and that Ptolemy, not Cleomenes, was responsible for the population transfers.

administration but are critical of his excesses, and finally apologists like Seibert[16] and Polyani (admittedly in the minority)[17] who, by emphasising the positive aspects of Cleomenes' achievement create a more flattering image.[18] Opinions range from "administrator of great vigour",[19] to "sharp man with a shrewd head for finance",[20] but it is worth quoting the vivid prose of Peter Green, who in his racy, journalistic style writes: "He [Cleomenes] saw that the key to success was hard cash, and (with the help of his military-cum-fiscal office) proceeded to amass it in great quantities. The story of his rapid rise to power, through robbery, blackmail, grain-profiteering and whole-sale extortion, is too complex, and marginal, to relate here. What does call for comment, however, is Alexander's reaction to it."[21]

Indeed, but apart from Alexander's response, I would also like to explore Ptolemy's reaction too, and his apparently systematic blackening of Cleomenes' reputation. The context of Alexander's correspondence with his governor is critical. In Arrian's text (7.23.8), he quotes Alexander's letter to Cleomenes directly:

> If I find these temples set in good order in Egypt, and these shrines of Hephaestion, whatever wrong you have hitherto done, I pardon it; and for the future, of whatever nature your fault may be, you shall receive no harm at my hands.[22]

Arrian remarks that he cannot approve such a mandate to a man who was not only ruling over such a large and populous area, but who was also nasty. So, Alexander appears to be giving a known criminal open approval to continue his career of exploitation and graft. There has been a lot of comment about this passage, including an intriguing (if peculiar) explanation by Joseph Vogt who argued that Alexander was acting like an Achaemenid king in dispensing whatever clemency or punishment he considered appropriate.[23] However, Mary Whitby pointed out in a recent article in *Electrum* (2004) that Alexander's letter is expressing not so much a clean slate for Cleomenes as rather conditional approval – if the *heroa* for Hephaestion are built to Alexander's satisfaction, then Cleomenes would have nothing to fear, but if not … then the consequences could be unpleasant to say the least.[24] Nevertheless, Alexander's response seems to be the opposite of his treatment of other satraps who were executed for mismanagement after the King's return from Babylon. In those instances – at least according to Arrian (6.27.5) the policy proved effective in convincing native peoples that corrupt or oppressive local regimes would be brought to justice.[25] In the case of Egypt's governance, Alexander seemed to be acting out of sheer personal expediency.

---

[16]   Seibert 1969, 39–51.
[17]   Polyani 1977, 240–251
[18]   Le Rider 1997, 71.
[19]   Fraser 1972, 6.
[20]   Lane Fox 1973, 198, 220.
[21]   Green 1974, 278.
[22]   τὰ ἱερὰ τὰ ἐν Αἰγύπτῳ καλῶς κατεσκευασμένα καὶ τὰ ἡρῷα τὰ Ἡφαιστίωνος, εἴ τέ τι πρότερον ἡμάρτηκας, ἀφήσω σε τούτου, καὶ τὸ λοιπόν, ὁπηλίκον ἂν ἁμάρτῃς, οὐδὲν πείσῃ ἐξ ἐμοῦ ἄχαρι. A. G. Roos and G. Wirth, *Flavii Arriani quae exstant omnia*, vol. 1. Leipzig: Teubner, 1967.
[23]   Vogt 1971, 155–157; see Burstein 2008, 193 n.29.
[24]   Whitby, 41–42. See also Müller 2003, 234–236.
[25]   Bosworth, forthcoming.

It is clear that Alexander not only wanted something important out of Cleomenes, but also that he was confident that the Greek satrap would deliver. Cleomenes is described as an architect or an engineer by Pseudo-Callisthenes, and it is evident that the construction of Alexandria was planned on an impressive scale;[26] how much of it had been built by the time of Alexander's death is another question. But there is the iconography of another monument, which is also thought to have been carved during Cleomenes' regime that offers a striking testimony of the satrap's capacity to realise projects – namely the beautiful representations of Alexander as Pharaoh on the Shrine of the Barque in Luxor, a temple dedicated to the cult of the royal ka.[27] A sanctuary to Amun Re had been constructed by Amenhotep III, but was rebuilt in the name of Alexander. The renovation involved removing four pillars enclosing the old inner sanctuary and constructing a new one for Amun's barque with caved reliefs on its walls. Although the question of whether Alexander was ever formally crowned Pharaoh is controversial,[28] the 52 panels from the shrine in the inner sanctum of the temple show the king being introduced to Amun-Re and to the ithyphallic Amun-Re Khamutef, honouring the deities with prayers and offerings, as well as receiving gifts – including Amun-Re's responsibility and his throne. The inscriptions appear to date to the 320s, and Andrew Stewart is probably right to say that initiative for the project was Alexander's.[29] But importantly the carvings and inscriptions demonstrate the legitimation of Alexander's rule by the Theban priests, and that for these people the images and their titulature had a mystical and ritual power.[30] Moreover, the priests of the temple had not conferred this kind of acceptance upon the Persian monarchs, who had desecrated Egyptian religious practices.

Cleomenes would no doubt have financed and perhaps supervised this work; it was an elaborate and expensive project. Although Pesudo-Aristotle claims that Cleomenes was also effective at extracting revenues from priests (in particular by outraging their religious sensitivities when he threatened a cull of crocodiles), he must have still been able to work productively with them, but whatever methods he used – perhaps a combination of bribery and intimidation – the stunning results speak for themselves.

Alexander did not live to see either the constructed city of Alexandria or the restored Shrine of the Barque, and it is not known what intelligence he had of their progress, but he would have had his informants. We know that the king was left bereft and highly distraught by the death of Hephaestion; what better way to ensure the construction of his dead friend's heroic shrines than to entrust them to the man who had bankrolled the renovation of the temple of the divine living ruler?[31]

This brings me to the question of the authenticity of Alexander's letter and Ptolemy's

---

[26] Burstein 2008, 186.

[27] Bell 1985, 251–294. See also the comprehensive study of Abd El-Raziq 1984.

[28] Burstein 1991, 139–145. Cf. Bosche-Puche 2008, 29–44; 2013, 131–154; and 2014, who argues convincingly for a new interpretation of Alexander's Egyptian reign and official titulature.

[29] Stewart 1993, 175 with n. 66. The date of the inscriptions was suggested by Burstein. Cf. Bosche-Puche 2008, 29–44.

[30] Collins 2009, 179–205. On this see Schäfer 2007, 54–74.

[31] On doubts concerning the historicity of the tradition that Hephaestion was Alexander's lover see Müller 2011, 429–456.

role in shaping the historiography about Cleomenes. Arrian seems to have accepted the correspondence as genuine, and it is possible that he believed that if Ptolemy had cited it, then it had to be true – at least if Arrian himself was adhering to the principle which he stated in his preface (1.1.2) – that it was more shameful (*aischroteron*) for a king to be caught in a lie. Modern scholars have been understandably sceptical; Hammond states outright that the letter was a forgery,[32] while in his forthcoming commentary Bosworth notes that Ptolemy, "a remarkably slippery customer", was not above using forgery if it suited his purpose; apart from Alexander's fictitious Will (the basis of the *Liber de Morte* and part of the Alexander Romance) which Bosworth thinks was concocted by Ptolemy's staff,[33] Soter also sent a false message before Ipsus reporting that Seleucus and Lysimachus had been beaten, which then gave him the justification to withdraw his forces from Syria (Diod. 20.113.1–2; 21.1.5–60). I might add that Ptolemy did not have a monopoly on false documents and he might have studied under Eumenes, who was also a master of duplicity.[34] Although we cannot prove whether Alexander's letter to Cleomenes was genuine or fake, in this instance, I am prepared to side with Arrian and accept it at face value.[35] When Ptolemy took over the satrapy there would have been an archive of documents – we know from Plutarch's Life of *Eumenes* (2.2) that satraps were expected to keep file copies of their correspondence with the King – and this was one occasion where Ptolemy could exploit a real communication to his advantage; as WikiLeaks has shown in our own time, disseminated official, but sensitive material can be nothing short of sensational. For Ptolemy, Alexander's letter was a pure gift; here was the great king himself openly acknowledging that Cleomenes was a delinquent who was exploiting his subjects – and, moreover, someone whom he fully expected would continue to do so. The letter alone would justify Ptolemy's action in ridding Egypt of such a gangster.

So, why did Ptolemy have Cleomenes killed? By now it might seem obvious that Cleomenes is 'quacking' on Pharos. Here we have an incoming new satrap, Ptolemy, who needs cash to enrol a mercenary army (Diod. 18.14.1); he is also faced with a full treasury and an apparently unpopular incumbent with a reputation for making money out of human misery. It stands to reason that Ptolemy would have had him quickly removed. However, there is a puzzling anomaly. We are told that at the distribution of the satrapies in Babylon after Alexander's death, Ptolemy was confirmed as satrap of Egypt and Cleomenes was meant to be his hyparch or adjutant (Just. 13.4.11; Arr. *Succ* 1.5; Dexippus FGrH 100 F8). Cleomenes does not seem to have offered any resistance to Ptolemy when he arrived, and given his acumen and achievements, he would have been useful to Ptolemy too – although one might say that Cleomenes' local knowledge and connections made him dangerous as well as useful. Pausanias (1.6.3) seems to indicate that Ptolemy and Cleomenes cooperated prior to Ptolemy's hi-jacking of Alexander's body and Perdiccas' invasion, but then Ptolemy had Cleomenes killed, not because of his previous administration of the

---

[32] Hammond 1993, 302–305; but cf. Hamilton 1953, 157 who accepts the correspondence as genuine.

[33] Bosworth 2000, 207–241.

[34] Prior to the battle of Gabiene, Eumenes concocted a false letter from Olympias which said that her forces had been victorious, in order to boost the morale of his own army (Diod. 19.23; Poly. *Strat.* 4.11.3).

[35] On Ptolemy honouring the memory of his friend Hephaestion see Müller 2013, 75–92.

satrapy but because he suspected Cleomenes of working for Perdiccas – so disloyalty, rather than mismanagement was Ptolemy's main motive.

Yet I find myself drawn to Arrian's description of Cleomenes as *aner kakos* – a 'bad man'. On one level, such a description is so broad as to be almost meaningless – after all, Greek literature is full of *andres kakoi*. But as noted earlier, the phrase has a surprisingly limited application in Arrian – occurring elsewhere only in connection with Tauriscus, the Greek who had led Harpalus astray. Harpalus, like Ptolemy, had been a boyhood friend of Alexander's and had been exiled with him by Philip II, but had been recalled and cherished by Alexander. Like his father, Philip, Alexander reinstated Harpalus, yet he was to betray his king and flee a second time, with a kit bag of 5,000 talents – with which to buy mercenaries. It is tempting to think that perhaps something of that nature – perhaps involving intended embezzlement and flight – happened in the case of Cleomenes. Unlike Alexander, Ptolemy would not give him a second chance.

I do not think we can take the investigation further, but for me *aner kakos* was a loaded statement. And more than four hundred years later, Arrian himself steeped in a world of verbal nuance was to pick it up and run.

Bibliography

Abd El-Raziq, M. (1984) *Die Darstellungen und Texte des Sanktuars Alexanders des Grossen im Tempel von Luxor.* Mainz am Rheim.

Basileios, A. K. and C. P Baloglou (2013) *Oeconomica. Introduction, Translation and Commentaries.* Athens.

Bell, L. (1985) Luxor Temple and the Cult of the Royal Ka, *Journal of Near Eastern Studies* 44, 251–294.

Boshe-Puche, F. (2008) L'autel' du temple d'Alexandre le Grand à bahariya retrouvé, *Le Bulletin de l'Institut Français d'Archéologie Orientale* 108, 29–44.

— (2013) The Egyptian Royal Titulary of Alexander the Great, I: Horus, Two Ladies, Golden Horus, and Throne Names, *Journal of Egyptian Archaeology* 99, 131–154.

— (2014) The Egyptian Royal Titulary of Alexander the Great II: Personal Name, Empty Cartouche, Final Remarks, and Appendix, *Journal of Egyptian Archaeology* 100 (in press).

Bosworth, A. B. (1980) *A Historical Commentary on Arrian's History of Alexander I.* Oxford.

— (2000) Ptolemy and the Will of Alexander. In A. B. Bosworth and E. J. Baynham (eds) *Alexander the Great in Fact and Fiction,* 207–241, Oxford.

— (forthcoming). *A Historical Commentary on Arrian's History of Alexander* iii. Oxford.

Burstein, S. M. (1991) Pharaoh Alexander: A Scholarly Myth, *Ancient Society* 22, 139–145.

— (2000) Prelude to Alexander: The Reign of Khababash, *Ancient History Bulletin* 14, 149–154.

— (2008) Alexander's Organisation of Egypt: A Note on the Career of Cleomenes of Naucratis. In T. Howe and J. Reames (eds) *Macedonian Legacies. Studies in Ancient Macedonian History and Culture in Honor of Eugene N. Borza,* 183–194, Claremont.

Collins, A. (2009) The Divinity of Alexander in Egypt: A Reassessment. In P. Wheatley and R. Hannah (eds) *Alexander and His Successors,* 179–205, Claremont.

— (2012) Cleomenes of Naucratis, Heroonopolis, and the Revenue from the Red Sea Trade under Alexander the Great, *ZPE* 180, 237–242.

Fraser, P. M. (1972) *Ptolemaic Alexandria.* Oxford.

Garnsey, P. (1988) *Famine and Food Supply in the Graeco-Roman World. Response to Risk and Crisis.* Cambridge.

Green, P. (1974) *Alexander of Macedon.* Harmondsworth.

Hamilton, J. R. (1953) Alexander and his 'So-Called Father', *CQ* 3, 151–157.

Hammond, N. G. L. (1993) *Sources for Alexander the Great.* Cambridge.

Heckel, W. (2006) *Who's Who in the Age of Alexander the Great.* London.

Hölbl, G. (1994) *Die Geschichte des Ptolemäerreichs.* Darmstadt.

Howe, T. (2013) Athens, Alexander and the Politics of Resistance, *Ancient World* 44.1, 55–65.

— (2014) Founding Alexandria: Alexander the Great and the Politics of Memory. In P. Bosman (ed.) *Alexander in Africa*, 72–91. Acta Classica Supplement V. Pretoria.

Immerman, R. H. (1982) *The CIA in Guatemala: the Foreign Policy of Intervention.* Austin.

Jacobs, B. (1994) *Die Satrapienverwaltung im Perserreich zur Zeit Dareios' III.* Wiesbaden.

Jaschinski, S. (1981) *Alexander und Griechenland unter dem Eindruck der Flucht des Harpalos.* Bonn.

Kloft, H. B. (1988) Kleomenes von Naukratis, *Grazer Beiträge* 15, 191–222.

Lane Fox, R. (1973) *Alexander the Great.* London.

Le Rider, G. (1997) Cleomene de Naucratis, *Bulletin de Correspondance Hellénique* 121, 79–83.

Müller, S. (2003). *Maßnahmen der Herrschaftssicherung gegenüber der makedonischen Opposition bei Alexander dem Großen.* Frankfurt.

— (2006). Alexander, Harpalos, Pythionike und Glykera. Überlegungen zu den Repräsentationsformen des Schatzmeisters in Babylon und Tarsos. In V. Lica (ed.) *Philia. FS Gerhard Wirth*, 71–106, Galatzi.

— (2011) In Abhängigkeit von Alexander? Hephaistion bei den Alexanderhistoriographen, *Gymnasium* 118, 429–456.

— (2013) Ptolemaios und die Erinnerung an Hephaistion, *Anabasis* 3, 75–92.

Oliver, G. J. (2007) *War, Food, and Politics in Early Hellenistic Athens.* Oxford.

Polyani, K. (1977) *The Livelihood of Man.* New York.

Rhodes, P. J. and R. Osborne (2003) *Greek Historical Inscriptions 404–323 BC.* Oxford.

Schäfer, D. (2007) Alexander der Große, Pharao und Priester. In S. Pfeiffer (ed.) *Ägypten unter fremden Herrschern zwischen persischer Satrapie und römischer Provinz*, 54–74, Frankfurt.

Seibert, J. (1969) *Untersuchungen zur Geschichte Ptolemaios' I* (Münchener Beiträge zur Papyrusforschung und antiken Rechtsgeschichte 56). Munich.

Stewart, A. (1993) *Faces of Power.* Berkeley and Los Angeles.

Vogt, J. (1971) Kleomenes von Naukratis – Herr von Ägypten, *Chiron* 1, 155–157.

Wheatley, P., W. Heckel, and J. Yardley (2011) *Justin* Epitome *of the* Philippic History *of Pompeius Trogus*, vol II Books 13–15. Translation and appendices by J. C. Yardley, commentary by Pat Wheatley and Waldemar Heckel. Oxford.

Whitby, W. (2004) Four Notes on Alexander, *Electrum* 8, 35–47.

Wiesehöfer, J. (1991) PRTRK, RB HYL, SGN und MR. Zur Verwaltung Südägyptens in achaimenidischer Zeit, *Achaemenid History* 6, 305–309.

CULT OF THE DEAD AND VISION
OF THE AFTERLIFE
IN EARLY HELLENISTIC MACEDONIA

Franca Landucci Gattinoni

In the geopolitical chessboard of the Aegean Sea, Macedonian power emerged and developed thanks to the extraordinary organizational and strategic ability of Philip II, who became king of Macedonia in 359 BCE. Until then, Macedonia had been relegated to the margins of Greek history, and the profits from the raw materials of its territory (mainly timber and precious metals) had benefited the Greek cities that controlled their trade.

Amidst the wreckage of contemporary Hellenistic historiography, Books 16–20 of the *Library* of Diodorus Siculus, the historian of the second half of the first century BCE, provide the widest and most ancient historical *continuum* on the years between 359 and 302.[1] In his account of the events, Diodorus sometimes mentions customs typical of the Macedonian tradition, with some references also to the official burial ceremonies for the deceased sovereigns.

These references became particularly significant in the last three decades of the twentieth century due to the archaeological discoveries of Manolis Andronikos at Vergina, where, in the excavations of the so-called Great Tumulus, an impressive number of ancient structures came to light: three underground tombs and a surface monument, identified as a *heroon*, *i.e.* a sacred building dedicated to the worship of one or more dead people inhumed in close proximity.[2] On the basis of typological and functional analyses of these exceptional finds, generally datable between the second quarter and the end of the fourth century BCE, it is now the accepted scholarly opinion that the Great Tumulus was the burial place of the Macedonian rulers of the time. Much has been debated, however, over the precise identification of the buried bodies: what is certain is that Alexander the Great's is definitely not among them, since about two years after his death in Babylon in June 323, his corpse was conducted to Alexandria of Egypt where he was laid to rest by the will of Ptolemy I.[3]

The findings at Vergina are well known, yet I think a brief description of the three tombs

---

[1]   For an initial approach to Diodorus's life and works, see Ambaglio *et al.* 2008.

[2]   The work of reference for the findings at Vergina is still Andronikos 1984, published by the discoverer as a preliminary report.

[3]   On the burial of Alexander the Great, see Adriani 2000, *passim*; Landucci Gattinoni 2008, 129–138.

could be useful at this point so as to make clearer the subsequent references to the structures.[4] Tomb I, the closest to the *heroon,* at the edge of the Great Tumulus, is an underground cist tomb consisting of a single burial chamber, 3.50 m by 2.10 m, and 3 m high: Pillaged in ancient times, it still displays marvellous paintings on three of its four walls. Tomb II, preserved intact at the center of the Great Tumulus, is a typical barrel-vaulted Macedonian tomb consisting of a main room and an antechamber, with a striking façade topped by a large Doric frieze, 5.56 m long and 1.16 m high, representing a hunting scene, which is still readable despite the ravages of time. The interpretation of the frieze has always been heavily dependent on the identification of the ruler, aged about fifty, whose ashes were in a golden urn found in the main room; another golden urn with the ashes of a young woman aged about twenty was in the antechamber. Also Tomb III, preserved intact and situated immediately north of Tomb II, is a typical barrel-vaulted Macedonian tomb, consisting of a main room and an antechamber, with a façade with no semi-columns and surmounted by a frieze now unfortunately completely unreadable;[5] the antechamber of the tomb was empty, while in the main room was found a silver hydria containing the ashes of a teenage boy known as the 'Young Prince'.

While the identity of the latter is undisputed – all scholars[6] agree that the young prince must be identified as the posthumous son of Alexander the Great, Alexander IV, murdered in 310 when he was about 13 years old (both the young prince and his uncle Philip III Arrhidaeus were Alexander the Great's heirs),[7] with regard to the identification of the remains in Tomb II scholars are divided into two factions bitterly hostile to each other.

On the one hand, the members of the 'oldest' faction, loyal to the thesis of the discoverer of the tombs,[8] believe that therein were buried Philip II and his last wife Kleopatra, shortly after their assassination, at Aegae, in 336.[9] The other faction, siding with a thesis proposed in 1980 by several scholars independently from each other,[10] believes Tomb II to be the burial

---

4   For an initial description of the three tombs, see Andronikos 1984, 55–83, 86–91, 97–100, 198–199; Touratsoglou 1995, 221–243; recapitulation of the issue in Landucci Gattinoni 2003, 44–56; a more recent comprehensive description in Borza, Palagia 2007, 81–125.

5   For a brief but clear analysis of the characteristics of Macedonian tombs, in addition to the now classic works of Andronikos 1993, 145–190, and Miller 1993, see also the recent (wide) collection of Brecoulaki 2006.

6   See, most recently, with ample discussion of bibliography, Landucci Gattinoni 2003, 44–56; Borza, and Palagia 2007, 81–125.

7   On the death of Alexander IV, see *Marmor Parium* in *FGrHist* 239FB18, which dates this event to the Attic year 310/09; Diod. 19.105.1–3; Paus. 9.7.2; Iust. 15.2.3. For an analysis of the problem, see Landucci Gattinoni 2003, 124–137; Landucci Gattinoni 2010, 113–121.

8   The prime supporter of the identification of the deceased buried in Tomb II as Philip II was M. Andronikos himself, who in all his interventions always insisted on this hypothesis (see in particular the reflections in Andronikos 1984, 218–235, several times repeated in numerous interventions); Hammond many times sided with this hypothesis (see most recently Hammond 1991, 69–82), while other scholars limited themselves to reaffirm Andronikos's thesis in individual interventions (see *e.g.* Green 1982, 129–151; Lavenne 1999, 71–74).

9   On the death of Philip, with extensive analysis of sources and bibliography, see Worthington 2008, 172–186, and most recently, Landucci Gattinoni 2012, 127–135.

10   After the first attempts, independent of each other, to identify the deceased in Tomb II as Philip III Arrhidaeus, all datable to 1980 (see Adams 1980, 67–72; Lehmann 1980, 527–531; Prestianni Giallombardo, and Tripodi 1980, 989–1001), several scholars have aligned themselves with this new hypothesis: see, in

site of king Philip III Arrhidaeus and his wife Eurydike. As stated by Diodorus (19.11.1–9), the two sovereigns were murdered in October 317, during the so-called Second War of Diadochi, by Alexander's mother, Olympias, eager to eliminate those that she considered the most dangerous rivals to her grandson Alexander IV. Diodorus (19.52.5) also reports that, about two years later, Cassander, Antipater's son, after taking control of Macedonia, buried with full honours the remains of Philip III and Eurydike, and condemned to death Olympias and her collaborators.[11] With respect to this issue, it must be pointed out that, while the former hypothesis, which identifies the remains in Tomb II as Philip II's, was vigorously sustained by Prof. Andronikos until his death, the latter seems to be based on arguments that, albeit not binding in themselves, form a coherent and homogeneous picture, so much so that even some among those who had first thought of Philip II now believe most likely the identification of the corpse in Tomb II as Philip III Arrhidaeus.[12]

Sic stantibus rebus, however, the identity of the person in Tomb I, whose importance – despite the lack of grave goods, plundered before the construction of the Great Tumulus[13] – is attested by the marvellous frescoes still visible on three of the four walls of the underground chamber, is still unclear.

Interestingly, the frescoes in Tomb I were described in detail by Andronikos,[14] who, besides presenting them as true masterpieces,[15] attributed the best preserved, the Rape of Persephone by Hades, to the painter Nicomachos, who, according to Pliny,[16] was the author

---

particular, the interesting reflections of Tripodi 1998, 99–109; for a detailed list, see Landucci Gattinoni 2003, 45, note 95; updates in Borza, and Palagia 2007, 81–125.

[11] On these events, see Landucci Gattinoni 2003, 39–43.

[12] For a recapitulation of the issue, with ample discussion of bibliography and the shared hypothesis that identifies the deceased inhumed in Tomb II as Philip III, see, besides Landucci Gattinoni 2003, 44–56, also Borza, Palagia 2007, 81–125. *Contra,* with arguments that are, in my opinion, not diriment, Daumas 2009, 139–165.

[13] See Andronikos 1984, 86–91.

[14] Andronikos 1984, 87–89: "The lower section of all the walls is painted in glowing red (Pompeian red). 1.50 m above the floor is a narrow frieze (0.22 m high; it narrows to 0.19 m on the south wall) which runs around three of the four walls – it is absent from the western side where there were 'shelves'. The same decorative theme, two griffins facing each other with a flower between them, repeats itself against a blue background. Above this frieze the plastering of the walls was white and on that were the paintings. On the long southern wall were three seated female figures. They are not very well preserved, the central one having suffered most. [...] I consider it highly probable that this trio represents the Three Fates. The centerpiece of the narrow eastern wall is a female figure depicted seated alone on a rock. It is very well preserved, even though the colors that filled in the outlines of the drawing have almost disappeared. [...] One's first reaction might be to take this female figure as a portrait of the deceased. But the rock on which she sits, and even more, the composition which occupies the north wall gives us, I think, the correct interpretation: she is Demeter, sitting on the 'mirthless stone', deeply mourning the loss of her daughter, abducted by Hades. This is exactly the scene which covers the long north wall: here we are confronted not by a magnificent depiction of isolated figures, but by an absolutely unique dramatic composition. Luck was particularly favorable to us, for almost all the figures, together with the color, were preserved in exceptionally good condition. [...] The entire composition is based first and foremost on the drawing. The artist, one of the greatest in his own time, drew with a sure hand, a meticulous eye and great feeling."

[15] For an interesting critical reflection on these wall paintings, see most recently Moreno 1998, with ample bibliography.

[16] Pliny *NH* 35.108.

of a painting with the same subject that, in the first century CE, was at the *Capitolium* in Rome. Since Nicomachos was active between 360 and 320 BCE,[17] the link between him and the paintings in Tomb I appears to authorize the hypothesis that identifies the person inhumed as Philip II, probably laid to rest with a young woman (his last wife Kleopatra?) and a child (their infant son?), as seems to be proven by the few human remains which survived the plundering and were found scattered on the floor of the tomb.[18] This hypothesis is obviously contested by those who identify the individual buried in Tomb II as Philip II. With respect to this controversy, it must be acknowledged that only Hammond has properly delved into the issue,[19] whereas others, beginning with Andronikos himself, have avoided the problem, generically referring to Tomb I as the 'Tomb of Persephone' on the basis of the episode portrayed in the fresco on the north wall, the Rape of Persephone by Hades. Further to that, it may be pointed out that Hammond has proposed to identify the individual buried in Tomb I as Amyntas III, Philip's father, yet with no compelling (and convincing) argument in support of his thesis.[20] In fact, the latter is contradicted, in particular by the chronology of the frescoes themselves, which the archaeologists seem to agree as dating to the second half of the fourth century, thus several years after the death of Amyntas in 369.[21]

As a confirmation of the fame that surrounded the deceased inhumed in Tomb it may also be the fact that only this tomb, among those of the Great Tumulus, was pillaged around 274 by the Gallic mercenaries of Pyrrhus, king of Epirus, who, according to Plutarch (*Pyrrh.* 26.6), after taking control of Aegae, let his men outrage the nearby royal tombs.[22] In effect, the Vergina excavations have proved that after plundering Tomb I the barbarians in the pay of Pyrrhus, even if hungry for treasures, did not even try to look for other tombs, which were indeed in close proximity, as if certain of having grasped most of the wealth stored *in loco*, a conviction that must derive from the belief of having already raided the tomb of the greatest of the Macedonian rulers buried in the royal cemetery at Aegae, namely that of Philip II, who was the true founder of the power of his people.

Within this picture fits well the *heroon*, of which few (and meagre) remains were found close to Tomb I. The *heroon* could in effect indicate the place of worship dedicated to the memory of Philip II by the will of his son, although this hypothesis should be proposed very prudently since, as recently pointed out by Mari,[23] no literary source confirms the existence of such a building near the royal tombs, and from an archaeological point of view, too, there may be doubts about the typology of the original structure.

---

[17]   See most recently Hoesch 2000, col.924.

[18]   The hypothesis of the identification of the deceased buried in Tomb I as Philip II, only passingly mentioned by Borza 1987, 105–121, in particular 188–119, then developed in Landucci Gattinoni 2003, 44–56, was recently revived by Borza, and Palagia 2007, 81–125.

[19]   Hammond 1982, 111–127, in particular, 115–117.

[20]   Hammond's thesis has been challenged, I think, effectively, most recently by Borza, and Palagia 2007, 81–125, with extensive discussion of bibliography.

[21]   On the date of Amyntas's death, see Diod. 15.60.3; on this historical figure, see most recently Bearzot 2005, 17–41.

[22]   See Andronikos 1984, 227–228; Carney 1992, 4–5.

[23]   Mari 2008, 225–226.

In any case, the hypothesis that identifies the dead in Tomb II as Philip III Arrhidaeus and his wife Eurydike has been challenged by an objection that, as I have argued elsewhere,[24] is not without foundation and thus deserves careful investigation. More specifically, some scholars[25] think that, if Tomb II preserved the two sovereigns eliminated by Olympias in 317 and buried therein by Cassander, it should also preserve the remains of Kynna, daughter of Philip II and mother of Eurydike based on the fact that Diodorus, in the description of the funeral of the two sovereigns (19.52.5), explicitly states that Cassander "buried also Kynna with them, according to royal custom." Yet, since in Tomb II only two gold funerary *larnakes* were found (and there was no trace of a third cinerary urn), the lack of Kynna's ashes seems to preclude the possibility of identifying this tomb as Philip III Arrhidaeus. In effect, it is true, as maintained by Adams,[26] that Diodorus's passage must not be interpreted as a sure indication of a *joint* burial for these three historical figures honored by Cassander; however, it is also true that the same passage *at least* implies the existence of *a nearby burial site* for Eurydike's mother, whose *status*, as Philip II's daughter, made her worthy of resting in the area of the Great Tumulus, that is, in a burial area reserved for the last representatives of the Temenid dynasty. In my view, a possible solution to the debate lies in a brief note drafted by Andronikos along with the description of the excavation campaigns carried out at the Great Tumulus of Vergina from 1976 to 1980.[27] Andronikos writes that in the summer of 1980, about thirty meters to the east of Tomb II, another 'Macedonian tomb' was excavated, which, unlike similar tombs, had a free colonnade on its façade, the sole remains of the original monument (the rest having been quarried and transferred, perhaps to be used elsewhere, in circumstances unknown to us).[28] This tomb, then, of which no further details are available about chamber and antechamber, could be the resting site for Kynna's mortal remains, buried with all honors near the richer and more important tomb of her son-in-law Philip III Arrhidaeus and of her daughter Eurydike. Kynna was indeed part of the royal family, although hierarchically subordinate to Philip III Arrhidaeus and Eurydike, who had officially been the king and queen (βασιλεῖς) of Macedonia, and were therefore worthy of royal burial as prescribed by tradition.

Once 'discovered' the possible burial site of Kynna thus solved any contradiction between archaeological evidence and Diodorus's text, and so nothing precludes, in my view, the identification of the inhumed in Tomb II as the royal couple, namely Philip III Arrhidaeus and his wife Eurydike. Indeed, for several decades Tomb II has been amazing

---

[24] See Landucci Gattinoni 2010, 113–121.

[25] See Green 1982, 148–149; Andronikos 1984, 228; Musgrave 1991, 5.

[26] See Adams 1991, 30–31, whose opinion is reinforced by Borza 1991, 39.

[27] See Andronikos 1984, 82–83.

[28] Andronikos 1984, 83. In the same page, the archaeologist concludes his description of this tomb, lamenting the severity of the damage done to the structure, but stressing the hope of being able to reconstruct its shape at least graphically, as its plan had been detected with great precision. Obviously, the premature death of Andronikos has so far prevented the realization of this project, as well as the definitive publication of all the findings of the excavations at Vergina. A brief reference to this tomb is also in Andronikos 1993, 161, but especially in Touratsoglou 1995, 242, at the end of the paragraph devoted to the tombs of the Great Tumulus (221–242) (*To the north of these three tombs was discovered a fourth, with a free colonnade on its facade. Apart from the stylobate, the columns and a few stones from the walls, the rest of the building has been destroyed and quarried for building material*).

the world for the imposing neatness of its architecture and the opulence of its contents, these being clear and everlasting signs of the extraordinary funeral honors granted to the royal couple by Cassander, son of Antipater, whom Diodorus (19.52.5) explicitly indicates as the organizer of obsequies celebrated according to Macedonian royal custom (καθάπερ ἔθος ἦν τοῖς βασιλεῦσι).

In particular, Diodorus inserts the latter piece of information in a long articulated passage (19.52.1–7) dedicated to the actions that Cassander undertook in order to sanction his definitive seizure of Macedonia after his three-year exile. In the passage, Diodorus, alongside the events, focuses on the theme of the management of sovereignty and on Cassander's wish to take possession of such sovereignty. The importance of this issue is emphasized at a linguistic level not only by the frequent and repetitive use of terms connected with the semantic field of 'sovereignty', but also by the continual references to the last representatives of the Argead dynasty, among whom Cassander aimed to present himself as the legitimate heir. In more detail, already at 19.52.1, we read, *in primis*, that "Cassander's ambitions included the kingdom of Macedonia" (περιελάμβανε ταῖς ἐλπίσι τὴν Μακεδόνων βασιλείαν) and, *in secundis*, that he decided to marry Thessalonike, daughter of Philip II, because he was "eager to appear as a relative to the royal house" (σπεύδων οἰκεῖον αὐτὸν ἀποδεῖξαι τῆς βασιλικῆς συγγενείας). Later, at 19.52.4, writing of the young Alexander IV and of his mother, the Persian princess Roxane,[29] Diodorus maintains that Cassander's conduct was aimed at "preventing the existence of successors in the kingdom" (ἵνα μηδεὶς ᾖ διάδοχος τῆς βασιλείας): to this purpose, he had decreed that the young Argead was to be given "no royal education but a common man's" (τὴν ἀγωγὴν οὐκέτι βασιλικήν, ἀλλ' ἰδιώτου τοῦ τυχόντος οἰκείαν ἐκέλευε γίνεσθαι). Finally, at 19.52.5, the historian reports that Cassander "already behaving like a king had Eurydike and Philip, the sovereign couple, buried in Aegae according to royal custom" (βασιλικῶς ἤδη διεξάγων τὰ κατὰ τὴν ἀρχὴν Εὐρυδίκην μὲν καὶ Φίλιππον τοὺς βασιλεῖς [...] ἔθαψεν ἐν Αἰγαιαῖς, καθάπερ ἔθος ἦν τοῖς βασιλεῦσι).

Thus, according to Diodorus, Cassander's 'hunt' for power in Macedonia was realized through two basic steps: on the one hand, the exclusion of Alexander IV, indelibly 'marked' by his mother's Persian nationality, from the line of succession to the throne; on the other, the creation of a series of ideal and familial ties with Philip II, with the tenaciously pursued aim of channelling towards himself those persistent feelings of nostalgia, devotion and respect for the man that all Macedonians considered the founder of their powerful kingdom.[30]

In light of such direct continuity between Cassander and Philip II, then, can also be read the funeral ceremonies that the Antipatrid organized to honor Philip III Arrhidaeus and his wife Eurydike. These were characterized by 'funeral games', the celebration of which must have been part of the traditional obsequies for the members of the royal family, if, according to Diodorus,[31] even Alexander himself on the point of dying had prefigured the *epitáphios agōn* that his heirs were to hold in his honor.[32] The funerals for Philip III Arrhidaeus and

---

[29] On Roxane, see Heckel 2006, 241–242.
[30] On Macedonian nostalgia for Philip II, see the anecdote mentioned in Plut. *Demetr.* 42.6–7.
[31] On this aspect, see Diod. 17.117.4; 18.1.4. On *epitáphios agōn*, in general, in Greek tradition, see Landucci Gattinoni 2007, 155–170.
[32] On this aspect, see Landucci Gattinoni 2008, 6–7.

his wife Eurydike are moreover mentioned also by Diyllus,[33] who substantially confirms Diodorus's words on the 'royal' nature of the burial ceremony of the sovereigns, a feature strongly pursued by Cassander with the clear aim of claiming Philip II's legacy.

As justly pointed out by Mari,[34] Diodorus's detailed description confirms that "the attention devoted to the funeral of the deceased sovereign was an important step in the acknowledgment of the legitimacy of the new king and, therefore, it was an essential part of the complex *nomos* which regulated the relations between the two fundamental bodies of the Macedonian state" (ὁ βασιλεὺς καὶ οἱ Μακεδόνες). Also Alexander, in effect, after the assassination of Philip, confirmed his *status* as legitimate heir by devoting himself to the funeral rites for his father.[35] It is noteworthy that Alexander, besides holding the obsequies, also punished the murderers of his father, whose sovereignty he had inherited, with a conduct similar to that of Cassander, who, besides celebrating the funeral of Philip III and Eurydike, had put to death Alexander the Great's mother, Olympias, who was responsible for the death sentence of the two sovereigns.[36] However, we must admit that devotion to funeral ceremonies and cult of the dead were typical characteristics not only of the royal family, but of all the Macedonian aristocracy, given the several monumental tombs (seventy, according to the latest calculations) discovered in Macedonian territory during the twentieth century besides those at the Great Tumulus.[37]

On the widespread presence of monumental tombs, Mario Torelli, in a convincing reflection, argues indeed that "in a society organized in an aristocratic structure governed by kinship [...], the aristocracy developed indestructible faith in life after death and in the maintenance of its rank after death".[38] Such faith was made visible and understandable through the building of monumental tombs; to this conviction these tombs' magnificent architecture and marvellous wall paintings have impressively born testament over the centuries.

Bibliography

Adams, W. L. (1980) The Royal Macedonian Tomb at Vergina: An Historical Interpretation, *Ancient World* 3, 67–72.
— (1991) Cassander, Alexander IV and the Tombs at Vergina, *Ancient World* 22, 27–33.
Adriani, A. (2000) *La tomba di Alessandro*. Rome.
Ambaglio, D., F. Landucci and L. Bravi (2008) *Diodoro Siculo*, Biblioteca storica. *Commento Storico. Introduzione generale*. Milan.
Andronikos, M. (1984) *Vergina. The Royal Tombs and the Ancient City*. Athens.
— (1993) Le 'tombe macedoni'. In R. Ginouvès (ed.) *I Macedoni. Da Filippo alla conquista romana*, trad. ital., 145–190, Milan (= Paris 1993).
Bearzot, C. (2005) Aminta III di Macedonia in Diodoro. In C. Bearzot, F. Landucci (eds) *Diodoro e l'altra*

---

[33] See Diyllus in *FGrHist* 73F1: Κάσσανδρος [...], θάψας τὸν βασιλέα καὶ τὴν βασίλισσαν ἐν Αἰγαῖς, [...] καὶ τοῖς ἄλλοις τιμήσας, οἷς προσῆκει, καὶ μονομαχίας ἀγῶνα ἔθηκεν, εἰς ὃν κατέβησαν τέσσαρες τῶν στρατιωτῶν. On Diyllus, see the brief notes in Tuplin 2007, 162–164.
[34] Mari 2008, 224–225.
[35] Diod. 17.2.1.
[36] For references and bibliography on the issue of succession, see Fernández Nieto 2005, 29–44.
[37] On the Macedonian tombs, see *supra*, note 5.
[38] Torelli and Mavrojannis 1997, 321.

Grecia: Macedonia, Occidente, Ellenismo nella 'Biblioteca storica'. Atti del convegno Milano, 15–16 gennaio 2004, 17–41, Milan.

Borza, E. N. (1987) The Royal Macedonian Tombs and the Paraphernalia of Alexander the Great, *Phoenix* 41, 105–121.

— (1991) Commentary, *Ancient World* 22, 35–40.

Borza, E. N. and O. Palagia. (2007) The Chronology of the Macedonian Royal Tombs at Vergina, *Jahrbuch des Deutschen Archäologischen Instituts* 122, 81–125.

Brecoulaki, H. (2006) *La peinture funéraire de Macédoine : emplois et fonctions de la couleur IVe–IIe s. av. J.-C.*, 2 vols. Paris.

Carney, E. D. (1992) Tomb I at Vergina and the Meaning of the Great Tumulus as an Historical Monument, *Archaeological News* 17, 1–10.

Daumas, M. (2009) *L'or et le pouvoir: armement scythe et mythes grecs*. Nanterre.

Fernández Nieto, F. J. (2005) La designación del sucesor en el antiguo reino de Macedonia. In V. Alonso Troncoso (ed.) *Διάδοχος τῆς βασιλείας: la figura del sucesor en la realeza helenística*, 29–44, Madrid.

Green, P. (1982) The Royal Tombs of Vergina: A Historical Analysis. In W. L. Adams and E. N. Borza (eds) *Philip II, Alexander the Great and the Macedonian Heritage*, 129–151, Washington, DC.

Hammond, N. G. L. (1982) The Evidence for the Identity of the Royal Tombs at Vergina. In Adams and Borza, 111–127.

— (1991) The Royal Tombs at Vergina: Evolution and Identities, *Annual of the British School at Athens* 86, 69–82.

Heckel, W. (2006) *Who's Who in the Age of Alexander the Great: Prosopography of Alexander's Empire*. Oxford.

Hoesch, N. (2000) in *Der Neue Pauly* 8 s.v. *Nikomachos* n.4, col.924.

Landucci Gattinoni, F. (2003) *L'arte del potere. Vita e opere di Cassandro di Macedonia*. Stuttgart.

— (2007) Polluce e l'Ellenismo. In C. Bearzot, F. Landucci, and G. Zecchini (eds) *L'Onomasticon di Giulio Polluce. Tra lessicografia e antiquaria*, 155–170, Milan.

— (2008) *Diodoro Siculo, Biblioteca storica. Libro XVIII. Commento storico*. Milan.

— (2010) Cassander and the Legacy of Philip II and Alexander III in Diodorus' Library. In E. Carney and D. Ogden (eds) *Philip II and Alexander the Great: Father and Son, Lives and Afterlives*, 113–121, Oxford and New York.

— (2012) *Filippo re dei Macedoni*. Bologna.

Lavenne, S. (1999) À propos d'un portrait d'Alexandre le Grand trouvé dans la Tombe II du Grand Tumulus de Vergina, *RAHAL* 32, 71–74.

Lehmann, P. W. (1980) The So-called Tomb of Philip II: A Different Interpretation, *American Journal of Archaeology* 84, 527–531.

Mari, M. (2008) The Ruler Cult in Macedonia. In B. Virgilio (ed.) *Studi ellenistici* 20, 219–268, Pisa – Roma.

Miller, S. G. (1993) *The Tomb of Lyson and Kallikles: A Painted Macedonian Tomb*. Mainz am Rhein.

Moreno, P. (1998) Elementi di pittura ellenistica. In A. Rouveret (ed.) *L'Italie Méridionale et les premières expériences de la peinture hellénistique. Actes de la table ronde organisée par l'École française de Rome (Rome, 18 février 1994)*, 7–67, Rome.

Musgrave, J. H. (1991) The Human Remains from Vergina Tombs I, II e III: An Overview, *Ancient World* 22, 3–9.

Prestianni Giallombardo, A. M., and B. Tripodi (1980) Le tombe regali di Vergina: quale Filippo? *Annali della Scuola Normale Superiore di Pisa* 3.3, 989–1001.

Torelli, M., and T. Mavrojannis (1997) *Grecia. Guida Archeologica*. Milan.

Touratsoglou, I. (1995) *Macedonia. History. Monuments. Museums*. Athens.

Tripodi, B. (1997) *Cacce reali macedoni. Tra Alessandro I e Filippo V*, Soveria Mannelli (CZ) (Pelorias, 3).

Tuplin, C. (2007) Continuous Histories *(Hellenica)*. In J. Marincola (ed.) *A Companion to Greek and Roman Historiography*, 159–170, Malden, MA.

Worthington, I. (2008) *Philip II of Macedonia*. New Haven.

THE CAREER OF SOSTRATOS OF KNIDOS: POLITICS, DIPLOMACY AND THE ALEXANDRIAN BUILDING PROGRAMME IN THE EARLY HELLENISTIC PERIOD

Alexander Meeus[1]

The prosopography of Alexander's Empire is very well-known and easily accessible, in large part thanks to the work of Waldemar Heckel.[2] No encompassing prosopography exists for the period of the Successors,[3] but here too Heckel has produced many fundamental studies showing the importance of analysing people's positions and relationships for a proper understanding of the history of their times.[4] It is a pleasure to follow in his footsteps with this study of the career of Sostratos, the son of Dexiphanes, of Knidos. The main issues will be Sostratos' role in the construction of the Pharos, his diplomatic activity, and the date of his career. Sostratos occurs comparatively regularly in the literary sources and in the epigraphical record, and although the references are far from as informative as we would wish, they do allow us to say more about Sostratos' career and the politics of his time than one might think at first sight.[5] Yet we must constantly walk the tightrope between making the most of the evidence and making too much of it. Therefore, I have left conclusions that may be considered all too risky for a separate section at the end.

Sostratos' involvement in the construction of the Pharos
Sostratos' greatest claim to fame is undoubtedly the construction of the Pharos at Alexandria,

---

[1] I would like to thank Charles Crowther for invaluable epigraphical advice, and the editors for their comments on this paper. I am, as always, also greatly indebted to Hans Hauben who supervised an early version of this paper as an undergraduate essay in 2001. This version has been produced during a fellowship funded by the Research Foundation – Flanders (FWO). Unless indicated otherwise, translations of inscriptions are my own, and those of literary sources are from the Loeb Classical Library. All dates are BCE.
[2] Heckel 1992 and 2006 and articles too numerous to list.
[3] There are, however, partial prosopographies such as those of Hauben 1975 (nauarchs), Heckel 1988 (the *Liber de morte*) or Billows 1990, 361–452 (friends and subordinates of Antigonos Monophthalmos), and several prosopographies of wider scope are relevant to the age of the Successors: *e.g.* Peremans *et al.* 1950–2002; Sandberger 1970; Olshausen 1974; Mooren 1975; Tataki 1998; Paschidis 2008.
[4] *E.g.* Heckel 1978, 1980a, 1980b, 1982, 1983, 1983–4, 1987, 1990, 2007 as well as 1988, 1992, *passim*, and 2006, *passim*.
[5] For overviews of the evidence known before 1978, Peremans *et al.* 1950–2002, no. 16555; Olshausen 1974, no. 24; Mooren 1975, no. 8. To these should now be added *SEG* XXVIII 60 (Shear 1978).

later included among the seven wonders of the ancient world.[6] It used to be almost universally accepted that Sostratos was the architect of the Pharos, and not without reason: this was stated by all sources that are unambiguously explicit about his involvement in the building project.[7] Wilamowitz, however, considered this view to be foolish, and claimed that Sostratos must have been the sponsor of the project rather than the architect.[8] After Fraser had argued for this view at some length, it became the most popular opinion,[9] until Bing recently added a third option to the debate: on the basis of Posidippus' dedicatory epigram (AB 115), he has argued that Sostratos only dedicated the statue of Zeus that crowned the Pharos and had nothing to do with the tower itself.[10]

I shall start with the question whether Sostratos was the architect.[11] The first source to claim that he was the Pharos' designer is Pliny (*NH* 36.18):

> Another towering structure built by a king is also extolled, namely the one that stands on Pharos, the island that commands the harbour at Alexandria. The tower is said to have cost 800 talents. We should not fail to mention the generous spirit shown by King Ptolemy, whereby he allowed the name of the architect, Sostratus of Cnidos, to be inscribed on the very fabric of the building. (…) The same architect is said to have been the very first to build a promenade supported on piers: this he did at Cnidos.[12]

Lucian (*Hist. Conscr.* 62) likewise claims that Sostratos was the building's architect, but has a different explanation of why his name was inscribed on the Pharos:

---

[6]   On the Pharos, see *e.g.* Clayton 1988; Empereur 2004; McKenzie 2007, 41–45; Hairy 2007; Giardina 2010, 57–63 (Giardina's book is useful as the most complete catalogue of ancient and mediaeval lighthouses, but otherwise unfortunately rather inadequate).

[7]   Plin. *NH* 18.83; Luc *Hist. Conscr.* 62; ΣLuc. *Icar.* 12 (ed. Rabe). See *e.g.* Perdrizet 1899; Holleaux 1907, 345; Tarn 1913, 386; Bürchner 1921, 918; Durrbach 1921, 32; Bevan 1927, 95; Amandry 1940/1, 63–64; Peremans *et al.* 1950–2002, no. 16555; Olshausen 1974, no. 21; Mooren 1975, no. 8; Préaux 1978, I, 222; Eckschmitt 1984, 189; Lauter 1986, 29; Müller 1989, 204–206; Bernand 1995, 50–53, 1996, 86–87 and 1998, 116–117; Sonnabend 1996, 237–243; McKenzie 2007, 42; Strootman 2007, 219; Giardina 2010, 57; Beresford 2013, 201 n. 109; Bruns Özgan 2013, 133. Often, however, the possibility that Sostratos was the architect is not even mentioned any more: *e.g.* Fantuzzi and Hunter 2004, 388, limiting themselves to a choice between the dedicant of the tower or of statue on top.

[8]   Wilamowitz 1924, I, 154 n. 2: "Immer noch begegnet man der Torheit, Sostratos wäre Architekt gewesen".

[9]   Fraser 1972, I, 19–20 and II, 50–51. See also *e.g.* Gow 1965, II, 490; Chamoux 1975, 221; Shear 1978, 23–24; Heinen 1981, 5; Bowman 1986, 206; Bengtson 1987, 174; Fernández-Galiano 1987, 93–94; Kerkhecker 1997, 134; Grimm 1998, 45; Huß 2001, 208 and 219; Lelli 2005, 87; Errington 2008, 151; Marquaille 2008, 60; Radt 2009, 413–414; Vandorpe 2010, 174; Constantakopoulou 2012, 58; Łukaszewicz 2014, 202.

[10] Bing 1998, 21–31; Empereur 2004, 16–17; Obbink 2004, 23; Nisetich 2005, 60; Thompson 2005, 270 n. 10 and 279; Ambühl 2007, 278 and 281 n. 20; Hairy 2007, 78; Guimier-Sorbets 2007, 173; Lang 2013, 246 n. 16.

[11] On the meaning of the terms ἀρχιτέκτων and *architectus*, see Donderer 1996, 15–24.

[12] magnificatur et alia turris a rege facta in insula pharo portum optinente alexandriae, quam constitisse dccc talentis tradunt, magno animo, ne quid omittamus, ptolemaei regis, quo in ea permiserit sostrati cnidii architecti structura ipsa nomen inscribi. (…) hic idem architectus primus omnium pensilem ambulationem cnidi fecisse traditur.

Do you know what the Cnidian architect did? He built the tower on Pharos, the mightiest and most beautiful work of all. (…) After he had built the work he wrote his name on the masonry inside, covered it with gypsum, and having hidden it inscribed the name of the reigning king. He knew, as actually happened, that in a very short time the letters would fall away with the plaster and there would be revealed: 'Sostratus of Cnidos, the son of Dexiphanes, to the Divine Saviours, for the sake of them that sail the sea'. Thus, not even he had regard for the immediate moment or his own brief life-time: he looked to our day and eternity, as long as the tower shall stand and his skill abide.[13]

A third reference to Sostratos as the architect of the Alexandrian lighthouse is to be found in the scholia to Lucian's *Icaromenippus* 12 (ed. Rabe), where the additional information about the tower's appearance suggests that Lucian's treatise on history was not the scholiast's source or at any rate not the only one:[14]

The building was initiated by an order of Alexander, the son of Philip and Olympias, and the architect was Sostratos the Knidian who inscribed in the stones of the tower 'Sostratos, the son of Dexiphanes, of Knidos on behalf of all mariners to the saviour gods'.[15]

(translation by the author)

All three authors explicitly state that Sostratos was the architect of the Pharos,[16] although Pliny and Lucian both seem to have been puzzled at the uncommon fact of the architect's name being inscribed on the building.[17] Indeed this is what has troubled moderns too, all the more so since Sostratos is known from other sources as an active Ptolemaic diplomat and 'friend of the kings' (cf. infra), for which reason scholars doubt that Sostratos could have been an '*ordinary* architect'.[18] To assume that Sostratos had to be either an architect

---

[13] ὁρᾷς τὸν Κνίδιον ἐκεῖνον ἀρχιτέκτονα, οἷον ἐποίησεν; οἰκοδομήσας γὰρ τὸν ἐπὶ τῇ Φάρῳ πύργον, μέγιστον καὶ κάλλιστον ἔργων ἁπάντων (…) οἰκοδομήσας οὖν αὐτὸ τὸ ἔργον ἔνδοθεν μὲν κατὰ τῶν λίθων τὸ αὐτοῦ ὄνομα ἔγραψεν, ἐπιχρίσας δὲ τιτάνῳ καὶ ἐπικαλύψας ἐπέγραψε τοὔνομα τοῦ τότε βασιλεύοντος, εἰδώς, ὅπερ καὶ ἐγένετο, πάνυ ὀλίγου χρόνου συνεκπεσούμενα μὲν τῷ χρίσματι τὰ γράμματα, ἐκφανησόμενον δέ, 'Σώστρατος Δεξιφάνους Κνίδιος θεοῖς σωτῆρσιν ὑπὲρ τῶν πλωϊζομένων.' οὕτως οὐδ' ἐκεῖνος ἐς τὸν τότε καιρὸν οὐδὲ τὸν αὑτοῦ βίον τὸν ὀλίγου ἑώρα, ἀλλ' εἰς τὸν νῦν καὶ τὸν ἀεί, ἄχρι ἂν ἑστήκῃ ὁ πύργος καὶ μένῃ αὐτοῦ ἡ τέχνη.

[14] It should be pointed out that the scholiast mistakenly attributes the Kolossos of Rhodes to Lysippos (ἔργον δὲ Λυσίππου τοῦ ἀγαλματοποιοῦ) just before discussing the Pharos. This can, however, be used to argue both ways: one may indeed stress that the scholiast misattributes another one of the seven wonders or one may suggest that his substituting the sculptor of the Kolossos with the latter's teacher reveals the desire to ascribe the works to famous men (as he does in ascribing the initiative for the Pharos to Alexander), Sostratos thus apparently being sufficiently famous as the architect of the Pharos (cf. infra).

[15] γέγονε δὲ προστάγματι μὲν Ἀλεξάνδρου τοῦ Φιλίππου καὶ Ὀλυμπιάδος, ἀρχιτεκτονήσαντος δὲ Σωστράτου τοῦ Κνιδίου, ὃς καὶ ἐπέγραψε τῷ πύργῳ ἐπὶ τῶν λίθων "Σώστρατος Δεξιφάνους Κνίδιος θεοῖς σωτῆρσιν ὑπὲρ τῶν πλωϊζομένων".

[16] Other sources are less explicit and mention Sostratos without shedding light on the question of his role: Steph. Byz. *s.v.* Φάρος; Suda, *s.v.* Φάρος (Φ114 Adler); Georgius Syncellus (*Ecl. Chron.* 516, p. 327 ed. Mosshammer). On Strabo 17.1.6, see below.

[17] On Greek building inscriptions, see *e.g.* Hesberg 1981 and 1994, 36–52; Donderer 1996, *passim*; Hellmann 1999, *passim*.

[18] Shear 1978, 24, emphasis mine. Cf. Wilamowitz 1924, I, 154 n. 2; Gow 1965, II, 490: "an eminent statesman and no mere architect"; Fraser 1972, I, 19 and II, 52 n. 116; Bing 1998, 23; Empereur 2004, 16: "il ne s'agit pas d'un simple architecte, (…), mais d'un personage important, d'un 'Ami des rois' (…)"; Lelli 2005, 87: "più che il semplice progettista del Faro (…) ne fu il committente e finanziatore (…)";

or a leading diplomat is to create a false dichotomy, however: the political and military staff of the Hellenistic kings included artists, writers, philosophers, both moral and natural, and physicians in no small number (Sonnabend 1996, *passim*; Habicht 2006, 31–32). Thus there is no reason why an architect would be excluded from becoming a royal *philos*, or why a *philos* of such background could not act as a diplomat.[19] Furthermore, Sostratos need not just have been an ordinary architect. Indeed, another text by Lucian confirms that he was much more than ordinary.

In the introduction to his *Hippias* (2), Lucian mentions that Sostratos helped Ptolemy to take Memphis without a siege by diverting the Nile, an anecdote that is difficult to put in context (cf. infra). Fraser (1972, I, 19; Marek 1984, 427 n. 281) suggests that Sostratos may have been in charge of the military operation rather than being the engineer (μηχανικός; cf. Donderer 1996, 16) devising and carrying out the plan, as Lucian has it. Such a conclusion seems to ignore the context of the statement. In this treatise Lucian praises Hippias, a contemporary architect who built a magnificent bathing complex. He starts the work (*Hipp.* 1) with the claim that the most praiseworthy men are those who not only know how to speak well but can also put their knowledge into practice. First he gives some general examples referring to the classic difference between those who eloquently discuss medicine and those who can actually heal their patients, and to those who can actually play an instrument well rather than just having a good ear for music. Next he mentions generals who are not only excellent at deploying and haranguing their troops but also bravely take part in the fighting themselves such as Agamemnon and Achilles of old and Alexander and Pyrrhos in more recent times. Lucian (*Hipp.* 2) then notes that he has not mentioned these names to display his knowledge of history, but because the same mastery of both theory and practice is also found among the best engineers: though famous for their knowledge they also left examples of their skill to posterity. He again lists some historical examples: Archimedes and Sostratos of Knidos. Sostratos is mentioned because he "took Memphis for Ptolemy without a siege by turning the river aside and dividing it" and Archimedes for "burning the ships of the enemy by means of his science". Next we get an anecdote about Thales of Miletos who also diverted a river in spite of not being an engineer, as Lucian explicitly adds. Lastly he mentions Epeios, who built the Trojan horse and then went into it to join the fighting. "Among these men", Lucian goes on to say (*Hipp.* 3), "Hippias, [his] own contemporary, deserves mention". Praising Hippias for his excellence in speech and even greater competence in action in all fields of science, Lucian sets out to

---

Errington 2008, 151: "There is a report that Sostratos was actually the architect of the Pharos, but given his other activities that is very improbable"; Łukaszewicz 2014, 202: "Il s'agit d'un puissant personnage politique plutôt que d'un simple architecte". *Contra*: Tomlinson 1992, 105, who states that this is to underestimate the status and the social class of ancient architects. Cf. infra n. 15. Bevan 1927, 96: limited himself to observing that an inscription of the architect's name was remarkable. That would indeed be rather exceptional: see Donderer 1996, 27–39.

[19] Another architect known to have acted as ambassador was Herakleides, a leading *philos* of Philip V: Plb. 13.4–5. Cf. Préaux 1978, I, 222; Habicht 2006, 31–32; Strootman 2007, 219: "Another important aspect is the fact that the sources show no indication that artists and intellectuals at court formed a special category as distinct from 'normal' courtiers. To all account they were first of all philoi of the king. It was not exceptional that philosophers or other writers were given political, diplomatic or military responsibilities".

describe "one of his achievements which [he] recently looked upon with wonder. Though the undertaking is a commonplace, and in [his] days a very frequent one, the construction of a bath, yet [Hippias'] thoughtfulness and intelligence even in this commonplace matter is marvellous" (*Hipp.* 4).

Lucian's aim in the introduction of the treatise is thus to compare Hippias with some of the greatest names of Greek history: the mention of Archimedes and Sostratos is meant immediately to convince his readers that Hippias is a great architect. At first sight Sostratos seems rather out of place here, as the other men listed as examples (Agamemnon, Achilles, Alexander, Pyrrhos, Archimedes and Thales) are still famous, while his fame is limited to a small group of historians of the early Hellenistic period. Yet the context clearly reveals that in Lucian's day Sostratos must have been one of the most famous Greek engineers, as he was the first to come to Lucian's mind after Archimedes.[20] Sostratos' fame should not surprise us, however, if he was the architect of the exceedingly famous lighthouse of Alexandria, an enormous building that "stood virtually intact for a thousand years, in spite of earthquakes, and retained much of its original shape for several more centuries".[21] It would seem then, that Sostratos is simply one of the many victims of the poor preservation of the ancient sources. If Lucian had merely wanted to list a great technical achievement of a man who was not an actual engineer, he would probably have said so – just as he does in the case of Thales.[22] The only possible conclusion seems to be that Sostratos was in fact an architect, so that there is no reason to doubt the claims that he was involved in the construction of the Pharos in this capacity.

Another building mentioned by Pliny (*NH* 36.83, quoted above) may have added to Sostratos' claim to architectural fame: the *pensilis ambulatio* (hanging promenade) at Knidos, which pseudo-Lucian calls the Stoa of Sostratos (*Am.* 11: Στοαὶ Σωστράτου).[23] That the latter text only explicitly mentions the stoa among the things that could give pleasure in Knidos, suggests that it was a well-known tourist attraction.[24] The evidence does not tell us in what way Sostratos was involved with the building; nothing precludes that he was its architect, but he may well have been the sponsor as well.[25] At any rate, if we are to believe

---

[20] Lauter 1986, 29; Winter 2006, 297 n. 194: "he was evidently one of the outstanding architect-engineers of the early Hellenistic age" cf. also 237; McKenzie 2007, 42: "an engineer of exceptional skill". On the necessity of choosing the best examples, see *e.g.* Isoc. 9.34.

[21] Lawrence 1996, 180. Caesar (*BC* 3.112.1) also expressed his admiration for it: "turris magna altatudine, mirificis operibus extructa" ("a tower of great height, a work of wonderful construction").

[22] This precision in the case of Thales suggests to me that in this instance we need not worry about the fact that, as Macleod (1991, 281–282) notes, "L[ucian] tends to be careless or cavalier in his use, adaptation or invention of historical examples to reinforce his argument".

[23] There is no consensus on which of the Knidian stoai this building might have been: both the stoa on the terrace of the temple of Dionysos, which is closer to the harbour, and the Doric stoa which lies more to the north, have been suggested. See Bürchner 1921, 917; Coulton 1976, 245–246; Lauter 1986, 123; Bruns-Özgan 2002, 39–45 and 2013, 133–134. Winter (2006, 297 n. 194) suggests that Sostratos may also have built a lighthouse in Knidos.

[24] Bruns-Özgan 2002, 45; Zwingmann 2012, 223.

[25] Perdrizet (1899, 261–2), Tarn (1913, 386), Lauter (1986, 29) and Zwingmann (2012, 222) consider him the architect. Fraser (1972, II, 50 n. 111), on the other hand, suggests on the basis of the name Stoa of Sostratos, which he likens to the 'Stoa of Attalos' in Athens, that Sostratos was the buidling's sponsor;

Pliny, the building was the first example of this particular type of stoa with two levels,[26] and is likely to have constituted another reason for Sostratos' fame as an architect.

Thus, Fraser's judgment (1972, I, 19) that the claim that Sostratos was an architect "lacks any real substance" is quite startling, and indeed after having needed an entire page to deconstruct the evidence that Sostratos was an architect, he still ends up – rightly – concluding that it would be "perverse to deny the possibility" (Fraser 1972, II, 50–51 n. 111). Like Fraser, Bing (1998, 23) stresses that we have no earlier evidence than Pliny, but I wonder what a history of the early Hellenistic period (*c.* 338–264 BCE) that discards everything that is not attested before the Roman era would look like. Diodorus (mid 1st century BCE), our earliest source for most of it, also acknowledges his debt to the libraries of Rome (1.4.2–4). More generally, if an explicit attestation by three sources that Sostratos was the architect of the Pharos, combined with a mention of further activity as an engineer, can no longer be considered evidence of at least some substance, we might better acknowledge that many entire fields in ancient history cannot be studied and focus our attention on some other pursuit, for instance one that *is* possible.

No source attributes the Pharos to any other architect than Sostratos, but the evidence for the building's sponsor is not as unanimous. According to the sources that unmistakably call Sostratos the architect, the dedicant was either a Ptolemy (Plin. *NH* 36.83; Luc. *Hist. conscr.* 62) or Alexander the Great (ΣLuc. *Icar.* 12). The latter option seems to be precluded by the date of construction of the lighthouse: the Suda (*s.v.* Φάρος [Φ114 Adler]) says it was built when Pyrrhos became king of Epeiros, *i.e.* in 297, while Eusebius (ed. Schoene, p. 118: Ol. 124, 2–3) gives a date of 283/2.[27] Respectively these may have been the start and end dates of the works;[28] at any rate the building seems to belong to the Ptolemaic era. Perhaps, then, Ptolemy I took the initiative, although the actual dedication may only have happened under Ptolemy II. Strabo (17.1.6), however, seems to suggest that it was Sostratos who dedicated the Pharos: τοῦτον δ᾽ ἀνέθηκε Σώστρατος Κνίδιος ('Sostratos the Knidian dedicated it'): as Fraser has stressed, ἀνέθηκε is the verb form commonly used for dedicatory activity.[29] That Posidippus' epigram only speaks about Sostratos without mentioning any king, seems to point in the same direction (Fraser 1972, I, 20), especially since he was a poet connected to the Ptolemaic court:[30]

thus also Kerkhecker 1997, 134. Fraser's point is sensible, but there is no reason why he would then have appointed anyone else as its architect, and Heichelheim (1940, 1222) plausibly suggests that he was both architect and sponsor.

[26] The precise meaning of *pensilis* in this context is not clear, though: Winter 2006, 293 n. 87. Similar buildings from around the same time existed at Athens, Corinth and Pella, and it is difficult to determine the question of priority with absolute certainty: Coulton 1976, 89–91; Lauter 1982, 718 and 1986, 121–124.

[27] Ammianus Marcellinus (22.16.9) mistakenly places the construction of the Pharos under Kleopatra VII. Fraser 1972, II, 57 n. 131: "This is one of the many legends which grew up around the person of Cleopatra in Roman and Byzantine times".

[28] Fraser 1972, I, 20 and II, 52 nn. 118–120; Eckschmitt 1984, 189; Daumas and Mathieu 1987, 44; Fernández-Galiano 1987, 93; Huß 2001, 218–9 with n. 3; Cohen 2006, 364.

[29] Fraser 1972, I, 19; Daumas and Mathieu 1987, 44; Fernández-Galiano 1987, 94; Bernand 2001, 25. For Sostratos as the sponsor of the Pharos, see also above, n. 8. Bernand (1996, 85), however, following the translation of Letronne, seems to interpret it as 'set up' or 'erected', making Sostratos only the architect and not the dedicant (cf. *ibid.*, 87).

[30] On Posidippus and the Ptolemaic court, see *e.g.* Kerkhecker 1997; Fantuzzi and Hunter 2004, 377–403;

As a saviour of the Greeks, this watchman of Pharos, was set up, lord Proteus
by Sostratos the Knidian, son of Dexiphanes.
Since in Egypt there are no lookout-points or mountains as on the islands,
but low lies the breakwater where ships take harbour,
for that reason, cleaving the air sheer and steep,
this tower shines forth across countless leagues
by day, and all night long quickly a sailor on the waves
will see the great fire blazing from its peak
and though he may run to the Bull's Horn itself, he would not miss
Zeus Soter, o Proteus, in sailing hither.[31]

(trans. Bing, adapted on the basis of Austin)

Bing, however, has recently argued that this poem only concerns the dedication of the statue
on top of the Pharos.[32] There seems no doubt that he is correct to identify the statue on top
of the Pharos, and indeed the god to whom it was dedicated, as Zeus Soter (Bing 1998,
23–25),[33] but I am less convinced by his argument that the epigram does not concern the
Pharos as a whole, *i.e.* both the tower and the statue. He argues that Ἑλλήνων σωτήρ in verse
1 and Ζεὺς Σωτήρ in verse 10 have the same point of reference, and that to treat them as if
they mean something different, as some have done, ignores "the plain sense of the words"
and weakens "the very carefully constructed frame of the poem, in which the invocation
of Proteus and mention of a saviour in the last line echo precisely these elements in the
first" (*ibid.*, 25). I absolutely agree with this analysis, yet I do not see why we should deny
Posidippus the further sophistication of playing with multiple parallel meanings in these
verses, in limiting this meaning to a reference to the statue atop the Pharos. If the poem
would be the dedicatory epigram of the statue alone, and not of the tower as a whole, six
out of the ten verses deal with what would on this interpretation only be the statue base.
While such a high tower would be a very impressive base, this reading weakens the poem
even more as it implies that the focus is all wrong. The claim that these verses explain why
the statue needed a tower does not explain the disproportion, and Zeus probably would
not be said to need a high tower to be able to exercise his saving powers.

It is, moreover, not only Zeus who acts as saviour, but also in part the tower itself,

---

Thompson 2005; Ambühl 2007; Müller 2014a and 2014b.

[31] Ἑλλήνων σωτῆρα, Φάρου σκοπόν, ὦ ἄνα Πρωτεῦ,
Σώστρατος ἔστησεν Δεξιφάνου[ς] Κνίδιος·
οὐ γὰρ ἐν Αἰγύπτωι σκοπαὶ οὔρεος οἷ' ἐπὶ νήσων
ἀλλὰ χαμαὶ χηλὴ ναύλοχος ἐκτέταται.
τοῦ χάριν εὐθεῖάν τε καὶ ὄρθιον αἰθέρα τέμνειν
πύργος ὅδ' ἀπλάτων φαίνετ' ἀπὸ σταδίων
ἤματι, παννύχιος δὲ θ[ο]ῶ[ς] ἐν κύματι ναύτης
ὄψεται ἐκ κορυφῆς πῦρ μέγα καιόμενον,
καί κεν ἐπ' αὐτὸ δράμοι Ταύρου κέρας οὐδ' ἂν ἁμάρτοι
Σωτῆρος, Πρωτεῦ, Ζηνὸς [ὁ] τῆιδε πλέων.

[32] Bing 1998, esp. 21–29. Cf. *supra*, n. 9.

[33] The plural in Luc., *Hist. conscr.* 62, ΣLuc *Icar.* 12, and Georg. Syncel. *Ecl. chron.* 516 (ed. Mosshammer
p. 327) is probably a mistake: Fraser 1972, I, 19; Guimier-Sorbets 2007, 173; cf. Bernand 2001, 25. For
different views, see recently *e.g.* Daumas and Mathieu 1987; Fernández-Galiano 1987, 93; Bernand 1996;
Hazzard 2000, 15–16; Müller 2009, 212 n. 376.

thanks to the light shining from its top that can be seen from very far due to its height, as is indicated in verse 8. Rather than taking the first and the last verses only as referring to the statue of Zeus, I would suggest that the statue and the tower, as well as Zeus himself are referred to simultaneously, which would definitely add to the epigram's force: Ἑλλήνων σωτήρ, Φάρου σκοπός and – as far as the tower is concerned, metonymically – also Ζεὺς Σωτήρ seem to carry all of these meanings at once. In Bing's view this is not possible, because if σωτήρ in verse one would refer to the lighthouse, it would require Ἑλλήνων to be an objective genitive, which would mean that the lighthouse only saves Greeks. Even assuming that Posidippus, who was obviously writing primarily for Greeks, realized the problem, one might wonder whether he would have cared about this technicality. Furthermore, the implication of Bing's reading would be that Zeus' power only works among the Greeks, which seems at least as problematic, if not more, especially given the importance of Zeus to Alexander and the Ptolemies.[34]

Furthermore, as Bing himself convincingly argues at some length, it seems quite likely that Strabo, in referring to the inscription on the Pharos, was merely paraphrasing Posidippus' epigram.[35] This very epigram, then, seems to have been the inscription on the Pharos. Yet Strabo (17.1.6) apparently saw only one inscription (ἡ ἐπιγραφή), and one may wonder why the tower would only carry an inscription commemorating the dedication of the statue on top of it, and no inscription about the construction or dedication of the tower itself. It seems inconceivable that a royal dedication would not be marked out as such,[36] yet both Pliny (*NH* 36.83) and Lucian (*Hist. conscr.* 62) likewise seem to suggest that there was only one inscription on the building, that of Sostratos. Thus, even regardless of the meaning of the epigram and its being the same as the inscription on the tower, the testimonies of Strabo, Pliny and Lucian demonstrate that Sostratos' name was inscribed where one would expect the dedicant. Although the 800 talents (20,688kg of silver) the tower is said to have cost by Pliny – perhaps exaggerating somewhat? – might make this difficult to believe,[37] the conclusion seems to be that Sostratos was both the architect

---

[34] Bing (1998, 30–31) offers a further argument on the basis of a dream of the scribe of the papyrus, which has preserved Posidippus' epigram (*P. Louvre* 7172, on which see Obbink 2004, 19–28), a certain Ptolemaios connected with the Memphite Serapeion in the second century BCE. Another papyrus (*UPZ* 78, l. 28–39) records a dream of the same Ptolemaios, imagining himself to be on top of a high tower in Alexandria: on the assumption that the tower was the Pharos and that being on top of it constitutes a correct interpretation of the epigram inscribed on the Pharos, the dream would confirm that the epigram only referred to the statue of Zeus that topped the Pharos. However, this leads to the question of what one should make of the fact that in Ptolemaios' dream there was a huge crowd to the north and east of him: if the tower was the Pharos, the crowd would for the most part have had to stand in the sea. Of course, in a dream everything is possible, but once this is acknowledged, it probably loses its evidentiary value for any such conclusions that one may wish to build on it (and see the questions Bing himself asks in the next paragraph for further problems with this interpretation). For Zeus and the Ptolemies, see Hazzard 2000, 91–92; Barbantani 2010, 238–242; Müller 2014a, at n. 96.

[35] Chamoux 1975, 220–221; Weber 1993, 333 n. 2; Bing 1998, 27–29; Obbink 2004, 22. *Contra*: Perdrizet 1899, 264; Bernand 2001, 26.

[36] On the importance of the dedicant and sponsor in architectural epigrams of the period, see Hesberg 1981, 67–68 and 81; cf. Hellmann 1999, 110.

[37] Wilamowitz (1924, I, 154 n. 2) refers to Apollonios the dioiketes as evidence that a courtier could have achieved such wealth; it is difficult to assess how normal Apollonios' situation would have been, as we cannot

and the dedicant of the Pharos.[38] He was certainly not the only Ptolemaic *philos* to have sponsored and dedicated a building.[39]

It is likely, though, that in planning the work, Sostratos worked closely together with Ptolemy (Huß 2001, 219), as the construction of the Pharos was important to the king in several different ways. Its primary function may have been, as Posidippus (AB 115, v. 3–10; cf. Str. 17.1.6; Plin. 5.34; Amm. Marc. 22.16.9; ΣLuc *Icar.* 12) suggests in the dedicatory epigram, to create a clearly visible landmark to guide ships to the harbour, which was one aspect that helped make the Alexandrian harbour very well suited for large-scale international trade (cf. McKenzie 2007, 74). But undoubtedly there was much more to it.[40] The construction of such a large structure helped to boost the monumental character of Alexandria, and the development of royal cities and the creation of all sorts of cultural prestige were at the heart of propagandistic royal display in the early Hellenistic period.[41] The idea that a splendidly adorned city deserved to rule the world already existed in Greece before the Hellenistic period and is found very explicitly in Isocrates (7.66 and very similar 15.234; cf. Hesberg 1981, 74–76):

> Who of my own generation does not remember that the democracy so adorned the city with temples and public buildings that even today visitors from other lands consider that she is worthy to rule not only over Hellas but over all the world (…)?[42]

It seems plausible that such ideas were only strengthened by the competition between the Hellenistic monarchies. As the first lighthouse of its kind and the inspiration to so many

---

even begin to compare our knowledge about any other Hellenistic official with the wealth of information available on Apollonios thanks to the Zenon archive. This view of Sostratos' wealth is also held by Tomlinson 1992, 105; Huß 2001, 219; Errington 2008, 151; Radt 2009, 413. Hölbl (1994, 66) and Bing (1998, 23 n. 10), on the other hand, doubt that Sostratos possessed the means to fund such a project. Cf. in general Hesberg 1994, 30.

[38] This view has been expressed before: Thiersch 1909, 31–32; Heichelheim 1940; Donderer 1996, 35 and 79–80; Hellmann 1999, 111 (with some reservations); Winter 2006, 93; Blasius 2011, 141. Cf. Gow (1965, II, 490) who deems it possible that Sostratos as sponsor might also have had his say in the design of the building.

[39] Hesberg 1981, 77 n. 74; Weber 1993, 333–334; Bing 1998, 23 n. 10. They may somewhat exaggerate the number of examples, though, and the exceptionality of the Ptolemaic court in this respect.

[40] See in general Beresford 2013, 201–202: "In many cases it is probable that ancient lighthouses were erected as much to reflect the political aspirations of rulers and/or cities as to provide navigational assistance to seafarers".

[41] See *e.g.* Heinen 1981, 4–6; Walbank 1984, 84; Davies 2005, 127–128; Guimier-Sorbets 2007, 174; Weber 2007; Lang 2013, 243–247; Anson 2014, 127; Łukaszewicz 2014, 192. Cf. Strabo 13.1.26 on Alexander honouring Ilion, amongst other things, "by improving it with buildings"; as Cohen (1995, 25–26) notes in this context, "Strabo's list may serve as a useful illustration of the types of benefits a city could expect. The example set by Alexander was in fact followed by his successors and in this way developed the tradition of Hellenistic kings and queens as benefactors and patrons" (25). The splendour of Alexandria was also celebrated in the poetry of Herondas (*Mim.* 1.26–33); cf. Murray 2008, 21.

[42] τίς οὐ μνημονεύει τῶν ἡλικιωτῶν τῶν ἐμῶν, τὴν μὲν δημοκρατίαν οὕτω κοσμήσασαν τὴν πόλιν καὶ τοῖς ἱεροῖς καὶ τοῖς ὁσίοις, ὥστ' ἔτι καὶ νῦν τοὺς ἀφικνουμένους νομίζειν αὐτὴν ἀξίαν εἶναι μὴ μόνον τῶν Ἑλλήνων ἄρχειν ἀλλὰ καὶ τῶν ἄλλων ἁπάντων (…).

subsequent ones,[43] the Pharos absolutely deserves a place among the many spectacular innovative ideas originating in Hellenistic Alexandria such as Eratosthenes' calculation of the circumference of the earth, Aristarchos' heliocentrism (if he worked in Alexandria at the time), or the advances in anatomy of Herophilos (Staden 1996, 85; Strootman 2007, 189). Obviously of lesser scientific importance than these, its conspicuous prominence in the Alexandrian cityscape and its practical application might well have made it more prestigious than all these others.[44] It is surely telling, though not unique, that the very first words of Posidippus' epigram, Ἑλλήνων σωτῆρα, address all Greeks rather than just the Alexandrians (Hesberg 1981, 68–69 and 73; Weber 1993, 332 with n. 6; Hellmann 1999, 110).

Finally, the Pharos probably also fulfilled an important military function, controlling the strategic location of the island of Pharos as a watchtower and perhaps also a signalling tower for communication with the Egyptian hinterland.[45] In this respect, Sostratos' setting up a lighthouse in the Alexandrian harbour that was both very prestigious and highly useful in many ways can be compared to another well-attested dedication by a Ptolemaic royal *philos*, the temple to Arsinoe Zephyritis by Kallikrates of Samos.[46] This shrine "became a focal point into which might flow, and from which might spread, the broad political/cultural interests of the Ptolemaic court", as Bing (2002/3, 264) aptly put it. Given the immense costs the kings already had to cover in constructing their new capitals (Davies 2005), it is not surprising that they also called on the help of wealthy courtiers or encouraged them to become involved.

Sostratos in the epigraphical record and his diplomatic activity

That Sostratos enjoyed some prominence at the Ptolemaic court as a Friend of the kings (Str. 17.1.6: φίλος τῶν βασιλέων) is suggested by the epigraphic record in which he appears regularly. He has been honoured by the League of the Islanders (*Choix Délos* 21/*IG* XI.4 1038), the people of Delos (*Choix Délos* 22/*IG* XI.4 563), the people of Kaunos (*Choix Délos* 23/*IG* XI.4 1130), the people of Delphi (*FD* III.1 299), the Kyrenaian citizen Etearchos (*Choix Délos* 24/*IG* XI.4 1190), and possibly also by the Delphic Amphiktyony (*CID* IV 26/*FdD* III.1 298) and by a Ptolemaic royal couple (*BCH* 64–65 1940/1, 63–65). Yet these

---

[43] Winter 2006, 93: "The influence of the Pharos in the Graeco-Roman, as well as the Arabic, world was substantial"; Giardina 2010, *passim*; Beresford 2013, 201.

[44] This was also the message of Posidippus' epigram. Cf. Obbink 2004, 22: "the capital of Ptolemy's realm is advertised as visible from afar, by a beacon of light that shines throughout the Greek world"; Lang 2013, 246: "The Pharos lighthouse itself (…) was a statement that relied partly on size, and consequently on implicit claims to wealth and state authority".

[45] Łukaszewicz 2014, 203–204: "avant tout une tour de guet". Although I do not see how *P.Oxy* X 1271, a mere permit to leave the harbour (cf. Str. 2.3.5), reveals anything about the military function of the Pharos, I find the suggestion utterly plausible. Cf., speculatively, Thiersch 1909, 91–94 and Green 1990, 159. On the strategic location of the Pharos, see Caes. *BC* 3.112.1–5; cf. J. *BJ* 4.10.5 (607 and 612), and the interest in the Pharos of the Roman ambassadors at D.S. 33.28b.2; Jähne, *Klio* 1981, 87; Green 1996, 10.

[46] For other donations of large building by members of the entourages of Hellenistic kings, see *e.g.* Lamia's stoa at Sikyon (Ath. 13.577c) or the bouleuterion of Miletos by the Seleukid Friends Timarchos and Herakleides (*Milet* I.2, no. 1 and 2).

honorary inscriptions shed very little light on the specific reasons for the honours, almost all attestations lack context and most can only be dated in the vaguest manner.[47] Most simply limit themselves to the standard indication that Sostratos was a good man who has continually paid excellent services to those who honoured him or their fellow citizens;[48] only the Nesiotic decree is slightly more specific in mentioning Sostratos' assistance to the Islanders who visited the Alexandrian court.[49] Apart from thanking the honorand for past services, such decrees also aimed at encouraging future goodwill.[50] The Delian decree might be the result of the Nesiotic one, as the latter stipulates that all the members of the league should pass their own decrees with the same honours for Sostratos (Durrbach, *Choix* 21, l. 31–37; Marek 1984, 279–280), though we cannot exclude that Sostratos was honoured more than once at Delos.[51]

The Nesiotai honoured Sostratos with πολιτεία (citizenship) in all member states for him and his descendants,[52] as well as, ἀτέλεια (tax exemption) for everything they imported and exported, προεδρία (front row seats) at all games, πρόσοδος (priority in the boule and the assembly – after religious matters); furthermore part of the offerings at every sacrifice would be sent to his house in Knidos for him and his family,[53] and he received a golden crown

---

[47] This is of course hardly exceptional, as Reger (1994, 64) remarks in the case of Delian honorary decrees: "individually they tend to be depressingly uninformative". For Delian decrees offering (somewhat) more specific reasons, see *e.g. IG* XI.4 573, 618, 627, 691. Of course, the reasons for granting proxeny and related benefits will have been thoroughly discussed in the assembly before taking the decision: Gschnitzer 1973, 704. That political activity forms the background for almost all of the honours for Sostratos, seems most likely (cf. Reger 1994, 65 on *Choix Délos* 22), though architectural activity cannot be ruled out (cf. infra, n. 59). The amphiktyonic decree seems to concern a donation of money for a specific purpose, perhaps the restoration of a statue, if the restorations are in any way correct: *FD* III.1 298, l. 4–6, ἐπειδὴ Ἀ[ρχίδαμος ......], Π[υθοκλῆς Σώστρατος Δεξιφάνους Κνίδιοι] ἐπαγγέλλονται τὸν Ἑρμῆν τὸν ἐναγώ]νιον τὸν ἐν τῶι Πυ[θικῶι σταδίωι ἐκ] τῶν [ἰδίων ἀναλωμάτων ἀναστήσειν]. Marek 1984, 412 n. 56 seems to express some doubt.

[48] *Choix Délos* 22, l. 2–8: ἐπειδὴ Σώστρατος Δεξιφάνους Κνίδιος ἀνὴρ ἀγαθὸς ὢν διατελεῖ περί τε τὸ ἱερὸν καὶ τὴν πόλιν τὴν Δηλίων καὶ ποεῖ ἀγαθὸν ὅ τι δύναται καὶ λόγωι καὶ ἔργωι τοὺς ἐντυγχάνοντας ἑαυτῶι Δηλίων· ἐπαινέσαι μὲν αὐτὸν ἀρετῆς καὶ εὐνοίας ἕνεκεν; *Choix Délos* 23, l. 3–4: ἀρετῆς ἕνεκεν καὶ [εὐνοίας] τῆς εἰς τὸν δῆμον; *Choix Délos* 24, l. 3–5: [ἀρε]τῆς ἕ[ν]εκ[εν κ]αὶ εὐεργεσίας [τῆ]ς εἰς ἑ[α]υτὸ[ν κ]αὶ [το]ὺς ἄ[λλ]ους [Κυρηναί]ους; *FdD* III.1 299: no reason stated.

[49] *Choix Délos* 21, l. 5–10 and 12–14: τήν τε εὔνοιαν [ἣν δια]τελεῖ ἔχων Σώστρατος πρὸς τοὺς νησιώτας καὶ ὅτι χρείας παρέχεται τοῖς ἀφικνουμένοις [π]ρὸς τὸν βασιλέα μετὰ πάσης προθυμίας καὶ [λέγων] καὶ πράσσων ὅ τι ἂν δύνηται ἀγαθὸν ὑπὲρ τῶν [νησιω]τῶν (...) ἀρετῆς ἕνεκα [καὶ εὐν]οίας ἧς ἔχων διατελεῖ ἐμ παντὶ καιρῶι εἰς [τὸν β]ασιλέα Πτολεμαῖον καὶ τοὺς νησιώτας.

[50] See *e.g.* Habicht 1970, 242; Marek 1984, 262; Ma 1999, 201–206. Cf. Constantakopoulou 2012, 55–61.

[51] Renewed or additional later honours were not at all uncommon in Delos or elsewhere, *e.g. IG* XI.4 664 and 665; *FD* III.1 38; below, n. 49. It is debated whether Delos was a member of the Nesiotic League, but there seems little reason to doubt that it was: Constantakopoulou 2012, 58 with n. 69 and 70.

[52] Constantakopoulou (2012, 59) seems to consider it the usual practice of the Nesiotai to grant its honorands citizenship in all member states of the league, but in that case we would expect it to occur in *IG* XII.5 817 as well.

[53] Holleaux 1907, 343–344 (followed by Roussel, *ad loc.*, and Durrbach 1921, 32) plausibly argues that this means a sum of money raised by the sale of the sacrificial meat, though this makes one wonder why there were so many recipients (Sostratos, his descendants and – the puzzling bit – his brothers); something of a more honorific nature may be meant.

of 3,000 drachmai (*IG* XI.4 1038).[54] This is more than what is awarded to the unknown contemporary honorand of *IG* XI.4 1039, who is only given citizenship in all member states, προεδρία and πρόσοδος (no ἀτέλεια, no part of the offerings, nor a crown), and the Thebans Hypostratos and Kaphisodoros (*IG* XI.4 1040), who only get προεδρία and πρόσοδος, though with ἀσυλία (freedom from seizure) added as well.[55] A Syracusan banker by the name of Timon, son of Nymphodoros, who had helped the league to buy grain in a time of urgency was honoured with a crown, the value of which is lost in a lacuna, proxeny and *euergesia* for him and his descendants, *prosodos* and an invitation to league festivals (*IG* XII.5 817).[56] His help in the most crucial aspect of life was clearly very much appreciated but he did not receive the same honours as Sostratos (no πολιτεία, no ἀτέλεια, no προεδρία, no part of the offerings). Although sufficiently well preserved examples are not very numerous, it would thus seem that the honours for Sostratos were very substantial.

In Delos (*Choix Délos* 22, l. 8–16), Sostratos and his descendants were given the titles of πρόξενος καὶ εὐεργέτης of the city and the sanctuary, and they were awarded πολιτεία (citizenship), ἀτέλεια πάντων (exemption from all taxes), προεδρία (front-row seats at religious festivals), γῆς καὶ οἰκίας ἔγκτησις (the right to own land and a house), πρόσοδος (priority – after religious matters) in the boule and the assembly, as well as τἄλλα ὅσαπερ τοῖς ἄλλοις προξένοις καὶ εὐεργέταις τῆς πόλεως δέδοται παρὰ Δηλίων (the other things that are given to *proxenoi* and *euergetai* of the city by the Delians). The award of citizenship was rather rare in Delian proxeny decrees, which shows the importance of Sostratos to the Delians: it usually seems to have been reserved for high officials of the kings holding hegemony over Delos (Antigonids or Ptolemies).[57] On the other hand, he was not granted the other rare honour of ἀσυλία (freedom from seizure).[58] For someone usually visiting the city as a royal ambassador, this may have been included in his diplomatic inviolability.[59] Alternatively, it may have been covered by τἄλλα ὅσαπερ τοῖς ἄλλοις προξένοις καὶ εὐεργέταις τῆς πόλεως δέδοται παρὰ Δηλίων, although Reger (1994, 72; *contra* Habicht 2002, 15) has argued that this is not necessarily to be taken as including all other honours.[60] Out

---

[54] Some years before the Nesiotai had voted an honorific crown of 1,000 staters for Ptolemy II (*SIG*³ 390, l. 42–45).

[55] Thrasykles, the honorand of *IG* XI.4 1043, only receives a crown, but other honours were voted in an earlier decree (cf. l. 5, τοῦ προτέρου ψηφίσματος, and l. 8–9, πάλι[ν] ἐπαινέσαι), which has not been preserved. *IG* XI.4 1041, 1042, 1044, 1045, 1046, 1048 are too badly damaged for the comparison to be useful, as further honours may or may not have been listed.

[56] Honorary decrees for him by the Delians and the Tenians have also been found: *IG* XI.4 759, XII.5 816 and 817.

[57] Durrbach 1921, 37; Reger 1994, 70–71; Habicht 2002, 15–16: only in 17 out of 508 decrees from the period of indepence is citizenship awarded to the honorand.

[58] Another rare award, that of ἰσοτέλεια (the right to be taxed like a Delian citizen), was obviously rendered irrelevant by the bigger grant of ἀτέλεια πάντων; for a *proxenos* awarded ἰσοτέλεια rather than ἀτέλεια, see *e.g. IG* XI.4 627. Cf. Reger 1994, 72.

[59] On diplomatic inviolability, see Mosley 1973, 81–92.

[60] This formula might simply refer to specific set of minor honours, like the right to participate in state banquets, sometimes granted as a specific honour to *non-proxenoi*: *e.g. IG* XI.4 511 if the restoration is correct ([καλέσαι] δὲ αὐτὸν ἐ[πὶ ξενία ἕως ἂν] ἐπιδημῆι). It is never explicitly included among the honours for proxenoi (Habicht 2002, 17), but it seems unlikely that more important honorands would not be invited to state banquets while they were present in the city when men of lesser status being present at the same

of the 508 honorands over a 148 year period collected by Habicht, only the 24 men who were awarded a crown are perhaps to be seen as honoured more highly (cf. Habicht 2002, 15–16). However, we must not forget that Sostratos was awarded a golden crown worth 3,000 drachmai by the Nesiotai at Delos (Durrbach, *Choix* 21, l. 14–17), whereas those honoured with a crown by the Delians receive a laurel wreath, with the single exception of Philokles of Sidon, the king of the Sidonians, an even higher Ptolemaic official, who was awarded a gold crown of 1,000 drachmai (*IG* XI.4 559, l. 16–22), but not the proxeny.[61] Out of 467 known Delian proxenoi only one, Admetos of Thessalonike (*c.* 240–230 BCE), was honoured with a statue, or rather two statues; together with the fact that he was honoured three times, this shows that he was extremely important to Delos (Habicht 2002, 17–18). Thus, although a few men received even higher honours, Sostratos is clearly amongst those honoured most highly by the Delians.

In Delphi, Sostratos received the following honours along with his proxeny (*FD* III.1 299): θεαροδοκία (the privilege of hosting sacred embassies)[62], προδικία (priority access to the courts), προεδ[ρία] (front-row seats at religious festivals), [ἀσ]υλία (freedom from seizure), ἀ[τ]έλεια πάντων (full exemption from taxes), τ[ἆλλα ὅσα καὶ τοῖς] ἄλλοις προξένο[ις καὶ εὐεργέ[ταις] ("the other things that are given to the other *proxenoi* and benefactors"), and probably also προμαντεία (priority access to the oracle).[63] Whether τ[ἆλλα ὅσα καὶ τοῖς] ἄλλοις προξένο[ις κα]ὶ εὐεργέ[ταις] might mean that he also received the title of εὐεργέτης is not clear.[64] All of those are quite standard (Bouvier 1978, esp. 104; Habicht 2002, 22), apart from the θεαροδοκία, which is only given in 35 out of the 649 Delphic proxeny decrees studied by Habicht (2002, 25), almost always in the third century. If the restoration of προμαντεία is as correct as it is likely, Sostratos is among the small group of 44 out the 282 third century honorands collected by Bouvier (1978, 104–105) who received not only the standard list of προξενία, προμαντεία, προεδρία, προδικία, ἀσυλία and ἀτέλεια (given to 221 of them), but at least one additional honour as well. Only 17 men out of the 282 received 8 different honours (*i.e.* one more than Sostratos) and only one received 9 different ones; of course the quality of the honours varies too, but it is difficult to create a qualitative hierarchy. We can only speculate on the nature of Sostratos' relations with Delphi; perhaps he had gained their gratitude by hosting Delphic *theoroi* in Alexandria, as the grant of the rather rare *theorodokia* might suggest.[65]

---

time would be welcome.

[61] Habicht 2002, 16. Marek 1984, 254, suggests that Philokles' status may have been considered too high to make him a proxenos. On Philokles, see Hauben 2004.

[62] On the *thearodokia*, see Rutherford 2013, 83–86. *Thearodokoi* were often wealthy and important people (*ibid.*, 84).

[63] The lacuna in l. 3 at any rate leaves space for one further honour, and comparison with other decrees makes the supplement προμαντεία virtually certain (cf. Bouvier 1978 and Habicht 2002, 22, on προμαντεία as a very common honour for proxenoi in Delphi).

[64] Bouvier 1978, 114–115: "Le sens de cette clausule ne nous apparaît pas nettement. (…) Dans l'état actuel de nos connaissances, nous ne pouvons guère voir autre chose dans cette formule qu'une clause de style qui laissait la porte ouverte aux rectifications possibles".

[65] Although Sostratos' involvement in such Knidian construction works would not be unlikely, there is no evidence for the oft-repeated view that Sostratos was honoured because of restoration works on the terrace of the Knidian lesche at Delphi: Perdrizet 1899, 271; Tarn 1913, 386; Bourguet *ad FdD* 299; Heichelheim

It seems to be generally accepted that Sostratos, along with one or two of his brothers, were honoured by the Delphic Amphiktyony for offering to pay for the restoration of the statue of Hermes Enagonios in the Pythian stadium (*CID* IV 26/*FD* III.1 298). The inscription is badly damaged, however, and the names of the honorands are lost apart from two letters. In *FD* III.1 298 (l. 4–5) they are restored as Ἀ[ρχίδαμος ....], Π[υθοκλῆς Σώστρατος Δεξιφάνους Κνίδιοι], while in *CID* IV 26/*FD* III.1 298 (l. 3–4) we read Ἀ[ρχίδαμος], Π[υθοκλῆς Σώστρατος Δεξιφάνους Κνίδιοι]. The basis of this restoration is threefold. First of all, the Amphiktyonic decree has been engraved on the Knidian treasury on the same badly broken stone (7 fragments preserved) as three individual decrees for Σωστρ[άτωι Δεξιφάνους] Κνιδίωι (*FD* III.1 299, l. 2), Πυθοκλε[ῖ .... Κνιδ]ίωι (*FD* III.1 300, l. 2), and [Ἀρ]χιδάμ[ωι ..... Κ]νιδίωι (*FD* III.1 301, l. 2). A second argument is that two letters, the Α and Π, match; the initial Α of the name in *FD* III.1 301 is itself the result of a restoration, but it seems a relatively certain one.[66] Thirdly, there is the fact that three older city decrees have been engraved beneath the more recent Amphiktyonic decree.[67]

There is, however, no reason why all texts on the same stone necessarily belong together, and it is not even certain that they were all engraved at the same time. The lettering of *CID* IV 26/*FD* III.1 298 and *FD* III.1 299 seems to suggest that they were not by the same cutter, and their position on the stone rather suggests that *CID* IV 26/*FD* III.1 was engraved later than *FD* III.1 299.[68] Another problem with the restoration of the names in *CID* IV 26/*FD* III.1 298 as those of the honorands of the three city decrees engraved below is that the lacuna is not long enough for three names and three patronymics, so we have

1940; Hesberg 1994, 30. *Contra*: Donderer 1996, 65 n. 229.

[66] The only names containing the letters χιδαμ, which I found in the PHI inscriptions database, Trismegistos and the TLG are Αἰχίδαμος, Ἀρχίδαμας, Ἀρχίδαμος, Εὐαρχίδαμος, and Γεχιδάμυς. Ἀρχίδαμος is by far the most common: the restoration in *FD* III.1 301 thus seems rather likely.

[67] Bourguet writes in his discussion of FD III.1 298: "Il me semble, puisque l'on trouve recopiés à la suite d'un décret amphictyonique des textes antérieurs, que l'on peut admettre sans difficulté que tous ces textes se rapportent aux mêmes personnages".

[68] The difference in letter shapes is particularly striking in the case of the chi. As to the order of engraving it seems telling that the space between the first line of *FD* III.1 299, containing the traditional invocation θ[εο]ί, and the rest of the text is rather wide (10–12mm), whereas the last line of *CID* IV 26/*FD* III.1 298 almost touches the θ[εο]ί on the first line of *FD* III.1 299, the space only being 1–2mm. It would thus seem that *FD* III.1 299 had already been engraved before the cutter of *CID* IV 26/*FD* III.1 298 started his task, taking little regard for the text already present lower on the stone: it would have been much easier for the cutter of *FD* III.1 299 to stay away from a text above it if the city decrees had not been inscribed yet, than for the cutter *CID* IV 26/*FD* III.1 298 to make sure his last line did not end being too close to the first of *FD* III.1 299 if that was already there. Discussing the problem of the order of texts on a stone, Daux (1943, 22) points out that "une prudence extrême est ici nécessaire: un texte gravé au-dessus d'un autre ne lui est pas toujours antérieur" and lists several Delphic cases in which it is certain that texts engraved above other texts have been added later. I would like to thank Charles Crowther for the opportunity to study a squeeze of part of this stone containing *FD* III.1 299 and the bottom two lines of *CID* IV 26/*FD* III.1 298 at the Centre for the Study of Ancient Documents in Oxford, and for his invaluable advice. A partial photograph of the squeeze I studied has been published in Fraser and Rönne 1957, pl. 20 no. 1, cf. p. 86 with n. 28; it shows the position of the iota of the θ[εο]ί of *FD* III.1 299 in relation to the lines above and below.

to assume that at least two of the men were brothers. As we do know from *IG* XI.4 1038 that Sostratos had brothers, this is definitely possible,[69] but not of course, necessary. If the number of dots in Bourguet's edition of *FD* III.1 300 and 301 accurately represents the number of missing letters, the length of these lacunae does not allow for the patronymics of Pythokles and Archidamos to be restored as Δεξιφάνους. In no. 300 there are 7 dots while Δεξιφάνους is 10 letters; in no. 301 there are only 6. The latter one is no problem for Bourguet as he assumes that only Pythokles and Sostratos were brothers, but Lefèvre in *CID* IV 26 considers all three of them to have been brothers (see above for their respective restorations). The length of the lines varies quite a lot in all texts, although no line is completely preserved; nevertheless the more formulaic ones are probably quite certain. In no. 300 a longer patronymic would diminish the difference in length between the lines, but in no. 301 a longer patronymic would make what is already the longest line in the text even longer and create a difference of 12 letters between the longest and the shortest one (barring the first, which only has θεοί, and the last one which obviously need not be as long). Thus, the possibility that Sostratos was honoured by the Delphic Amphiktyony in this decree exists, but with not a single letter of Sostratos' name surviving, and the part containing the honours and their inspiration being badly damaged, I shall not dwell on this text any further.

We face a very similar set of problems with another text from Delphi that is usually connected with Sostratos of Knidos, a broken slab of limestone preserving the top and left margins and – partially – the words Σώστρατο[ς] on the first line and βασίλισ[σα] on the third line (Amandry 1940/1, 63–65). In between, a second line has been chiselled away and no trace of its text survives; the two lines that remain seem to have been cut by different hands and the position of the letters on the third line (starting at the very edge of the stone and closer to each other) suggests that the third line was longer than the text it replaced. The lettering is clearly of the third century, probably the first half of it, and Sostratos of Knidos is the only royal agent among the *Sostratoi* known to have been connected with Delphi in this period. Amandry therefore identified him as the Sostratos of the inscription, and suggested that Sostratos had dedicated a statue of Ptolemy II to which he later, after the sibling marriage, added a statue of Arsinoe II, hence the longer third line. He thus restored the text as follows:

> Sostrato[s, the son of Dexiphanes, of Knidos] (dedicated a statue of)
> {King Ptolemy to Apollo}
> Quee[n Arsinoe and King Ptolemy to Apollo].[70]

This is an attractive hypothesis,[71] but its foundations are shaky. There is no need to assume that the Sostratos of this inscription was a royal agent. And even if the restorations would be largely correct, the question remains whether Sostratos could have put his name before

---

69 For examples of brothers being honoured in a single decree, see *e.g. SGDI* 2674 and *IG* II² 6; if the restorations in *Agora* XVI 37 would be correct, this decree offers another example.
70 Σώστρατο[ς Δεξιφάνους Κνίδιος]
    {βασιλέα Πτολεμαῖον Ἀπόλλωνι}
    βασίλισ[σαν Ἀρσινόην καὶ βασιλέα Πτολεμαῖον Ἀπόλλωνι]
71 It has been accepted *e.g.* by Shear 1978, 24 n. 45 and Marquaille 2008, 60.

that of the queen, for which reason Fraser suggested that it was Arsinoe who dedicated a statue of Sostratos.[72] Such honours for *philoi* by Hellenistic monarchs are certainly not unseen,[73] but one may wonder why the name of the dedicant would have been adjusted in this scenario. On Fraser's interpretation the stone would give us a fascinating insight into the prominence of Sostratos at the Ptolemaic court, but it must remain entirely speculative.

We are on more sure footing, but unfortunately still not well-informed, with two statue bases from Delos, one set up by the people of Kaunos (*IG* XI.4 1130) and another by the Kyrenaian citizen Etearchos son of Damylos (*IG* XI.4 1190):[74] they respectively honour Sostratos for ἀρετή and a lost quality (εὐνοία?) displayed toward the demos, and [ἀρε]τή and εὐεργεσία towards the dedicant and his fellow citizens. Both cities stood under Ptolemaic control for at least some time, so Sostratos probably had entertained relations between them and the court in Alexandria, but that is all we know.

Sostratos is one of the best-attested Ptolemaic royal Friends in the epigraphic record after Kallikrates of Samos.[75] The geographical distribution of the communities honouring him (all Cycladic islands, Delos, Delphi, Kaunos and Kyrene) suggests that Sostratos was one of the leading Ptolemaic diplomats (cf. Durrbach 1921, 32; Marek 1984, 343), and testifies to the extent of Ptolemaic interests in the Eastern Mediterranean world.[76]

The honorary decree for Kallias of Sphettos, first published in 1978, perhaps sheds more light on Sostratos' diplomatic career (Shear 1978; *SEG* XXVIII 60). It also gives us some insight into the nature of his diplomatic activity, brief though the reference is. The inscription gives a detailed account of the career of Kallias, an Athenian in the service of the Ptolemies (Marek 1984, 253–254; Paschidis 2008, 145–150). In describing the

---

[72] 1972, II, 53 n. 121; Kerkhecker 1997, 134. Shear 1978, 24.

[73] Weber 1997, 59 with n. 142; Habicht 2006, 35–36; Ma 2013, 184–185 with n. 171. I single out one example here, the statue Ptolemy II erected for his naval architect Pyrgoteles (*OGIS* 39): [Β]ασιλεὺς Πτολεμαῖος | [Πυρ]γοτέλην Ζώητος ἀρχιτεκτονήσ[αντα] | τὴν τριακοντήρη καὶ εἰκ[ο]σ[ήρη], 'King Ptolemy (dedicated a statue of) Pyrgoteles, the son of Zoetos, who was the engineer of the *triakonteres* and the *eikoseres*'. Thus, the possibility of Arsinoe dedicating a statue of Sostratos, might not be as hard to believe as Shear (1978, 24 n. 45) seems to think.

[74] This Etearchos is not otherwise known, but it has been suggested that he is to be identified with the Etearchos who dedicated a phiale in the temple of Apollo at Delos which is first mentioned in the inventories of 279 (*IG* XI.2 161 B, l. 75): Durrbach 1921, 33; Marek 1984, 427 n. 281; Criscuolo 2003, 324–6, who also identifies him with the Etearchos of Posidippus' epigram AB 76. Thompson (2005, 27), however, rather thinks that the epigram concerns the Alexandrian Etearchos, son of Kleon, who was nomarch of the Arsinoite nome (Peremans *et al.* 1950–2002, no. 00883 = 10080 = 12361).

[75] Cf. Perdrizet 1899, 271: "sur aucun grand fonctionnaire de Philadelphe, on n'a maintenant plus de details que sur Sostrate". Wallace (2013, 153) in his study of Adeimantos of Lampsakos, probably the best documented *philos* of Sostratos' time, writes that "perhaps the only early Hellenistic *philos* about whom a diversity of sources exists comparable to those pertaining to Adeimantus is Sostratos of Cnidus, a high-ranking Ptolemaic courtier of the early third century". He then goes on to describe how uninformative the sources are about Sostratos' specific activities as royal *philos* compared to Adeimantos (cf. *ibid.*, 142). On Kallikrates, see Hauben 1970 and 2013; Mooren 1975, no. 10; Bing 2002/3.

[76] On the wide-ranging interests of the Ptolemies in the Eastern Mediterranean, see most recently Hauben 2014; Meeus, 2014; Strootman 2014, 314–315. For a different, but not necessarily incompatible perspective, see Meadows 2006, 2008, 2012, 2013a. For a very different perspective: Pébarthe 2014, esp. 81–83.

aftermath of the Athenian revolt against Demetrios of 287 or 286,[77] the decree mentions that (l. 32–40):

> And when King Ptolemy dispatched Sostratos to negotiate in the city's interests, and Sostratos summoned an embassy to meet him at Peiraieus with which he would discuss terms of peace with Demetrios on behalf of the city, Kallias complied with the request of the generals and the Council, acted as envoy for the Demos, and worked in every way for the city's interests, and he remained in the City with his mercenaries until the peace had been concluded (…)[78] (trans. Shear, adapted)[79]

Although the name Sostratos is not uncommon, it seems more than likely that we are dealing with Sostratos of Knidos here.[80] As Shear (1978, 23) noted,

> there is every indication that our man was a personage of great eminence: he was dispatched personally by the king; he was received in the Peiraieus (line 35) despite control of the port by Demetrios' hostile forces; and he was sufficiently well known so as to be recognizable to the average Athenian without his patronymic and ethnic. Even if formal demonstration is not possible, we can accept with confidence his identification as Sostratos, son of Dexiphanes of Knidos, a man of great wealth and high rank at the court of Alexandria.[81]

Furthermore, Ptolemy had every reason to send a leading diplomat: he had unsuccessfully attempted to intervene on Athens' behalf in an earlier conflict with Demetrios less than a decade before (Plut. *Demetr.* 33.7), and could not afford to disappoint the Athenians again without jeopardizing his prestige and influence in the Greek world (Habicht 1979, 66–67; Dreyer 1996, 64). With both the Sostratos of the Kallias decree and Sostratos of Knidos being high Ptolemaic diplomats active in the 280s there is little reason to doubt that we are dealing with one and the same man.

The precise nature of Sostratos' negotiations in the Peiraieus is debated. Assuming that the peace Sostratos concluded with Demetrios on behalf of the Athenians (τὴν εἰρήνην ὑπὲρ τῆς πόλεως πρὸς Δημήτριον, l. 35–36) was the same as the peace Demetrios made with Pyrrhos (Plut. *Demetr.* 12.5), Shear (1978, 75 cf. 22) argued that Sostratos is likely

---

[77] Shear (1978, 61–73) dated the revolt to 286, but after the reactions of Habicht (1979, 48–62) and Osborne (1979) a broad consensus seemed to have grown on 287: *e.g.* Buraselis 1982, 97; Green 1990, 128; Dreyer 1996; Sonnabend 1996, 238. Recently, however, Shear (2010) has made an interesting case for 286, but this immensely complex problem cannot be discussed here.

[78] καὶ τοῦ βασιλ{ιλ}έως Πτολεμαίου ἀποστείλαντος Σώστρατον τὰ συμφέροντα πράξοντα τεῖ πόλει, καὶ Σωστράτου μεταπεμπομένου πρεσβείαν πρὸς ἑαυτὸν εἰς Πειραιᾶ μεθ' ἧς συνθήσει τὰ περὶ τὴν εἰρήνην ὑπὲρ τῆς πόλεως πρὸς Δημήτριον, ὑπακούσας εἰς ταῦτα τοῖς στρατηγοῖς καὶ τεῖ βουλεῖ Καλλίας καὶ πρεσβεύων ὑπὲρ τοῦ δήμου καὶ [π]άντα πράττων τὰ συμφέροντα τεῖ πόλει, καὶ συμπαραμ[ε]ίνας ἐν τῶι ἄστει μετὰ τῶν στρατιωτῶν ἕως ἡ εἰρήνη σ[υ]νετελέσθη (…).

[79] On the question whether συντίθημι should here be translated as 'to conclude' or 'to discuss', see Paschidis 2008, 147 n. 6.

[80] Shear 1978, 22–23; Habicht 1979, 62; Osborne 1979, 188 n. 22; Buraselis 1982, 166; Marek 1984, 175–176; Sonnabend 1996, 238; Huß 2001, 208; Paschidis 2008, 147; Wallace 2013, 153.

[81] Cf., on Graeco-Roman Egypt, Depauw 2014, 88: "Globally, however, the frequency of the patronymic and the precise modalities of its presence or absence have barely been studied. As a general rule, it seems that the patronymic could be omitted for important people, even in an official context." Cf. Wallace 2013, 153 on Adeimantos of Lampsakos in Strabo 13.1.19.

to have brought about an agreement between Demetrios and all those who had previously allied against him (Plut. *Demetr.* 44.1), *i.e.* Ptolemy, Lysimachos, Seleukos and Pyrrhos.[82] However, the parallel case of the Third Diadoch War suggests that this is not necessarily the case: the ultimatum of 315 pitted Ptolemy, Kassandros and Lysimachos against Antigonos (D.S. 19.57.1–2), yet they did not originally make peace all at the same time (*OGIS* 5, esp. l. 26–31; cf. Simpson 1954). Habicht's interpretation that these were separate negotiations between Demetrios and Ptolemy, represented by Sostratos, seems much more in tune with the phrasing of the decree.[83] It is striking, though, that Athens does not seem to have been an equal partner in the negotiations about its own fate: Sostratos did not only represent Ptolemy's interests but those of the Athenians as well, and it was Sostratos who asked a delegation from the city to discuss the Athenian terms with him (Paschidis 2008, 147 with n. 6). What we are to make of this, is not clear, but it is surely crucial to realize that the Kallias decree only focuses on the role of Kallias: we know from Plutarch (*Demetr.* 46.3) that there had been at least one embassy from Athens to Demetrios, which contributed to the peace (Paschidis 2008, 150–152). During the previous big conflict between Athens and Demetrios in 295/4, the situation seems to have been rather different: the Athenians sent a delegation that negotiated directly with Demetrios, though it was supported by at least one courtier of Demetrios, Herodoros, who helped the demos to establish friendship with the king (*IG* II² 646, l. 15–23).[84] Buraselis (1982, 94) assumes that Sostratos acted as a neutral negotiator between Athens and Demetrios and therefore suggests that Ptolemy and Demetrios had already concluded peace. It cannot be excluded, however, that Athens was not given the right to participate in the final negotiations:[85] according to Habicht (1979, 62 with n. 75; Dreyer 1996, 64) Demetrios might have refused to negotiate with a city that had been rebelling for the second time in such a short span of time. At any rate, Sostratos' negotiations were of vital importance for the city: the performance of roles like this partially explains why these royal diplomats were honoured all over the Greek world, and there is no doubt that Sostratos will have been honoured by the Athenians (Osborne 1981–1983, II, 163 n. 732 and III, 190 n. 41). Only one other diplomatic mission is explicitly attested (S.E. *M.* 1.276), but here as well Sostratos' patronymic and demotic are missing, so that the identification cannot be absolutely certain (see below, section 4). Although Sostratos is regularly described as admiral in the secondary literature,[86] nothing

---

[82]   Gabbert 1997, 18 does not mention Seleukos but apparently accepts Shear's argument that Lysimachos was included in the peace via his agent Artemidoros of Perinthos.

[83]   Habicht 1979, 45–46 and 63; Buraselis 1982, 94 n. 234; Hölbl 1994, 25–26; Dreyer 1996, 49 with n. 36 and 1999, 219; Paschidis 2008, 143 and 147. That one of the rulers was represented by ambassadors in such negotiations does not seem to have been uncommon: see again *OGIS* 5, with Hauben 1987. For direct negotiations, see *e.g.* D.S. 19.64.8.

[84]   All of this is obviously conditional on the correctness of the restorations in the decree for Herodoros and the match between reality and the literal meaning of texts in both his decree and that for Kallias.

[85]   One should of course take into account the unequal power relationship between kings and cities: see recently Paschidis 2013. For a different view, see *e.g.* Giovannini 2004.

[86]   *E.g.* Wilamowitz-Moellendorf 1881, 118; Hiller von Gaertingen 1899, 164 n. 113; Hunter 2003, 166; Errington 2008, 56. The anecdote about Sostratos from Sextus Empiricus (*M.* I 276) discussed below may be the basis for viewing Sostratos as admiral, but he only acts as diplomat there, not even necessarily in the aftermath of a seabattle.

in the sources points in this direction: his attested activities are all situated in the spheres of architecture, engineering and diplomacy.

The date of Sostratos' career

The present analysis of Sostratos' activities as diplomat and engineer also affects the chronology of his career, which is usually dated to the 280s and the 270s.[87] It seems difficult to believe, though, that Sostratos built the Pharos early in his career: while he may have been able to fund the project through inherited wealth, he must have been relatively experienced as an architect to design such an extraordinary building as the Pharos. Thus, if the construction of the Pharos started in 297, at least Sostratos' career as an architect will have started long before 297.[88] The first dateable event in Sostratos' diplomatic career is his mission to negotiate in Athens in 287/6. Since this mission was of the highest importance for maintaining Ptolemaic influence in Greece (cf. supra), it seems highly likely that Sostratos was an experienced diplomat at this time.[89]

Other dates in Sostratos' career are much more difficult to establish as none of the inscriptions honouring him can be assigned a precise date. The Amphiktyonic decree *CID* IV 26, from the archonship of Eudokos at Delphi, belongs to 272/1 or 271/0 (Dreyer 1999, 398–404), but as we have seen, there is no reason to assume that this text actually honours Sostratos. Only in the case of the Nesiotic decree can we at least establish somewhat precise termini. It is usually assumed that this decree must postdate the so-called Nikouria decree (*Syll.*³ 390) and pre-date the marriage of Ptolemy II to his sister Arsinoe II but neither assumption seems absolutely necessary to me.[90] The first one is based on the sole mention of divine honours for Ptolemy Soter in the Nikouria decree, while the decree for Sostratos mentions honours for Ptolemy II as well. In the Nikouria decree, however, the divine honours for Soter are mentioned only in the context of the Ptolemaia in Alexandria, in which the local honours for Ptolemy II on Delos would be irrelevant, even when they existed. Indeed in the decree for Sostratos they are only mentioned because of the part of the offerings made "to the other gods and to Ptolemy Soter and king Ptolemy" (l. 24–25: τοῖς τε ἄλλοις θεοῖς καὶ Σωτῆρι Πτολεμαίωι καὶ βασιλεῖ Πτολεμαίωι) which will be sent by

---

[87] See *e.g.* Perdrizet 1899, 262: "il appartient plutôt au temps des Épigones". Peremans *et al.* (1950–2002), no. 16555, and Daumas and Mathieu 1987, 44: 290–260. Fraser 1972, I, 20 and Fernández-Galiano 1987, 93: around 280–270. Mooren 1975, no. 8 and Hauben 2004, 42 n. 94: first decades of the third century. Müller 1989, 204: first half of the third century. Rare exceptions are Daux (1943, 29) who suggests an earlier start ("La carrière de Sostratos a commencé bien avant cette date [=285]") and Olshausen (1974, no. 21) who notes the *termini* as 305 and 246.

[88] Fraser (1972, I, 20) argues for the reliability of the date because the return of Pyrrhos to Epeiros in 297 by which the Suda dates the construction of the Pharos "was not one of the stock parallellisms of Hellenistic chronology" which suggests it goes back to an Alexandrian chronological source.

[89] Buraselis (1982, 166) states that Sostratos would have been *at least* 25 years old at the time and much older if the construction of the Pharos had started in 297. Indeed 25 seems a rather low estimate as ambassadors were usually older men: both experience (Mooren 1979, 263–264) and age (Mosley 1973, 46) were important factors in the choice of ambassadors.

[90] For the *c.* 279–274/3 date, see *e.g.*: Fraser 1954, 61 n. 1; Habicht 1970, 111–112; Buraselis 1982, 180; Hauben 2004, 42 n. 94.

Sostratos every year. Thus the only certain *terminus post quem* for the Nesiotic Sostratos decree is the accession of Ptolemy II, or perhaps the foundation of the league if that occurred only under Philadelphos, as has been argued recently.[91] There is, on the other hand, no need why the Nesiotes should have divinised Arsinoe II immediately when she married her brother, though probably they could not stay behind when Ptolemy instituted the state cult for the *Theoi Adelphoi* in 272/1 (Buraselis 2008, 298–299; Carney 2013, 97), so the decree must pre-date that year. The text also mentions the nesiarch Bakkhon, but the dates of his career are even more uncertain than those of Sostratos (Hauben 2004, 41 n. 85; Meadows 2013b, 28; *contra* Hazzard 2000, 173–174).

Delphi honoured Sostratos under the archonship of Ornichidas, but the year in which he held office is uncertain (Fraser 1954, 61 n. 1).[92] The chronological indications in the other inscriptions are not more helpful. The proposer of the Delian decree, Amnos son of Dexikrates, also proposed another undateable decree (*IG* XI.4 564) and occurs in an account that is usually dated to 304 (*IG* XI.2 144 A14; Théreux 1976, 85; Reger 1994, 337; Vial 2008, 17), but we do not know whether that was early or later in his career; the decree for Sostratos is likely to be at least some two decades later, as the Ptolemies only controlled the Aegean islands from the mid 280s onward. The career of Etearchos, son of Damylos, of Kyrene who honoured Sostratos in *IG* XI.4 1190, cannot be dated either. The Kaunian honours, in turn, probably belong in either of the two periods of Ptolemaic control in Kaunos, *i.e.* a brief period after the conquest of 309 or after 285 (Meadows 2006, 462–463; Hauben 2014, 245), but we do not know which one.[93] On this basis we cannot conclude much more than that Sostratos' architectural career had already started some time before the end of the fourth century, and that the period of his activity as a diplomat must at least span the first quarter of the third century since he was an experienced diplomat by 287/6. Although Sostratos is very often described as a courtier of Ptolemy II, it seems that most of his career is to be situated under Soter.[94]

Some speculations on early Hellenistic history

Two obscure episodes from Sostratos' career may well offer us valuable information on international politics in his times. In an undated and contextless anecdote in the

---

[91] If this is correct we need not detain ourselves here with Hazzard's (2000, 47–58 and 168–175) new date for the Nikouria decree since it is no longer to be considered a *terminus post quem* for our decree. At any rate, it seems rather unlikely that this downdating of the Nikouria decree is correct: Hauben 2004 and 2010; Constantakopoulou 2012, 65 n. 41; Meadows 2013b, 28. Meadows (2013b) argues that the Nesiotic League may only have been founded in 282. This too goes against the *communis opinio*, but the problem is too large to be addressed here: see Huß 2001, 149 n. 435 with further references.

[92] Marek (1984, 175–176) argues that Sostratos was honoured at Delphi around the same time as his Athenian negotiations of 287/6, but there is no reason why Sostratos would have contacts with the Greek mainland only on this occasion.

[93] That the Kaunian statue was set up in Delos might rather point to the second period when the Ptolemies were in control of Delos too, but this is not necessary. Ptolemy himself had sacrificed on Delos in 309: Hauben 2014, 251–252.

[94] For Sostratos as a contemporary of Ptolemy II, see *e.g.* Tarn 1913, 386; Clayton 1988, 144; Errington 2008, 151; Blasius 2011, 141. For the perhaps substantially earlier start of his career in 323, see below, section 4.

introduction of his *Hippias* (2), which has been discussed above for the light it sheds on Sostratos' role as an engineer, Lucian tells about Sostratos of Knidos helping Ptolemy to capture Memphis without a fight by changing the course of the Nile and thus flooding the city.[95] Scholars have placed this anecdote in the context of Alexander's arrival in Egypt (Clayton 1988, 144–145), of Perdikkas' attack on Egypt in 320 (Droysen 1878, 128 n. 1), or of Ptolemy II's actions against the Galatians mentioned by Pausanias (1.7.2; Fraser 1972, II, 51 n. 111), but Litvinenko (2001) has recently shown that none of these interpretations is satisfactory. He proposes a fascinating new hypothesis of his own: he dates the episode to Ptolemy's arrival in Egypt in 323 (accepted by Hauben 2004, 42–43 n. 94; Schäfer 2011, 92–93). Although it cannot be conclusive due to the scanty nature of the evidence, this hypothesis is very attractive: it is difficult to see at what other time during Sostratos' career Memphis was not in Ptolemaic hands.

Admittedly, there are two fundamental problems that Litvinenko did not address, but neither seems insurmountable. The first one concerns the date of Sostratos' career, which is usually placed in the first half of the third century. As we have seen above, however, it seems that Sostratos must have been active as an architect well before 297, and nothing precludes that his political and military career had already started in the fourth century. The second problem is Diodorus' statement that Ptolemy arrived in his satrapy ἀκινδύνως (18.14.1). It should be noted that Diodorus regularly uses the word κίνδυνος to mean battle and the adverb ἀκινδύνως can thus mean without a fight, including situations where a battle was only prevented at the very last moment, for instance by means of a stratagem.[96] The latter, of course, exactly fits the situation we are facing here: the capture of a city without fighting thanks to its being flooded. While it seems too bold to consider Diodorus' language as positive evidence for Litvinenko's hypothesis, it is at any rate clear that there is no necessary contradiction between Diodorus and Lucian.

The consequences of this hypothesis, if correct, are of enormous significance: the episode would throw a whole new light on how we understand the relationships between Alexander's Successors, especially Perdikkas and Ptolemy, immediately after the king's death. Pausanias' description of Ptolemy's arrival in Egypt, admittedly chronologically very compressed, seems to offer more detail (Litvinenko 2001, 816): he claims that Ptolemy "crossed over to Egypt in person, and killed Kleomenes, whom Alexander had appointed satrap of that country, considering him a friend of Perdikkas, and therefore not faithful to himself".[97] It

[95] It should be noted that this interpretation is based on the emendation of what seems to be a suspicious manuscript reading: the τὸν Κνίδιον Σώστρατον, τὸν μὲν Πτολεμαῖον χειρωσάμενον καὶ τὴν Μέμφιν ἄνευ πολιορκίας ἀποστροφῇ καὶ διαιρέσει τοῦ ποταμοῦ of the paradosis has been emended to τὸν Κνίδιον Σώστρατον, τὸν μὲν Πτολεμαίῳ χειρωσάμενον τὴν Μέμφιν ἄνευ πολιορκίας... in modern editions of the text.

[96] See *e.g.* 15.33.1, 16.52.7 and 19.94.1 for such use of ἀκινδύνως; at *e.g.* 11.77.4, 16.66.5, 17.49.2 and 19.11.4 we find χωρὶς κινδύνων with this same meaning. Cf. Palm 1955, 191.

[97] Paus. 1.6.3: αὐτὸς δὲ ἐς Αἴγυπτον διαβὰς Κλεομένην τε ἀπέκτεινεν, ὃν σατραπεύειν Αἰγύπτου κατέστησεν Ἀλέξανδρος, Περδίκκᾳ νομίζων εὔνουν καὶ δι' αὐτὸ οὐ πιστὸν αὑτῷ (...). That the sentence continues with the body-snatch that took place some two years later indicates the degree of chronological compression, but it is not impossible that Kleomenes was killed soon after Ptolemy's arrival, as seems to be suggested by the first part of the sentence. At any rate there is an indication that the problems between Ptolemy and Perdikkas existed before the hi-jacking of Alexander's funeral cart.

is often assumed that tensions between Ptolemy and Perdikkas only arose in 321, after the hi-jacking of Alexander's funeral cart (*e.g.* Schäfer 2002, 59; Rathmann 2005b, 74; Anson 2014, 49 and 53). There are, however, other indications of a very strained relationship between both men. Apart from the brief period of compromise between the nobles against the infantry, they mostly seem to have opposed each other in the debates of the organisation of the empire after Alexander's death (Anson 2004, 61–2; Meeus 2008, 48–50 and 70–6). Diodorus informs us that upon his arrival in Egypt Ptolemy immediately tried to set up an alliance with Antipatros "since he knew well that Perdikkas would attempt to wrest from him the satrapy of Egypt".[98] That the enmity existed before the body snatch is also suggested by Arrian's (*Succ.* 24.1) comment that after this episode Perdikkas desired even more (ἔτι μᾶλλον) to remove Ptolemy from power in Egypt (ὡς Πτολεμαῖον μὲν ἀφελόμενος τὴν ἀρχὴν τῶν ἑαυτῷ τινα ἐπιτηδείων καταστῆσαι Αἰγύπτου ὕπαρχον). If Perdikkas had indeed instructed Kleomenes to hold Memphis against Ptolemy and try and prevent Ptolemy from taking over the satrapy, as the combination of Luc. *Hipp.* 2 and Paus. 1.6.3 seems to suggest, the conflict was much more intense and overt from early on than has usually been thought.[99]

If, as seems likely from all of the above, his career was already well underway in 323, that also impacts the interpretation of another contextless and undated anecdote about Sostratos: Sextus Empiricus (*M.* 1.276) relates how Sostratos, sent by Ptolemy to Antigonos concerning some royal affair (βασιλικῆς τινος ἕνεκα χρείας), made the latter change his mind after a rash reply by citing some verses from the *Odyssey* with which Zeus' messenger Iris asks Poseidon to reconsider the answer he gave to Zeus' message.[100] Unfortunately Sextus has not specified the identities of the Antigonos, Ptolemy and Sostratos. Sostratos of Knidos is the only Ptolemaic diplomat of that name famous enough not to have needed further identification,[101] but this still leaves two possibilities for each of the kings: Soter and Philadelphos on the one hand and Monophthalmos and Gonatas on the other. Because of the implicit comparison of Antigonos to Poseidon, the episode has usually been situated after a sea battle, either Salamis in 306 or Kos in 261 or 255 (cf. Meeus 2014, 300 n. 134).

---

[98] D.S. 18.14.2: σαφῶς εἰδὼς ὅτι Περδίκκας ἐπιβαλεῖται παρελέσθαι τὴν τῆς Αἰγύπτου σατραπείαν. This has often been considered an anticipatory doublet of the diplomatic contacts between Ptolemy and Antipatros on the eve of the First Diadoch War, but Diodorus (18.25.4) notes that Antipartos already knew at that time that Ptolemy was hostile to Perdikkas and well-disposed towards him and Krateros: ὄντα τοῦ μὲν Περδίκκου παντελῶς ἀλλότριον, ἑαυτοῖς δὲ φίλον. There seems no reason to presume that we are facing a doublet here: Meeus 2014, 271 n. 28.

[99] If this is correct, Ptolemy would probably not have needed to find a reason to execute Kleomenes as is for instance suggested by Bingen 2007, 23.

[100] Hom. *Il.* 15.201–3: οὕτω δὴ κέλεαι, γαιήοχε κυανοχαῖτα; τόνδε φέρω Διὶ μῦθον ἀπηνέα τε κρατερόν τε; ἦ τι μεταστρέψεις; στρεπταὶ μέν τε φρένες ἐσθλῶν ("Am I then to carry, o dark-haired, earth-encircler, this word, which is strong and steep, back to Zeus from you? Or will you change a little? The hearts of the great can be changed", trans. R. Lattimore).

[101] The identification of Sextus' Sostratos with the Knidian is widely though not universally accepted. In favour of this identification, see *e.g.* Perdrizet 1899, 265; Tarn 1913, 386–387; Heichelheim 1940, 1222; Peremans *et al.* (1950–2002), no. 16555; Gow 1965, II, 490; Sonnabend 1996, 241; Dreyer 1999, 366 ('eventuell'); Lelli 2005, 87 ('probabile'); Wallace 2013, 153; Meeus 2014, 299 n. 133 with further references for both views.

With Sostratos' career having started in or before 323, the battle of Kos or even any point in the Chremonidean war, as Dreyer (1999, 366–368) recently suggested, seem improbably late. Although I recently suggested that the aftermath of Antigonos' failed invasion of Egypt later in 306 might be an even more suitable context (Meeus 2014, 300), I now wonder whether it is really necessary to situate the anecdote shortly after a sea battle or whether it is even possible to connect it to any specific known occasion.[102] I am certainly not convinced by the attempt to connect this passage to the Athenian negotiations of 287/6 on the implausible assumption that these constitute Sostratos' only diplomatic activity.[103] Surely the epigraphic texts suggest that Sostratos was a regular diplomat, and while a mistake is always possible, there is no reason to assume that Sextus meant Demetrios when he wrote about Antigonos. At any rate, the story gives us a glimpse of Sostratos' diplomatic talent or, if it is unhistorical, of his reputation as a diplomat. Given the importance of Zeus to all Macedonian dynasties, Argeads and Antigonids (Le Bohec-Bouhet 2002) as well as Ptolemies (see above, n. 29), such a comparison placing Ptolemy-Zeus above Antigonos-Poseidon, if that is the implication of the quotation, throws an interesting light on the way the Ptolemies saw themselves (Meeus 2014, 299–300).

Conclusion

Even for a relatively well-attested – compared to many other courtiers – individual like Sostratos, the evidence does not allow for a very clear picture of his career as a whole. Nevertheless some aspects of it emerge quite clearly from the sources. There is no reason to doubt that he was an architect, and indeed he seems to have been a very famous one: no doubt this is primarily due to the construction of the lighthouse of Pharos, but the stoa of Knidos seems to have been a well-known building too. It is probably as a military engineer that he entered the service of the Ptolemies, given the early stage of his career at which he fulfilled this role in 323. Later he also became a diplomat and his contacts with Kyrene, Delos, the Cycladic islands, Delphi, Athens, Kaunos and the Antigonid court suggest that, as a Friend of the King, he was an important figure representing Ptolemaic interests all over the Greek world in the first quarter of the third century and perhaps before. Yet his support of the Ptolemies was not limited to the fields of war and diplomacy: his sponsoring the Pharos clearly fits in with the royal policy for the development of Alexandria, and it seems likely that as a *philos* he was acting in close collaboration with Ptolemy here. No precise dates for Sostratos' career can be established, but it seems that he was active from at least 323 to the 270s and spent all this time in Ptolemaic service.

Bibliography

Amandry, P. (1940/1) Dédicaces delphiques, *BCH* 64–65, 61–75.
Ambühl, A. (2007) Tell, All Ye Singers, My Fame. Kings, Queens and Nobility in Epigram. In P. Bing and J. S. Bruss (eds), *Brill's Companion to Hellenistic Epigram*. Leiden, 275–294.

---

[102] Perdrizet (1899, 265) simply situates it in the reign of Gonatas.
[103] Sonnabend 1996, 242–243. Paschidis (2008, 147 n. 4) considers the view that Sextus refers to the negotiations of 287/6 "attractive but uncertain".

Anson, E. M. (2004) *Eumenes of Cardia. A Greek among Macedonians* (Ancient Mediterranean and Medieval Texts and Contexts. Studies in Philo of Alexandria and Mediterranean Antiquity 3). Boston.

— (2014) *Alexander's Heirs. The Age of the Successors*. Chichester.

Barbantani, S. (2010) Idéologie royale et littérature de cour dans l'Égypte lagide. In I. Savalli-Lestrade and I. Cogitore (eds) *Des Rois au Prince. Pratique du Pouvoir Monarchique dans l'Orient Hellénistique et Romain (IVe Siècle avant J.-C.–IIe Siècle après J.-C.)*. Grenoble, 227–252.

Bengtson, H. (1987) *Die Diadochen: die Nachfolger Alexanders des Großen*. München.

Beresford, J. (2013) *The Ancient Sailing Season* (Mnemosyne Supplements 351). Leiden.

Bernand, A. (1995) *Alexandrie des Ptolémées*. Paris.

— (1996) Les veilleurs du Phare, *ZPE* 113, 85–90.

— (1998) *Alexandrie la Grande*. Paris.

Bernand, É. (2001) *Inscriptions grecques d'Alexandrie ptolémaïque* (Bibliothèque d'étude de l'Institut français d'archéologie orientale 133). Cairo.

Bevan, E. (1927) *A History of Egypt under the Ptolemaic Dynasty*. London.

Bing, P. (1998) Between Literature and the Monuments. In M. A. Harder *et al.* (eds), *Genre in Hellenistic Poetry* (Hellenistica Groningana. Proceedings of the Groningen Workshops on Hellenistic Poetry 3). Groningen, 21–43.

— (2002/3) Posidippus and the Admiral: Kallikrates of Samos in the Milan Epigrams, *Greek Roman and Byzantine Studies* 43, 243–266.

Bingen, J. (2007) *Hellenistic Egypt. Monarchy, Society, Economy, Culture*. Edinburgh.

Blasius, A. (2011) *"It was Greek to me…"* – Die lokalen Eliten im ptolemäischen Ägypten. In B. Dreyer and P. F. Mittag (eds), *Lokale Eliten und hellenistische Könige: zwischen Kooperation und Konfrontation*. Berlin, 132–190.

Bouvier, H. (1978) Honneurs et récompenses à Delphes, *ZPE* 30, 101–118.

Bowman, A. K. (1986) *Egypt after the Pharaohs. 332 BC–AD 642 From Alexander to the Arab Conquest*. London.

Bruns-Özgan, C. (2002) *Knidos. Ein Führer durch die Ruinen*. Konya.

— (2013) *Knidos. Ergebnisse der Ausgrabungen von 1996–2006* (Knidos-Studien 4). Istanbul.

Bürchner, L. (1921) Knidos (1), *RE* XI.1, 914–921.

Buraselis, K. (1982) *Das hellenistische Makedonien und die Ägäis. Forschungen zur Politik des Kassandros und der drei ersten Antigoniden im Ägäischen Meer und in Westkleinasien* (Münchener Beiträge zur Papyrusforschung und antiken Rechtsgeschichte 73). München.

— (2008) The Problem of the Ptolemaic sibling marriage: a Case of Dynastic Acculturation? In McKechnie and Guillaume (2008), 291–302.

— (2013) *et al.* (eds) *The Ptolemies, the Sea and the Nile: Studies in Waterborne Power*. Cambridge.

Carney, E. D. (2013) *Arsinoë of Egypt and Macedon: A Royal Life*. Oxford.

Chamoux, F. (1975) L' epigramme de Poseidippos sur le Phare d' Alexandrie. In J. Bingen *et al.* (eds), *Le monde grec: pensée, littérature, histoire, documents. Hommages à Claire Préaux* (Universtité Libre de Bruxelles, Faculté de Philosophie et Lettres 62). Brussel, 214–222.

Clayton, P. A. (1988) The Pharos at Alexandria. In P. A. Clayton and M. J. Price (eds), *The Seven Wonders of the Ancient World*. London, 138–157.

Cohen, G. M. (1995) *The Hellenistic settlements in Europe, the Islands, and Asia Minor* (Hellenistic Culture and Society 17). Berekeley.

— (2006) *The Hellenistic Settlements in Syria, the Red Sea Basin, and North Africa* (Hellenistic Culture and Society 46). Berkeley.

Constantakopoulou, C. (2012) Identity and Resistance: The Islanders' League, the Aegean Islands and the Hellenistic Kings, *Mediterranean Historical Review* 27, 51–72.

Coulton, J. J. (1976) *The Architectural Development of the Greek Stoa*. Oxford.

Criscuolo, L. (2003) Agoni e politica alla corte di Alessandria. Riflessioni su alcuni epigrammi di Posidippo, *Chiron* 33, 311–333.

Daumas, F. and B. Mathieu (1987) Le Phare d'Alexandrie et ses dieux: un document inedit, *Academiae Analecta* 49, 43–55.

Daux, G. (1943) *Chronologie delphique* (*FdD* III, Fasc. hors série). Paris.

Davies, J. (2005) The Economic Consequences of Hellenistic Palaces. In Z. H. Archibald *et al.* (eds), *Making, Moving and Managing. The New World of Ancient Economies, 323–31 BC.* Oxford, 117–135.

Depauw, M. (2014) Elements of Identification in Egypt, 800 BC–AD 300. In M. Depauw and S. Coussement (eds.), *Identifiers and Identification Methods in the Ancient World* (Orientalia Lovaniensia Analecta 229). Leuven, 75–102.

Donderer, M. (1996) *Die Architekten der späten römischen Republik und der Kaiserzeit. Epigraphische Zeugnisse* (Erlanger Forschungen, Reihe A, Geisteswissenschaften, 69). Erlangen.

Dreyer, B. (1996) Der Beginn der Freiheitsphase Athens 287 v. Chr. und das Datum der Panathenäen und Ptolemaia im Kalliasdekret, *ZPE* 111, 45–67.

— (1999) *Untersuchungen zur Geschichte des spätklassischen Athen (322–c. 230 v. Chr.)* (Historia Einzelschriften 137), Stuttgart.

Droysen, J. G. (1878) *Geschichte des Hellenismus* II, *Geschichte der Diadochen*. 2 Halbbände, Gotha.

Durrbach, F. (1921) *Choix d'inscriptions de Délos*. Paris.

Eckschmitt, W. (1984) *Die sieben Weltwunder. Ihre Erbauung, Zerstörung und Wiederentdeckung* (Kulturgeschichte der antiken Welt. Sonderband). Mainz am Rhein.

Empereur, J.-Y. (2004) *Le Phare d'Alexandrie. La Merveille retrouvée*. Paris.

Errington, R. M. (2008) *A History of the Hellenistic World 323–30 BC* (Blackwell History of the Ancient World). Oxford.

Fernández-Galiano, E. (1987) *Posidipo de Pela* (Manuales y anejos de 'Emerita' 36). Madrid.

Fraser, P. M. (1954) Two Hellenistic Inscriptions from Delphi, *BCH* 78, 49–67.

— (1972) *Ptolemaic Alexandria*. 3 vols. Oxford.

Fraser, P. M. and T. Rönne (1957) *Boeotian and West Greek Tombstones* (Skrifter utgivna av Svenska Institutet i Athen 4°, VI). Lund.

Gabbert, J. J. (1997) *Antigonus II Gonatas. A Political Biography*. London.

Giardina, B. (2010) *Navigare necesse est. Lighthouses from Antiquity to the Middle Ages: History, Architecture, Iconography and Archaeological Remains* (BAR International Series 2096) Oxford.

Giovannini, A. (2004) Le traité entre Iasos et Ptolémée Ier (IK 28, 1, 2–3) et les relations entre les cites grecques d'Asie Mineure et les souverains hellénistiques, *EA* 37, 69–87.

Gow, A. S. F. (1965) and D. L. Page, *The Greek Anthology. Hellenistic Epigrams*. 2 vols. Cambridge.

Green, P. (1990) *Alexander to Actium. The Historical Evolution of the Hellenistic Age* (Hellenistic Culture and Society 1). Berkeley.

— (1996) Alexander's Alexandria. In Hamma (1996) 3–25.

Grimm, G. (1998) *Alexandria: die erste Königsstadt der hellenistischen Welt. Bilder aus der Nilmetropole von Alexander dem Grossen bis Kleopatra VII* (Zaberns Bildbände zur Archäologie. Sonderhefte der Antiken Welt). Mainz am Rhein.

Gschnitzer, F. (1973) Proxenos, *RE* Suppl. XIII, 629–730.

Gutzwiller, K. (ed.) (2005) *The New Posidippus. A Hellenistic Poetry Book*. Oxford.

Guimier-Sorbets, A.-M. (2007) L'image de Ptolémée devant Alexandrie. In Massa-Pairault and Sauron (2007) 163–176.

Habicht, C. (1970) *Gottmenschentum und griechische Städte* (Zetemata 14), München.

— (1979) *Untersuchungen zur politischen Geschichte Athens im 3. Jahrhundert v.Chr.* München.

— (2002) Die Ehren der Proxenoi. Ein Vergleich, *MH* 59, 13–30.

— (2006) *The Hellenistic Monarchies. Selected Papers*. Ann Arbor.

Hairy, I. (2007) Pharos, l'Égypte et Platon. In Massa-Pairault and Sauron (2007), 61–89.

Hamma, K. (ed.) (1996) *Alexandria and Alexandrianism*. Malibu.

Hauben, H. (1970) *Callicrates of Samos. A Contribution to the Study of the Ptolemaic Admiralty* (Studia Hellenistica 18). Leuven.

— (1975) *Het vlootbevelhebberschap in de vroege diadochentijd (323–301 vóór Christus). Een prosopografisch en institutioneel onderzoek* (Verhandelingen van de Koninklijke Academie voor Wetenschappen, Letteren en Schone Kunsten van België. Klasse der Letteren 77). Brussels.

— (1987) Who is Who in Antigonus' Letter to the Scepsians (OGIS 5 = Welles, *Royal Correspondence* 1), *EA* 9, 29–36.

— (2004) A Phoenician King in the Service of the Ptolemies: Philocles of Sidon Revisited, *AncSoc* 34, 27–44.

— (2010) Rhodes, the League of the Islanders, and the Cult of Ptolemy I Soter. In A. M. Tamis *et al.* (eds), *Philathenaios. Studies in Honour of Michael J. Osborne*. Athens, 101–119.

— (2013) Callicrates of Samos and Patroclus of Macedon, Champions of Ptolemaic Thalassocracy. In Buraselis (2013), 39–65.

— (2014) Ptolemy's Grand Tour. In Hauben and Meeus (2014), 235–261.

Hauben, H. and A. Meeus (eds) (2014) *The Age of the Successors and the Creation of the Hellenistic Dynasties (323–276 BC)* (Studia Hellenistica 53). Leuven.

Heckel, W. (1978) On Attalos and Atalante, *Classical Quarterly* 28, 377–382.

— (1980a) Kelbanos, Kebalos or Kephalon?, *BN* 15, 43–45.

— (1980b) Marsyas of Pella, Historian of Macedon, *Hermes* 108, 444–62.

— (1982) The Career of Antigenes, *SO* 57, 57–67.

— (1983) Adea-Eurydike, *Glotta* 61, 40–42.

— (1983–1984) Kynnane the Illyrian, *RSA* 13–14, 193–200.

— (1987) A Grandson of Antipatros at Delos, *ZPE* 70, 161–2.

— (1988) *The Last Days and Testament of Alexander the Great. A Prosopographic Study* (Historia Einzelschriften 56). Stuttgart.

— (1990) Peithon, Son of Agenor, *Mnemosyne* 43, 456–9.

— (1992) *The Marshals of Alexander's Empire*. London.

— (2006) *Who's Who in the Age of Alexander the Great. Prosopography of Alexander's Empire*. Oxford.

— (2007) Nikanor Son of Balacrus, *Greek Roman and Byzantine Studies* 47, 401–412.

Heichelheim, F. (1940) Sostratos (11a), *RE* Suppl. VII, 1221–1222.

Heinen, H. (1981) Alexandrien – Weltstadt und Residenz. In N. Hinske (ed.) *Alexandrien. Kulturbegegnungen dreier Jahrtausende im Schmelztiegel einer mediterranen Großstadt* (Aegyptiaca Treverensia 1), Mainz am Rhein, 3–12.

Hellmann, M.-C. (1999) *Choix d'inscriptions architecturales grecques traduites et commentées* (Travaux de la Maison de l'orient méditerranéen 30). Lyon.

Hesberg, H. von (1981) Bemerkungen zu Architekturepigrammen des 3. Jahrhunderts v. Chr., *JdI* 96, 55–119.

— (1994) *Formen privater Repräsentation in der Baukunst des 2. und 1. Jahrhunderts v. Chr.* (Arbeiten zur Archäologie). Köln.

Hiller von Gaertingen, F. (1899) Geschichte der Stadt Thera. In F. Hiller von Gaertingen (ed.) *Die Insel Thera in Altertum und Gegenwart*, Berlin, 141–184.

Hölbl, G. (1994) *Geschichte des Ptolemäerreiches. Politik, Ideologie und religiöse Kultur von Alexander dem Großen bis zur römischen Eroberung*. Darmstadt.

Holleaux, M. (1907) Inscriptions anciennement découvertes à Délos, *BCH* 31, 335–377.

Hunter, R. (2003) *Theocritus, Encomium of Ptolemy Philadelphus* (Hellenistic Culture and Society 39). Berkeley.

Huß, W. (2001) *Ägypten in hellenistischer Zeit. 332–30 v. Chr.* München.

Jähne, A. (1981) Die Ἀλεξανδρέων χώρα, *Klio* 63, 63–103.

Kerkhecker, A. (1997) Μουσέων ἐν ταλάρῳ – Dichter und Dichtung am Ptolemäerhof, *Antike und Abendland* 43, 124–144.

Lang, P. (2013) *Medicine and Society in Ptolemaic Egypt* (Studies in Ancient Medicine 41). Leiden.

Lauter, H. (1982) Struktur statt Typus. Zu einem hellenistischen Architekturmotiv, *AA*, 703–724.

— (1986) *Die Architektur des Hellenismus*. Darmstadt.

Lawrence, A. W. (1996) *Greek Architecture* (Pelican History of Art 11) [revised by R. A. Tomlinson]. New Haven.

Lelli, E. (2005) Posidippo e Callimaco. In M. Di Marco *et al.* (eds) *Posidippo e gli altri. Il poeta, il genere, il contesto culturale e letterario* (Appunti Romani di Filologia 6 [2004]). Pisa, 77–132.

Litvinenko, Y. (2001) Sostratus of Cnidus, Satrap Ptolemy, and the Capture of Memphis. In I. Andorlini *et al.* (eds) *Atti del XXII Congresso Internazionale di Papirologia. Firenze, 23–29 agosto 1998*. Firenze, 813–820.

Łukaszewicz, A. (2014) Sur les pas de Ptolémée Ier. Quelques remarques sur la ville d'Alexandrie. In Hauben and Meeus 2014, 189–205.

Ma, J. (1999) *Antiochos III and the cities of Western Asia Minor*. Oxford.

— (2013) *Statues and Cities. Honorific Portraits and Civic Identity in the Hellenistic World* (Oxford Studies in Ancient Culture and Representation). Oxford.

MacLeod, M. D. (1991) *Lucian: A Selection* (Aris and Phillips Classical Texts). Warminster.

Marek, C. (1984) *Die Proxenie* (Europäische Hochschulschriften, Reihe 3, vol. 213). Frankfurt am Main.

Marquaille, C. (2008) The Foreign Policy of Ptolemy II. In McKechnie and Guillaume (2008), 39–64.

Massa-Pairault, F.-H. and G. Sauron (2007) (eds) *Images et Modernité Hellénistiques. Appropriation et Représentation du Monde d'Alexandre à César* (Collection de l'École française de Rome 390). Rome.

McKechnie, P. and P. Guillaume (2008) (eds) *Ptolemy II Philadelphus and his World* (Mnemosyne Suppl. 300). Leiden.

McKenzie, J. S. (2007) *The Architecture of Alexandria and Egypt c. 300 BC to AD 700* (Pelican History of Art). New Haven.

Meadows, A. (2006) The Ptolemaic Annexation of Lycia: *SEG* 27.929. In K. Dörtlük *et al.* (eds) *The IIIrd Symposium on Lycia, 07–10 November 2005, Antalya. Symposium Proceedings*. 2 vols. Antalya, 459–470.

— (2008) Fouilles d'Amyzon 6 Reconsidered: The Ptolemies at Amyzon, *ZPE* 166, 115–120.

— (2012) *Deditio in Fidem*: The Ptolemaic Conquest of Asia Minor. In C. Smith and L. Yarrow (eds), *Imperialism, Cultural Politics, and Polybius*, Oxford, 113–133.

— (2013a) Two 'Double' Dedications at Ephesus and the Beginning of Ptolemaic Control of Ionia, *Gephyra* 10, 1–12.

— (2013b) The Ptolemaic League of the Islanders. In K. Buraselis (2013), 19–38.

Meeus, A. (2008) The Power Struggle of the Diadochoi in Babylon, 323 BC, *AncSoc* 38, 39–82.

— (2014) The Territorial Ambitions of Ptolemy I. In H. Hauben and A. Meeus (2014), 263–306.

Mooren, L. (1975) *The Aulic Titulature in Ptolemaic Egypt. Introduction and Prosopography* (Verhandelingen van de Koninklijke Academie voor Wetenschappen, Letteren en Schone Kunsten van België. Klasse der letteren 78). Brussels.

— (1979) Die diplomatische Funktion der hellenistischen Königsfreunde. In E. Olshausen (ed.) *Antike Diplomatie* (Wege der Forschung 462), Darmstadt, 256–290.

Mosley, D. J. (1973) *Envoys and Diplomacy in Ancient Greece* (Historia Einzelschriften 22). Wiesbaden.

Müller, C. (1989) *Architekten in der Welt der Antike*. Zürich.

Müller, S. (2009a) *Das hellenistische Königspaar in der medialen Repräsentation. Ptolemaios II. und Arsinoë II.* (Beiträge zur Altertumskunde 263). Berlin.

— (2014a) Poseidippos of Pella and the Memory of Alexander's Campaigns at the Ptolemaic Court. In W. Heckel *et al.* (eds), *The Many Faces of War in the Ancient World*, Cambridge (forthcoming).

— (2014b) Poseidippos, Ptolemy, and Alexander. In K. Nawotka *et al.* (eds), *Alexander and the East: History, Art, Tradition*. Wiesbaden (forthcoming).

Murray, O. (2008) Ptolemaic Royal Patronage. In McKechnie and Guillaume (2008), 10–24.

Nisetich, F. (2005) The Poems of Posidippus. In Gutzwiller (2005), 17–64.

Obbink, D. (2004) Posidippus on Papyri then and Now. In B. Acosta-Hughes *et al.* (eds), *Labored in Papyrus Leaves: Perspectives on an Epigram Collection Attributed to Posidippus (P.Mil.Vogl. VIII 309)* (Hellenic Studies 2). Washington, DC, 16–28.

Olshausen, E. (1974) *Prosopographie der hellenistischen Königsgesandten I, Von Triparadeisos bis Pydna* (Studia Hellenistica 19). Leuven.

Osborne, M.J. (1979) Kallias, Phaidros and the Revolt of Athens in 287 BC, *ZPE* 35, 181–194.

— (1981–1983) *Naturalization in Athens* (Verhandelingen van de Koninklijke Academie voor Wetenschappen, Letteren en Schone Kunsten van België: Klasse der letteren, jrg. 43 nr. 98–jrg. 44 nr. 101–jrg. 45 nr. 109). 3 vols. Brussels.

Palm, J. (1955) *Über Sprache und Stil des Diodoros von Sizilien. Ein Beitrag zur Beleuchtung der hellenistischen Prosa.* Lund.

Paschidis, P. (2008) *Between City and King. Prosopographical Studies on the Intermediaries Between the Cities of the Greek Mainland and Aegean and the Royal Courts in the Hellenistic Period (322–190 BC)* (Meletemata 59). Athens.

— (2013) Φίλοι and φιλία between *poleis* and kings in the Hellenistic period. In M. Mari and J. Thornton (eds) *Parole in Movimento. Linguaggio politico e lessico storiografico nel mondo ellenistico* (Studi ellenistici 27). Pisa, 283–298.

Pébarthe, C. (2014) Les Cyclades dans la tourmente des thalassocraties. Approche comparatiste des dominations athénienne (Ve siècle) et lagide (IIIe siècle). In G. Bonnin and E. Le Quéré (eds) *Pouvoirs, îles et mer. Formes et modalités de l'hégémonie dans les Cyclades antiques (VIIe s. a.C.–IIIe s. p.C.)* (Scripta Antiqua 64). Bordeaux, 81–99.

Perdrizet, P. (1899) Sostrate de Cnide, architecte du Phare, *REA* 1, 261–272.

Peremans, W. *et al.* (1950–2002) *Prosopographia Ptolemaica* (Studia Hellenistica). 10 vols. Leuven.

Préaux, C. (1978) *Le monde hellénistique. La Grèce et l'Orient de la mort d'Alexandre à la conquête romaine de la Grèce (323–146 av. J.-C.)* (Nouvelle Clio. L'histoire et ses problèmes). 2 vols. Paris.

Radt, S. (2009) *Strabons* Geographika, vol. VIII, *Buch XIV–XVII: Kommentar.* Göttingen.

Reger, G. (1994) *Regionalism and change in the economy of independent Delos, 314–167 B.C.* (Hellenistic Culture and Society 14). Berkeley.

Rutherford, I. (2013) *State Pilgrims and Sacred Observers in Ancient Greece. A Study of Theōriā and Theōroi.* Cambridge.

Sandberger, F. (1970) *Prosopographie zur Geschichte des Pyrrhos.* diss. Stuttgart.

Schäfer, C. (2002) *Eumenes von Kardia und der Kampf um die Macht im Alexanderreich* (Frankfurter Althistorische Beiträge 9). Frankfurt am Main.

Schäfer, D. (2011) *Makedonische Pharaonen und hieroglyphische Stelen. Historische Untersuchungen zur Satrapenstele und verwandten Denkmälern* (Studia Hellenistica 50). Leuven.

Shear, J. (2010) Demetrios Poliorketes, Kallias of Sphettos, and the Panathenaia. In G. Reger *et al.* (eds) *Studies in Greek Epigraphy and History in Honour of Stephen V. Tracy* (Études 26). Bordeaux, 135–152.

Shear, T. L. (1978) *Kallias of Sphettos and the Revolt of Athens in 286 BC.* (Hesperia. Supplement 17). Princeton.

Simpson, R. H. (1954) The Historical Circumstances of the Peace of 311, *JHS* 74, 25–31.

Sonnabend, H. (1996) *Die Freundschaften der Gelehrten und die zwischenstaatliche Politik im klassischen und hellenistischen Griechenland* (Altertumswissenschaftliche Texte und Studien 30). Hildesheim – Zürich – New York.

Staden, H. von (1996) Body and Machine: Interactions between Medicine, Mechanics and Philosophy in Early Alexandria. In Hamma (1996), 85–106.

Strootman, R. (2007) *The Hellenistic Royal Court. Court Culture, Ceremonial and Ideology in Greece, Egypt and the Near East, 336–30 BCE.* diss. Utrecht.

— (2014) 'Men to Whose Rapacity neither Sea nor Mountain Sets a Limit': The Aims of the Diadochs. In Hauben and Meeus (2014), 307–322.

Tarn, W. W. (1913) *Antigonos Gonatas.* Oxford.

Tataki, A. B. (1998) *Macedonians Abroad. A Contribution to the Prosopography of Ancient Macedonia* (Meletemata 26). Athens.

Théreux, J. (1976) Observations sur l'Amphictyonie attico-délienne, *Études d'archéologie classique* 5 (Annales de l'est 53), 87–95.

Thompson, D. J. (2005) Posidippus, Poet of the Ptolemies. In Gutzwiller (2005), 269–283.

Tomlinson, R. A. (1992) *From Mycenae to Constantinople. The Evolution of the Ancient City.* London.

Vandorpe, K. (2010) The Ptolemaic Period. In A. B. Lloyd (ed.) *A Companion to Ancient Egypt* (Blackwell Companions to the Ancient World). Malden, 159–79.

Vial, C. (2008) *Inscriptions de Délos. Index* II, *Les Déliens.* Paris.

Walbank, F. W. (1984) Monarchies and Monarchic Ideas. In F. W. Walbank *et al.* (eds) *The Cambridge Ancient History* VII².1, *The Hellenistic World.* Cambridge, 62–100.

Wallace, S. (2013) Adeimantus of Lampsacus and the Development of the Early Hellenistic Philos. In V. Alonso Troncoso and E. M. Anson (eds), *After Alexander. The Time of the Diadochi (323–281 BC)*. Oxford, 142–157.

Weber, G. (1993) *Dichtung und höfische Gesellschaft. Die Rezeption von Zeitgeschichte am Hof der ersten drei Ptolemäer* (Hermes Einzelschriften 62). Stuttgart.

— (1997) Interaktion, Representation und Herrschaft der Königshof im Hellenismus. In A. Winterling (ed.) *Zwischen 'Haus' und 'Staat'. Antike Höfe im Vergleich*. München, 27–71.

— (2007) Die neuen Zentralen, Hauptstädte, Residenzen Paläste und Höfe. In G. Weber (ed.) *Kulturgeschichte des Hellenismus. Von Alexander dem Großen bis Kleopatra*. Stuttgart, 99–117.

Wilamowitz-Moellendorf, U. von (1881) *Antigonos von Karystos* (Philologische Untersuchungen 4). Berlin.

— (1924) *Hellenistische Dichtung in der Zeit des Kallimachos*. 2 vols. Berlin.

Winter, F. E. (2006) *Studies in Hellenistic Architecture* (Phoenix Suppl. 42). Toronto.

Zwingmann, N. (2012) *Antiker Tourismus in Kleinasien und auf den vorgelagerten Inseln. Selbstvergewisserung in der Fremde* (Antiquitas I, 59). Bonn.

WHAT DID ARSINOE TELL LYSIMACHUS ABOUT PHILETAERUS?

Daniel Ogden[1]

Strabo's note on the origin of the Pergamene state is full of interest for the history of the Diadochic world:

> Pergamum was the treasury [γαζοφυλάκιον] of Lysimachus, the son of Agathocles, one of the Successors to Alexander, and it consists of a settlement upon the very top of the mountain. The mountain is cone-shaped and tapers to a sharp point. *Philetaerus was entrusted with the guarding of this fort and its money (there were 9,000 talents). He came from Tieum, and he was a eunuch [θλιβίας] from his boyhood. For it happened that a great crowd had gathered to watch at some funeral, and the nurse who was carrying Philetaerus, who was still an infant, was caught back in the crowd and was crushed so hard [συνθλιβῆναι] that the child was maimed. But although he was a eunuch [εὐνοῦχος], he was reared in a decent fashion [τραφεὶς δὲ καλῶς] and appeared worthy of being entrusted with the citadel. For some time he remained well disposed [εὔνους]*[2] *towards Lysimachus, but then he fell at variance with his wife, Arsinoe, who was slandering [διαβάλλουσαν] him, and detached the place from his rule.* He continued to govern it in a fashion that best suited the circumstances, since, as he could see, change was in the air. For Lysimachus' household had fallen into disarray, and he had been compelled to kill his son Agathocles. Then Seleucus came and destroyed him, only to be destroyed himself, deceitfully murdered by Ptolemy Ceraunus. In the midst of all this turmoil, the eunuch continued in control of the fort and managed it by making promises to or by paying court to whoever was powerful or in the offing at any one time. That is how he maintained charge over the castle and the money for twenty years.
>
> (Strab. C623)

The two themes of this passage upon which I wish to concentrate initially are the eunuchism of Philetaerus and the slander of Arsinoe, the historical setting for the latter of which, since it is closely associated with the death of Agathocles, seems to be *c.* 283–2 BCE.

It is possible to historicise both of these themes. As to the eunuchism, Pausanias too asserts that Philetaerus was a Paphlagonian eunuch, though he offers a seemingly incompatible,

---

[1] It is a pleasure and a privilege to be able to offer this paper in celebration of Prof. Heckel's inspirational and indispensible scholarship.
[2] Wordplay, evidently.

and rather more demeaning, account of how he came by that status: he was in origin the eunuch slave of one Docimus, a general of Antigonus.[3] If Pausanias is right, and he is not merely reflecting a piece of hostile propaganda generated at some indeterminate point in the Attalid era, then Strabo's story of the crushing at the funeral would be exposed as the engaging fiction we might in any case suspect it to be. Philetaerus' eunuchism can be contextualised historically in other ways too. First, eunuchs were particularly associated with the role of treasurer. Accordingly, we are told by Phylarchus and Plutarch that Demetrius Poliorcetes used to abuse Lysimachus as a mere 'treasurer' (γαζοφύλαξ), a term which angered Lysimachus precisely because eunuchs were particularly associated with the role, being considered, as they were, particularly loyal and reliable.[4] Secondly, Cybele, patron goddess of the eunuch *galli*, was the object of the most prominent cult at Pergamum under Philetaerus and his successors. Philetaerus himself dedicated a temple to the goddess, the 'Megalesium', where dedications to and statuettes of Attis have been found, as well as one to Demeter, in honour of his mother Boa, and one to 'the Mother of the Gods' at Mamurt-Kaleh.[5] It is possible to read these two contexts both forwards and backwards, as it were. Both of them could indicate that Philetaerus' eunuchism, however acquired, was a historical fact. Alternatively, both could provide the starting-point and justification for the tradition's misrepresentation of Philetaerus as eunuch.[6] It is, accordingly, impossible to know whether the historical Philetaerus was a eunuch or not. Another type of evidence to which one might think of turning here, the iconography, is indecisive: the statuary and the coin portraits alike represent him as corpulent, certainly, though there is nothing further about them specifically to indicate eunuchism.[7]

It is possible to historicise the dispute between Arsinoe and Philetaerus by putting it into a broad historical context. This friction is testified to also by Pausanias, who states that, after the murder of Agathocles, Philetaerus transferred his allegiance to Seleucus because he was suspicious of the treatment he would receive from Arsinoe (τὰ παρὰ τῆς Ἀρσινόης ὕποπτα ἡγούμενος).[8] Lysimachus had given some cities in north west Asia Minor to Arsinoe, including the cities of Heraclea and Amastris, the latter named for the widow of Dionysius,

---

[3] Paus. 1.8.1. Luc. *Macr.* 12 also describes Philetaerus as a eunuch in passing. Compatible with Pausanias' claim, in detail and tone, is Athenaeus 577b (= Carystius of Pergamum *FHG* iv p.358 F12, later second-century BCE), where we are told that Philetaerus was the son of a Boa, flute-girl courtesan (ἑταίρα). His mother's Paphlagonian origin (Tieum) at any rate is testified to more neutrally at Strabo C543 and C623 (as quoted), and *IvP* ii. 613 (= *OGIS* 264) lines 14–15. His father was Attalus, seemingly, therefore, a Macedonian: *OGIS* nos. 748–9. Cf. Beloch 1912–27, iv.2 207–8; Hansen 1971, 17; Allen 1983, 182–4; Kosmetatou 2003, 159–61.

[4] Plut. *Dem.* 25 and Ath. 261b (incorporating Phylarchus *FGrH* 81 F31).

[5] See Hansen 1971, 17–18, 26, 51, 127–8, 237–42, 284, 299, 438, 446, 456–7 and Allen 1983, 183 and 200–7.

[6] Cf. Beloch 1912–27, iv.2, 208; Hansen 1971, 15, 17; Guyot 1980, 219–20; Ogden 1999, 199–201; Tougher 2002, 147.

[7] See Hansen 1971, 20–2; Gans 2006, 11–17, with further bibliography. Davis and Kraay 1973, 250–1: "It was said that he was a eunuch, having been injured in infancy, but his career as a mercenary officer in the army of Antigonus the One-eyed and the burly, aggressive head on his portrait coins bespeak a most masculine man" (!).

[8] Pausanias 1.10.4–5.

tyrant of Heraclea, and sometime wife of Lysimachus himself. Amastris had created it through a synoecism that had briefly encompassed Philetaerus' birthplace of Tieum, and the city was managed by one Eumenes, probably Philetaerus' own brother. Arsinoe's rule in the region was evidently meddlesome and harsh: Upon Heraclea she imposed a brutal tyrant, Heraclides of Cyme. This would seem to offer cause enough for friction between Arsinoe and Philetaerus, whether or not Arsinoe was attempting to exert direct control over Pergamum itself. But why are we told that Arsinoe 'slandered' him? Slander seems to speak of a more personal tale, and one of intrigue. What might have been the supposed content of this mysterious slander?[9]

Moreover, Strabo's passage takes on a rather different light when read in conjunction with Lucian's tale of Stratonice and Combabus in his poem *On the Syrian Goddess*. Here we are told how Stratonice, the young wife of Seleucus, dreams that Hera (Atargatis) orders her to build a temple for her in Hierapolis (Bambyce), with threats of punishments should she not do so. She ignores the dream at first but eventually confesses it to Seleucus, who bids her go up to Hierapolis and build the temple. The king orders his friend Combabus to escort her, together with the treasure she has to take to fund the operation. He begs him not to send him for fear of jealousy, but the king insists, and so he seeks a week's deferment, castrates himself, preserves his testicles in a pot of honey, seals it with his ring, and gives it to the king as a great treasure to guard whilst he is gone. The king additionally seals it with his own signet ring. Combabus works for three years with Stratonice in building the temple, and she begins to fall in love with him. At first she conceals her love, but in the end determines to get drunk and declare it. Combabus rudely rejects her advances and tells her off for drunkenness. When she threatens to kill herself, Combabus tells her what he has done. People returning from Hierapolis regale the king with rumours of an affair. So the king summons Combabus before the work is finished. An untrue story, Lucian adds, tells that Stratonice herself wrote letters to the king accusing Combabus of trying to rape her, just as in the mythical stories of Anteia-Stheneboea and Phaedra.[10] But anyway, Combabus returns and the king imprisons him. Seleucus accuses him of threefold wrongs, adultery, disloyalty and impiety before Hera, and resolves to execute him. Combabus asks the king to bring forth the pot, and they break the seal. Upon discovering the contents, the king embraces Combabus, weeps and undertakes to execute the false accusers. He offers Combabus wealth and promises that he will never leave his side, even when he sleeps with

9 Strab. C544, Memnon *FGrH* 434 FF4–5, 9 (F9 for Eumenes); discussion at McShane 1964, 31–3; Longega 1968, 44–54; Hansen 1971, 15–17; Allen 1983, 11–14; Mehl 1986, 291–2, 319; Hammond and Walbank 1988, 240 ("The quarrel perhaps arose out of an attempt by Arsinoe to get possession of the town of Amastris, as she had done that of Heraclea – if indeed the Eumenes to whom Lysimachus had entrusted the town… was Philetaerus' brother"); Brodersen 1989, 184; Grainger 1990, 194–5; Lund 1992, 193–5; Virgilio 1993, 14–19; Müller 2009, 42–3; Carney 2013, 37–8, 45. Macurdy 1932, 113–14 and Burstein 1982, 199–200 are oddly silent on the matter.

10 Anteia-Stheneboea: Hom. *Il.* 6.155–205; Eur. *Stheneboea.* (FF661–71 *TrGF*); Apollod. 2.3.1; Zenobius *Centuriae* 2.87; Hyginus *Fabulae* 57, *Astronomica* 2.18; Tzetzes on Lycophron *Alexandra* 17, *Chiliades* 7 no. 149. Phaedra: Soph. *Phaedra* (FF677–693a *TrGF*); Eur. *Hipp.*; Diod. 4.62; Ov. *Heroides* 4; Sen. *Phaed.*; Apollod. *Epit.* 1.18–19; Paus. 1.22, 2.32; Hyginus *Fabulae* 47; Servius on Virg. *A.* 6.445 and 7.761; Tzetzes on Lycophron *Alexandra* 1329, *Chiliades* 6 no.56; schol. Hom. *Od.* 9.321; schol. Plat. *Laws* 931b.

his wife. Combabus returns to complete the temple. He is rewarded with a bronze statue in the sanctuary – a woman in shape, but clothed like a man.[11]

Lucian's tale can hardly be regarded as historical in any meaningful sense. Were we to insist on historicising it, the action would have to have fallen between 298 BCE, when Seleucus married Stratonice, and 292 BCE when he passed her on to his son Antiochus.[12] The tale is usually said to be unique in terms of the Greek tradition (we shall qualify this shortly), but it is rather less so in the context of Near Eastern and Asian tradition more generally, where a number of parallels have been identified:[13]

- A Persian tale first fully preserved in Arabic in al-Tabari's *History* of *c.* 915 CE, and then in Persian in Ferdowsi's *Shahnameh* of 1010 CE, but evidently already lurking behind the Pahlavi *Deeds of Ardeshir* of *c.* 600 CE. According to this story, King Ardeshir has asked his chief mage, Harjand (or perhaps Abarsam) to execute his wife, either because she has attempted to poison him or because he has discovered that she is the daughter of his erstwhile enemy, the supplanted king Ardevan. But when the mage learns that she is pregnant, he resolves, in an extraordinary act of loyalty, to keep her secretly in a cellar and rear her child, Shapur, there. In the meantime he castrates himself and gives his genitals, preserved in salt, to the king in a sealed casket. When, years later, the king regrets his sonlessness and repents of his order to execute the woman, the mage brings the pair forth, revealing all, and is rewarded with a share of the king's rule and the construction of the city of Jundishapur in his honor.[14]
- A Tocharian B tale recorded by Xuan Zang in *c.* 630 CE in the city of Kucha (Kuqa) in Turkestan (Xinjiang). When the king of the land is to leave his palace to go on a Buddhist pilgrimage, he puts his younger brother in charge. The brother castrates himself and gives his testicles to the king in a golden casket, who entrusts it to a guard. Upon the king's return, craftsmen slander the brother, telling him he has brought debauchery to the inner palace. The brother prevails upon the king to open the casket before he punishes him. The brother is rewarded with the free run of the inner palace.[15]
- A Turkish tale recorded by Paul Lucas in Iconium in 1705 CE. When a former governor of Iconium, Mullak Onker, wishes to make the pilgrimage to Mecca, he leaves the city and his house in the hands of his friend, the Christian bishop Epsepi. As Mullak Onker is departing Epsepi castrates himself and gives him his genitals in a little box to store in a secure place until his return. Epsepi proceeds to make many enemies in the course of his administration, including even in the harem, and these enemies determine to destroy him. Upon Mullak's return they tell him that Epsepi has been debauching his womenfolk, including his mother. The women of the harem endorse the accusations, and throw themselves upon Mullak complaining of Epsepi's brutality. Epsepi avoids the decreed beheading by asking Mullak to look inside the box first. Mullak makes a vow of eternal friendship with Epsepi, and they are eventually buried side by side.[16]
- A Kannada tale recorded by Captain W. H. Sykes in his camp at Bejapoor (Bijapur) in 1818. Mohammad-Shah (Muhammad b. 'Ibrahim b. Tahmasp, whose historical rule spanned 1626–56 CE) dispatches his

---

[11] Luc. *Syr. D.* 19–27, with Lightfoot 2003 *ad loc.*
[12] See Ogden 1999, 119–24.
[13] Discussed at Benveniste 1939, 251; Krappe 1946; Lightfoot 2003, 384–8, the latter of whom also gives attention to more recent literary adaptations of Lucian's tale.
[14] Al-Tabari *History*: 823–4; pp. 26–8 in the Nöldeke trans.; vol. 5 pp. 24–6 in the Bosworth trans. Ferdowsi *Shahnameh*: C1392–7; vol. 6 pp. 259–66 in the Warner and Warner trans.; pp. 554–60 in the abridged Davis trans. *Deeds of Ardeshir*: cc.10–11, pp. 96–107 Grenet (with French trans.). Cf. Benveniste 1939, 252–3; Krappe 1946, 193; Lightfoot 2003, 385. The historical Ardeshir I, founder of the Sassanid dynasty, ruled 224–39 CE; for discussion of other traditional stories with Greek affinities associated with him in the *Deeds*, see Ogden 2011, 72–6 and 2012.
[15] Xuan Zang at Lévi 1913, 358–9. Cf. Benveniste 1939, 254–5; Krappe 1946, 194–5; Lightfoot 2003, 385–6.
[16] Lucas 1712, 193–9. Cf. Krappe 1946, 189–90 and Lightfoot 2003, 387

friend Mulik from Bejapoor to fetch a new concubine for him from Sungul Deep. Mulik castrates himself and gives his genitals to the king in a casket. Upon his return his enemies tell the king that Mulik has anticipated him with the woman. He avoids beheading by asking the king to examine the contents of the casket first. The king rewards him by building the magnificent Taj Bowree cistern in his name.[17]

Most of these tales function as aetiologies: Lucian's as an aetiology of the cult of Hera-Atargatis at Hierapolis-Bambyce and of her eunuch devotees; the Persian tale as an aetiology of the foundation of Jundishapur; the Turkish tale as an aetiology of a curious pair of tombs; the Indian tale as an aetiology of the Taj Bowree.[18] But the overriding theme of all these tales is, manifestly, the absolute loyalty of the courtier-figure to his king, loyalty even to the point of self-harm.

Lucian's tale of Combabus has hitherto been regarded as the earliest attested example of the eunuch-slander story-type.[19] But, for all that Strabo's account of Philetaerus and Arsinoe lacks the motifs of auto-castration and casket, I suggest that the elements of the story-type nonetheless lurk behind it, and this, of course, pushes the attestation of the story-type back at least to the late Augustan or Tiberian age.

The content of Arsinoe's slander is not so mysterious after all: it is the same as that of Stratonice's slander against Combabus in Lucian's less preferred variant, the same as that of Sthenoboea's against Bellerophon, and the same as that of Phaedra's against Hippolytus: Philetaerus had attempted to force himself upon her. This accusation will have been rebutted by the late revelation of Philetaerus' eunuch condition. And Arsinoe – or rather the figure of Arsinoe as represented elsewhere in the tradition – gratifyingly has form in the levelling of such accusations. For, in an episode which has its own striking resonances with the Combabus tale, we are told by Pausanias that after failing in her attempt to seduce Agathocles, Lysimachus' son and seeming heir, and her own stepson, she had similarly slandered him:

> Many disasters are wont to arise for men on account of love. For although Lysimachus was already advanced in age, although he himself was considered fortunate in his children, and although Agathocles already had children himself by Lysandra, he married Lysandra's sister Arsinoe. It is said that this Arsinoe was frightened on behalf of her children, lest they should fall under the power of Agathocles after Lysimachus' death, and it is said that for this reason she plotted against Agathocles. People have written too that Arsinoe fell in love with Agathocles, but that since her love was unrequited she plotted death for him. And they say that Lysimachus later realised what his wife had dared to do, but that it was no use to him, now that he was completely bereft of friends...
>
> (Pausanias 1.10.3–4)

This episode in turn exhibits further gentle resonances with the Seleucus tradition, the well known and oft-told story of Seleucus' son Antiochus falling in love with his young step-mother Stratonice.[20]

---

[17] Sykes 1823, 64–5. Cf. Benveniste 1939, 253–4 and Krappe 1946, 195–6; Lightfoot 2003, 385–6.
[18] Lightfoot 2003, 384–8.
[19] Benveniste 1939, 256–8; Lightfoot 2003, 387–8.
[20] V. Max. 5.7 ext.1; Plin. *Nat.*7.123; Plut. *Dem.* 38; Rufus of Ephesus pp. 607–8 Daremberg-Ruelle; App. *Syr.* 59–61; Luc. *Syr. D.* 17–18 (cf. *Calumny* 14; *Icaromenippus* 15; *How to Write History* 35); Gal. *On*

What of the remainder of the tale of Arsinoe and Philetaerus? Under what circumstances might he have acted as her guardian or chaperone in the absence of the king? Perhaps the context, half fictive, half historical, was a visit by Arsinoe to Asia Minor to inspect or administer the possessions that Lysimachus had bestowed upon her there.

It is conceivable that the Arsinoe-Philetaerus tale, like the Stratonice-Combabus tale, did at some point in its archaeology contain an episode in which the adult Philetaerus advisedly castrated himself prior to chaperoning Arsinoe, giving Lysimachus the pot and revealing the contents at the appropriate time. In that case we would have to suppose that Strabo's story of the accidental childhood castration of Philetaerus was a variant fiction developed to explain the same fact, if fact it was, that of Philetaerus' eunuchism. But Occam's razor, and the proximity in Strabo's text of the childhood tale, which is clearly sympathetic towards Philetaerus, and the slander of Arsinoe invite us to suppose rather that it was precisely the accidental childhood castration that was the object of the revelation in the tale all along. Closer inspection of Strabo's words suggests that it could quite appropriately have functioned in this way. The claim that Philetaerus was reared 'in a decent fashion' implies that Philetaerus was brought up as, and lived the life of, a man rather than as a eunuch. Accordingly, Philetaerus' longstanding eunuchism would have remained a secret until the point of Arsinoe's accusation, when it had to be brought out into the light.

In what dramatic fashion was this eunuchism then revealed, with no pot to show? It can hardly have been seemly to have Philetaerus hoicking up his tunic before an assembled court. Perhaps a clue lurks in the figure of the nurse. Was she brought before Lysimachus' court to confess her story? One thinks here of the nurses found so frequently on the Menandrian stage (a stage, as it happens, quite contemporary with the lives of Arsinoe and Philetaerus), who often have a key role in revealing a long-lost secret from a baby's childhood.[21] In the fragmentary *Titthe* the titular 'Nurse' confessed in the prologue either to having borrowed or lent a baby (presumably on a permanent basis), and must have contributed to the revelation of that baby's true identity in adulthood in the course of the play.[22] In the *Eunuch*, which was adapted by Terence, the nurse Sophrona is brought in to identify the recognition tokens of the (unnamed) long-lost girl at the centre of the action, who will go on to marry Chaerea.[23] In the *Heautontimorumenos*, also adapted by Terence, Sostrata

---

Prognosis/De Praecognitione 6 (= *CMG* V 8.1, pp. 100–5); *Commentary on Hippocrates'* Prognosticus/ *In Hippocratis* Prognosticum 1 (= *CMG* V 9.2, pp. 206–7); Jul. *Mis.* 17 (= 347a-348a); Syncellus' *Ecclesiastical Chronicle* 520 (p. 330.13–17 Mosshamer); *Suda* s.v. Ἐρασίστρατος; Tzetzes *Chiliades* 7 no. 118. The many discussions of this tale include: Mesk 1913; Breebart 1967; Fraser 1969; Amundsen 1974; Landucci 1978; Marasco 1982, 104–114; Brodersen 1985; 1989, 168–77; Mehl 1986, 230–68; Kuhrt and Sherwin-White 1991; Goukowsky 2007, 156–9. I find the frequent comparison of the tale of Stratonice and Antiochus to that of Phaedra and Hippolytus to be over-egged. The comparability of the Phaedra myth is rather, as we have seen, with the Combabus tale.

[21] In addition to the three Menandrian plays mentioned in this paragraph, note also the roles of nurses in *Anepsioi, Epitrepontes, Heros, Misoumenos, Pseuderacles, Rhapizomene, Samia*. Webster 1974, 111–93 offers convenient summaries and reconstructions of the plots of these fragmentary plays. One thinks more generally of the shepherds brought on stage to reveal what happened to the baby Oedipus in their care in Sophocles' *Oedipus Tyrannus*.

[22] Reconstruction at Webster 1974, 193.

[23] Ter. *Eu.* 806–7, 910–15; cf. Webster 1974, 139–41 for the reconstruction of the underlying Menandrian

confirms the identity of her long-lost daughter Antiphila with the help of a recognition token in the form of a ring and the recollections of the girl's former nurse.[24]

Whatever the historical pegs upon which the story of Arsinoe and Philetaerus was hung, why was it developed? We may offer two reasons. The first is that it adds drama to what could be seen as a critical moment in Lysimachus' tragic end, and his annihilation by Seleucus. As Strabo and Pausanias indicate, Philetaerus could be seen as instrumental in allowing Seleucus to prevail over Lysimachus by transferring himself and Pergamum from the suzerainty of the latter to the former. The crucial transfer of resources aside, it was this change of allegiance that prompted Lysimachus to cross over into Asia and so enter the battle with Seleucus, Corupedium, in which Seleucus was to kill him.[25]

The second is that it functions as part of a wider parallelism established in tradition between Lysimachus and Seleucus. Just as Seleucus had his wife Stratonice fall in love with, be rejected by, and slander the secret eunuch Combabus, so Lysimachus was to have his wife Arsinoe fall in love with, be rejected by, and slander the eunuch Philetaerus. An explicit parallelism between Seleucus and Lysimachus survives in Appian's account, in the course of his so-called 'Seleucus excursus', of the fateful battle of Corupedium and its aftermath, in which Seleucus was himself then killed by the wicked Ptolemy Ceraunus. Appian works hard to manufacture a parallelism between the immediate fates of the two kings' bodies after their death. First he tells, in finishing off his biography of Seleucus, how Philetaerus used his vast wealth to ransom Seleucus' body from Ptolemy Ceraunus, how he cremated it, and sent the urn to his son Antiochus, who installed it in a hero-shrine, the 'Nicatoreum', in the city named for Seleucus, Seleucia-in-Pieria. But then Appian curiously travels back in time to speak of the prior fate of the body of Lysimachus on the battlefield of Corupedium. Lysimachus' body was guarded where it lay by his loyal dog, until it could be retrieved by his son Alexander, who installed it in a hero-shrine, the 'Lysimacheum', in the city named for Lysimachus, Lysimachia.[26]

In three of the four stories mentioned here, that of Stratonice and Combabus, that of the dead Seleucus and Philetaerus, and that of the dead Lysimachus and his dog, the central

---

play. The titles of these plays are merely coincidental for present purposes.

[24] Ter. *Hau.* 614–17; cf. Webster 1974, 144–6 for the reconstruction of the underlying Menandrian play.

[25] Paus. 1.10.4–5; cf. 1.8.1.

[26] App. *Syr.* 62–4. Discussion at Marasco 1982, 117–40; Brodersen 1989, 178–90; Goukowsky 2007, xviii, 161–4. The last contends that the parallelism between the description of the placing of Seleucus in the Nicatoreum of Seleucia (he wrongly locates in Antioch) and that of the placing of Lysimachus in the Lysimacheum of Lysimachia suggests that Appian's treatment of these matters may have originated in an epideictic oration he had given in one or other of the cities, to glorify the relevant founder.

Appian also makes another parallelism between Lysimachus and Seleucus at this point by telling, with little warrant in context, the tale of how Lysimachus had been given an omen of his future kingship, or even predestined for it, when Alexander had placed his diadem on his head to staunch a wound; this picks up the tale Appian has told at c.56, in accordance with which Seleucus was given an omen of his future kingship, or even predestined for it, when he placed Alexander's diadem on his own head in order to retrieve it from the marsh into which it had been blown.

For Lysimachus' loyal dog, which is also said to have committed suttee on his pyre, see also Duris *FGrH* 76 F55 (= Plin. *Nat.* 8.143; the dog was called 'Hyrcanus'); Phlegon of Tralles *FGrH* 257 F9; Ael. *NA.* 6.25; Tzetzes *Chiliades* no. 132.

theme is manifestly ultimate loyalty. We may presume that it was also the central theme of the Arsinoe and Philetaerus story, but that in this case the great loyalty of the eunuch figure was crucially sacrificed. And so it was that this loyalty was transferred to Seleucus, to be demonstrated so strikingly in the redeeming of his body, but, before that, and signally, to set in chain the series of events that led to Lysimachus' own downfall.

This thematic cluster leads me to suppose that the tale of Arsinoe and Philetaerus originated in the rich fictive traditions that developed around the figure of Seleucus, as indeed seems to have been the case with the tale of the dead Lysimachus and his dog, which is found, as we have noted, in Appian's Seleucus excursus. (In any case, what reason might one have, after the death of Lysimachus and with it the extinction of his dynasty, for developing traditions focusing upon him in his own right?) The evidently once very rich fictive traditions about Seleucus are refracted still not only in Appian, but also Libanius, John Malalas and many others.[27] Without reference to these other texts, a glance at Malalas aside, Peter Fraser found the fictive elements of the Seleucus excursus alone so striking that he hypothesised their derivation from a lost 'Seleucus Romance', a text supposedly resembling the *Alexander Romance*.[28]

Abbreviations

CMG	*Corpus medicorum Graecorum* 1907–
FGrH	Jacoby *et al.* 1923–
FHG	Müller 1878–85
IvP	Fränkel *et al.* 1890–
OGIS	Dittenberger 1903–5

Bibliography

Allen, R. E. (1983) *The Attalid Kingdom. A Constitutional History.* Oxford.

Amundsen, D. W. (1974) Romanticizing the Ancient Medical Profession: The Characterization of the Physician in the Graeco-Roman Novel, *Bulletin of the History of Medicine* 48, 320–37.

Beloch, K. J. (1912–27) *Griechische Geschichte*. 2nd edn. 4 vols. 8 parts, Strasburg.

Benveniste, E. (1939) La légende de Kombabos. In *Mélanges syriens: offerts à M. René Dussaud*. 2 vols. I, 249–58, Paris.

Bosworth, C. E. trans. (1999) *The History of al-Tabari. v. The Sasanids, the Byzantines, the Lakhmids, and Yemen.* New York.

Breebart, A. B. (1967) King Seleucus I, Antiochus, and Stratonice, *Mnemosyne* 20, 154–64.

Brodersen, K. (1985) Der liebeskranke Königssohn und die seleukidische Herrscahftsauffassung, *Athenaeum* 63, 459–69.

— (1989) *Appians Abriss der Seleukidengeschichte (Syriake 45,232–70,369): Text und Kommentar*. Münchener Arbeiten zur alten Geschichte Band 1. Munich.

Burstein, S. M. (1982) Arsinoe II Philadelphos: a revisionist view. In W. L. Adams and E. N. Borza (eds) *Philip II, Alexander the Great and the Macedonian Heritage*, 197–212, Lanham, NY.

[27] I would point in particular to Euphorion of Chalcis F119 Lightfoot (*c.* 200 BCE); Diod. 19.55 (*c.* 30 BCE); Just. 15.3–4, 17.1–2 (iv CE?), after Trogus (*c.* 20 BCE); Plut. *Dem.* 31–2, 38, 47–52 (*c.* 100 CE); App. *Syr.* 52–63 (130s–160s CE); Polyaenus *Strategemata* 4.9 (*c.* 163 CE); Luc. *Syr. D.* 17–27 (*c.* 170s CE); Libanius *Orations* 11 (*Antiochicus*) 76–105 (356 CE); John Malalas *Chronicle* 197–203 (vi CE), after Pausanias of Antioch/Damascus *FGrH* 854 F10 (before 358/9 CE?).

[28] Fraser 1996, 36–9; approved by Stoneman 2008, 61.

Carney, E. D. (2013) *Arsinoe of Egypt and Macedon*. New York.

Corpus medicorum Graecorum (1907–) Berlin.

Davis, D. trans. (2006) Abolqasem Ferdowsi, *Shahnameh. The Persian Book of Kings*. London.

Davis, N, and C. M. Kraay (1973) *The Hellenistic Kingdoms. Portrait Coins and History.* London.

Dittenberger, W. (1903–5) *Orientis graeci inscriptiones selectae*. 2 vols. Leipzig.

Fränkel, M., *et al.* (eds) (1890–) *Die Inschriften von Pergamon*. 3+ vols. Berlin.

Fraser, P. M. (1969) The career of Erasistratus of Ceos, *Istituto Lombardo-Accademia di Scienze e Lettere, Rendiconti, Classe di Lettere* 103, 518–37.

— (1996) *The Cities of Alexander the Great*. Oxford.

Gans, U.-W. (2006) *Attalidische Herrscherbildnisse. Studien zur hellenistichen Porträtplastik Pergamons*. Wiesbaden.

Goukowsky, P. (1978) *Essai sur les origins du mythe d'Alexandre*. 2 vols. Nancy.

Grainger, J. D. (1990) *Seleukos Nikator: Constructing a Hellenistic Kingdom*. London.

Grenet, F. (2003) *Le geste d'Ardashir fils de Pâbag. Kārnāmagi–Araxšeri–Pābagān*. Die.

Guyot, P. (1980) *Eunuchen als Sklaven und Freigelassene in der griechisch-römischen Antike*. Stuttgart.

Hammond, N. G. L., and F. W. Walbank, (1988) *A History of Macedonia* iii. Oxford.

Hansen, E. V. (1971) *The Attalids of Pergamon*. 2nd edn. Ithaca.

Jacoby, F., *et al.* (1923–) (eds) *Die Fragmente der griechischen Historiker*. Multiple volumes and parts. Berlin and Leiden.

Kosmetatou, E. (2003) The Attalids of Pergamon. In A. Erskine (ed.), *A Companion to the Hellenistic World*, 159–74. Oxford.

Krappe, A. H. (1946) Seleukos and Kombabos, *Byzantina-Metabyzantina* 1, 189–99.

Kuhrt, A., and S. Sherwin-White (1991) Aspects of Seleucid Royal Ideology: the cylinder of Antiochus I from Borsippa, *Journal of Hellenic Studies* 111, 71–86.

Landucci, F. (1978) Problemi dinastici e opinion pubblica nel 'caso' di Stratonice. In M. Sordi (ed.) *Aspetti dell'opinione pubblica nel mondo antico, Vita e Pensiero*. CISA 5, 74–84, Milan.

Lévi, S. (1913) Le 'Tokharien', langue de Koutcha, *Journal Asiatique* 2, 311–380.

Lightfoot, J. L. (2003) *Lucian. On the Syrian Goddess*. Oxford.

Longega, G. (1968) *Arsinoe II*. Rome.

Lucas, P. (1712) *Voyage de sieur Paul Lucas fait par ordre du Roy dans la Grèce, l'Asie Mineure, la Macédoine et l'Afrique*. Vol. i. Paris.

Lund, S. (1992) *Lysimachus*. London.

MacShane, R. B. (1964) *The Foreign Policy of the Attalids of Pergamum*. Urbana.

Macurdy, G. H. (1932) *Hellenistic Queens*. Baltimore.

Marasco, G. (1982) *Appiano e la storia dei Seleucidi fino all' ascesa al trono di Antioco III*. Florence.

Mehl, A. (1986) *Seleukos Nikator und sein Reich: Teil 1: Seleukos' Leben und die Entwicklung seiner Machtposition*. Louvain.

Mesk, J. (1913) Antiochus und Stratonike, *Rheinisches Museum* 68, 366–94.

Müller, C. (*i.e.* K.) (ed.) (1878–85) *Fragmenta historicorum Graecorum*. 5 vols. Paris.

Müller, S. (2009) *Das hellenistische Königspaar in der medialen Repäsentation – Ptolemaios II und Arsinoë II*. Beiträge zur Altertumskunde 263. Berlin.

Nöldeke, T. (1879) trans. *Tabari. Geschichte der Perser und Araber zur Zeit der Sasaniden*. Leiden.

Ogden, D. (1999) *Polygamy, Prostitutes and Death: the Hellenistic Dynasties*. London.

— (2011) *Alexander the Great: Myth, Genesis and Sexuality*. Exeter.

— (2012) Sekandar, Dragon-Slayer. In R. Stoneman, K. Erickson and I. Netton (eds) The Alexander Romance *in Persia and the East*. Ancient Narrative Supplementum 15, 277–94, Groningen.

Stoneman, R. (2008) *Alexander the Great: A Life in Legend*. New Haven.

Tougher, S. (2002) In or out? Origins of court eunuchs. In S. Tougher (ed.) *Eunuchs in Antiquity and Beyond*, 143–59, Swansea.

Virgilio, B. (1993) *Gli Attalidi di Pergamo. Fama, Eredità, Memoria*. Pisa.

Warner, A. G., and E. Warner trans. (1912) *The Sháhnáma of Firdausí*. 9 vols. London.

Webster, T. B. L. (1974) *An Introduction to Menander*. Manchester.

POLYBIUS
ON NAVAL WARFARE

Philip de Souza[1]

Introduction

This paper addresses a basic question – how useful and reliable are Polybius' accounts of naval warfare for the modern historian. Traditionally he has been considered one of the best of all the ancient historians, particularly when it comes to aspects of warfare. One leading modern scholar sums him up thus: "On the whole Polybios is a remarkably sober historian – some would say too sober – and this inclines one to trust him."[2]

Eric Marsden's seminal paper on Polybius' merits as a military historian offers a general starting point.[3] Marsden argues that, like all historians, military historians need to be selective, and that Polybius should be judged on how well he has selected his material. Marsden offers a three-part classification of the ways that information is presented in military history narratives. The first of these is through accounts of planning, build-up and operations with comments.[4] The second is through accounts devoid of comment, "probably because the writer held the significance of the military concepts involved to be sufficiently obvious." The third is also through accounts without comments, but in this case it is "because the writer considers his information interesting and possibly instructive, but cannot see clearly and precisely where or in what its importance lies." Marsden draws attention to the topos of the inclusion of comments and to the fact that Polybius may seem, at times, to over-emphasise, perhaps even to distort, particular features of warfare,

[1] I am delighted and honoured to be part of this celebratory volume for a scholar whose work I have read, used and admired for many years. Earlier versions of this paper were given in Liverpool University at the Polybius 1957–2007 colloquium in honour of Frank Walbank, and in University College Dublin at the Dublin Classics Seminar in 2012. Thanks are due to the organisers of both events and to the participants who offered numerous helpful comments. This short paper is part of a much larger study of ancient naval warfare that was partly funded by the Irish Research Council for the Humanities and Social Sciences.
[2] Lazenby 1996, 6. Note also the approval of Morrison and Coates 1996, xiv.
[3] Marsden 1974.
[4] (Marsden 1974, 273–4). As an example of this approach Marsden cites Polybius' comments on the significance of superior numbers of cavalry at the battle of Cannae, and in warfare generally (Polyb. 3.117.4–5). Marsden himself comments that "It is most difficult to agree with this view, but he is certainly entitled to his opinion, and it is not without value" Marsden 1974, 274, n. 1.

both in his selection and his arrangement of the material. This is seen, above all, when he comments directly on the lessons that can be learned from the events he has described. Marsden is aware of the potential for distortion, he does not, however, see this as a major problem:

> As he wanted to be, Polybius is a veritable mine of information for the military man. It may be a positive advantage that he did not include more interpretative sections, which might have contaminated the factual evidence rather than clarified it. It was possibly the economy of his work, imposed by himself, that forced him to be so selective that some modern readers will greatly regret the numerous detailed omissions. However at the very least, he began the breakthrough into more advanced, even modern, military history.[5]

In the recorded discussion following Marsden's paper François Paschoud asked whether Polybius, like many other ancient historical writers, seeks primarily to create a 'purple passage' (*morceau de bravoure littéraire*) when describing battles. To which Marsden countered that "Polybius does not appear to be concerned with just an attractive literary account, his style remaining solemn and dry." Frank Walbank suggested that Polybius is imposing order on confusion, in order to create an accepted version of events. Walbank added, "I would say Polybius was certainly not interested in fine writing in the sense that Livy was in his elaboration of material; and unlike Livy he knew what a battle was."[6]

Although Marsden had not explicitly addressed naval warfare, Paul Pédech argued that there are strong indications of the importance of naval warfare to Polybius, pointing out that, as one would expect from a native Greek, Polybius is just as interested in naval warfare as he is in terrestrial warfare. Pédech argued that in his account of the First Punic War Polybius emphasises the naval encounters, especially during the command period of Hamilcar Barca, when a series of naval battles were fought. He suggested that the war between Rome and Antiochus III can be characterised by a similar series of naval encounters, but for these we are largely reliant upon Livy's version (Livy 36.43–45; 37. 23–24 and 28–30). Pédech also suggested that Polybius' focus is very much on the innovative methods of combat (*moyens de combat inédits*) and tactical manoeuvres employed in these encounters, such as; the introduction of the Roman *corvus* at the battle of Mylae (Polyb. 1.22), the Rhodian use of flaming pots at Panormus and Myonnesus (Polyb. 21.7), the Romans' triangular formation at Ecnomus (Polyb. 1.27–28), and Adherbal's skilful manoeuvres to avoid being trapped by the Roman fleet at Drepana (Polyb. 1.49–51). I will examine some of these in more detail below.

Comparative aspects

Polybius is clearly very interested in comparing the details of various aspects of the technology of warfare. A good example is his discussion of the differences between Roman and Greek palisade stakes (χάραχες), which he thinks shows the Roman version to be superior both because of its ease of transport and the clever way in which the Romans intertwine them to make stronger palisades (Polyb. 18.18). Pédech incorporated this example into his wide-

---

[5]   Marsden 1974, 294–5.
[6]   Marsden 1974, 298–99.

ranging discussion of Polybius' comparative approach to the writing of history.[7] He saw the comparison of military systems as an integral part of Polybius' historical method:

> Le sujet que Polybe avait choisi offrait de multiples occasions de comparer les forces de Rome avec celles de ses adversaires; chaque bataille était une expérience nouvelle où se vérifiaient les qualités des uns et les faiblesses des autres; chacun jetait toutes ses ressources dans les plateaux de la balance; l'historien n'avait qu'à en faire l'inventaire pour commenter le résultat.[8]

This comparative approach is also prominent in Polybius' presentation of naval warfare. It must, of course, be linked with his desire to write history that is a suitable means of education and training for those who wish to embark on a political career:

> Had previous chroniclers neglected to speak in praise of History in general, it might perhaps have been necessary for me to recommend everyone to choose for study and welcome such treatises as the present, since men have no more ready corrective of conduct than knowledge of the past. But all historians, one may say without exception, and in no half-heated manner, but making this the beginning and end of their labour, have impressed on us that the soundest education and training for a life of active politics is the study of History, and that the surest and indeed the only method of learning how to bear bravely the vicissitudes of fortune, is to recall the calamities of others.
>
> (Polyb. 1.1.1–2)[9]

Pédech concluded his contribution to the discussion of Marsden's paper by saying, "*Polybe et donc un historien militaire complet. Il va jusqu'à mettre une certaine coquetterie à s'entendre sur les operations navales.*"[10] Marsden's own final comments also drew attention to the limitations of Polybius experience, which might have implications for his reliance on his sources: "Polybius criticized Ephorus's treatment of land warfare, but praised his accounts of naval fighting, possibly because Polybius had little or no experience at sea and therefore did not understand so well the employment of warships and what happened in action."[11]

Polybius' military experience (and understanding of military matters)

Since the issue of personal experience has been raised it is appropriate at this point to consider not only what experience Polybius had, but also how important such experience was to the historian. Polybius himself concludes his harsh critique of Callisthenes' error-strewn account of the Battle of Issus in 333 by saying: "We are bound to attribute the mistake to the writer, and to think that his inexperience blinded him to the difference between what is possible and what is impossible in warfare" (Polyb. 12.22.5–6).[12] Later in the same book, towards the end of what survives of his denunciation of the Sicilian historian Timaeus, Polybius claims that one of the things that makes him a poor historian is his self confessed lack of experience (Polyb. 12.25h.1).[13] He goes on to insist that an

---

7   Pédech 1964, 405–26.
8   Pédech 1964, 424.
9   Translation Paton, Walbank, Habicht, 2010, 3. See also Polyb. 12.15.
10   Marsden 1974, 300.
11   Marsden 1974, 300. The passage criticizing Ephorus that he refers to (Polyb. 12.25f) is quoted below.
12   Translation Waterfield 2010, 431.
13   For an analysis of what Polybius has to say about him see Brown 1958, 93–106. Timaeus is not the only

historian must have personal experience of the kinds of things he writes about, so that readers find in his writing the same vividness as is found in Homer:

> …vividness of the kind that would make a reader declare, when the topic is politics, the writer must have gained experience, as a politician himself, of how public life works; or, when the topic was warfare, that the writer had served in the forces and seen action; or when the topic was private life, that the writer had raised children and lived with a woman
>
> (Polyb. 12.25.h5)[14]

Further on he castigates Timaeus for choosing an easy life of research compiled solely from the works of others, rather than undertaking the rigours of personal enquiry and autopsy (12.26e–27.7). And he cites with approval Theopompus' dictum that, "the greatest military expert is the man who has witnessed the most battles" (Polyb. 12.27.8).[15] He then starts what for us is the last section of Book 12 by declaring that the way to end errors among historians is for men who have held public office to take up history writing, or for prospective writers to gain political experience (Polyb. 12.28.3–6). Thus Polybius sets out his manifesto for the ideal historian, who should be a man of action and experience – a man like himself.

It is beyond dispute that Polybius was well versed in politics, but how much experience did he have of warfare?[16] We can assume, given his family background, that he was trained in the use of arms and that he learnt the basics of strategy and tactics from an early age. Depending on when he was born, he could have participated in Achaean League actions in the early or late 180s, but nothing survives from his *Histories* to indicate how much, if any, action he saw in his youth. He was clearly experienced enough, both politically and militarily, to be elected *hipparchos* for the Achaean League in 170/169, which effectively made him second-in-command to Archon, the *strategos* (Polyb. 28.6.9). He was part of the embassy sent to conduct negotiations with the Roman consul Quintus Marcius Philippus regarding Achaean assistance against king Perseus of Macedon (Polyb. 28.12.4–7). He says that he was also charged with reconnoitring the route that an Achaean army would take to Thessaly and ensuring that adequate supplies and markets would be available, should their presence be required by the Roman commander. Thus he shows us that his fellow Achaeans were prepared to place a considerable amount of trust in his understanding and judgement of military and political matters.

Polybius says that, on finding Philippus already on the offensive, he and his colleagues "shared the perils of the invasion of Macedonia" (Polyb. 28.13.2), although what that entailed is unclear.[17] The consul eventually declined the Achaean offer, but Polybius did not return immediately to Achaea with the rest of the embassy. Instead, Polybius tells us that he remained with Philippus and implies that he played some kind of military role, perhaps attached to the consul's staff, in the ensuing events, although the surviving excerpts from his

---

writer to be criticised in Book 12, but he takes the brunt of Polybius wrath against 'couch' historians.

14 Translation Waterfield 2010, 437.
15 Translation Waterfield 2010, 443.
16 On Polybius' life see Walbank 1957–67–79, vol. I, 1–6; Walbank 1972, 6–13; McGing 2010, 130–47.
17 Livy makes no mention of Polybius or the Achaean embassy, but he does give a fairly detailed account of the campaign, which must be based on Polybius (Livy 44.2–8).

work offer no details (Polyb. 28.13.7).[18] There were no opportunities for Polybius to gain further, direct military experience. In 168 BCE he and his father Lycortas were ready to lead an Achaean force to help King Ptolemy VI and his son deal with an invasion by Antiochus IV, but were dissuaded from doing so by a message from Philippus (Polyb. 29.23–25).

Although Polybius was among the thousand Achaean exiles deported to Rome after the Roman victory at Pydna in 168, he was not forced to spend his time reclining on a couch and reading about great events. His friendship with Scipio Aemilianus enabled him to leave Italy, probably visiting Spain with Scipio in 151 and witnessing the fall of Carthage in 146, where he may even have been involved in the fighting. The 4th century CE Latin historian Ammianus Marcellinus claims that the Emperor Julian personally led an attack on the gates of the citadel of Pirisabora on the Euphrates in CE 363, and was ashamed that it failed because he had read of a similar exploit at Carthage involving Scipio Aemilianus and Polybius that succeeded (Amm. Marc. 24.2.14–17). Ammianus seems to imply that the anecdote that inspired Julian was recounted by Polybius, but it is not among the surviving fragments of his *Histories,* nor is it mentioned by any other source. Ammianus insists that it was a genuine incident, but he does so in order to convince his readers of the authenticity of his story about Julian, which leaves both tales open to doubt.[19]

I am inclined to reject the Scipio story as an invention, or an elaboration of a much less exciting account, not least because Polybius praises both Scipio Africanus and Hannibal for their cautious approach to leading from the front (Polyb. 10.13.1–3; 10.33), and castigates Marcus Claudius Marcellus for his brainlessness in getting killed in action unnecessarily (Polyb. 10.32.1–9). There is no good reason, however, to disbelieve the Elder Pliny's statement that, "When Scipio was in command in Africa he provided Polybius the annalist with a fleet for the purpose of sailing around the continent to explore it" (Plin. *HN.* 5.9). Polybius himself says that, in the pursuit of the historical and truthfulness and authority geographical autopsy is central:

> I accepted all the hazards of travelling in Libya, Iberia and Gaul, and sailing the sea that washes the outer coastline of these places. I wanted to correct the mistaken notion of my predecessors, and give the Greeks reliable information about these parts of the world too.
>
> (Polyb. 3.59.7–8)[20]

Given that Polybius was elected as *hipparchos* of the Achaean League in 169 we can reasonably assume that he was well acquainted with the methods and principles of land, and especially cavalry warfare. He comments in the context of Hannibal's victory at the Battle of Cannae in 216 that:

> The battle taught later generations that in wartime it is better to have half as many infantry as the enemy, and overwhelmingly cavalry superiority, than to have exactly the same numbers as the enemy in all respects
>
> (Polyb. 3.117.4–5)

---

[18] McGing plausibly suggests that he was one of the consul's advisers and adds: "This may well have given him the chance to make battlefield notes" (McGing 2010, 143).

[19] "It is difficult to believe this, although, of course, impossible to disprove it" (McGing 2010, 142).

[20] Translation Waterfield 2010, 175.

This seems to reflect a personal conviction, rather than a commonly held belief, and it is perhaps indicative of the kind of thing that was included in his lost work on *Tactics* that he refers to in Book Nine of his *Histories* (Polyb. 9.20.4).[21] There is, however, no evidence that Polybius ever actively participated in a naval warfare, although his expedition around Africa would have given him a fair amount of maritime experience, especially if he were in overall command. Would Polybius, because of his relatively limited experience, have considered himself less capable of explaining or commenting on naval warfare than on land warfare? Given the nature of his remarks on the importance of personal experience, military, political or domestic, I suggest not. He does not claim that the historian needs to be an expert on every aspect of military matters, only that he needs to have personal experience of warfare.

Historians of naval warfare

How and where did Polybius learn about the practice of naval warfare? A logical answer, consistent with his own recommendation to his readers, would be that he obtained guidance from suitably experienced writers. One of these must surely have been Thucydides, whose work was Polybius' principal model in terms of both his subject matter and his approach to the writing of history.[22] Thucydides' narrative is a treasure-trove of comments on naval warfare and tactics (*e.g.* Thuc. 2.83–91; 7.36 and 70). We can assume that Polybius also learnt quite a lot from Xenophon, the first two books of whose *Hellenica* are replete with descriptions of naval warfare. Polybius cites him as an authority on ancient Sparta (Polyb. 6.45.1) and he quotes Xenophon's description of Ephesus as a "workshop of war," likening New Carthage after its capture by Scipio Africanus in 209 to the Greek city when it was Agesilaus' base in 395 (Polyb. 10.20.7; Xen. *Hell.* 3.4.16–18; Xen. *Ages.* 1.26). Another of Polybius' literary instructors was the fourth century historian Ephorus of Cumae, whom he criticises vehemently on other matters, but whom he somewhat grudgingly praises for his knowledge of naval warfare: [23]

> I get the impression from his battle passages that he had an adequate understanding of naval operations, but had no experience at all of land battles. If we focus on sea battles, then, such as the one fought off Cyprus or the battle of Cnidus, we are bound to be impressed by Ephorus' competence and expertise, and we learn a great deal that will serve us well in similar circumstances.

(Polyb. 12.25f)[24]

Of course, when it comes to the details of events that he narrates in the *Histories*, Polybius will have taken much of his understanding of the strategic situations and the specific tactical insights from the written sources that he used.[25] For the First Punic War the key sources were the Roman senatorial historian Quintus Fabius Pictor and the Greek Philinus of Acragas.

---

[21] For what may be a summary of parts of that work see Polyb. 9.12–20.

[22] See Walbank 1972, 32–48.

[23] See Pedech 1964, 26–33, 60–2, 356–8, 407–8.

[24] Translation Waterfield 2010, 436.

[25] For detailed discussion of Polybius' use of his sources see Walbank 1957–67–79, *ad loc*. For a general appraisal see Walbank 1972, 77–84.

Polybius describes these two as the best sources for the war, who, despite their respective pro-Roman and pro-Carthaginian biases, were not likely to have deliberately falsified anything (Polyb. 1.14.1–3). He does criticize Philinus for inaccuracy regarding a supposed treaty between Rome and Carthage (Polyb. 3.26), but he had clearly read his work in detail and made considerable use of it. Probably the most important indicative examples for this paper, however, are the Rhodian historians Zeno and Antisthenes, who are the subject of some typically double-edged comments in the course of book 16 of the *Histories*:

> Since some authors of particular histories have dealt with this period comprising the attempt on Messene and the sea battles I have described, I should like to offer a brief criticism of them. I shall not criticize the whole class, but only those whom I regard as worthy of mention and detailed examination. These are Zeno and Antisthenes of Rhodes, whom for several reasons I consider worthy of notice. For not only were they contemporary with the events they described, but they also took part in politics, and generally speaking they did not compose their works for the sake of gain but to win fame and to do their duty as statesmen. Since they treated some of the same events as I myself I must not pass them over in silence, lest owing to their being Rhodians and to the reputation of the Rhodians for great familiarity with naval matters, in cases where I differ from them students may be inclined to follow them rather than myself. Both of them, then, declare that the battle of Lade was not less important than that of Chios, but more severe and terrible, and that both as regards the issue of the separate contests that occurred in the fight and its general result the victory lay with the Rhodians. Now I would admit that authors should have a preference for their own country but they should not make statements about it that are contrary to facts."
>
> (Polyb. 16.14)[26]

Polybius then describes the extent of the Rhodian naval losses at the Battle of Lade and gives an account of the victory celebrations of Philip V following that battle. He continues as follows:

> After telling us all these things, which obviously are symptoms of defeat, they nevertheless declare that the Rhodians were victorious both in the particular engagements and generally, and this in spite of the fact that the despatch sent home by the admiral at the very time to the Rhodian senate and prytaneis, which is still preserved in the prytaneum at Rhodes, does not confirm the pronouncements of Antisthenes and Zeno, but my own.
>
> (16.15.7–8)[27]

This is a heavily qualified recommendation, but Polybius is never at his most fulsome when commenting on the merits of other historians. Nevertheless, it can be taken as evidence that he did follow their accounts, and it might be inferred, on the basis of what has been argued above, that he followed them quite closely, not merely because they were the principal sources for the naval encounters of this period, but also because he was acutely aware that they knew much more than he did about naval warfare.[28]

---

[26] Translation Paton 1922–7, vol. V, 27–29.
[27] Translation Paton 1922–7, vol. V, 31.
[28] On Rhodian historiography of this period see Wiemer 2001, chs. 4–5.

The nature of ancient naval warfare

The remainder of this paper will examine a few examples of Polybius' treatment of naval warfare, beginning with one of his most influential accounts, that of the Romans' momentous decision to challenge the Carthaginians at sea in the First Punic War. At this point, however, it is important to note that my own approach to the subject of ancient naval warfare differs markedly from that of many modern scholars in one important respect: I do not make the assumption that the fleets of Classical Antiquity were primarily intended to engage in naval warfare in the early modern sense of ship to ship combat. Rather they were designed and used for what modern military specialists would term 'amphibious strike operations,' their primary function was to transport fighting men by sea to attack targets on land. [29] Very large warships, which were developed in the fourth century BCE could act as platforms for missile weapons and siege machines, giving them a major role in attacks on coastal cities.[30]

Nowadays such operations are typically conducted using aircraft as well as ships and ground forces, but the basic analogy is sound. Most of the men who made up the crews of ancient warship were therefore not simply 'oarsmen', but were infantrymen. They were deployed as 'light troops', the usual Greek words for which are *psiloi* or *kouphoi*, and the usual Latin word is *velites*. They could be used to ravage and plunder enemy territory, to assault poorly defended settlements, thereby diverting enemy forces from other areas of combat. They also routinely constructed fortifications and siege works and, when necessary, they would engage in skirmishes and provide missile fire and harrying actions in pitched battles. Ship to ship combat was only the secondary function of ancient warships, and was rarely the primary purpose for the creation and deployment of ancient war fleets, nor the typical manifestation of ancient naval warfare. That is not to say that ship to ship combat might not play an important, even crucial role in a particular conflict, especially when the key theatres of war were coastal, and when both sides had reason to attempt to intercept each other's fleets at sea, as was the case for much of the Punic Wars, and occasionally in the wars of the Hellenistic states that Polybius covered in his *Histories*.

The Romans first take to the sea

That Polybius was well aware of the primary function of naval forces is obvious from his explanation of why the Romans decided to build a large fleet in 261. He introduces the creation of the first major Roman fleets thus:

> As long as the Carthaginians had undisputed dominance at sea, the outcome of the war hung in the balance. For, as time passed and the Romans retained possession of Acragas, many inland towns were alarmed enough about the Romans' land forces to join their side, but more coastal towns were frightened enough of the Carthaginian fleet to secede from them. The scales of war were constantly tipping one way or the other, with increasingly larger fluctuations. Under

---

[29]   Traditionally, scholars working on maritime aspects of warfare in Antiquity, myself included, have focused so much on combat between warships that they have often underestimated the extent to which warships were used to convey military forces in order to fight on land. Recent studies that have challenged the accepted orthodoxy include van Wees 2004, 62–4, 222–4; Krentz 2007, 172; Murray 2012; de Souza 2013.

[30]   See de Souza 2007a and 2007b; Murray 2012.

these circumstances, the Romans committed themselves to taking to the sea along with the Carthaginians. A factor that influenced their thinking was how commonly Italy was raided by naval forces, while Libya remained completely untouched. Here we have the issue that prompted me to cover this war in greater detail: I did not want anyone to be ignorant of how and when and why the Romans first took to the sea.

(Polyb. 1.20.5–8)[31]

This famous passage clearly shows how Polybius conceptualizes naval warfare as a distinct and specialised form of warfare, and thus why he attaches so great a significance to the Romans' deliberate decision to become a sea power. It is likely that he modelled it on Thucydides' paradigm of Athenian sea power versus Spartan land power, which he uses extensively in his account of the Peloponnesian War (Thuc. 1.18; 1.80–81; 1.141–3; 2.62; 2.89; 4.12; 4.55).

There are problems with the manner in which Polybius emphasises this momentous event, that is, in Marsden's terms, with the comments he makes:

It was, therefore, because the war was dragging on that they first applied themselves to building ships – 100 quinqueremes and 20 triremes. They faced great difficulties because their shipwrights were completely inexperienced in the building of a quinquereme, since the vessels had never before been employed in Italy. Yet it is this fact that illustrates better than any the extraordinary spirit and audacity of the Romans' decision. It was not a question of having adequate resources for the enterprise, for they had in fact none whatsoever, nor had they ever given a thought to the sea before this. But once they had conceived the idea, they embarked on it so boldly that without waiting to gain any experience in naval warfare they immediately engaged the Carthaginians, who had for generations enjoyed an unchallenged supremacy at sea.

(Polyb. 1.20.9–12)[32]

Can we take all of this at face value? The answer must be an emphatic no. To say that the Romans had never given thought to the sea is a huge exaggeration, given the considerable evidence for Roman naval activities and the development of a small but significant naval infrastructure prior to 264.[33] Instead this 'purple passage' must be seen primarily in the context of Polybius' historiographical methodology. It provides him with a way of comparing and contrasting the Romans with the Carthaginians, thereby allowing him to develop several themes: the Romans' drive and determination, which borders on arrogance; their sudden rise as a sea power to challenge Carthage; the twist of fate (*tyche*) that allows them to learn from their enemy.[34] For the modern historian, trying to establish the details of Roman naval capacity at the start of the First Punic War, Polybius' historiographical structure is highly problematic. For example, is the claim of a lack of available shipwrights who knew about building 'fives' likely to be true? It does not seem unreasonable, given that the only direct evidence that we have of their use the in the Western Mediterranean before this

---

[31] Translation Waterfield, 19, adapted.
[32] Translation Scott-Kilvert 1979, 62.
[33] See, briefly, de Souza, 2013, 382–3; for a more detailed and optimistic assessment see Steinby 2007, 29–86.
[34] On the importance of *tyche* in the Histories see Pédech 1964, 331–54; Walbank 1972, 59–65; McGing 2010, 195–201.

point is by Dionysius I and II of Syracuse in the first half of the fourth century (Diod. 14.41–42; 14. 58.2; 15.73.2), and perhaps by Agathocles and Pyrrhus in the first quarter of the third century (Diod. 21.16.1; 22.8.5). Ancient warships were relatively complex to design and construct. Having limited uses and being made from perishable materials they were not kept around indefinitely unless they were needed (See de Souza 2007a, 361–7; 2013, 381). The story that Polybius tells of exactly how the Romans went about building a fleet is a plausible one:

> One piece of evidence of their extraordinary daring, and of the truth of my account, is this. When they first ventured to transport their forces to Messana, not only had they no decked ships, but no warships at all, not so much as a single galley. They merely borrowed penteconters and triremes from the Tarentines, and the Locrians, and the people of Elea and Neapolis, and ferried the troops across at great risk. It was on this occasion that the Carthaginians sailed out to attack them as they were crossing the straits, and one of their decked ships, in their eagerness to overtake the transports ventured too near the shore, ran aground and fell into the hands of the Romans. It was this ship which they proceeded to use as a model, and they built their whole fleet according to its specifications; from which it is clear that but for this accident they would have been prevented from carrying out their programme for sheer lack of the necessary knowledge.
>
> (Polyb. 1.20.13–16)[35]

However, the topos of Romans learning from their enemies is a common one, and certainly not unique to the Romans.[36] So we must be wary of accepting it at face value. On the other hand it is more than just a literary topos – it is a sound military practice, which is exactly the kind of thing that Polybius ought to be providing for his readers. Thus we see that Polybius is not above exaggerating and embellishing to make his points, but he does offer a plausible account of events and selects and comments on his material in keeping with his didactic aims.

Returning to Polybius' version of the events in the early years of the First Punic War, after explaining how the Romans had acquired their ships, he goes on to describe the training of the crews on land before putting them out into ships at sea, which was a sound move in the circumstances (Polyb. 1.21.1–3). Next he introduces the famous 'raven' or *corvus*, the boarding bridge which has become a symbol of Roman naval ingenuity. There is no need to dwell on the details of this device, but it is important to note that it is a technical innovation that Polybius describes in some detail – for the instruction of his readers – although he cannot have actually seen it for himself.[37] It seems to have had an immediately successful impact, but it was a hastily devised piece of equipment, and was short-lived as a tactical weapon, being abandoned only a few years after its introduction, probably because it depended for its effectiveness on its novelty, and once the surprise wore off the Carthaginians were able to devise suitable tactics to counter its use.[38] Polybius does

---

[35] Translation Scott-Kilvert 1979, 62–3.

[36] *E.g.* Sall. *Cat.* 51.37–39 – Caesar's speech on the punishment of the Catilinarian conspirators; see Walbank 1957–67–79, I, 75.

[37] See Lazenby 1996, 68–72.

[38] See de Souza 2007b, 437–9.

not tell us exactly when or why the *corvus* was discarded, but he has plenty more to say about naval warfare in the First Punic War.

The Battle of Ecnomus

This major naval battle, which took place in 256 BCE, involved two huge fleets, each comprising more than 300 warships carrying more than 100,000 men.[39] The Romans departed from Messana and headed west. Their intention was to invade North Africa. The Carthaginians seem to have been heading for the cities of Eastern Sicily, or perhaps even Southern Italy, but they were aware of the Roman fleet's position and moved to intercept it. The battle that ensued when the two fleets met off Cape Ecnomus in Southern Sicily is presented by Polybius as a set piece featuring an example of a Roman tactical innovation (Polyb. 1.26–28). His account of it is a good example of what Marsden classifies as "accounts of planning, build-up and operations with comments."[40] Polybius' introductory comments emphasise the strategic and tactical issues facing the Romans:

> Now the Romans' plan of campaign was to sail to Africa and shift the whole scene of operations to that country; they wished to make the Carthaginians feel that the war no longer threatened Sicily but their own territory. The Carthaginians, on the other hand, were determined to prevent this. They knew that Africa was extremely vulnerable to attack, and that the population would offer little resistance to any invader who succeeded in getting ashore; this was a situation which they could not allow to arise and they were eager to risk a battle at sea. Since the one side was determined to force a landing and the other to prevent one, it was clear that this inexorable clash of purposes would produce the struggle that followed. ... The Romans had to reckon with two difficulties: first that their course lay across the open sea, and secondly that their enemies possessed the faster vessels, and they therefore took great pains to devise a formation that would remain unbroken and would be difficult to attack.
>
> (Polyb. 1.26.1–4 and 10)[41]

Polybius then describes how the Romans adopted an unusual, innovative formation which he calls a wedge, or triangle.

This wedge may have been, in practice, similar to the crescent or arc formation known from early modern naval warfare, but with the variation that its rear was 'closed' with an extra line of ships, acting as a protective reserve for the very slow, vulnerable ships towing horse-transports.[42] The way that Polybius describes the action, with fast Carthaginian ships trying to harass and pick off the Romans also resembles the clash between the Great Armada and the English fleet in the English Channel in CE 1588:

> The battle that followed was fiercely fought. The Carthaginians' superior speed enabled them to sail round the enemy's flank as well as to approach easily or to beat a rapid retreat. But for their part the Romans were equally confident of victory; as soon as the vessels came to close quarters the contest became one of sheer strength since their 'ravens' grappled each ship the moment it came within striking distance, and besides this they were fighting under the eyes

---

[39] For a full discussion see Lazenby 1996, 81–96.
[40] Marsden 1974, 274.
[41] Translation Scott-Kilvert 1979, 68–9.
[42] See Martin and Parker 1999, 145–59.

of both their consuls, who were taking part in the battle in person. This at any rate was the state of affairs in the centre.

(Polyb. 1.27.11–13)

Polybius describes the rest of the battle as effectively three separate engagements, with the two sides evenly matched, but the Romans gaining an advantage in part because the Carthaginian captains were reluctant to bring their ships within range of a *corvus* (Polyb. 1.28.11). He concludes that it was a Roman victory because of the numbers of ships lost or captured, and because the Romans were able to proceed to Africa (Polyb. 1.28.13–29.1). In this 'account with comments' Polybius introduces a strategic problem that is quite likely to occur when the territory of two warring states is separated by open sea, and then picks out a tactical naval innovation designed to overcome a disparity in skill and experience, thereby providing a highly instructive example for his readers of how to conduct naval warfare successfully.

The Battles of Drepana and the Aegates Islands

We can see Polybius using a similar approach in his accounts of naval engagements towards the end of the First Punic War. In a highly didactic account of the Battle of Drepana in 249, Polybius emphasises the speed of the Carthaginian ships, which he says was due both to their better construction and to the better quality of their rowers (Polyb. 1.51.4). He takes great pains to explain how the inshore position that was taken by the Roman ships limited their capacity for evasive manoeuvres, whereas the Carthaginians could make the most of the open sea behind them (Polyb. 1.51.5–8). But the most impressive aspect of his narrative is how well, in a few words, Polybius outlines two of the most basic of ancient ship to ship combat tactics, the so-called *diekplous* and *periplous* manoeuvres:

> The Carthaginians could use their superior speed to retire in safety to open water. There they could put about and attack the foremost of their pursuers, either working round astern of them (περιπλέοντες), or attacking them from the beam (πλάγιοι προσπίπτοντες). ... One of the most effective manoeuvres in sea battles, that of sailing through (διεκπλεῖν) the enemy's line and reappearing astern of ships which are already engaged with others, was ruled out for the Romans because of the weight of their vessels and the inferior training of their crews.
>
> (Polyb. 1.51.6 and 9)

Thus Polybius effectively characterizes how one side was superior in comparison to the other in terms of both equipment and tactics.[43] In keeping with his emphasis on the vicissitudes of *tyche*, and his narrative theme of a contest for 'thalassocracy', Polybius indicates that, after their victory at Drepana, the Carthaginians went into another encounter off Gela feeling contemptuous of the Romans as naval enemies (1.53.9). Their hopes of regaining their thalassocracy were then restored by the subsequent losses of Roman ships to storms (Polyb. 1.55.1–2). He says of the Romans that at this point: "they disembarked from the sea" (ἐκ μὲν τῆς θαλάττης ἐξέβησαν), whilst continuing to operate on land. This statement is clearly intended as a stark counterpoint to his declaration of their zeal to take to the sea in 260 BCE (Polyb. 1.21.7–8).

---

[43] On these tactics see de Souza 1996; Lazenby 1987.

It is also clear that Polybius' account of the Roman disaster at Drepana and its aftermath is intended to set up a complete reversal of fortunes in the final, decisive naval encounter of the Punic War – the Battle of the Aegates Islands in 241. The theme of learning from the enemy is picked up with the detail that the new Roman fleet was modelled on the ship of Hannibal the Rhodian (Polyb. 1.59.8), which was captured at Lilybaeum, after successfully running the Romans' blockade of the harbour on several occasions in 250 BCE (Polyb. 1.46–47). As the two fleets come in sight of each other Polybius describes the Carthaginians lowering their masts before engaging the Roman fleet (Polyb. 1.61.1). This phrase indicates that either the Carthaginian fleet was under sail, and thus entirely unprepared for combat at sea, or, less probably, that they were under oars, but the commanders had made a grave mistake in not stepping the masts and leaving them on the shore. Polybius goes on to describe how the battle went in favour of the Romans because, in complete contrast to the situation at Drepana, their ships were well built, lighter and ready for battle, being manned by well trained crews and unyielding marines. On the Carthaginian side, however, the ships were heavily laden, unprepared for combat and manned by untrained, inexperienced men (Polyb. 1.61.1–4). In summing up the battle, Polybius blames the Carthaginian defeat on their arrogant underestimation of the Romans:

> The fact is that, owing to their never having expected the Romans to dispute the sea with them again, they had, in contempt for them, neglected their naval force. So that immediately on engaging they had the worst in many parts of the battle and were soon routed, fifty ships being sunk and seventy captured with their crews.
>
> (Polyb. 1.61.5–6)

We have seen from these few examples that from the beginning of his *Histories* Polybius narrates the build-up and the operations of naval warfare with an air of confidence and authority, commenting freely on those aspects that he thinks are important. A few examples from his later books will show that the same pattern seems to have continued, but there are additional problems for the modern reader caused by their fragmentary nature.

The Battle of Chios

Polybius' account of the battle of Chios in 201, fought between the fleet of Philip V of Macedon and the combined fleets of Attalos I of Pergamon, the Rhodians and the Byzantines includes vivid, episodic descriptions of the action and is the earliest surviving account of a 'Hellenistic' naval battle. As with previous examples we have examined, Polybius describes the build-up and the initial action involving large warships, noting that, "Among the other ordinary ships of the fleet the contest was equal; for the advantage that Philip had in the number of his galleys was balanced by Attalus' superiority in decked ships." (Polyb. 16.4.1)

Polybius' narrative focuses on particular aspects of the battle which offer potential as 'lessons' for his readers. For example:

> Now had not the Macedonians interspersed their galleys (λέμβους) among their decked ships (καταφράκτωννεῶν) the battle would have been quickly and easily decided, but as it was these galleys impeded the action of the Rhodian ships in many ways. For once the original order of

battle had been disturbed in their first charge, they were utterly mixed up, so that they could not readily sail through (διεκπλεῖν) the enemy's line nor turn their ships round, in fact could not employ at all the tactics in which they excelled, as the galleys were either falling foul of their oars and making it difficult for them to row, or else attacking them in the prow and sometimes in the stern, thereby hindering both the helmsmen and the rowers in their work.

(Polyb. 16.4.8)[44]

He goes on to describe a highly specialised Rhodian naval tactic, which only seems to have been used in this battle, apparently because they were prevented from using the *diekplous* and *periplous* tactic, that he commented on at length in his account of the battle of Drepana:

When it came to the prow to prow clashes the Rhodians employed a certain technique. For by causing their own ships to receive blows above the water at the prow, but striking the enemy ships below the water, they caused ruptures that were beyond repair.

(Polyb. 16.4.11–12)

It is very hard to establish the mechanics of this technique, and modern scholars are divided in their opinions.[45] Polybius, however, does not seem to think that it was a vital one:

But they rarely used this mode of attack; for as a rule they avoided close contact with the enemy, as the Macedonian soldiers offered a valiant resistance from the deck in such close combats. [14] For the most part forcing their way through the enemy's line (τοὺς διέκπλους παρασύροντες) and put his banks of oars out of action, afterwards turning and sailing round again (ἐκπεριπλέοντες) and attacking him sometimes in the stern and sometimes in the beam while he was still turning; thus they made breaches in some of the ships and in others damaged some necessary part of the gear. Indeed by this mode of fighting they destroyed quite a number of the enemy's ships.

(Polyb. 16.4.13–14)

Thus, although he seems quite fascinated by this innovation, Polybius does not allow it to distort his description of the battle and emphasizes the use of more orthodox tactics. However, he then describes the *aristeia* of three Rhodian quinqueremes captained by Theophiliscus, Philostratus, and Nicostratus, whose helmsman was called Autolycus. This is something of a 'purple passage'; it is so heavily biased in favour of the Rhodians that it can be assumed to derive closely from the Rhodian sources that Polybius is heavily reliant upon. We in turn are at the mercy of the tenth century CE Byzantine excerptors who have selected certain sections of the Polybian narrative for their compilations, and may well have garbled some key phrases in the process.

Polybius was most likely using a Rhodian account here, written by Zeno or Antisthenes.

---

[44] Translation Paton 1926, 11.

[45] Walbank 1957–67–79, 508 suggests, "Perhaps Polybius has not fully understood his source." Livy might have appreciated the irony of that one, but for the modern historian trying to make sense of what remains this is scant consolation. Morrison and Coates (1996, 364) suggest that the bows of the Rhodian could be dipped "by moving the men on deck forward, which is likely to have had the effect described, *if it could be carried out in the heat of the battle*." (The italics are mine). Alternatively, they suggest that it was simply a case of the Rhodian ships' prows being designed to force an enemy ram upwards, above the waterline, which would in turn make the ram of the Rhodian vessels strike below the enemy's waterline. Such an explanation is rational, but it does not fit well with the Polybian text as we have it.

Rhodian authors writing about Rhodian naval matters ought to have been reliable, by his standards, but this passage may have been corrupted in transmission, perhaps by omissions, or by mistakes made by inexpert copyists. The whole passage serves as a salutary warning about the perils inherent in using the fragments of Polybius.

Rhodian naval innovation

However, we should not be too pessimistic. Another fragment, taken from Polybius' 21st book and quoted in the *Suda*, describes an ingenious system for dropping fire on enemy ships. It was devised in 190 BCE by the Rhodian admiral Pausistratus, when his small fleet of around 30 ships was trapped in the harbour of Panormus on the north coast of Samos by the Seleucid fleet, commanded by a Rhodian exile called Polyxenidas:

> The fire-carrier, which Pausistratus the Rhodian admiral deployed, was funnel-shaped. On either side of the prow two brackets were set into the gunwale, protruding out from the sides, into which were fitted poles projecting forwards and out to sea. At the tip of these the funnel-shaped pot, full of fire, was attached by an iron chain, in such a way that, in the course of frontal or broadside ramming, the fire was tipped out into the enemy's ship, but at a point well away from one's own, thanks to the inclination.
>
> (Polyb. 21.7.1–4)

Livy and Appian, whose principal source must have been Polybius, narrate these events at greater length, explaining that Pausistratus (Appian calls him Pausimachus) was tricked into relaxing his guard by Polyxenidas, who pretended he was willing to hand the Seleucid fleet over to his fellow-Rhodian. Livy and Appian describe the fire-carrying devices in a similar fashion to the fragment of Polybius, saying that they were successful in enabling the seven ships that carried them to escape, although Pausistratus was killed before he could see the devices in action (Livy 37.10–11; App. Syr. 24).[46]

We have yet another fragment, clearly from close by in the same book, preserved partly in the Suda and partly in a section of the *Excerpta Antiqua* on the virtues and vices of great men.[47] Here it is said that Pausistratus was appointed as Rhodian *nauarchos* ahead of the less talented, but more circumspect Pamphilidas (an error for Eudamas), because Pausistratus was a bold man of action (διὰ τὸ πρᾶξιν ἔχειν τινὰ καὶ τόλμαν), but the defeat at Panormus caused the Rhodians to regret their decision (Polyb. 21.7.5–7). Livy describes how the Rhodians now appointed Eudamos to lead another, smaller fleet that continued their participation in the war against Antiochus III.[48] What we can reconstruct of Polybius' 'comments' here is minimal, but they seem designed to emphasize what Polybius construes as correct or incorrect behaviour in times of war.

---

[46] Appian's version is especially interesting here because, in addition to showing the inventiveness of the Rhodians, it presents 'Pausimachus' (*i.e.* Pausistratus) as a conscientious commander: "Pausimachus trained his soldiers by repeated exercises, and constructed machines of various kinds. He attached iron vessels containing fire to long poles, for suspending over the sea, so as to hang clear of his own ships and fall upon those of the enemy when they approached" (App. *Syr.* 24). Livy, perhaps more inclined to deviate from the Polybian line, makes Pausistratus out to have been negligent (Livy 37/10–11).

[47] See Walbank 1957–79 ad loc. and vol. III, 5–6.

[48] For further details see de Souza 2002, 84–6.

Conclusions

It would seem that Polybius' accounts of naval warfare fulfil his didactic purposes very well. He selects and presents useful information regarding warfare, narrating and commenting on it to highlight good and bad aspects of leadership and military practice in general and naval tactics in particular. He structures his accounts to emphasize tactical and technical innovations, as well as comparative aspects of military history, and he integrates his thematic concerns like a contest for thalassocracy between Rome and Carthage, and the significance of *tyche* very effectively. He comes across as both knowledgeable and authoritative in his appraisals. We should bear in mind that he had no direct experience of naval warfare, but that is not a reason to rate him as a less reliable source than the likes of Thucydides and Xenophon.

Bibliography

Andreau, J. and Virlouvet, C. (eds) (2002) *L'information et la mer dans le monde antique*. Rome.

Brown, T. S. (1958) *Timaeus of Tauromenium. University of California Publications in History Volume 55*. Berkeley and Los Angeles.

Campbell, B., and L. A. Tritle (eds) (2013) *The Oxford Handbook of Warfare in the Classical World*. New York and Oxford.

Casson, L. (1971) *Ships and Seamanship in the Ancient World*. Princeton.

de Souza, P. (1996) diekplous. In S. Hornblower and A. Spawforth (eds) *The Oxford Classical Dictionary*, 3rd edn, 468, Oxford.

— (2002) Beyond the headland: locating the enemy in ancient naval warfare. In Andreau and Virlouvet, 69–92.

— (2007a) Naval forces in the Hellenistic World and Roman Republic. In P. Sabin, H. van Wees and M. Whitby (eds) *The Cambridge History of Greek and Roman Warfare. Volume I: Greece, the Hellenistic World and the Rise of Rome*, 357–67, Cambridge.

— (2007b) Naval battles in the Hellenistic World and Roman Republic. In Sabin, van Wees and Whitby, 434–47.

— (2013) War at Sea. In Campbell and Tritle, 369–94.

— (forthcoming) Raiders from the Sea: the Maritime Context of the *Poliorcetica*. In M. Pretzler and E. Gabba (ed.) *Polybe. Entretiens Fondation Hardt XX*. Geneva.

Hornblower, S., and Spawforth, A. (eds) (2005). *The Oxford Classical Dictionary*, 3rd edn. Oxford.

Krentz, P. (2007) Archaic and Classical Greek War. In Sabin, van Wees and Whitby, 147–85.

Krentz, P. and Wheeler, E. L. (eds) (1994) *Polyaenus, Stratagems of War*. Chicago.

Lazenby, J. F. (1987) The diekplous, *Greece & Rome* 34, 169–77.

— (1996) *The First Punic War*. London.

Marsden, E. W. (1974) Polybius as a military historian. In E. Gabba (ed.) *Polybe. Entretiens sur l'Antiquité Classique* 20, 267–301.

Martin, C. and Parker, G. (1999) *The Spanish Armada²*. Manchester.

McGing, B. (2010) *Polybius' Histories*. Oxford.

Morrison, J. S. and J. F. Coates (1996) *Greek and Roman Oared Warships 399–30 BC*. Oxford.

Murray, W. M. (2012) *The Age of Titans: the Rise and Fall of the Great Hellenistic Navies*. New York and Oxford.

Paton, W. R. (ed.) (1922–27) *Polybius: the Histories*, 6 vols. Cambridge MA and London.

Paton, W. R., F. W. Walbank, and C. Habicht (eds) (2010) *Polybius: The Histories Books 1–2*. Cambridge, MA.

Pédech, P. (1964) *La méthode historique de Polybe*. Paris.

Pretzler, M. (ed.) (forthcoming) *Aeneas Tacticus: War, Politics and Literature in Classical Greece*. Leiden.

Sabin, P., H. van Wees, and M. Whitby (eds.) (2007) *The Cambridge History of Greek and Roman Warfare. Volume I: Greece, the Hellenistic World and the Rise of Rome*. Cambridge.

Sacks, K. (1981) *Polybius on the Writing of History*. Berkeley and Los Angeles.

Scott-Kilvert, I. (ed.) (1979) *Polybius: The Rise of the Roman Empire*. London.

Steinby, C. (2007) *The Roman Republican Navy: From the sixth century to 167 BC*. Helsinki.

Thiel, J. H. (1954) *A History of Roman Sea-Power before the Second Punic War*. Amsterdam.

van Wees, H. (2004) *Greek Warfare: Myths and Realities*. London.

Walbank, F. W. (1957–67–79) *A Historical Commentary on Polybius*. 3 vols. Oxford.

— (1972) *Polybius*. Berkeley and Los Angeles.

Walton, F. R. (1957) *Diodorus of Sicily. Books XXI–XXXII*. Cambridge, MA and London.

Waterfield, R. (2010) *Polybius: The Histories. Translated by Robin Waterfield, with an Introduction and notes by Brian McGing*. Oxford.

Wheeler, E. L. (1988) *Stratagem and the Vocabulary of Military Trickery*. Leiden.

Wiemer, H.-U. (2001) *Rhodische Traditionen in der hellenistischen Historiographie*. Frankfurt am Main.

ROME'S APPARENT DISINTEREST IN MACEDONIA 168–148 BCE

John Vanderspoel[1]

One of the curiosities surrounding the Roman defeat of the Macedonian king Perseus in 168 at Pydna was the victorious state's apparent complete disinterest in the incorporation of the conquered territory into its sphere of direct control. To outward appearances, Rome had been interested merely in ensuring that Macedonia was no longer interfering or perhaps no longer capable of interfering in the continuous geopolitical struggles in the eastern Mediterranean during the early part of the second century, as the Seleucid kingdom, Rhodes, Pergamum and others fought for supremacy under the watchful eye of Rome.[2] In the years before 168, Perseus, like his father Philip V, had shown a tendency to aggression against friends of Rome in the Greek world and a willingness to challenge Rome's self-proclaimed guardianship over the Greek states and their freedom.[3] As was certainly to be expected in international politics and diplomacy, not every Greek state had been in favor of Rome's interference and declarations. Some, as a consequence, were not unwilling to support, in the background or more openly, the ambitions of Perseus, on the assumption, often made but rarely realized, that it would be possible to remove without much difficulty a new overlord who had assisted in the removal of the old oppressor. Once war broke out between Perseus and Rome, it was simply a matter of time before the Macedonian king emulated his father's ultimate lack of success in battle against Roman armies.

---

[1] I am very pleased to be able to contribute to a volume honoring a colleague and friend of nearly thirty years, whose guitars I have also begun, in more recent years, to accompany with my bass guitar. Because the topic of the volume falls outside my normal range of academic activity, I have chosen to offer a paper that is primarily an essay of interpretation; for that reason, annotation is representative enough to establish standard views as necessary, but not comprehensive. In particular, the bibliography on Roman imperialism is vast; I have tended to cite some early work to show the history of the scholarship, along with some recent work that has helped to shape my views.

[2] The most recent full treatment of the eastern Mediterranean in this period is Eckstein 2008. Though Eckstein offers a theoretical perspective that not all will accept, his book nevertheless provides a full account of the events and of the interpretations of scholars in the past, and it offers full reference to primary sources and to previous studies. For a preliminary treatment of some of the elements of his thesis, see Eckstein 2006, 567–589.

[3] For the relationship of Rome and Macedonia before 168, see, recently, Eckstein 2010, 225–50.

After the battle of Pydna, the members of the dynasty were transported to Rome. They included Perseus himself, a half-brother named Philip, and Perseus's young son Alexander, along with another son and a daughter.[4] After the triumph of their conqueror L. Aemilius Paullus Macedonicus,[5] they were kept under guard at Alba. Perseus (and possibly the other children) soon died, but Alexander eventually tried his hand at several occupations, in the correct belief that he would never be permitted return to Macedonia as king: he learned the trade of working in precious metals and also established himself as a *notarius* at Rome.[6]

Because Rome chose to put an end to the dynasty instead of establishing or supporting a replacement for Perseus,[7] it made a series of other arrangements for Macedonia. Unlike the procedure that they had adopted for Spain about three decades earlier, the Romans chose not to transform the region into a province or otherwise assume direct control of the territory.[8] Acting with the advice of a senatorial commission, L. Aemilius Paullus had exacted one hundred talents from Macedonia (reportedly half of the annual taxes to the king) and allowed the Macedonians to live as free and independent inhabitants in their cities, towns and lands.[9] The Romans also established the prominence, as independent entities, of four *merides*, the four 'parts' by which the Macecdonian kings had traditionally governed Macedonia.[10] The autonomy of each *meris* was a main principle of the arrangement, and, at least initially, trade between *merides* and even intermarriage appear to have been forbidden. In addition, Macedonians most likely paid some kind of annual tribute to Rome, though this has been disputed.[11] Possibly, like Carthage (also not yet part of any province) but certainly with less formality, the Macedonians were permitted or required to pay a sum designated as war indemnity[12] in a series of annual instalments, a procedure that is not specifically attested in the sources but would have the advantage of allowing regular supervision of Macedonia by Roman officials. Over time, some of the restrictions, especially those on trade and intermarriage, were relaxed somewhat.[13]

Evidently, Rome was expecting, or at least hoping, that the Macedonians might enjoy their new-found local autonomy enough to abandon any idea of a 'national' identity, and in particular, any idea of a 'national' identity that resulted in a 'national' leader, be he a dynast or some other figure. The intended model was, perhaps, Italy itself, where towns

---

[4] Plut. *Aemilius Paullus*, 33.6–8. The place, Alba, is mentioned in Livy 45.42.

[5] On whom, see Reiter 1988.

[6] Plut. *Aemilius Paullus*, 37.2–4; his brother and sister died young, and Perseus apparently starved himself to death, though a story did arise that he was kept awake by his guards, who were annoyed with him for some reason, and therefore died, in effect, of weariness.

[7] On the unusual nature of Rome's actions at this time, see Gruen 1982, 257–67.

[8] Plut. *Aem.* 28; the gentle dealings with Macedonia were, unfortunately marred by the vicious treatment of Epirus by Aemilius Paullus, who enslaved 150,000 and sacked 70 cities.

[9] Plut. *Aem.* 28.6

[10] For details of the *merides*, including their specific locations, and other aspects of the settlement, see Hammond and Walbank 1988.

[11] For the arrangements put in place by Rome and the tribute, see Eckstein 2010, 245.

[12] See Badian 1968, 19, citing Tenney Frank, for the suggestion that the halved tribute was, in effect, war indemnity. My suggestion is, in effect, that an annual tribute may have disguised a war indemnity paid over a period of years – not more than 20, as it turned out.

[13] See Eckstein 2010, 246–7.

with a high degree of local autonomy had for the most part co-existed peacefully alongside each other and in relative harmony with Rome in regional groups for more than a century (other than brief moments of disquiet during the Punic wars), but a traditional arrangement of towns and cities in Macedonia, even under the kings, also lay behind the new reality.

Rome imposed other strictures as well. The most important of these were the restrictions on the military capacity of the region. Essentially, the Macedonians were prohibited from raising a military force, except for some small forces at the level of the *merides* to deal with frontier security: there was to be no 'national' army. From one point of view, this makes sense, since Rome was attempting to ensure that the Macedonians would not interfere yet again in the Mediterranean, annoy the friends of Rome or Rome itself, or supply military support to others who might interfere in one or another of these ways. The consequence, however, was that the region could not defend itself very effectively against external enemies, for Rome, though presumably guaranteeing the safety of the region, did not leave behind a military force to assist the Macedonians against their enemies. Perhaps this was a deliberate ploy to keep Macedonia occupied enough with its own troubles to forestall any thoughts of interfering elsewhere in the eastern Mediterranean world.

Less than 20 years later, Rome's arrangements proved to be completely ineffective, for two main reasons. In the first place, claimants to the Macedonian throne gained enough support to create problems within Macedonia. Some claimants boasted of an association with Perseus, like, for example, Andriscus, who claimed to be the former dynast's son, propaganda that was bolstered by his apparent likeness to the former king. Secondly, the borders of the *merides* were under constant attack, and the local military forces limited by Roman strictures were unable to cope. Rome was obliged, of course, to deal with the claimants, but initially took diplomatic measures that were not particularly effective. For example, P. Cornelius Scipio Nasica Corculum, sent as ambassador, discovered that remonstrations were having little effect, and he was even forced to put together a force of Achaean soldiers to defend Thessaly against Andriscus, who had managed to raise an army comprised in large part of Thracians. Most likely in 148,[14] Andriscus defeated a Roman army sent out under P. Iuventius Thalna, praetor for 149, but probably still in command in Macedonia. His victory sealed his fate – and that of Macedonia. In the allocations of commands for 148, Rome gave Macedonia to the praetor Q. Caecilius Metellus, who arrived with a much larger army. He soon defeated Andriscus at Pydna; the pretender fled to Thrace, but was soon handed over. Then Rome did what it might have done 20 years earlier: in 148 it created the province of Macedonia.[15]

The main points of the military history, that is, the two victories at Pydna in 168 BCE and 148, are established well enough that no further comment is needed here. The details of what happened in Macedonia during these two decades are not the subject here either, largely because a lack of evidence prevents a comprehensive discussion. With that said,

---

[14] The date is a subject of some disagreement, but most scholars place the event in 148; see, for example, Astin 1967, 74; Eckstein 2010, 247.

[15] For the events of the last years before the province, see Eckstein 2010, 246–8, and Vanderspoel 2010, 251–2, which goes on to detail the story of Macedonia as a Roman province. Whatever the specifics of the creation of the province (on which historians differ), the Roman era in Macedonia began in 148.

the rest of this paper will address Rome's apparent disinterest in Macedonia after the first victory at Pydna.

The most obvious point is a Roman unwillingness to do in 168 what it was forced to do in 148, that is, to create the province of Macedonia. After all, as noted already, the Romans had begun to add provinces well beyond the immediate area of Italy (that is, beyond Sicily, Sardinia and Corsica) very early in the second century (in other words, the two Spanish provinces).[16] Yet the point is not as obvious as it might at first appear to be. Elsewhere, I have suggested that Rome's primary concern after the Punic wars was the ability of Carthage to acquire the territorial (and perhaps other) resources to challenge Rome again in the western Mediterranean.[17] That would account for the creation of Sicily, Sardinia and Corsica as provinces after the First Punic war, since Carthage had held all or parts of these before, during, and even after the war.[18] The establishment of the two Spains as provinces similarly put under Roman domination more territory that Carthage had employed as a resource and as a base of operations before and during the Second Punic war.

While Philip V had cooperated with Hannibal against Rome, that had been a diplomatic agreement and was never a territorial arrangement. Rome, naturally, dealt as needed with Philip V, but it made no effort, as it did in Spain, to take Macedonia for itself, during or after the Second Punic war. Rather, the Romans seem to have regarded Philip not as a threat to Rome, but as an enemy of Rome's friends and a friend of Rome's enemies. Macedonia was, after all, not located at Rome's boundaries or at the boundaries of areas under Roman control: it was separated from Rome and Italy by Illyria and western Greece, areas where Rome was far more inclined to engage in diplomatic and even occasional military interference. Essentially, from the Roman perspective, Philip V was an annoyance largely because he insisted on interfering in places where Rome preferred to interfere unchallenged. In short, Roman actions against Philip were always a reaction, designed to stop him from doing what he was doing, not an attempt to accumulate territory, tribute or anything else along those lines.

By extension, the attitude to Macedonia reflected the attitude to Philip.[19] When Philip gave way to Perseus, Rome's view did not change much. The Romans had preferred Perseus's brother Demetrius, who, as a hostage in Italy, had become relatively philo-Roman, and were annoyed with Perseus for his role in the elimination of Demetrius, but they did not interfere in the transition to Perseus, nor did they attempt to eliminate him. They did view Perseus as somewhat anti-Roman and regarded his dynastic marriage with some suspicion, but the main consequence was closer scrutiny of his activities. Warfare against Perseus did not break out until Macedonia's own actions required it (from a Roman point of view), for the Romans were essentially as uninterested in achieving direct control of Macedonia as they were of achieving direct control elsewhere in the eastern Mediterranean. At this

16 On the acquisition of the provinces, the background and later developments, see Richardson 1987.

17 Vanderspoel 2010, 256; the current essay is, essentially, an expansion of the remark made there.

18 For an interesting study of the relationship between the imperialism and the concept of province, see Richardson 2008, esp. ch. 2 (10–62), for the Republican period.

19 For Rome and Philip, see Walbank 1940, which is still regularly cited; also Gruen 1973, 123–36, which argues that Philip did not have an alliance with Rome after 196; and, more recently, Eckstein 2008, 77–118, 273–305, and *passim*.

stage, Rome had not yet become aggressively imperialistic in an eastwards direction.[20] Indeed, it was not imperialistic in the western Mediterranean either: it had not taken direct control of any territory in Africa, while allowing Massinissa and his Numidians to circumscribe Carthage on its behalf. Neither had Rome placed Italy under direct control, even if it dominated the latter with its military capacity and by the establishment of colonies throughout the peninsula.

In other words, during the first part of the second century Roman foreign policy (as we may call it) was dominated by thoughts of Carthage and the fearsome prospect of yet another war with its long-time enemy. To deal with that, Rome took direct control of territory as needed (in their view). Secondarily, Rome was interested in a peaceful Mediterranean, where its friends, as well as shipping and trade, could flourish and where no nation or empire was more powerful than Rome. This is the attitude that lies behind the declaration of freedom for the Greeks; this is the attitude that lies behind the attempts to regulate the expansionist behavior of the various kingdoms in Thrace, Asia Minor, the islands and the Near East; this is the attitude that lies behind the interactions with Philip during the 190s.

The only deviation from this policy, and even then it is only a partial deviation because the other points remain valid, is the Roman reaction to Hannibal's flight to Antiochus and to the Carthaginian general's encouragement of further war with Rome. Whether or not Hannibal, in the company of new friends, represented a serious threat to Roman security, his presence in the east excited Rome's primary foreign policy consideration and, briefly, drew to the eastern Mediterranean what was essentially an issue more relevant to the west. Potentially, of course, Roman senators more interested than some of their fellows in eastern expansion or domination could employ Hannibal as propaganda to generate a harder line, but the Carthaginian's value was transitory: as he passed from view and from the earth, Rome's brief fright settled down again into the established pattern of attempts to keep the eastern Mediterranean and its surrounding lands as peaceful, and also as fragmented, as possible.[21]

There were other considerations in 168, among them the bureaucratic burden of the administration of a new province. The creation of the first four provinces (Sicily, Sardinia and Corsica, two Spains) had required more praetors and quaestors than had been needed earlier as governors of provinces and to serve on the accounting staffs. Additional praetorships and quaestorships had been created to fill the need, but a potential requirement to create even more positions so soon will certainly have met with reluctance in some quarters. By nature, the Roman nobility was not inclined to allow too many opportunities for glory and renown; new praetorships would create that possibility for men whose careers would

---

[20] A classic early treatment of Roman imperialism is Harris 1979. On the relationships between Rome and the east, Gruen 1984 remains important and highly useful, though it focuses more on the earlier period than on the 2nd century BCE. Kallet-Marx 1995 treats Macedonia in the provincial period and much more besides, but does not offer a detailed treatment of the earlier half of the 2nd century BCE. The most recent survey of the period under consideration here is Eckstein 2008 which argues a thesis while offering a comprehensive account of the historical details and reference to earlier scholarship.

[21] Badian 1958, 99–104, suggests that Rome's intervention in the east became "more brutally direct" (100) after the defeat of Perseus, but it was also "still unwilling to undertake the burdens of direct administration" (104).

otherwise not have progressed beyond the lower offices – exactly where the higher nobility wanted them to remain. In fact, in the early part of the second century BCE, a shortage of praetors already existed, and the Romans regularly prorogued the terms of praetors to deal with the situation. Partly, of course, prorogation would permit some continuity of leadership in, for example, Spain; at the same time, it allowed a few men to achieve a level of military success in two years that they could not have achieved during a single year in office.

Rivalries within the aristocracy contributed to a tendency to limit that type of opportunity as much as possible to the senatorial group in the ascendancy at any given moment or to its relatives in the first instance and to its friends in the second. Any third instance was to be avoided, if at all possible, and a reluctance to add more praetors and quaestors was one way to prevent, for as long as possible, random nobles from achieving glory and renown. Had Macedonia been created as a province in 168 it would have offered its governors constant opportunities for military glory, given the regular incursions of Thracians, Turdetani and others. Indeed, as the Romans were to discover later when it was a province, Macedonia's military situation offered Roman generals more than adequate scope for glory and renown – and for defeat and death in battle.[22]

The events leading up to the renewal of war with Carthage suggest a change of attitude at Rome in the late 150s and early 140s. For several years before the outbreak of the Third Punic war, Roman foreign policy, especially as it related to Carthage, was a contest between two factions led by two prominent members of the Roman aristocracy. One was the famous M. Porcius Cato,[23] whose persistent call for the destruction of Carthage was countered by arguments that '*Carthago delenda est*' was premature, since Carthage had not yet given a justification for war. The leader of the faction opposed to Cato was P. Cornelius Scipio Nasica Corculum, who, as one of Rome's leading statesmen, was regularly chosen as a diplomat and negotiator. Like others in his extended family (the Cornelii Scipiones; the Aemilii Paulli), he had long held to a less aggressive point of view when discussing the need or desirability of Roman expansion;[24] even after the initial *deditio* of Carthage, he seems to have argued for a moderation of terms while others, Cato with his theatrics naturally among them, pressed increasingly harsh demands that led to the actual outbreak of the Third Punic war.

The outbreak of war with Carthage changed Rome, or so it appears. Cato's perspective and that of like-minded senators clearly gained the upper hand. The new direction was responsible for the war itself, in the sense that Carthage had surrendered but was pushed into an eventually foolhardy self-defence against Roman demands. Though he was no friend of Carthage and merely had not yet reached that conclusion that war was necessary, Scipio Nasica could no longer hold back his fellow-senators, despite his prominence among them.[25] He nevertheless retained considerable influence: when the threat posed by Andriscus became severe enough to require Roman attention, Scipio Nasica travelled to Greece to

---

[22] For a brief survey of the early years of the province, Vanderspoel 2010, 260–4.

[23] On whom, Astin 1978 is still the most useful full treatment.

[24] See Astin 1967, 48–54, 276–80, for a discussion of opposing attitudes at Rome just before the outbreak of war; also Astin 1978, 126–30.

[25] He had been named *pontifex maximus* in 150 and became *princeps senatus* in 147. See the remarks of Astin 1967, 54.

organize resistance and, probably, to ensure that neither Greece nor Macedonia assisted Carthage.[26] In fact, it is possible that Scipio Nasica had already been sent to Greece to secure the loyalty of its various regions because of the impending war with Carthage when Andriscus emerged as a threat. As mentioned above, his diplomatic initiatives met with failure,[27] and he was reduced to begging the Senate to send out a significant military force while gathering what Achaean forces were available for the defence of Thessaly.

In a sense, Rome's negotiations, on the one hand, achieved what they were designed to achieve by their instigators (that is, the provocation of Carthage to war) and, on the other, failed miserably for Scipio Nasica (that is, his inability to stop Andriscus). It is as if peace negotiations themselves were under fire from every side: Cato and his supporters attacked the peace-proposing policy of Scipio Nasica and his cohorts, while Andriscus simply ran roughshod over the diplomacy offered by the Roman statesman. As he saw his own best efforts come to naught, Scipio must have wondered what had changed and why so many of his fellow senators were now actively propounding a more aggressive foreign policy. 149 was, after all, also the year when Ser. Sulpicius Galba massacred the Lusitanians and, through bribery and by milking the sympathies of the jury by presenting his pitiable children and an orphaned relative, was acquitted of the charges brought against him.[28]

In the first years of the 140s, to all outward appearances, Rome became aggressive, it became violent, it tolerated war crimes, and its fuse grew shorter and shorter. These were not good years to be an enemy of the most powerful state in the Mediterranean, as both Carthage and Corinth were to discover in 146. If we can most reasonably understand Ser. Sulpicius Galba's actions as his brutal personal response to a defeat inflicted on him by the Lusitanians previously, the first region in the 140s to feel the wrath of Rome as a state was Macedonia. The inevitable defeat of Andriscus led to the creation of the province of Macedonia, presumably over a period of time in terms of its details, but not in principle, since the Roman era begins in 148.

Somewhat curiously, the destruction of Corinth a couple of years later did not lead to the creation of another province. On the other hand, territory in Africa was taken under Rome's direct control in 146, as a province was created from Carthage and its territory. If, as I have suggested above, Rome's willingness to create provinces was a consequence of its tempestuous relationship with Carthage, the creation of the new province of Africa has an obvious, if surprisingly late, genesis. Since Macedonia became a province a couple of years earlier, either it must be shown to relate to Rome's problems with Carthage in some way or the thesis falters, at least for the 140s, if not necessarily for the third century and the 190s. How, then, might the war against Andriscus and the creation of the province of Macedonia be connected to the Third Punic war?

One obvious point is the timing of Andriscus's challenge to Rome's generic overlordship of Macedonia. Though he must have begun to accumulate power, support and men

---

[26] The latter point is nowhere stated (and Scipio Nasica as ambassador is mentioned by name only in Zonaras, 9.28), but the example of Philip V would certainly be on Roman minds.

[27] Less an indication of weaker support (note his appointment as *princeps senatus*) than senatorial preoccupation with Carthage.

[28] See, briefly, Curchin 1991, 33–5, and Richardson 1987, 136–40.

somewhat earlier, his challenge to Rome occurred in 149, the year that Carthage took up armed hostilities. His rejection of Roman attempts to negotiate terms occurred in the very same year that Carthage rejected Rome's (so-called) diplomacy. Even though the demands were very different and made in very different ways, it will not have been difficult at Rome to point to the coincidence in time and to make more of it than it actually was. Presumably, Andriscus thought that Rome was too busy with Carthage to respond to him with force. At the same time, it will have been a simple matter to suggest that Andriscus was intending to emulate Philip V and act in concert with Carthage. Rome had a long collective memory: The mere mention of Gauls, as the war with the Cimbri and Teutones in 104 indicates, caused irrational fears and desperate searches for geese to post as security cameras.

Moreover, because the tide of opinion had turned to a harshness that had not existed even as late as the later 150s, the atmosphere was primed for the fearful determination that all Rome's enemies were cooperating with each other against her. It does not matter whether that was true or not; what matters is what the Romans thought or feared or could convince themselves or their fellow Romans to think or fear. And it matters immensely that Andriscus was defeated in 148: The war with Carthage was still raging, and in the new environment that now represented Roman foreign policy, Macedonia could not be permitted to find itself in a position to render assistance to the main enemy. Thus, the Romans immediately created the province in principle, even if many details were still to be worked out after 146.

In conclusion, it is the argument of this essay that Rome did not transform Macedonia into a province in 168, as it could easily have done, for the simple reason that Macedonia did not at that time pose any kind of threat or danger in relation to Rome's primary enemy in the Mediterranean, the Carthaginians.[29] Twenty years later, in 148, Macedonia and especially its revolutionary leader were defeated in the middle of a war with Carthage. Given this simple, not necessarily dangerous, coincidence of timing, Rome might have created a province even before its attitude changed. In the new more aggressive environment of the early 140s that decision was almost inevitable. Once taken, the province of Macedonia was created, unlike in Greece, which was allowed to remain free after its 'revolt' (if that term can be applied here) was quashed in 146. By that point, the war with Carthage was no longer the danger that it had been only a short time earlier,[30] and never in any of Rome's wars with Carthage had Greece done anything to interfere in any way on behalf of Carthage.

Perhaps also the aggressiveness of Rome's foreign policy died down somewhat with the defeat of Carthage. Certainly, the Romans continued to find places to fight, particularly to protect or expand the boundaries in Spain and Macedonia, but these did not result in new provinces. The next province was Asia, a legacy from King Attalus; at that point, the willingness to create provinces for a new reason emerged for the first time. All six of the provinces acquired previously (Sicily; Sardinia et Corsica; Hispania Citerior; Hispania

---

[29] Compare Astin's remark at 1967, 76, when hinting that Scipio could be seen as a new Aemilius Paullus: "...Carthage ranked well below Macedonia among the heirs of Greek civilization; but as an enemy of Rome it was more ancient and more feared than Macedon; ...."

[30] Astin 1967, 75, notes that the final moments of the Third Punic war took place "probably a little earlier" than the campaigns of Metellus and Mummius against the Achaeans.

Ulterior; Macedonia; Africa) were obtained in the context or aftermath of the three wars Rome fought with Carthage, curiously enough at an exact pace of two provinces per war. On that view, Rome was not interested in transforming Macedonia into its own territory, as a province or otherwise, until it posed a danger that coincided directly with a war against Carthage.

Bibliography

Astin, A. E. (1967) *Scipio Aemilianus*. Oxford.

— (1978) *Cato the Censor*. Oxford.

Badian, E. (1958) *Foreign Clientelae (264–70 BC)*. Oxford.

— (1968) *Roman Imperialism in the Late Republic*, 2nd edn. Oxford.

Curchin, L. A. (1991) *Roman Spain: Conquest and Assimilation*. London and New York.

Eckstein, A. M. (2006) Conceptualizing Roman Imperialism under the Republic: An Introduction. In N. Rosenstein and R. Morstein-Marx (eds) *A Companion to the Roman Republic*, 567–89, Malden, MA.

— (2008) *Rome Enters the Greek East: From Anarchy to Hierarchy in the Hellenistic Mediterranean, 230–170 BC*. Malden, MA.

— (2010) Macedonia and Rome, 221–146 BC. In J. Roisman and I. Worthington (eds), *A Companion to Ancient Macedonia*, 225–50, Malden, MA.

Gruen, E. S. (1973) The Supposed Alliance between Rome and Philip V of Macedon, *California Studies in Classical Antiquity* 6, 123–36.

— (1982) Macedonia and the Settlement of 167 BC. In W. L. Adams and E. N. Borza (eds) *Philip II, Alexander the Great, and the Macedonian Heritage*, 257–67, Washington, DC.

— (1984) *The Hellenistic World and the Coming of Rome*, 2 vols. Berkeley and Los Angeles.

Harris, W. V. (1979) *War and Imperialism in Republican Rome, 327–70 BC*. Oxford.

Kallet-Marx, R. M. (1995) *Hegemony to Empire: The Development of Roman Imperialism in the East from 148 to 62 BC*. Berkeley and Los Angeles.

Hammond, N. G. L. and F. W. Walbank (1988) *A History of Macedonia*, Vol. 3. Oxford.

Reiter, R. (1988) *Aemilius Paullus: Conqueror of Greece*. London and New York.

Richardson, J. S. (1987) *Hispaniae: Spain and the Development of Roman imperialism, 218–82 BC*. Cambridge.

— (2008) *The Language of Empire: Rome and the Idea of Empire from the Third Century BC to the Second Century AD*. Cambridge.

Vanderspoel, J. (2010) *Provincia Macedonia*. In J. Roisman and I. Worthington (eds) *A Companion to Ancient Macedonia*, 251–75, Malden, MA.

Walbank, F. W. (1940) *Philip V of Macedon*. Oxford.

INDEX